INSIGHT GUIDE

NORMANDY

APA PUBLICATIONS   L

Part of the Langenscheidt Publishing Group

INSIGHT GUIDE
NORMANDY

Editorial
Editor
Pam Barrett
Editorial Director
Brian Bell

Distribution

UK & Ireland
GeoCenter International Ltd
The Viables Centre, Harrow Way
Basingstoke, Hants RG22 4BJ
Fax: (44) 1256-817988

United States
Langenscheidt Publishers, Inc.
46–35 54th Road, Maspeth, NY 11378
Fax: (1) 718 784-0640

Canada
Thomas Allen & Son Ltd
390 Steelcase Road East
Markham, Ontario L3R 1G2
Fax: (1) 905 475 6747

Australia
Universal Press
1 Waterloo Road
Macquarie Park, NSW 2113
Fax: (61) 2 9888 9074

New Zealand
Hema Maps New Zealand Ltd (HNZ)
Unit D, 24 Ra ORA Drive
East Tamaki, Auckland
Fax: (64) 9 273 6479

Worldwide
**Apa Publications GmbH & Co.
Verlag KG (Singapore branch)**
38 Joo Koon Road, Singapore 628990
Tel: (65) 865-1600. Fax: (65) 861-6438

Printing

Insight Print Services (Pte) Ltd
38 Joo Koon Road, Singapore 628990
Tel: (65) 865-1600. Fax: (65) 861-6438

©2002 Apa Publications GmbH & Co.
Verlag KG (Singapore branch)
All Rights Reserved

First Edition 1994
Second Edition 2002

CONTACTING THE EDITORS
We would appreciate it if readers
would alert us to errors or out-
dated information by writing to:
**Insight Guides, P.O. Box 7910,
London SE1 1WE, England.
Fax: (44) 20 7403-0290.**
insight@apaguide.demon.co.uk

www.insightguides.com

ABOUT THIS BOOK

This guidebook combines the interests and enthusiasms of two of the world's best known infor- mation providers: Insight Guides, whose titles have set the standard for visual travel guides since 1970, and Discovery Channel, the world's premier source of nonfiction tele- vision programming.

The editors of Insight Guides pro- vide practical advice and general understanding about a destination's history, culture, institutions and people. Discovery Channel and its Web site, www.discovery.com, help millions of viewers explore their world from the comfort of their own home and also encourage them to explore it first hand.

How to use the book

This fully updated edition of *Insight Guide: Normandy* is carefully struc- tured to convey an understanding of Normandy and its culture and to guide readers through its sights and activities:

◆ The **Features** section covers the history and culture of the region in a series of informative essays.

◆ The main **Places** section is a complete guide to all the sights and areas worth visiting. Places of spe- cial interest are coordinated by number with the maps.

◆ The **Travel Tips** listings section provides a handy point of reference for information on travel, hotels, shops, restaurants and more.

The contributors

This edition of *Insight Guide: Nor- mandy* was revised by **Pam Barrett**, a London-based editor, supervised by managing editor **Cathy Muscat** at Insight Guides. It has been com-

EXPLORE YOUR WORLD

pletely updated with the invaluable help of a number of writers and researchers.

The current edition builds on the solid foundations created by the editors and writers of previous editions. These include **Rowlinson Carter**, who wrote about the region's history from the very beginnings to D-Day; **Roger Williams**, editor of the first edition of *Insight Guide: Normandy*, who contributed features on Impressionism and Normandy's great abbeys and the chapter on Deauville and the Côte Fleurie; **Roland Collins**, whose original chapters on Rouen, Dieppe and its environs, Le Havre and the Seine Valley provided a firm base to build on; and **Nigel Tisdal**l, who contributed the original chapters on Caen, the D-Day beaches, and the Cotentin peninsula.

Other writers whose revised contributions appear in this edition include **Marie-Pierre Moine**, a former editor of *Taste* magazine who wrote the features on Food and the Norman character; **Jamie Reid**, former racing correspondent, who contributed a feature about horses; **John Ardagh**, who considered the influence of Normandy on some of France's finest writers; and writer-photographer **John Lloyd**, who wrote about the Orne region and Suisse Normande.

All the chapters in the **Places** section of the book have been thoroughly updated and expanded by several people: **Christopher and Melanie Rice**, authors of previous books on the area; **Emily Hatchwell**, who has edited and contributed to numerous Insight Guides, and who visited Western Normandy to check information for this edition; and **Joby Williams**, who concentrated her research chiefly on the Seine Valley, the Côte Fleurie and the Channel ports,

All these researchers also contributed vital new information to the expanded **Travel Tips** listings section at the back of the book.

Most of the stunning photography in this as in the earlier editions of the guide, is the work of **Lyle Lawson**, an American photographer based in England, but there are also numerous contributions from Dutch photographer **Jeroen Snijders**, the US-based **Dave Houser** and others.

Thanks also go to **Penny Phenix** for proofreading and indexing this latest edition of the book.

Map Legend

——	Regional Boundary
– – – –	Département Boundary
–•–	National Park/Reserve
– – – –	Ferry Route
✈ ✈	Airport: International/Regional
🚌	Bus Station
❶	Tourist Information
✉	Post Office
✝ ✝ ✝	Church/Ruins
✝	Monastery
☾	Mosque
✡	Synagogue
🏰	Castle/Ruins
🏛	Mansion/Stately home
∴	Archaeological Site
∩	Cave
🗿	Statue/Monument
★	Place of Interest

The main places of interest in the Places section are coordinated by number with a full-colour map (e.g. ❶), and a symbol at the top of every right-hand page tells you where to find the map.

CONTENTS

Maps

Introduction

History

Features

The harbour
at Honfleur.

A CIVILISED PEOPLE

Normandy is a region with a long, proud history and

the ability to overcome the harshest adversity

The Normans have a special place in Europe. They are descended from the Viking Norsemen, one of the most ruthless and uncivilised peoples, who became, through force of arms, riches and conscience, one of the most astonishingly civilised builders in history. They had a mercurial genius. In less than two centuries, they had blossomed, spread their empires to the four corners of the continent, from England to the Middle East, and then declined, leaving quietly like well-behaved party guests.

Suddenly this brilliant race had gone. But it had not disappeared: it was subsumed as part of the Frankish Empire. Mixed with the Gaulish tribes they had conquered, these conservative, hard-working, stubborn people retained their ancient stock down the centuries, cultivating the rich land that had first brought their ancestors along the Normandy coast and up the River Seine.

Apart from the 100 years they spent fighting off their English cross-Channel neighbours, their life went on largely undisturbed. They could live off the land, developing their shrewd market skills while their sailors discovered Quebec and other foreign lands. Only the French themselves upset the status quo – in the 16th-century Wars of Religion and (against the wishes of the local Royalist Chouans) during the 18th-century Revolution when monasteries were once again destroyed, as they had been by the Vikings.

The time for the Normans once more to take centre-stage came on 6 June 1944, when the entire Allied effort against the Third Reich was concentrated on landing troops on occupied continental Europe. Normandy's beaches were the target. It was the biggest military manoeuvre in history and, though successful, its effect was devastating. Centuries of endeavour were wiped from the map. Whole towns disappeared. The landscape was ruined.

The stubborn, sturdy Normans kept their heads. Patiently the towns were rebuilt. Traditions were not allowed to die. Parisians, who had long been partial to the Normandy coast and countryside, returned for holidays in the twinkling resorts of Deauville and Honfleur. Many bought second homes on the coast and among the tumble of old farmhouse buildings. Here they rediscovered a nostalgic France, of shrimp nets and sandy shores, and a rural idyll of half-timbered farms where the produce – milk, cream and cheese, apples, cider and Calvados – seemed as bounteous as it did to the early invaders. After more than 1,000 years, the region's charms and promise are still hard for any visitor to resist. ❑

PRECEDING PAGES: the imposing bulk of Château Gaillard; low tide at Diélette; a toll house on the Seine at Vernon; overlooking Dieppe harbour
LEFT: a young participant in Rouen's Joan of Arc pageant.

Decisive Dates

EARLY DAYS

56 BC: Romans under Julius Caesar conquer resident Celtic tribes and establish regional capital at Rotomagus (Rouen).

52 BC: Romans found the towns of Harfleur and Lisieux.

2nd century AD: Christianity spreads throughout Normandy.

AD 260: St Mellon becomes the first bishop of Rouen.

486: Normandy conquered by Frankish Merovingian Empire under King Clovis.

649: Abbeys of St-Ouen in Rouen and St-Wandrille at Fontenelle founded.

708: Abbey of Mont-St-Michel founded.

VIKINGS AND CONQUERORS

820: First Viking raids up the Seine valley.

841: Vikings plunder the abbey at Jumiège.

911: Under the Treaty of St-Clair-sur-Epte, signed with French king Charles la Simple, the Viking leader Rollo becomes the first duke of Normandy.

933: Accession of William Longsword; monastery rebuilding begins.

1027: Birth of William the Conqueror in Falaise.

1066: Duke William defeats Harold at the Battle of Hastings and conquers England.

1180–1223: Philippe-Auguste, king of France, reinforces castles in Normandy.

1195: Richard Lionheart, king of England, builds Château Gaillard.

1204: Château Gaillard captured by Philippe-Auguste, who goes on to conquer all Normandy except for the Isles Normandes (Channel Islands) and the duchy is united with French crown.

1315: Normandy awarded provincial status.

HUNDRED YEARS' WAR

1337–1453: Hundred Years' War fought against England, after the English king, Edward III, revived his claim to the throne of France.

1346: English victory at the Battle of Crécy.

1415: Henry V of England arrives at Honfleur and takes all Normandy.

1431: Joan of Arc, accused of witchcraft and heresy, is burned at the stake in Rouen.

1437: Caen University founded.

1453: The whole of France, apart from Calais, is back in French hands.

1459: English defeated at Formigny, a postscript to the war.

1469–1763: WARS OF RELIGION

1469: The French monarchy gives up the title to the duchy of Normandy.

1517: Le Havre founded by François I.

1572: The St Bartholomew's Day Massacre of Protestant Huguenots; thousands are killed throughout France, 500 in Rouen alone.

1598: Protestants fight back, and with Huguenot Henri of Navarre on the throne, the Edict of Nantes grants the Huguenots religious and civil liberties.

1608: Samuel de Champlain founds the Canadian city of Quebec on his third voyage to the Americas.

1630–36: Serious outbreaks of plague strike the whole of Normandy.

1643–1715: Louis XIV, the Sun King. During his reign his chief minister, Colbert, sets up Haras du Pin (the "Versailles of Horses"), expands the port of Honfleur and initiates a lace-making industry at Alençon that continues today.

1685: Bowing to pressure from the powerful Jesuits, Louis XIV revokes the Edict of Nantes and the persecution of the Huguenots recommences.

1692: A fleet under the Count of Tourville sets sail from La Hougue to restore James II to the English throne; it is disastrously defeated.

1756–63: Seven Years' War with England.

REVOLUTION AND EMPIRE

1789–92: The Revolution leads to the First Republic. Monasteries are destroyed. Normandy ceases to exist as a province and is replaced by the five *départements* that still exist today.

1790s: Caen welcomes Girondin refugees. Local woman Charlotte Corday, shocked at the assassination of Girondins in Paris, murders the minister of the interior, Jean-Paul Marat. She is executed, unrepentant. Loyalist supporters in Lower Normandy, calling themselves Chouans (screech-owls), gather support, attacking Briouze, La Ferté-Macé and Flers, and besieging Vire. They are finally defeated in 1799 and their leaders executed at Verneuil. Napoleon takes the Bayeaux tapestry to Paris where it is displayed to reinforce his plans to invade England.

1804–14: The First Empire is established under Napoleon Bonaparte.

1830: Charles X goes into exile in Cherbourg.

1848: Rioting in Rouen. King Louis-Philippe leaves Honfleur for exile in Britain.

1848–52: Second Empire.

WRITERS AND ARTISTS IN NORMANDY

1843: Rouen–Dieppe railway built and the Normandy coast becomes fashionable. Around this time Deauville is founded and becomes popular with Emperor Napoleon III and Empress Eugénie.

1850: The writer Guy de Maupassant is born in the château of Miromesnil, near Dieppe.

1856: *Madame Bovary* by Gustave Flaubert published, outraging the citizens of Rouen.

1870–71: Upper Normandy is occupied during the Franco–Prussian war.

1872: Claude Monet, who is living in Honfleur, paints *Impression: Soleil Levant*, the picture that gave Impressionism its name.

1890: Monet settles in Giverny, where he lives until his death in 1926.

Early 20th century: Raoul Dufy paints pictures of boats in Le Havre and racehorses at Deauville.

20TH CENTURY: WAR AND RECONSTRUCTION

1914–18: World War I. Ground fighting does not reach Normandy but the Channel ports are vital for supplies to the Anglo-French campaign.

1923: Paris–Deauville motorway begun.

1932: Ocean liner *Normandie* breaks records.

1939–45: World War II.

1940: France capitulates to Germany and all of France is occupied. Towns and cities in Haute Normandie ravaged by fire.

1942: Abortive Canadian raid on Dieppe results in huge loss of life.

1944 (6 June): D-Day. Allied forces land in the biggest movement of military manpower in history. Bitter fighting culminates in the Falaise Pocket, 22 August. Most of Caen is reduced to rubble.

1957: France is a founder member of the European Economic Commumity (later Economic Union).

1967: Nuclear reprocessing plant at La Hague starts operating.

1971: France's first nuclear submarine launched at Cherbourg.

1977: Autoroute de Normandie and the Pont de Brotonne completed.

1994–95: The Channel Tunnel, linking England and France, opens to the northeast; the new Pont de Normandie spans the Seine estuary between Le Havre and Honfleur.

1994: 50th anniversery of the D-Day landings celebrated; new museums and memorials founded.

2000: Terrible storms devastate France, damaging forests in the region and the roof of Rouen cathedral. The old Pegasus Bridge, casualty of the D-Day landings, is re-erected next to the newer one and a new museum opens on the site. ❑

PREDEDING PAGES: 17th-century map of Normandy.
LEFT: William the Conqueror.
RIGHT: bridge in Le Havre's Bassin du Commerce.

BEGINNINGS

The Romans founded Rouen as their regional capital, the Vikings established a duchy, and William the Conqueror, born in Falaise, rose to prominence here

Eight centuries after surrendering their sovereignty to France, the Normans retain a powerful sense of identity. "A turbulent race," commented the Norman chronicler Ordericus Vitalis in the days of independence, "and unless restrained by firm rule they are always ready for mischief." French chroniclers were blunter: Normandy, named after Viking Norsemen, was "a den of pirates".

The region has been through several metamorphoses, but it is the duchy of Normandy as it existed between AD 911 and 1204 that underpins the Norman identity and provides the most impressive monuments. This era is most remarkable for the way four characters rose more or less simultaneously to transform a disreputable corner of France into the most powerful force in Western Europe, utterly eclipsing the nascent kingdom of France proper.

They were William the Bastard, Robert Guiscard, his brother Roger, and Bohemund, the conquerors of England, Italy, Sicily and Syria respectively. Such power was not achieved by wearing kid gloves. "They were all," says one authority, "in varying degrees personally repellent, cruel and coldly unscrupulous."

Roman springboard

Normandy has no obvious natural boundaries, but Julius Caesar pegged it out as a single administrative entity after defeating the resident Celts in 56 BC. He saw it as a springboard for his designs on Britain. The Romans turned the former Celtic stronghold into their regional capital and named it Rothomagus. Diocletian (AD 245–313) came up with the name Lugdunensis Secunda, or Lyonnaise II, reflecting the region's second-place ranking among the 17 departments of Roman Gaul. Substantial Roman relics in Normandy are rare, one notable exception being the amphitheatre at Lillebonne, formerly Juliobona, in the Seine Valley.

Saxon pirates, precursors of the Germanic

hordes who crushed the Roman Empire in the 5th century, had a toehold in the Bessin and Cotentin 300 years earlier. Christianity was also early on the scene. St Mellon was reputedly invested as bishop of Rouen in about AD 260, in other words some 50 years before Emperor Constantine made Christianity official. This

bishop is a flimsy figure, historically speaking, but there is definite substance to St Victrice whose St-Gervais church in Rouen, built in 386, is one of the oldest in France.

Roman Empire and Germanic tribes co-existed long enough for some of the latter to abandon their guttural speech in favour of colloquial Latin. Throwing in some extra ingredients, they concocted the recipe for French. The Angles and Saxons who crossed the Channel did not adopt Latin quite so wholeheartedly and their hybrid became English. Back on the Continent, tribes accepting or rejecting Latin came to be distinguished as Franks and Germans respectively. The Bayeux Tapestry refers to

LEFT: the arrival of the Viking Norsemen.
RIGHT: a Roman floor mosaic from Lillebonne.

William the Conqueror and his men not as Normans but as "Franks".

The Merovingian Clovis (AD 465–511) overthrew the Gallo-Romans at Soissons in 486 and rapidly took possession of the whole country between the Somme and the Loire, later extending his specifically Frankish domain as far as Bordeaux and Toulouse. The former Lugdunesis Secunda was incorporated in a western kingdom which Clovis called Neustria. Clovis married Clotilde, the pious Christian daughter of the king of Burgundy, and was infected by her enthusiasm for building abbeys. Their example was followed avidly in Normandy

during the next two centuries, particularly by St Aubert, Bishop of Avranches.

Viking raids

For the Vikings who descended like thunderbolts in the 9th century, unfortifed abbeys crammed with treasure were irresistible. They conducted their raids like routine summer outings, and prayers went up everywhere for deliverance from their lusty throat-cutting. Charles I of France, known as Charles the Bald, tried bribing Viking chieftains to do their raping and pillaging elsewhere – he especially recommended England. The prospect of being paid not to lift a finger brought a growing number of

Viking chieftains to their island base in the Seine. Among them was Rolf, son of the Norwegian Earl Rognwald of More, who needed a new home because he had been banished from Norway for stealing the king's cattle. In these somewhat shady circumstances, the foundations of the duchy of Normandy were laid.

The legendary leader

Rollo, the Gallicised form of "Rolf", is the stuff of Norse legend, a man of such immense size that there was supposedly not a horse in Norway big enough to carry him without his feet dragging along the ground. Obliged to walk, he came to be known as Rollo Ganger ("the Marcher"). Very little is known about his early years in France, but sycophantic court chroniclers later made up the deficit with all sorts of fanciful nonsense, including his portrayal as some kind of Christian messiah.

Chronicles make no mention of Rollo until AD 890, 25 years after his banishment from Norway. He evidently took part in an unsuccessful attack on Paris, consoling himself in defeat by then marching across country to the Cotentin where he sacked St-Lô and perhaps Bayeux as well. Two years later he was involved in a siege of Évreux. The resident Count Berenger was killed, and Rollo's share of the booty included the count's daughter, Popa. He was now sufficiently notorious to qualify for a bribe from the king of France, Charles the Simple, who was prepared to recognise Rollo as the ruler of the territories around Rouen and Évreux in order to be left alone with the rest of his kingdom.

The pirates settle down

Rollo did not take the title Duke of Normandy but was called Patrician. The piratical Viking turned his sword into a ploughshare, donned the traditional white robe and presented himself barefoot for baptism as a Christian. On the question of marriage, however, he went his own way. The captured concubine, Popa, commanded his love and bore his children, while Gisella, Charles the Simple's daughter, whom he married to cement their treaty, died of neglect. Her father went to the length of sending two emissaries to lodge a formal protest over her treatment. Rollo had the ambassadors removed from his presence and summarily beheaded.

The hallmark of Rollo's government was

autocracy. While elsewhere in France feudalism was taking shape, Rollo and his successors kept power in their own hands and set their faces against the creation of powerful barons capable of challenging them. The worst crime was theft, a more serious matter than murder, and it is said that Rollo demonstrated his successful prosecution of theft by leaving a gold armlet dangling from a tree for three years.

Although "Norman" was derived from "Northmen", the latter never constituted more than a modest minority among the indigenous Celtic-Roman-Frankish stock. Norwegians like Rollo were a minority among a minority as

guage. The Rouen Scandinavians were rapidly Christianised; those in Bayeux clung to pagan beliefs. The scene at Rollo's deathbed (circa AD 930) demonstrated the conflict. Having made a generous gift to the Church for the good of his soul, he gave orders for the sacrifice of a number of Christian slaves to the gods Odin and Thor, just to be on the safe side.

The House of Rollo

With a crypto-pagan Norwegian aristocrat for a father and a French Christian concubine for a mother, Rollo's son and successor, William Longsword, personified the confused identity

most new immigrants were Danes or Anglo-Danes. But the Norwegians were mostly nobles, whereas the Danes came from a lower social strata. In both cases, they settled in towns, leaving rural areas to Frankish peasants.

Rouen and Bayeux were very different. In the former, Norse was barely used by the second generation of Scandinavian Normans, whereas Bayeux had a large Saxon population; as Norse and Saxon were mutually intelligible, there was less reason to abandon the old lan-

LEFT: a Viking ship depicted in a window of St-Rémy church, Dieppe.
ABOVE: a priest blessing the abbey at Jumiège.

of the second generation of Normans. The schism between Rouen and Bayeux deepened, and at one point the latter contingent threatened to brush the dust of Normandy from their feet and go home, which in some cases meant England. The French made it plain that the best possible outcome from their point of view would be to see the back of the whole lot of them.

Territorially speaking, however, Longsword's reign got off to a brisk start with sharp military actions followed by the annexation of the Cotentin, the Channel Islands and the Avranchin. During the course of his Avranchin campaign, which fixed the Norman-Breton frontier along the River Couesnon, Longsword espied Sprota, a Breton girl, and took her as a concubine, his reputation as an exceptionally pious Christian notwithstanding. With Sprota in tow, he took up residence at Fécamp and began rebuilding the ancient monastery destroyed by his Viking forebears. Sprota soon bore him a son, Richard. Destined to become the first duke of Normandy proper, he was known as Richard the Fearless.

Competition between the Carolingian Louis d'Outremer and the Capetian Count Hugh of Paris for the kingdom of France was an issue which did not particularly interest Longsword, but he could not help becoming embroiled and

one of the most highly feudalised states in Europe. Richard jealously guarded his role as the supreme spiritual as well as secular power in the land and saw to it that the Norman Church was generously maintained. He expanded the Fécamp monastery founded by his father and regenerated Mont-St-Michel and St-Ouen at Rouen. He was, in short, the patron of the school of Norman architecture which became so famous.

Brothers in conflict

Richard II, an illegitimate son, inherited a state whose Frenchness was no longer questionable.

in so doing lost his life to four assassins. His young son, Richard, was at once kidnapped by King Louis, but was rescued by a loyal courtier and carried away in a truss of hay.

Richard the Fearless

Richard thus survived to reign for 50 years, during which the French seemingly came to accept that the "pirates" were there to stay. Under Richard, Normandy became a powerful and wealthy state while remaining relatively small. He was responsible for introducing feudalism, which had gone against the grain of the Viking pioneers.

Over the next 70 years, Normandy became

He broke new ground for a Norman ruler by marrying the mother of his children, instead of settling for a "Danish marriage" neither sanctioned nor solemnised by the Church.

Their children, the future Richard III and Robert I, were the only legitimate dukes of Normandy. On the former's succession in 1026, he was immediately in dispute with his brother Robert over possession of Falaise. Reconciliation called for a boisterous party in Rouen, after which the young king and several guests took ill and died. Robert was suspected of poisoning them, but even if he was responsible there were insufficient grounds to prevent him from succeeding as Robert I.

The Atheling princes

Falaise, the cause of the fraternal quarrel, stands high above the Ante, a tributary of the River Dives. Robert had a castle here, and the story goes that from one of the windows he was bewitched by the sight of a girl paddling in the river below. She was Arletta, the daughter of a tanner in an age when tanning was a despised trade, if only because of the smell. Arletta gave Robert two children, William the Bastard (later the Conqueror), and one daughter.

After uninterrupted success both in war and internal administration, Robert's reign ran into difficulties over two refugees who took shelter in Rouen, the so-called Atheling princes of England, the sons of Ethelred the Unready and Robert's aunt, Emma. She had subsequently married Canute, Ethelred's successor as king of England, who had a son, Harold, by his previous marriage. At its simplest, Emma wished to get rid of Harold to further the interests of the Athelings, her children by Ethelred.

Robert was cajoled into threatening Canute with war if he did not put the Athelings in line for the English throne, and he went as far as assembling a fleet at Fécamp before adverse winds made him change his mind. The impossible odds against success made some of his advisers wonder about his sanity. When he then announced that he wished to go to Jerusalem instead, their convictions were strengthened.

Carried by devils

The duke at least made arrangements in case he did not come back. Young William was nominated as his heir with the duke of Brittany the regent-designate. Between Constantinople and Jerusalem Robert met a Norman pilgrim on the way home. By then Robert could no longer ride and was being carried in a litter by black slaves. The returning Norman asked whether he could take back any messages. "Tell them," Robert replied, "you saw me being carried to Paradise by devils." He managed to reach Jerusalem but died and was buried at Nicaea on the return journey. The reference to devils may explain why he is sometimes called "Robert the Devil" rather than "Robert the Magnificent", the title he preferred.

LEFT: wall relief from William the Conqueror's castle in Dives-sur-Mer.
RIGHT: William, the first Norman king of England.

William the Conqueror

The future William the Conqueror was just eight years old when word was received of Robert's death. The general population welcomed his succession, but ruthless ambition flared and a number of barons closed in for a quick kill. As William's tutor and bodyguards, one of whom slept in the same room, were murdered one after another, his regent the duke of Brittany appealed for reason and was himself poisoned. William's mother spirited him away to a succession of peasant communities in remote parts of the country. This peripatetic upbringing among Frankish peasants isolated

William from the influence of the Scandinavian military caste, but at the same time it deprived him of the formal education which had been a feature of his immediate predecessors. When time was ripe for him to make his first public appearance as the duke, William was 14 and his character was already set in stone. He was taciturn, bitter and ambitious.

Revenge on the Angevins

At 19, he crushed the so-called Great Revolt of the Barons at Val-ès-Dunes, and not long afterwards was provoked into an outrage which was to haunt him for the rest of his life. During a siege of Angevin forces occupying Alençon, the defenders beat the skins stretched along the top of the walls to deflect fire bombs and set up a chant of "Skins, skins, plenty of skins for the tanner!" William took this, no doubt correctly, as a slur on his mother. He ordered the hands and feet of 33 Angevin prisoners to be hacked off and their eyes put out. The wretches were then made to crawl back to their position as best they could.

Marriage and consolidation

Legend has it that William mellowed on falling in love with Matilda, daughter of Baldwin of Flanders. He urgently needed an heir: unclear

vassal, not a rival. Two French invasions were seen off at Mortemer and Varaville, and William's conquest of Maine in 1062 neatly rounded off Normandy's borders. In 1066, when he felt ready to turn his attention to other matters, William had been ruler of Normandy for 20 years – and was still only 38. His plans for the conquest of England were galvanised by the death of Edward the Confessor on 5 January 1066, ending the line of Danish kings.

Edward left a widow, Edith, daughter of Godwin, the earl of Kent and effectively Edward's prime minister. Godwin was one of the few Anglo-Saxons to hold high political of-

succession was a recipe for intrigue and treachery. The Count of Arques was one who fancied himself as a candidate, and was presumed to be among those who persuaded, or bribed, Pope Leo IX to forbid the proposed marriage on the spurious grounds of consanguinity. William and Matilda went ahead anyway with a ceremony at Eu and a writ of excommunication soon followed. This was lifted by Leo's successor, Pope Nicholas II, after William had agreed to build in Caen the Abbaye-aux-Hommes for himself and the Abbaye-aux-Dames for Matilda.

William's *modus vivendi* with King Henry I of France was undermined by Normandy's increasing prosperity. The king wanted a feudal

fice under the Danish kings; he represented an Anglo-Saxon revival keen to reclaim the English throne, especially as Edward's policy of conjugal self-denial meant that he had died without issue.

Hereditary wrangles

The Anglo-Saxons wanted Godwin's son Harold to rule, but Duke William believed he had a hereditary right to the throne through his father's aunt, the indefatigable Emma.

An enormous amount of ink has been expended on whether Edward wished Harold or William to succeed him. It hardly mattered, because the decision rested not with him but the Witan, a kind of privy council which the Anglo-Saxons dominated.

There is also the thorny question of whether Harold, under oath, had forfeited his claim to the throne to William. It seems that Harold was blown ashore in France by a storm and ended up as William's prisoner. The oath was the price of his freedom. According to one of the more colourful versions, the oath was sworn on a table covered by a cloth and might have been a casual affair had not William whipped the cloth aside to reveal that the oath had been taken on the relics of saints, a different kettle of fish altogether.

1,000 cavalry – and while the majority of the troops were Normans, they were joined by mercenaries and freebooters from all over the Continent. Rémi of Fécamp had William's promise of an English bishopric in exchange for providing one ship and 20 men-at-arms. William himself had in his pocket a Papal Bull, investing him with the title of king of England.

William's victory – and Harold's death – at the Battle of Hastings in 1066 gave him the English crown on Christmas Day. Thereafter William lived a double life, commuting between his roles as duke of Normandy and king of England. Much of what happened to William

Conquest of England

In any case, Harold had a head start by being in England when Edward died. The Witan rushed through Harold's election and he was crowned the same day by the Archbishop of York. William was out hunting when the news reached Normandy, and it is said he sat for some hours in silent thought. The outcome was the assembly of the largest invasion force the English Channel had seen – between 600 and 700 ships carrying some 7,000 men, including

LEFT: the Norman fleet sails across the Channel.
ABOVE: William's brother, Odo, presides over a feast; both as depicted in the Bayeaux Tapestry.

after 1066 belongs to the history of England rather than Normandy. However, September 1087, saw him engaged in a punitive raid against the French in Vexin. He was watching Nantes go up in flames when his horse trod on live coals and sent its rider crashing to the ground. The internal injuries proved terminal, but the long weeks before his death in the Abbey of St-Gervais in Rouen enabled William to put his affairs into order as best he could.

A tale of three brothers

Robert, William's oldest son, was to become duke of Burgundy and William Rufus, his second son, king of England. Henry, the third son, had to be content with a substantial sum of silver. "What shall I do with that gift," he complained, "if I have no land to live in?" William advised him to be ready to step into either brother's shoes. He indicated that, sadly, the need would not be long in arriving and that Henry would surpass his elder brothers in both riches and power.

Robert set Normandy on the road to ruin from the moment he took over. He was as courageous as his ancestors but also, unfortunately, "prodigal, inconsiderate, a slave to sensual passions, irresolute and vacillating". With his ready stockpile of silver, all Henry needed

that it would soon be his, expanded the duchy to include Nantes and Vexin.

The end of William Rufus

William was back in England contemplating further acquisitions when his customary spot of hunting after dinner went awry. A companion's cross-bow bolt may or may not have ricocheted off a deer, but in any case William Rufus was stretched out dead. His brother Henry – curiously – happened to be in England and at once galloped to Winchester where the royal treasure was kept. Three days later he was crowned king of England. "Thus," says a

was a little patience. When the inevitable happened and Robert applied for an urgent loan, Henry drove a hard bargain: 3,000lb of silver (three-fifths of his inheritance) for the Cotentin, which amounted to one third of Normandy.

Robert then announced he was going off on the First Crusade. Taking the Cross was an expensive enterprise, however, and he pawned his remaining share of Normandy to William Rufus. If he failed to return from the Holy Land or for any other reason failed to redeem the loan within five years, William Rufus would become duke of Normandy as well as king of England.

In Robert's absence, William Rufus paid frequent visits to Normandy and, fully confident

chronicler, "was Robert a second time deprived of the crown of England by a younger brother."

A deal is done

Robert returned exhausted from the Holy Land just a month later, landing at Mont-St-Michel. After attending to one or two local emergencies, he mounted the second substantial Norman invasion of England and landed safely at Portsmouth in 1101.

The great Norman families had estates on both sides of the Channel and would not happily sacrifice either, so Robert and Henry were persuaded to negotiate a settlement by which Robert dropped his claim to the English throne while Henry ceded the Cotentin he had bought from him, together with all other possessions in Normandy bar Domfront.

By fortifying Domfront with Château Tinchebrai, Henry was plainly waiting for Robert to bring such despair to Normandy that he could step in and be welcomed as a saviour. He made his move in August 1106. "I have not resolved on despoiling you of your duchy," he informed his brother on landing with his army, "but, invoked by the tears of the poor, I desire to succour the church of God, which, like a vessel without a pilot, runs great danger in the midst of a stormy sea."

ment of William, his 18-year-old son, as duke of Burgundy, and arrangements were in hand to have his younger son, Richard, acknowledged as his heir to the English throne. With his affairs in France neatly in order, Henry was feeling at "the pinnacle of human grandeur" as he prepared to sail from Barfleur for England. But the ship carrying his two sons was wrecked on tidal rocks, and Henry never smiled again.

The end of a dynasty

The drowning signalled the end of the dynasty founded by Rollo because Henry had no other children and the best he could do was arrange a

Henry offered to settle for just half of Normandy. Robert refused, and the Battle of Tinchebrai was joined on Michaelmas Eve 1106. Its outcome left Henry in full possession of Normandy, as his father had correctly foretold. Henry I of England thus became the ninth Duke of Normandy.

Henry ruthlessly defended both kingdom and duchy. Robert was blinded and spent the remaining 27 years of his life in the castle at Cardiff. Henry got France to affirm the invest-

second marriage for his daughter Matilda, widowed young by the death of the German emperor, Otto. Her new husband was Geoffrey the Fair, Count of Anjou, who, by wearing a sprig of broom in his cap, earned a resounding nickname, Plantagenet (Fr. *genet* = broom).

The transition was far from smooth as Stephen of Blois, William the Conqueror's nephew, seized both Norman and English crowns on Henry's death. Geoffrey concentrated on regaining Normandy while Matilda worked on England. Both achieved their objectives but Matilda quickly fell out of favour in England and was driven out to make way for the return of Stephen of Blois. Geoffrey's son,

LEFT: Henry II bids farewell to Thomas Becket.
ABOVE: Richard the Lionheart faces Philippe-Auguste on the battlefield of Gisors.

Henry, therefore succeeded as tenth Duke of Burgundy but not to the English throne.

Eleanor of Aquitaine, divorced in disgrace from Louis VII of France because of an affair with her uncle Raymond of Antioch during the Second Crusade – she went along dressed as an Amazonian warrior – took a fancy to Henry. She brought to their marriage a dowry which made him ruler of all western France from Flanders to Spain. This gave him the strength to exact from Stephen of Blois an undertaking that, on Stephen's death, he would inherit the English throne. The thrones were thus reunited.

Plots and rebellions

Henry's attempts to limit the power of the Church led to the exile, then the martyrdom, of his Archbishop of Canterbury, Thomas Becket. A number of Norman churches claim connection with the saint from his time in exile. Meanwhile, Henry's unbridled infidelities provoked Eleanor into a rebellious plot which was uncovered and resulted in her being locked up indefinitely. The untimely deaths of two older brothers made Richard heir apparent. Father and son fell out when Richard learned that the woman he was to marry, Alice, sister of Philippe-Auguste of France, had been seduced by his father while she was a minor in his care.

Henry was still fuming on his death-bed: "Cursed be the day of my birth, cursed be the sons I leave behind."

The second surviving son whom Henry cursed was John Lackland, who plotted with Philippe-Auguste while Richard Coeur de Lion (Lionheart) was winning glory on the Third Crusade. News of John's activities brought Richard hurrying home, a return delayed by his incarceration by the German emperor, pending payment of a colossal ransom.

Richard eventually reached England in 1194 and sailed from Portsmouth the same year with a fleet of 100 ships. Landing at Barfleur, he meant to deal with both John and Philippe-Auguste. The former, who had been installed as governor of Évreux, capitulated almost at once, but the campaign against Philippe-Auguste continued. In 1198 Richard "fell like a lion upon its prey" at Gisors, where Philippe had to be dragged out of the river at the town's gate to add to his humiliating defeat.

The following year, while besieging Chalus castle in the Limousin, Richard was hit by an arrow. His wound turned gangrenous and he died on 6 April 1199. His will bestowed 18,000 gallons of wine a year on Rouen cathedral and another 6,000 gallons on the archbishop, consignments which continued to arrive and were consumed until 1553. The larger matter of the duchy of Normandy and kingdom of England was settled in favour of his nephew, Arthur, Duke of Brittany, as Richard died childless.

Foul murder

Arthur was only 14 and John Lackland was not ready to abide by Richard's will. The Archbishop of Rouen also defied Richard's wishes to invest John as Duke of Normandy, and the Archbishop of Canterbury followed suit by crowning him at Westminster. Arthur's fate was sealed. John personally dragged him out of his Rouen cell, plunged a sword through his heart and dumped the body in the Seine. While some historians argue that Arthur was murdered at Cherbourg and dumped in the sea, there is no dispute that John's hand struck the fatal blow.

John's poor record

John's reign in Normandy was if anything more wretched than his performance in England which resulted in his being forced to sign the barons' Magna Carta in 1215. Philippe-Auguste was not slow to exploit the disaffection, with visible preparations to seize Normandy. John was curiously indifferent to the threat.

"Let Philippe proceed," he remarked, "I will recover more in a day than he can gain in a year." Twelve months later, however, his possessions in France were reduced to Rouen, Verneuil and Château Gaillard, the great castle Richard had built overlooking the River Seine.

The issue was effectively settled at Château Gaillard after a heroic defence lasting six months. That left only Rouen, and a plea for help by the city deputies was received with the same indifference. John was playing chess when they arrived and made them wait until the game was finished. He said he could do nothing, and they should look after themselves. Their reaction was to hand over the keys to Rouen without further resistance, thus reversing in 1204 the independence Charles the Simple had ceded to Rollo 282 years earlier. ❑

RIGHT: detailed figurative columns in the Abbaye St-Georges at St-Martin-de-Boscherville.

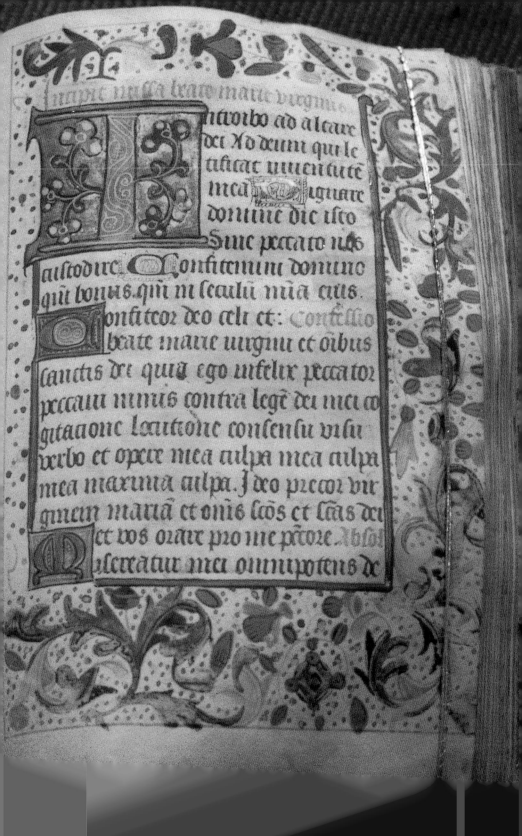

Introibo ad altare
dei Ad deum qui le
tificat iuuentutem
meam Dignare
domine die isto
Sine peccato nos
custodire. Confitemini domino
quia bonus.quia in seculum misericordia eius.
Confiteor deo celi et: Confessio
beate marie virginis et omnibus
sanctis dei quia ego infelix peccator
peccaui nimis contra legem dei mea co
gitatione locutione consensu visu
verbo et opere mea culpa mea culpa
mea maxima culpa. Ideo precor vir
ginem mariam et omnis sanctos et sanctas dei
et vos orare pro me peccatore. Absol
Misereatur mei omnipotens de

A FRENCH PROVINCE

The 14th to 16th centuries were a turbulent period, fraught by the Hundred Years' War with England and the Wars of Religion between Catholics and Huguenots

Normandy's relatively quiet life as a province of France ended in 1346 when Edward III of England landed his army in the Cotentin. Normandy was dragged into the Hundred Years' War between England and France. By ignoring William the Conqueror's citadel in Caen and making straight for the town's commercial centre, Edward showed he was more interested in plunder than conquest. The booty included 40,000 pieces of cloth and filled 100 English ships.

After giving Rouen the same treatment, Edward meant to go home but found that the Seine bridges had been cut behind him. Pursued by a French army 30,000 strong, he turned to face them just north of the forest of Crécy near Abbeville. Here the new English longbows demonstrated their phenomenal range. Some 1,500 French knights were brought down before reaching the English lines.

Henri of Navarre, the French king's disloyal brother, dragged Normandy deeper into the war by allowing the English to use his Norman holdings as a base. After several decades of inconclusive fighting, Henry V, the last great English Plantagenet, was determined to settle the matter once and for all by conquering the whole of France. In August 1415, he set out from Southampton with 1,500 ships and nearly 10,000 men. Thanks to Shakespeare, his encouragement to the troops as they stormed Harfleur's defences has gone into the English language in the play of *Henry V*: "Once more unto the breach, dear friends, once more...".

The Battle of Agincourt

The garrison at Rouen was a tougher nut to crack, particularly as dysentery reduced Henry's army to only 6,000 men in any condition to fight. Thinking the port of Calais would be a softer target, Henry was well on his way when

he was pulled up short by a French army five times the size of his own. The battle fought on St Crispin's Day was Agincourt, and Henry's pep-talk to the troops inspired Shakespeare to even greater heights of patriotic rhetoric.

The stunning victory at Agincourt persuaded the previously reluctant English government to

give Henry the money needed to complete the conquest of France. He returned in 1417 and quickly captured Caen, Bayeux, Falaise and Cherbourg. Rouen held out under siege for six months. Henry's ambition was within his grasp when the 1420 Treaty of Troyes promised him the French throne on the death of the lunatic incumbent Charles VI. But Charles outlived Henry, albeit by a few days, and his successor, Charles VII, immediately tore up the treaty.

Divine guidance

Henry's dying words to his brother, the Duke of Bedford, were to hang on to Normandy at all costs. The duke repulsed a Franco-Scottish attack in 1424, but the focus of the war then moved to an Orleans peasant girl who said she could hear the voices of St Michael, St Catherine and St Margaret. They were telling her, Joan of Arc, that her destiny was to rid France of the English. Brushing aside the barriers that denied peasants a royal audience, Joan not only got to see the future Charles VII but talked him into putting 4,000 troops at her disposal to lift the siege of Orleans.

According to Bedford, the white suit of armour she affected made the English troops believe that they were up against some kind of divine Amazon.

VOICE OF THE ERA

The Norman poet Alain Chartier spoke for the French conscience during the Hundred Years' War. Born in Bayeux and educated at the University of Paris, Chartier wrote a Quadrilogue Invective (1422) blaming nobility and peasants equally for France's ills. "Seek," he cried sarcastically, "seek, ye Frenchmen, the savour of delicious meats, long periods of repose from toil borrowed by the night from day, outrageous garments and trinkets, the caresses and delights of womankind. Fall into slumber, like to swine, amid dirt and the vileness of those horrible sins that have brought you so near to the end of all your days."

Trial by the Inquisition

The English were beaten and Joan, with her banner aloft, took pride of place next to Charles as he was crowned in the cathedral at Reims, to the east of Paris, on 20 July 1429. Slightly wounded in an attempt to retake Paris, Joan recovered to take part in an action at Compiègne against the Duke of Burgundy, England's ally. She was captured while leading a sortie and had a ransom of 10,000 crowns put on her head. Charles VII was not interested but the English certainly were.

She was taken to Rouen to face charges of heresy and sorcery. The trial was before an ecclesiastical court of the Inquisition under Pierre Cauchon, Bishop of Beauvais, who had designs on the archbishopric of Rouen.

Cauchon planned to trick Joan into an admission of guilt, but he under-estimated her quick-wittedness. Unchastened, Joan was taken back to the castle to examine various instruments of torture while she still had time to change her plea. This underestimated her courage.

Found guilty when the trial resumed, she was led to a waiting stake in the cemetery of the Abbey of St-Ouen. Joan then broke down, made a wild recantation and was escorted back to her prison cell with the sentence commuted to life imprisonment. This pleased neither Cauchon nor the English.

The martyred maid

On Trinity Sunday, 1431, guards entered Joan's cell and told her to change into male clothing. She refused to budge until, at midday, "for bodily necessities she was constrained to rise and put on the said clothes". The guards sprang into action. At her trial she had specifically renounced women who wore male clothing – like white suits of armour – and she had now gone back on this solemn undertaking. A second trial in the archbishop's chapel pronounced the death sentence, because of her relapse into "heresy and schism".

Joan was brought under heavy guard the following day to the Rouen market place where a large crowd had gathered round a pyre. The death sentence was confirmed aloud but there was no repetition of the previous breakdown. Joan went serenely to the flames and afterwards her ashes were cast into the Seine. Curiously, she was designated Venerable only in 1904 and was not canonised until 1920.

England in retreat

Joan's execution coincided with the Duke of Burgundy's switch of allegiance from England to France and the death of the Duke of Bedford from exhaustion. England was now in retreat, and in 1436 Paris hooted a contemptuous farewell to the last English troops.

For Normandy this was not quite the end of the war because for eight more years the English fleet buzzed about the Channel, and fortresses like Honfleur frequently changed hands. Nevertheless, Joan's martyrdom in the place du Vieux-Marché in Rouen was the symbolic turning-point.

by an unamused king of Castile. The French as a whole both hated and feared the sea, but the Normans, who routinely fished off Newfoundland and Iceland, were at ease with it.

In spite of the lurking hazard of the English fleet, the Ango family of Dieppe built up an impressive merchant fleet during the latter stages of the Hundred Years' War. Jean Ango, born in 1481, expanded the business by leaps and bounds so that King François I, perennially short of money and therefore obliged to ingratiate himself with wealthy subjects, made him Viscount of Dieppe. Ango commissioned two Florentine brothers, Giovanni and Giro-

The great explorers

While the Normandy countryside took a battering during the Hundred Years' War, Norman seafarers ran the gauntlet down the English Channel to greater things. In 1362, a party of Dieppe traders sailed down the African coast as far as what is now Sierra Leone and established a colony that they called Petit Dieppe. A century or so later, John de Béthencourt discovered the Canary Islands and triumphantly proclaimed himself king, soon to be dethroned

lamo da Verrazano, to investigate the east coast of America. Their trips were fruitful: Giovanni discovered the bay of Manhattan and came across the future site of New York. Another Ango captain, Jean Fleury, captured three caravels off the Azores in 1521. It transpired that they were carrying Montezuma's treasure back from Mexico.

The Parmentier brothers, also in Ango's pay, sailed round the Cape of Good Hope to Sumatra and Java in the year of 1529. Paulmier de Gonneville, "gentleman of Honfleur", steered his ship *Espoir* to Brazil while Jean Denis, merely "sailor of Honfleur", explored the mouth of the St Lawrence River.

LEFT: Joan of Arc, dressed for battle.
ABOVE: Philippe-August's castle, where the maid was kept before being burned on a pyre.

Power goes to Ango's head

Back in Dieppe, Ango invested some of his great fortune in a magnificent house built out of carved oak. It was named, like his flag-ship, *La Pensée*. This house perished in the Anglo-Dutch bombardment of Dieppe in 1694, but the contemporary and equally grand Manoir d'Ango at Varengeville near Dieppe, which he had built by Italian craftsmen in the Renaissance style with an exotic dovecote, still survives *(see page 215)*.

Being granted letters of marque by François seemed to go to Ango's head. While he is reckoned to have seized 300 ships belonging to

At his death in 1551, the family silver had gone and the Manoir d'Ango had been stripped of its celebrated art collection. Luckily, an impressive tomb in the church of St-Jacques in Dieppe, where he had been mayor, had been paid for in advance. The French Wars of Religion wiped out most of the Norman toe-holds abroad, and it was only afterwards that business returned to normal.

Exploring the New World

Samuel de Champlain was born in Bordeaux but established a ship-building business in Dieppe which provided him with the means to

others, when Portugal captured two of his, he ordered his captains to bombard Portuguese coastal villages and threatened to blockade Lisbon. King John of Portugal backed down, but Ango's dealing with the French kings were less satisfactory.

Having lent vast sums to François I, he was unable to recover the money from his successor Henri II. To compound his misery, the many commercial enemies he had made over the years found that with Henri II nodding appreciatively in the background, the courts were sympathetic to their grievances and ready to award exemplary damages. Ango watched his fortune evaporate in a welter of litigation.

explore the Canadian coast. On the third of these voyages, in 1608, he founded Quebec and from there set out to map large tracts of the virgin interior. Normans were a large contingent among the Frenchmen who flocked to join him. In 1612 Champlain was appointed lieutenant of Canada, and when Quebec was seized during the subsequent Anglo–French war, it was largely his artful diplomacy that returned the province to French sovereignty.

Pierre Belain of Esnambuc took possession of Martinique and Guadeloupe in the name of France in 1635, and Cavelier de La Salle of Rouen, after investigating the site of Chicago, sailed down the Mississippi to map Louisiana.

This second wave of overseas exploration needed French settlers to constitute a viable empire, and the intolerable climate in France during the Wars of Religion provided the impetus. Thousands of Canadians today can trace their families back to Normandy.

Revolt against Rome

In spite of 88 burnings at the stake, Calvinism had made considerable progress in France over a period of some 20 years before Henry II's death in 1559. Calvinists, followers of the religious reformer John Calvin, who was born Jean Cauvin in neighbouring Picardy, were called

in brothels or taverns and sometimes went years without saying Mass.

By the mid-16th century, Huguenots were challenging Roman Catholicism's traditional hold on the French establishment. Aristocrats banded together on either side of an increasingly hostile religious divide. François, Duke of Guise, and his brother Charles, Cardinal of Reims, led the Catholics.

The mere fact that the Huguenots were critical of the king endeared them to the rival Bourbons, notably Antoine of Navarre and his brother Louis, Duke of Condé. A third group were Catholic by faith but could not stand the

Huguenots in France. They had powerful friends in the army, in the establishment generally, and among the provincial gentry. Their strongholds in Normandy were Rouen and Caen University.

Calvinism was an intellectual revolt against sloth and corruption in the Roman Church. In the latter respect, the Church in Normandy had its own critic in Eude Rigaud, archbishop of Rouen. His *Journal of Pastoral Visits* is a sorrowful account of priests who spent their lives

LEFT: St Bartholomew's Day Massacre in 1572.
ABOVE: the busy river port of Rouen
in a 17th-century painting.

Queen Mother or the Guises. Gaspard de Coligny, Admiral of France, emerged as the leader of these so-called Politiques, and as far as the Catholics were concerned, they were worse than Huguenots.

The widespread suspicion that Catherine de'Medici, Queen Mother and Regent to the young Charles IX, was softening her attitude towards Huguenots, sent the Catholics running to Spain for armed support. The Huguenots in turn looked to England and were prepared to make a gift of Le Havre as an inducement. The prospect of Protestant English pouring into Le Havre looked like the Hundred Years' War all over again: the religious dam burst.

The Wars of Religion

In Caen, Catholics held William the Conqueror's citadel and were attacked from the spire of St-Pierre opposite by snipers. The Catholics replied with a cannon and nearly brought the spire down. With the capture of Rouen and the defeat of the forces of Admiral Coligny and the Duke of Condé at Dreux, the war was going well for the Catholics, but they lost momentum with the assassination of the Duke of Guise. An attempt was made on Coligny's life, backed by the Queen Mother, who wanted to abort his scheme for the Huguenot Henri of Navarre, to marry her daughter, Margaret.

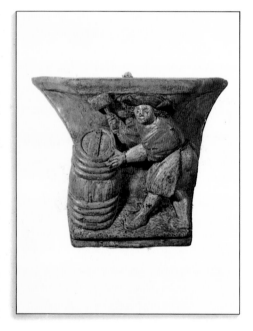

The dreaded wedding went ahead, however, and it was the sight of so many prominent Huguenots assembled in Paris for the occasion that prompted the Queen Mother to issue orders, on 24 August 1572, for the notorious St Bartholomew's Day Massacre. Among the thousands of Huguenots butchered in France that day was Admiral Coligny, whose head was chopped off and sent to the pope for approval.

The massacre provoked an orgy of reprisals wherever there was a significant Huguenot presence, and in Normandy that meant Rouen especially. When Henri III, the last of Catherine de'Medici's sons, was hacked to death by a Jacobin, Henry of Navarre came to the throne.

Henry's rule

Arques-la-Bataille in Normandy, the castle built in the 11th century by William the Conqueror's uncle, Guillaume de Talou, was the test of Henri's ability to rule over the objections of the Catholic League. In the event, the defeat he inflicted on the military pride of the League at Arques put an end to taunts about "the king without a throne". Nevertheless, he had to renounce Protestantism and besiege Paris for eight months before he could properly rule as Henri IV, and by placating the Catholics he antagonised the Huguenots.

The Huguenots had a battle-hardened army of 25,000 and could not be trifled with. They were granted the Edict of Nantes, guaranteeing them freedom of worship in their castles and other specified places, equality of civil rights, judicial protection and the right to garrison more than 100 fortified towns. It created, in short, a Huguenot state-within-a-state. The Catholics insisted on a *quid pro quo* – the recall of the Jesuits, earlier banished from France as "corrupters of the young, disturbers of public order and enemies of both king and state".

Marvellous ruin

The Jesuits were to wield enormous influence under Henri's successor, Louis XIV. They assured him that revoking the Edict of Nantes would bring the Huguenots back into the Roman Church. When in 1685 Louis bowed to the pressure, the court preacher rejoiced: "This is the worthy achievement of your reign and its true character... heresy is no more. God above has made this marvel." What happened was that the Huguenots, the brains and wealth of France, packed their bags and left. For Rouen, "God's marvel" was an economic disaster.

Another miscalculation of Louis's reign was getting involved in attempts to restore the exiled James II to the English throne. An army was made ready in 1692 to carry James back. The French fleet nosed out of port to see if the coast was clear. It was not. An Anglo-Dutch fleet was lying in wait. Valour took precedence over discretion and Admiral Tourville's flagship was knocked out of action. From the village of Quineville James watched the destruction of his hopes, and wept. ❏

LEFT: 17th-century carving shows a cooper at work.
RIGHT: colourful depiction of Boucher in Canada.

MANOIR DE BOUCHERVILLE CANADA

NOTRE DAME DE BOULOGNE

1662 PARTANT POUR LE CANADA

PIERRE BOUCHER DE LA ROCHELLE

ACCOMPAGNE DE COLONS ET DE SOLDATS

EN 1652 PIERRE BOUCHER DEFEND VICTORIEUSEMENT TROIS RIVIERES CONTRE LES IROQUOIS

LOYAL ROYALISTS

Girondins and Chouans both used Normandy as a base during the French Revolution. A century later, it was attracting writers, artists and high society

The fabulous court Louis XIV maintained at Versailles tends to disguise the fact that under him and his immediate successors France was practically bankrupt. Economics and efficient taxation were a blindspot, and the kings were also curiously blind to the lessons of history. An attempt to tax salt in western France in 1639 resulted in rebellion by the Avranches salt-workers. Armed bands led by Jean Quetil, "John Barefoot", went on the rampage, at one point holding the villages of Mortain and Pont-orson to ransom. Draconian measures were needed to rescue the country from the so-called Barefoot Peasants' War.

The higher clergy and nobility, who could afford to pay taxes, paid none at all. In 1789 the Third Estate, the social ranking lower than aristocracy and clergy, proclaimed a National Assembly and converged on the tennis court at Versailles to demand a new constitution. When it became apparent that the king would side with the aristocracy against them, the crowd's rage boiled over into the storming of the Bastille and the unfurling of the tricolor.

Normandy abolished

In one single night the National Assembly formally abolished everything redolent of the *ancien régime,* and that included Normandy and the other provinces. Normandy ceased to be a legal entity and was replaced by the five *départements* which still exist.

Province or not, Normandy had a special role in the French Revolution as a bed of counter-revolutionary activity when, it seemed to the majority of provincial people, the Revolution had been commandeered by the Paris mob.

To begin with, however, leadership of the 1791 Assembly was assumed by a body of young, middle-class men drawn from the Gironde in southwest France – hence the name

"Girondins". They regarded themselves as evangelists of a new international order, and it was not an order that rang sweetly in the ears of the autocratic heads of surrounding states. The naivety of the Girondins was their Achilles' heel when it came to coping with the likes of Robespierre and the Jacobins. In the latter's company, the Girondins were a voice of moderation and, when the Terror commenced, that was enough to condemn them, together with the royals and royalists, to the unforgiving power of the guillotine.

The People's Friend

The chief tormentor of the Girondins was Jean-Paul Marat, a long-time insurrectionist who had spent so much time hiding in rat-infested sewers that he contracted "a loathsome skin disease, making his naturally ugly face hideous and horrible". Marat ran a militant newspaper, *Ami du Peuple,* and by transmutation himself became "The People's Friend".

PRECEDING PAGES: inaugurating a statue of Admiral Duquesne in Dieppe.
LEFT: celebrating the fêtes de St-Louis in Caen.
RIGHT: traditional dress for a 19th-century rider.

Caen opened its gates to Girondist refugees and they fired the imagination of a young woman named Charlotte Corday, whose family history in Normandy could be traced back to the 11th century. She was descended from the dramatist Pierre Corneille and educated at the Abbaye-aux-Dames in Caen, where her cousin was the last abbess. She became devoted to the ideals of Voltaire and Jean-Jacques Rousseau.

Having made the acquaintance of the Girondin circle in Caen, Charlotte was shocked to learn that another batch of Girondins had been sent to the scaffold in Paris. She slipped secretly out of her father's house. "I am leaving without your permission," she said in a note, "without seeing you, because I should be so sorrowful. I am going to England." It was reputed to be the only lie she ever told. Charlotte was in fact going to Paris, and her purpose was to avenge the death of the Girondins.

Marat was not at the Ministry of Interior when Charlotte called in. He was working from home, being nursed through a recurrence of his sewer complaint by his mistress Simone Évrard. Charlotte tracked down his flat at 30 rue des Cordeliers but was twice refused admittance. She then decided to send a note by ordinary post: "Citizen, I come from Caen. Your love for your country makes me think you would like to know the miserable events in that part of the Republic. I shall present myself at your house at seven o'clock; have the goodness to receive me and grant me a moment's interview. I shall put you in a position to render a great service to the country."

Charlotte presented herself as promised but was again refused entry. She kicked up such a fuss that Marat, lying in a warm bath, asked Simone to find out what was happening. On hearing that it was the young woman who had written the note, he asked for her to be shown in. Charlotte found him in the bath with a board set up as a writing desk.

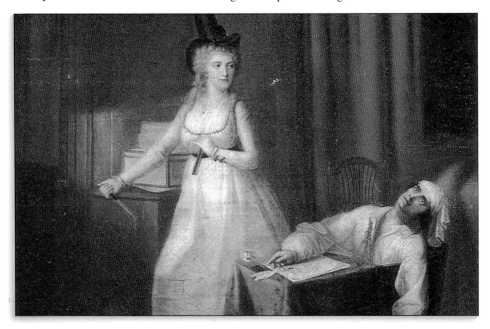

Charlotte told him that Caen was sheltering 18 dangerous Girondins. Marat asked for their names and when she reeled them off he passed summary judgement: "They will be guillotined." This was Charlotte's cue. She whipped out a kitchen knife she had purchased earlier in the day and plunged it into the heart of the People's Friend. He died at once.

Unrepentant murderess

At her trial, Charlotte expressed no remorse: "I have killed one man to save a hundred thousand," she said. Seeing an artist sketching the trial, she struck a proud pose. The sentence of death was assured. She was just 25 years old.

"Upon the stage of her execution," a newspaper reported, "her face had still the freshness and colour of a pleased woman." As her head rolled off, a carpenter named Legros picked it up and thumped the ears, a gesture which won the approval of the crowd but earned him the pillory and a term of imprisonment on the grounds that an inanimate head could not be guilty of conduct deserving such punishment.

The Chouan revolt

The Girondins were not alone in using Normandy as a base for counter-revolutionary activities. A second movement owed its origins

to wage a classic guerrilla campaign, disappearing into the landscape or friendly houses when the enemy approached in strength, regrouping later for surprise attacks elsewhere. If the Chouans wore any identifying insignia it was a white cockade, the antithesis of the republican tricolor. To be caught wearing the cockade carried an automatic death sentence.

Like most guerrilla wars, the Chouan campaign resulted in atrocities by both sides, although these have been obscured by the romantic gloss put on the business by the writer Jules-Amédée Barbey d'Aurevilly, whose *petite noblesse* Norman family was closely involved

to peasants in La Vendée who opposed the Revolution because it made the clergy subject to civil authority. A proposed tax increase in February 1793 inflamed their discontent into a rebellion which royalists were quick to exploit. When the revolt reached Brittany and Normandy, it was spearheaded by the "Catholic and Royal Army" known by the Bas-Breton word for screech-owls, "Chouans".

Chouans used their local knowledge of heaths, marshes, woods and hedge-bound fields

with the Chouans. Another of the renowned aristocratic rebels was Count Louis de Frotte, whose family still owns the château of Couterne near Bagnoles.

While the worst of the Terror ended when Robespierre went to the scaffold, Chouan resistance continued against the five-man Directory which took over. Count Louis was eventually betrayed and, with seven companions, fell before a firing squad at Verneuil.

Napoleon in Normandy

The signature on Count Louis's death warrant belonged to the Director who proposed, within a short space of time, to dispense with the

LEFT: Charlotte Corday murders Jean-Paul Marat.
ABOVE: *The Blacksmith*, a painting by Alexandre le Carpentier.

services of his colleagues and run the country his own way: Napoleon Bonaparte.

Napoleon came to Normandy in person to plan his invasion of England. He inspected Cherbourg as a possible springboard for the invasion. The port facilities did not amount to much, heavy seas having frustrated an attempt by the 17th-century engineer Vauban to build an artificial harbour. Napoleon promised that he would give Cherbourg something to rival "the marvels of Egypt". In practice, the project was no more realised than the invasion of England. The docks and a mole were completed on a more modest scale 50 years later.

outfit, would ceremonially welcome his friends of old, beginning with the Prince of Wales. The room was, of course, empty, and the charade ended with Brummell sinking into his one armchair in tears.

He died peacefully in the Bon Saveur asylum in May 1839, leaving a disciple, Barbey d'Aurevilly, the previously mentioned author of tales about the Chouans, who aped Brummell's dress. While the residents of Caen quite admired the style as worn by Brummell, it was not considered suitable for a local man. "At a time when nothing any longer appeared ridiculous," Sainte-Beuve wrote, "Barbey found the

Fashion and style

The story of Normandy in the early 19th century is brightened, but hardly ennobled, by George Bryan "Beau" Brummell, the London dandy who fled to France to avoid creditors and for a while was British consul in Caen. He checked into the now defunct Hôtel de la Victoire near St-Pierre's church and, with barely a penny to his name, breezily ordered "the best rooms, the best dinner and the best Lafitte".

As debts mounted he was relegated to the tattier Hôtel d'Angleterre, where he lost hold of his senses. He would have the room specially furnished with chandeliers, candlesticks and flowers, and then, wearing his most splendid

means of appearing so. An intelligent man would blush to cross Paris with him, even during the Carnival." The Duchesse de Berry turned heads in the same period when she introduced sea-bathing at Dieppe. After undressing in a bathing hut, she was transported to the water's edge in a sedan chair carried by the wives of local fishermen.

Celebrity visitors

The Normandy coast became increasingly fashionable as a summer resort when it was linked by rail to Paris in 1843. Proust revelled in being able to leave the Gare St-Lazare on the 1.22pm train and be at the Grand Hotel in Cabourg in time to dress for dinner. By 1854, when the Rev. George Musgrove dropped in, Dieppe had acquired an ornate casino, "where a thousand ladies in their morning or evening costume may sit at their ease, with book, crochet, or fan in hand, in a long gallery of glass, like fair flowers in a conservatory, awaiting admiration".

With Trouville-Deauville coming on stream, the coast attracted many of the most famous artistic names of the day. Among them were Dumas, father and son, Strindberg, Henry James, George Moore, Proust, Max Beerbohm, Saint-Saens, Debussy, Grieg, Diaghilev and almost all the well-known painters of the time.

Ignominious retreats

The Château d'Eu, originally built by Rollo, the scene of William the Conqueror's wedding to Matilda, and Joan of Arc's stop-over on her way to Rouen, became one of the favourite residences of King Louis-Philippe, after the restoration of the monarchy. Queen Victoria, landing from her yacht at Le Tréport, was twice his guest. But the circumstances in which Louis-Philippe last stayed at the château could hardly have been more ignominious. Driven out of Paris by the mob in 1848, the king and his family were taken secretly to Dreux where he was able to borrow some money from a ten-

Playwright Oscar Wilde made a bee-line for Dieppe on being released from prison in England and was urged by friends to pay a visit to a brothel to rehabilitate his reputation. A crowd of well-wishers accompanied him and waited outside. Wilde let them down. He emerged shaking his head and mumbling something about "cold mutton". Unlike Wilde, the Prince of Wales, the future Edward VII, who would arrive by yacht, passed his time vigorously, in the company of the Duchess of Caracciolo.

FAR LEFT: young Camembert queen.
LEFT: a dairymaid perched on a donkey.
ABOVE: most farms had their own cider press.

ant. They paid a farewell visit to the Château d'Eu before making their way, partly on foot, to Honfleur. An English steamer was at the wharf to take them off. The king and queen left France as Mr and Mrs William Smith, to be replaced by Louis Napoleon and the Second Empire.

The Second Empire ended with the surrender of Napoleon III at the final battle of the Franco-Prussian war (at Sedan) in 1870, but that left the Empress Eugénie still at the Tuileries. She guessed that something serious had gone wrong when breakfast failed to arrive at her chamber at the customary hour. The servants, it transpired, had heard the result of the battle and were too busy pillaging her wardrobe. Realising that she would have to flee, the empress complained that she had nothing to wear. American dentist, Dr Thomas Evans, smuggled Eugénie to Deauville where Sir John Burgoyne, on a yachting holiday, agreed to take her to England.

The Foreign Office was surprised to hear from Sir John that Eugénie was his passenger. Two English agents had been sent to Paris specifically to rescue her and had reported their mission accomplished. It turned out that they had rescued the wrong woman, a surprised but grateful Princess Clotilde. Louis-Napoleon and Eugénie were reunited and spent the rest of their days in Chislehurst, Kent.

Gambetta and the communards

Normandy played only a minor role in the Franco–Prussian war of 1870. The French army capitulated after defeat at Metz, but Paris was still in French hands and irregular bodies of volunteers popped up everywhere. The soul of continued resistance was Léon Gambetta, a fiery orator who, when the Prussians finally encircled Paris, escaped in a balloon, a feat commemorated in the balloon museum established by American publishing tycoon Malcolm Forbes at the Château de Balleroy in Calvados.

Gambetta landed in Rouen and within six weeks raised an army of 180,000 men. This army ended up fighting not the Prussians but

the Paris Communards, a fanatical minority who wanted to secede from France and found a Utopia based on the abolition of property, patriotism, religion, the family, rulers, armies, upper classes and "every species of refinement". At least 14,000 died before they were crushed.

The Great War

When hostilities began in 1914, the German strategy was to put France out of action as quickly as possible in order to deal with the Russians in the east. The French high command initially committed every possible mistake and it looked as if the Germans would take Paris. The capital was saved by Joffré's decisive victory in the valley of the Marne. Having failed to capture Paris, the Germans were denied the Channel ports, and their advance was halted at Ypres.

The Western Front then settled down into a notorious war of attrition between almost static trenches. The ground fighting never reached Normandy. Instead, the Channel ports well behind the lines kept the Anglo-French campaign going with supplies from Britain and later America. The significance of this vital role made a deep impression, some years later, on Adolf Hitler.

Queen of the sea

In the 1930s the name of *Normandie* was spread across the world when the transatlantic liner of that name sailed into the record books. She was then the longest liner in the world and France's pride and joy. Her luxury suites included the Deauville, the Trouville, the Caen and the Rouen, the last of which had four bedrooms and four bathrooms for which more than US$9,000 a head was charged on a memorable cruise to Rio's carnival. She left Le Havre in May 1932 on her maiden voyage in which she crossed the Atlantic and won the blue riband, breaking three records: for the fastest crossing, highest speed and longest day's run.

The *Normandie* was in New York when France fell, and was commandeered by the US navy, but a fire broke out in February 1942 and she was gutted and capsized. After her giant bulk was salvaged she became a troop transport ship, renamed the *Lafayette*. ❑

LEFT: setting off on the transatlantic crossing.
RIGHT: the *Normandie* was the pride of France.

L'ILLUSTRATION

LE PAQUEBOT
"NORMANDIE"

PRIX 5 frs

1er JUIN 1935

D-DAY

The summer of 1944 was the beginning of the end of World War II but for Normandy it was a time of terrible destruction and suffering

One of the arresting moments in the classic film based on Cornelius Ryan's equally gripping book, *The Longest Day*, is a German officer in a cliff-top observation post above a Normandy beach making a final scan of the English Channel before going off duty. The dawn mist is lifting and, sweeping across the horizon, his binoculars suddenly freeze. "The invasion," he gasps down the line to headquarters, "ten thousand ships." Headquarters are sceptical. The Allied invasion of France was not expected yet and in any case would not be in Normandy. "Which way are these ships heading?" a voice asks. The officer lifts his binoculars for another look. "Straight at me."

The degree to which the Germans were taken by surprise is summed up by the fact that Field Marshal Erwin Rommel, the legendary "Desert Fox" to whom Hitler had given the specific task of preparing for the Allied invasion, had two days earlier – on 4 June 1944 – decided it was safe to drive to Germany for his wife's birthday. Hitler and the high command were sure the Allies would land further east at Pas de Calais. The Channel crossing at that point was shortest, as was the distance across the plain of northern France to the German frontier.

Ingenious defences

Nevertheless, Rommel had gone to extraordinary lengths to fortify the Normandy coastline. A string of his own inventions complemented a line of concrete fortresses and blockhouses. Devices planted in the sand between the high and low water lines were designed to destroy landing craft or at least impale them as sitting ducks for shore batteries which had plotted the range of every square inch on the beaches. Around 60 million anti-tank and anti-personnel mines were laid. Some beaches concealed a web of piping which, connected to paraffin tanks,

would at the touch of a button spit out walls of flame. Areas suitable for parachute landings were flooded or laced with explosive stakes nicknamed "Rommel's asparagus".

"The first 24 hours of the invasion will be decisive," Rommel had warned. "The fate of Germany depends on the outcome... For the

Allies, as well as Germany, it will be the longest day."

The war whose end Rommel could foresee in 1944 had, of course, begun in 1939 with Hitler's invasion of Poland. France was invaded in May 1940, the 250,000-strong British Expeditionary Force being evacuated from Dunkerque as Rommel himself entered Cherbourg with his 7th Panzer Division. Hitler seemed to hold all the cards, but in reality the continued presence of a belligerent Britain a few miles away meant he had to defend his Continental conquests. Europe had to become a fortress behind an "Atlantic Wall" running from Norway to Spain.

PRECEDING PAGES: US transporter and landing craft: 7,000 ships and 200,000 men were in the first wave.
LEFT: British troops disembark.
RIGHT: Field Marshall Rommel inspects his defences.

The Dieppe Raid

Compared with the small cloak-and-dagger commando operations that had preceded it and the massive scale of the D-Day landings afterwards, the Dieppe raid on 19 August 1942 looks, in retrospect, says historian John Keegan in his admirable *Six Armies in Normandy*, "so recklessly hare-brained an enterprise that it is difficult to re-construct the official state of mind which gave it birth and drove it forward". The 2nd Canadian Division, as Keegan puts it, "was to sally forth in high summer from ports only 113 km (70 miles)

from the German-occupied coastline and disembark on the esplanade of a French seaside resort." As Dieppe was excluded from the 1944 landings and consequently spared the bombardment, the port is still recognisably as it was in 1942, and it is possible to form a picture of Operation Jubilee.

Commandos went in first, scaling the cliffs that line the Arques River to silence the German gun positions covering the port entrance. This brave and successful assault did not account for other German gunners, some of whom, when the Royal Regiment of Canada moved into the mouth of the gully leading into the cliffs at Puys and dropped the ramps of their landing craft, could aim right down the open mouths of the vessels. A handful of

Canadians survived the solid sheet of fire to reach the shelter of the sea wall and, using "bangalore torpedoes", blew a hole through the barbed wire crowning it. To mount the wall and crawl through the hole, however, was to be exposed to close-range machine-gun fire. Landing craft brought in second and third waves of men to repeat the same futile exercise. Every one of the 554 men who tried was killed or captured.

Ten LCTs (Landing Craft Tanks), each carrying three Churchill tanks, undertook a direct assault on the harbour and promenade. Fifteen of the tanks managed to get as far as the promenade, only to discover that access to the town was blocked by concrete obstacles which shrugged off the sappers' explosives. Trapped in the open, the tank crews kept on firing in support of the infantry until, one by one, they were knocked out. None got away. Deprived of this small measure of covering fire, the infantry on the beaches were mown down. A German gunner later recalled: "I knew as an infantryman I wouldn't have wanted to be in the places of those Canadians, lying on those damned stones, not only having the fire come at them, but with fragments of stone flying everywhere."

Only at Pourville beach, west of town, did the assault parties have any kind of shelter, but even so the casualties were fearsome. *Above them one of the war's most costly dogfights took place between the RAF and the Luftwaffe: 106 Allied planes were lost, 48 German planes shot down.

Of the 4,963 Canadians who set sail from England, only 2,110 returned, and of these 378 were wounded. Of those left behind in Dieppe, 1,874 were prisoners, but many of them were wounded and 72 died of their wounds. Proportionally, the operation ranked with the first day of the Battle of the Somme in World War I as the blackest in British military history.

Arguments about the rationale behind the raid have not yet been resolved. The majority view, perhaps, is that it was undertaken to prove to those calling for a Second Front in 1942, particularly Stalin, that the timing was wrong and that in any case frontal assaults on heavily defended Channel ports would not work. Others have said it taught important lessons about amphibious operations. About as illuminating, says Keegan, as to say that the *Titanic* "taught important lessons about passenger liner design". ❏

LEFT: a Canadian prisoner, one of many captured in the Dieppe Raid.

While Hitler was preoccupied in Russia, the German garrison in Normandy had a significant proportion of second-rate units, composed of men who were on the whole either too young or too old to fight on the Eastern Front, or were convalescing from wounds already received.

With the United States entering the war after the Japanese attack on Pearl Harbor in December 1941, Roosevelt and Churchill were under relentless pressure from Stalin to relieve the strain on Russia by opening a Second Front in the West. The Americans were sympathetic to the idea of a cross-Channel invasion while Churchill argued that a premature assault would

unloading of troops and stores until a nearby port could be captured.

Chosen beaches

The Normandy beaches situated in the western half of the Bay of the Seine – with Cherbourg and Le Havre close at hand – were just the ticket in all but one respect – the weather. Meteorological records revealed that even in June, the most likely month for an invasion, fair weather could not be relied on for more than three consecutive days, not nearly enough time to be sure of taking a port. That was a distinct problem for the planners.

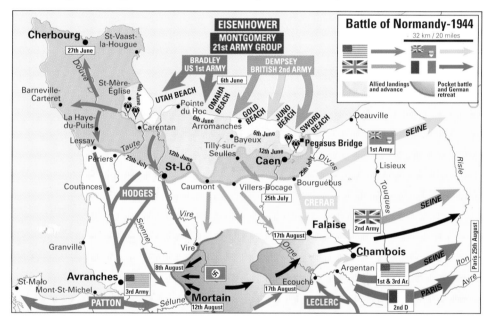

be repulsed with demoralising effect by the German forces already stationed in France.

It is said that the ill-fated Canadian raid on Dieppe *(see facing page)* went ahead to underline, especially for Stalin's benefit, that an effective Second Front in France would require an immense amount of planning and preparation. Landings in France would have to be within the operational radius of fighter bases in southern England, not more than 320 km (200 miles). Moreover, the beaches would have to be sufficiently long and sheltered for the

ABOVE: the troops spread out over Normandy: hundreds of towns and villages were devastated.

The answer to problems with the weather was that the landing forces would have to take artificial harbours ("Mulberries") with them. The idea was that old ships ("Gooseberries") would be sunk in line to form an outer breakwater. Within them was a semi-circle of of hollow concrete boxes, "Phoenixes", the largest displacing 6,000 tonnes. They were connected to the shore by floating roadways, "Whales".

The components for two Mulberries were constructed in England in great secrecy. Starting on the afternoon of D-Day, they were to be towed across the channel at 1½ knots then assembled on site, one for the Americans and one for the British.

In the event, the American Mulberry at Omaha Beach was destroyed in the Great Storm of D-Day+13, but its British counterpart, in a more sheltered position off Arromanches, survived (as pieces still do) to provide 39,000 vehicles and 220,000 men with dry landings.

Imminent action

Coded messages broadcast by the BBC warned the French Resistance that invasion was imminent. The first went out on 1 June 1944 as the opening line of Paul Verlaine's *Song of Autumn*: "The long sobs of the violins of autumn…". It was followed up on 5 June with the second line:

"Wound my heart with a monotonous langour". Admiral Wilhelm Canaris, chief of German Intelligence, had been tipped off about the significance of these messages and told monitors to keep an ear open for them. They were identified and reported, but to no avail. The Allies, it was said, were hardly likely to announce their arrival in France on the radio.

The first wave of the invasion was already in motion for a 5 June landing when deteriorating weather caused General Eisenhower, Chief of the Allied Expeditionary Force, to agonise over whether he ought to call a postponement. In the event, the main body was turned

PROPHETIC NAME

The code-name "Mulberry" for the artificial harbours contributed, as we shall see later, to a minor but intriguing aspect of war-time Intelligence. It was, in fact, chosen from a list of deliberately meaningless possibilities, and it was only after the war that one of the principal architects, Colonel V.C. Steer-Webster of the Royal Engineers, came across a biblical quotation from Luke XVII, 6:

"And the Lord said, If ye have the faith of a grain of mustard-seed, ye might say unto this Mulberry tree, Be thou plucked up by the root, and be thou planted in the sea; it will obey you."

back but there was no way of communicating with two midget submarines whose job was to surface less than a nautical mile offshore and transmit directional signals to the approaching fleet. The five-man crews of the two submarines, each squeezed into a tiny, single cabin, spent a tough night and day on the seabed off Ouistreham and Le Hamel, 32 km (20 miles) apart, not knowing what was going on.

Day One

Operation Overlord began in earnest as the clock struck midnight to herald 6 June. At its simplest, the plan called for a vanguard of airborne troops and commandos to secure the flanks of the beach-head and neutralise the gun batteries trained on it. The US 82nd and 101st Airborne Divisions were to seal off the north-western perimeter against counter-attacks by German forces concentrated around Cherbourg. The British 6th Airborne was to hold the eastern approaches. The five beaches within the corridor thus created were Utah and Omaha, for the 1st American Army, and Gold, Juno and Sword, for the 2nd (predominantly) British Army. The intention was to break out as quickly as possible with the Americans curling round to take Cherbourg and the British going straight for Caen, the German strongpoint.

grenades, slabs of TNT, a spade, blanket and raincoat, one change of socks and underwear, five days' rations and two cartons of cigarettes. They could barely stand up under the weight. Landing in water, they drowned.

British paratroopers used hunting horns to find one another in the darkness; the Americans clicked toy crickets. Wooden gliders, towed across the Channel by bombers and then unhitched for powerless descent, carried about 30 men each. Their night's work began with a crash landing – there was no other way – sometimes right on top of the positions they planned to take.

Poor visibility and high winds played havoc with the initial airborne landings so that paratroopers were scattered all over the place, some as far as 40 km (25 miles) off-target. The unluckiest fell into flooded areas. The typical American paratrooper had a jump-suit over his battledress and wore or carried a helmet, boots, gloves, main and reserve parachute, mae west, rifle and pistol with anything up to 700 rounds of ammunition, a selection of knives and a machete, an anti-tank mine and up to a dozen

LEFT: US naval guns pound the coast.
ABOVE: Allied troops in the ruins of Hermanville on 6 June 1944.

There were many acts of valour in the early hours of D-Day. A British glider unit is credited with the first victory: a blinding 10-minute fight which captured the vital Pegasus Bridge near Bénouville. Thanks to *The Longest Day*, one of the most unfortunate of the early American air drops became one of the most celebrated: Private John Steele, dangling helplessly from the Ste-Mère-Église, his parachute wrapped around the steeple.

Essential secrecy

Secrecy about the place and timing of the invasion had been maintained to a miraculous degree. Rommel was driving to Germany. All but two of the 124 aircraft of the Luftwaffe's 26th Fighter Wing had the previous afternoon been moved from their base near Lille.

The crack 21st Panzer Division, veterans of Rommel's Afrika Korps, were alerted to what was happening and, 40 km (25 miles) southeast of Caen, had their engines running. They received no orders to move, perhaps because bombing had neutralised much of the German communication network. Three serviceable boats of 5th E-boat Flotilla at Le Havre represented the sum strength of the German navy. They went into immediate action, pounding towards the biggest fleet ever assembled.

The vanguard of the invasion fleet consisted of 7,000 ships, of which 713 were warships including a number of battleships with guns capable of pounding Caen 24 km (15 miles) inland from off-shore stations. Some 11,500 aircraft and 200,000 sailors and soldiers made up the order of battle in the first wave alone, the landing forces being mustered in 59 separate convoys, each preceded by minesweepers and organised to land in the correct sequence.

The first wave

As the fleet approached the beaches, mother ships disgorged square-faced landing craft under an umbrella of shells from battleships and cruisers and salvoes of rockets from specially converted barges. Landing craft, said to have "a capacity for rolling all ways at once", quickly filled with water to the acute discomfort of the troops who, almost to a man, were wretchedly seasick. Several craft sank, and worse was in store as the water grew shallower and the craft triggered Rommel's devices. The force of one explosion blew an amphibious tank 30 metres (100 ft) into the air.

The opposition was stiffest at Omaha Beach in the American sector. Fewer than a third of the men survived the wade from their landing craft to dry land under withering fire from the cliffs above. Only half the tanks made it ashore. Ironically, the landings at Utah Beach were relatively easy because troops were put ashore in the wrong place. Brigadier-General Theodore Roosevelt, at 57 the only general to land with the first wave, was not too bothered. "We'll start the war from here," he announced.

At Sword Beach, Lord Lovat's 1st Special Service Brigade was piped ashore (*Highland Laddie* followed by *The Road to the Isles*) by a kilted William Millin waist-deep in water. At Gold Beach, the 47th Royal Marine Commandos lost all but one of their landing-craft and had to swim ashore under machine-gun fire. "Perhaps we're intruding," one remarked. "This seems to be a private beach." At Juno, the Canadian 3rd Division fought through a maze of pillboxes and trenches.

Even at 10,000 to 12,000 Allied casualties (killed and wounded), the cost was lighter than feared. The Germans are thought to have lost between 4,000 and 9,000 men, but that would not have concerned Hitler. "If only they would land half a million men," he had once mused, "and then foul weather and storms cut them off in the rear. Then everything would be all right."

Day Two

Many of the men at D-Day later said they were so keyed up that they could not think beyond the actual landing. The troops awoke on the blustering morning of 7 June cold, stiff and dirty after a fitful sleep in a shallow hole in French soil, in most cases their first on *terra firma* for three days.

Field Marshal Montgomery, in command of the Anglo-American troops, arrived off the Normandy beaches before dawn, having crossed from Plymouth in the destroyer HMS

Faulkner. His intention was to consolidate the five landing beaches into a continuous secure beach-head then strike hard while the Germans were off-balance and wondering whether the Normandy landings were a diversion for an invasion in the Pas de Calais.

The British 50th Division at Gold Beach stormed on to liberate Bayeux which, being taken so early, was the only town in Normandy to escape heavy damage. The Canadian Division at Juno managed to seize part of the Caen–Bayeux road

SOME STATISTICS

In the 87 days after landing, the Allies put ashore 2,052,299 men, 3,098,259 tons of stores, and 438,471 vehicles. The stores alone would have filled a goods train 1,450 km (900 miles) long.

Rommel returns

Rommel returned from his ill-timed trip to Germany on D-Day+2. The German High Command was still inclined to view the Normandy landings as a diversion, and within these constraints Rommel saw his duty as confining the Allies to the smallest possible area as he brought up a panzer force strong enough to drive them back into the sea. With one hand tied behind his back by the Allied air forces and pinpoint naval bombardment, Rom-

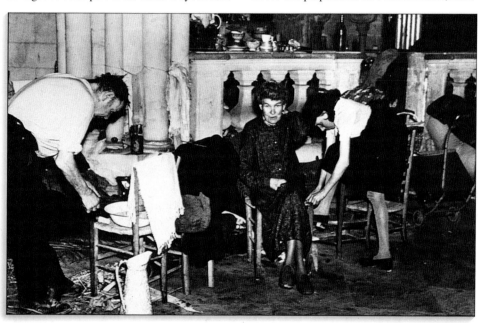

and railway line but plans for the swift capture of Carpiquet airport proved to be naive, as was the hope that the British 3rd Division at Sword could snap up Caen.

At Utah Beach, where the landing had been relatively comfortable, the main task was to consolidate the scattered landings of the two Airborne Divisions. At Omaha Beach, where the reception had been hottest, the Americans had to fight inland from their shallow beachhead against a crack German infantry division.

LEFT: a gift from the US 8th AAF.
ABOVE: citizens of Caen seek shelter in the Abbaye-aux-Hommes.

mel had the other shackled by Hitler. In response to desperate appeals for the release of panzer units still being kept in reserve for the "real" invasion around Calais, Hitler's unhelpful order was that "every man shall fight and die where he stands".

Hitler had another compelling reason for protecting the Pas de Calais at the expense of his forces in Normandy. It was the launching pad for the secret weapon that he believed would turn the tide of the war regardless of D-Day, the V1 "doodle-bug" rocket. To witness the start of the V1 bombardment of England and perhaps emulate Churchill's visit to Normandy on 10 June, Hitler went to France. Conferring with

Rommel in a bunker near Soissons, he wanted only to talk about the rocket. The next day, one of the rockets went berserk and crashed by the bunker. Hitler returned to East Prussia and never again set foot in France.

At the time of Hitler's brief visit, the Americans had taken Carentan, thereby joining up Utah and Omaha beaches and cutting the Cotentin peninsula in half, isolating the German forces in Cherbourg. In the British sector, however, things were not going at all well. Montgomery's plans to take Caen with an elaborate pincer movement failed, giving the newly arrived 51st Highland Division, veterans of the

all the more imperative. This was accomplished on 27 June, but only after the Germans had done such a thorough demolition job that the port was not serviceable for several weeks.

The Caen front still showed no improvement and the Allied air forces needed Carpiquet airport as badly as their navies needed Cherbourg. On 26 June Montgomery launched Operation Epsom with a view to encircling Caen from the west and attracting German armour to the British sector, thereby improving the chances of an American break-out. The offensive focused on capturing and holding "Hill 112" overlooking the airport. This was done, but the

Western Desert, a bitter taste of the very different conditions in Normandy.

Summer storms

During the middle of June, the Normandy campaign threatened to become a war of attrition. This was to the Allies' advantage as long as their replacements and supplies came across the English Channel faster than the Germans could receive theirs, but on 19 June the worst summer storm in living memory struck the coast. The American Mulberry at Omaha was damaged beyond repair and no fewer than 800 supply ships were driven ashore. The loss of the Mulberry made the capture of Cherbourg

BATTLING THROUGH *BOCAGE*

Memoirs of the Normandy fighting are haunted by the word bocage – small fields enclosed by hedgerows, "ridges on a monstrous waffle". Hedgerows grown since Celtic times had so stiffened the banks with their roots that the Americans had to improvise a special kind of bulldozer to cut through them. In the meantime, troops working their way through bocage confronted at intervals of 90 metres (100 yards) an interminable succession of perfect defensive positions for snipers, machine-gunners or worse. The roadways between the hedgerows had been worn so deep beneath the level of the surrounding fields that they could conceal a defensive tank.*

hill was almost immediately lost to a ferocious counter-attack. So much firepower was trained on it that neither side dared occupy it. Epsom did not win Caen but it did succeed in drawing a total of 725 panzers, which left the Americans with only 140 to worry about.

Sacking Field Marshal von Rundstedt, his Commander-in-Chief West, Hitler decided operations in Normandy required his personal attention. While his field staff recommended drawing back the German line so that it was out of range of naval bombardment, Hitler hated the idea of giving up any territory. "The present positions are to be held," he ordered.

The American and British armies had a more or less common problem in their sectors. The market town of St-Lô controlled the main road out of the Cotentin in the same way that Caen controlled the road network in the east, and both remained in German hands, as did Carpiquet airport. Omar Bradley and Montgomery arrived at the same conclusion: St-Lô and Caen would have to be pulverised.

The bombing of Caen

On the evening of 7 July, 267 bombers dropped more than 2,500 tons of bombs on Caen. The infantry were not sent in until the following

Cardboard army

That order applied also to the 15th Army, still chained to the Pas de Calais in anticipation of the arrival of "Patton's Army". The Germans assumed that General George Patton, whom they knew all too well from Italy, would be given a decisive role in the invasion of France. "Patton's Army" was apparently still poised on the Kent beaches ready for a Channel crossing. In reality, the force was a decoy army of cardboard cut-outs.

LEFT: Eisenhower with Ernest J. King, CIC US Fleet.
ABOVE: Montgomery with Winston Churchill during the latter's fleeting visit on 10 June.

morning, by which time the Germans had recovered. If anything, the destruction hampered the attackers. Craters blocked the path of vehicles, whole streets had been reduced to rubble, maps had no meaning. Only after two days of street fighting was the town north of the River Orne captured, as was the airport. Ominously, the Germans managed to hang on to high ground south of Caen and so commanded the gateway to the coveted Caen-Falaise plain.

After a similar aerial bombardment, St-Lô fell to the Americans on 18 July, the day Montgomery launched the Goodwood offensive to get the Germans away from Caen and open the way for the push on to the Caen-Falaise plain.

The simultaneous American offensive was to be Cobra, a punch through the German defences in the west to enable them to move into Brittany.

Goodwood began with the biggest air operation in support of ground troops in the entire war – 1,600 heavy bombers, 400 light bombers, and 2,500 fighters and Typhoon rocket aircraft. Nearly 750 guns lent their support. On the ground, the assault was led by three armoured divisions (750 tanks) and infantry divisions accompanied by a further 350 tanks. Rommel was waiting for them with several hundred tanks, 200 guns, about 100 of the wickedly effi-

above the road, came up to within 500 metres of us and the first one opened fire." Rommel and his driver were both hit and the car overturned. He was dragged out of the wreckage unconscious and seriously wounded. Rommel eventually recovered but took no further part in the war. He committed suicide in October rather than face charges of complicity in the von Stauffenberg plot to blow up Hitler three days after his encounter with the Spitfire.

With or without Rommel, the German defences managed to hold out against Goodwood. The British lost 400 tanks in the process, but these could be repaired or replaced. The

cient 88mm anti-tank guns, some 270 multibarrelled *nebelwerfers* ("Moaning Minnies") and a strong body of infantry in well-prepared defensive lines 16 km (10 miles) deep.

Rommel wounded

On the eve of what was going to be the major offensive of the campaign, Rommel had been out as usual to inspect the defences. On his way back to headquarters near the Seine, his spotter warned that two Spitfires were flying in his direction. "The driver was told to put on speed and turn off on to a little side road," an officer in the car recalled. "Before we could reach it the enemy aircraft, flying at great speed just

Germans lost far fewer, but they could not be. If there was any doubt left in Hitler's mind about the authenticity of the Normandy campaign, it would have been banished by the knowledge that Cobra, the American counterpart to Goodwood, was to employ the services of Patton and a real-life 3rd Army.

After an initial error that killed 558 American troops, the bombs went in on target and obliterated the Panzer Lehr, a significant proportion of the reduced tank force on the American front. Coutances was captured on 28 July and Avranches two days later. It was now time for Patton to show his long-awaited hand. In three days he manoeuvred 100,000 men and 15,000 vehicles down the single road out of Avranches and by 4 August had reached Rennes, the capital of Brittany. The 3rd Army then wheeled towards an emotive destination: Paris.

Montgomery switched his push east of Caen to the western flank, enabling the British 2nd Army and the American 1st to drive south almost side by side. The newly-established 1st Canadian Army – about half the men were British or belonged to the 1st Polish Armoured Division – was left with the problem of fighting through German defences to drive down the Caen–Falaise road. It was only 32 km (20 miles), but every inch would be contested.

The battle for Normandy was moving towards a climax. Patton had surged as far as Chartres and Orleans when it appeared that the German forces in Normandy could be encircled. Patton was told to change direction and begin a pincer movement aimed at snapping the trap in what became known as the Falaise Pocket. On 15 August the Allies landed in the south of France. Victory was coming closer.

German retreat

In Normandy, the German retreat was in full swing. "The floor of the valley was alive with stuff," a British gunner noted. "Men marching,

Canadian vendetta

For the Canadians, the slog down the Falaise road was a personal vendetta. On D-Day they had come up against the 12th SS Panzer Division, formed of fanatical Hitler Youth, by the Abbey of Ardenne near Caen. Twenty-three Canadians were captured, led into the abbey and shot. In their second encounter, nearby, another 45 prisoners were taken and shot. Barring the way to Falaise was the 12th SS again, but this time they met on more equal terms.

LEFT: an American MP lends a helping hand.
ABOVE: family life survived, somehow, in the most difficult of circumstances.

cycling and running, columns of horse-drawn transport, motor transport, and as the sun got up, more and more targets came to light. Soon the whole Regiment was banging away with all it had, and the cry for more ammunition went up on all sides. It was a gunner's paradise and everybody took advantage of it."

The Canadian Army still had the 12th SS Panzer Division between it and Falaise but not for much longer. Entering Falaise on 17 August they closed in on the last of the Hitler Youth. In the end, only four of them were alive to be captured, and they were all wounded. That did not quite end the Normandy campaign for the Canadians, and in fact a Canadian major went on to win the Victoria Cross in three days of hand-to-hand fighting at St-Lambert.

Polish bravery

The smallest contingent among the Allied forces, the 1st Polish Armoured Division, was among the heroes of the final phase of the battle for Normandy. While waiting to go into action they listened to news of the Warsaw Uprising which began on 1 August. When, on 17 August, they received their battle orders, some couldn't wait for the 2am start and went off without a re-supply of fuel or ammunition.

The Poles took up positions on a "long

whale-like ridge" with a commanding view of the valleys and roads around Chambois. The position, called The Mace, was excellent, but it was isolated and lay within German-held territory. Germans were pouring by on all sides and their only hope was to stay put with their 1,500 infantry and 80 tanks despite serious shortages of supplies and ammunition. The Germans saw the Poles as an obstacle between them and escape from the Falaise Pocket, so the position was engulfed in fire from all sides.

On 20 August the Germans directed their heaviest attack on The Mace. The assault was supported by armour, the fresh 2nd SS Panzer Division just arrived to spearhead a desperate German counter-offensive. They penetrated The Mace perimeter that evening. "Gentlemen," the Polish commander told his troops, "all is lost. I do not think the Canadians can come to our rescue. We have no food and very little ammunition... Fight all the same. There is no question of surrender. Tonight we shall die."

The night passed quietly, but in the morning the Germans meant to finish off the Poles. A supply drop by American Dakotas, the last hope, landed 8 km (5 miles) away. The garrison commander had signalled he could "no longer stand up from physical exhaustion" when the sound of Sherman tanks was heard – the Canadian Grenadier Guards. "The scene," one Grenadier recorded, "was the most savage the regiment had encountered... There were corpses everywhere, unburied and dismembered."

The huge sense of relief was ruined by the news that the Warsaw Uprising was doomed. It was left to Royal Canadian Engineers to mark the spot where the Polish exiles had played their heroic part. It simply read, in English, "A Polish Battlefield".

The battle's end

Hitler's keen prospect of destroying 500,000 Allied troops on the beaches of Normandy was heading rapidly towards disaster. The battle of the Falaise Pocket had annihilated Army Group B, the largest in his Army. The 2nd SS Panzer Division, which had only just arrived when it went into action against the Poles on The Mace, was down to 450 men and 15 tanks.

All in all, the battle for Normandy cost Germany 300,000 casualties. The figure for the Allies who, being on the offensive, would have expected more, was 209,672, including 36,976 killed. The German formations in Normandy remained a fighting force until 27 August, but it was really all over at Falaise on the 22nd.

General Eisenhower said that only Dante could have adequately described the scene. "It was literally possible to walk for hundreds of yards at a time stepping on nothing but dead and decaying flesh." A reconnaissance pilot flying over the battleground said that at 450 metres (1,500 ft) the stench penetrated the cockpit and assailed his nose. ❑

LEFT: Général de Gaulle in Bayeux, the first time he had been in France since the occupation began.
RIGHT: devastated Caen after two months' fighting.

AFTER THE WAR WAS OVER

When the hostilities ended, the period of reconstruction began. The task was huge and it was two decades before Normandy returned to normality

On 1 September 1944, the Battle of Normandy, which had started on the morning of 6 June on the beaches of Calvados and the Manche, finally ended. Normandy was liberated, but at a price. The cost of the battles, which for nearly three months had been contested on Norman soil between the troops of the Third Reich and those of the American, Canadian and British armies, was appalling.

Counting the cost

Added to the damage caused by the German invasion in 1940 was the damage by the seaborne landing missions, and by the airforce and artillery that assisted the Allies' breakthrough. It left towns and cities, industrial sites and communication systems totally or partially destroyed. Worst affected were St-Lô, Caen, Lisieux, Vire, Falaise, Rouen and Le Havre where it would be two years before ships could use the port again. In many places Normandy had been deprived forever of priceless riches, of works of art and, particularly, architecture. Whole towns of half-timbered buildings had disappeared.

The Norman countryside had also been a stage for fierce fighting which left a trail of destruction. In the Argentan-Chambois area in the *département* of Orne, the fighting in August 1944 was so violent that Germans who had taken part in the invasion of the Soviet Union unhesitatingly compared the Battle of the Falaise Pocket to that of Stalingrad.

After four years of occupation, many Normans became hostages of the retreating German army, innocent victims of both warring sides. Thousands of men, women and children either became refugees, or were killed or wounded by the aerial bombardments and artillery. In the *départements* of Calvados and the Manche alone, civilian casualties amounted to about 10,000 dead and 35,000 wounded.

LEFT: the people of Falaise return to what is left of their homes.
RIGHT: the American cemetery at Omaha Beach.

Dark days

Once the terrors of the war were over the Normans slipped into a dark period lasting many years, while reconstruction took place. Before 1939, Normandy was the most prosperous region in France. World War II put paid to that and seriously jeopardised the region's future.

This once-hospitable place and fashionable tourist centre was reduced to an enormous field of ruins, littered with masses of debris.

As soon as the fighting ended the Normans set to work clearing away the ruins to build a new region that would combine 20th-century living with cherished values from the past. No one was in any doubt about the enormity of the task. Over nearly the whole of Normandy reconstruction was needed. The economy of town and country, public services and the environment, were all victims of the war. What was worse, the communications systems, without which the economy could not begin to take off, were virtually unusable in most areas.

Financial problems

These huge undertakings could not be financed without big loans, but central government had requests for money from many quarters, compounding frequent political crises, and it turned a deaf ear. What money it did give was for bare necessities and was only a drop in the ocean. The Normans had to wait 20 years before their region was back to anything like normal.

Most of the other French regions developed, modernised their industry, agriculture, communications systems and exchanges, and set off to win new markets. In the meantime, Normandy was growing poorer, losing its trump

unable to find employment or had decided to leave their trade for something better paid.

The numbers of unemployed in Normandy increased every year until the end of the 1960s. The decline in the number of vacancies in agriculture and building forced workers to leave for other places, just as those with qualifications had already done. Thus a large part of Normandy was further depopulated.

Rural decline

As agriculture went into recession, the rural community felt it was being dragged into an inexorable decline. Until 1960, the shortage of

cards one by one. It watched its skilled workers set off for Paris or other cities which offered employment. With them went the hopes for its textile industry, boat building, ironworks and transport sectors.

If the competition against the other French regions became particularly strong, the difficulties encountered in trading with other countries was formidable. The only consolation the Normans had was the creation of a large number of temporary, unskilled jobs in the construction industry or in maintenance work for the public sector. This enabled a large number of labourers to get back to work and also attracted agricultural workers who were either

raw materials, the cessation and then control of trade and the decrease in buying power brought hard times for Normandy's "home-made" products: its meats, ciders, Calvados and cheeses which previously had made it a fortune.

The rural exodus also took away the large number of labourers essential just to carry out the various jobs on the smallholdings. A farm of an average 30–40 hectares (75–100 acres) once had up to 15 workers. Now that number was reduced to two or three: the owner, his wife and perhaps a part-time helper.

Production methods were mechanised and livestock farmers stopped making their own products, selling instead the raw materials directly to the increasing number of dairies and industrial cider plants.

Since the 19th century the mixture of flat, open country and wooded hills has provided for two types of agriculture in Normandy: arable farming and livestock farming of both beef and dairy cattle which has gone hand-in-hand with apple orchards and cider. Until 1939, livestock farms were the most profitable but, after the war, mechanisation and the expansion of the cereal market favoured arable farmers. The livestock regions, located in the most beautiful countryside and picturesque places, would have to await the increases in tourism for a new rise in fortune.

In spite of the difficulties, agriculture remains the driving force in Normandy, and, in the decades since the beginning of the 1980s, the pace of decrease in land-holdings has slowed, mainly as a result of farmers beginning to specialise. In terms of turnover, however, tourism is now running a close second.

Industrial revival

While agriculture was suffering in the 1950s, industry, business and communications began to revive around Caen, Rouen and Le Havre. To complement traditional enterprises and make up for the reduction of others (iron works at Caen, passenger transport to the US from Le Havre) these towns took on new industrial developments: petrochemicals and mechanical and electronic engineering. The Le Havre-Rouen basin expanded with refineries at Gonfreville, Notre-Dame-de-Gravenchon, Petite Couronne and Port-Jérôme, where the first synthetic rubber factory outside the US was built.

The construction of the Paris–Rouen motorway, later extended to Caen, the linking of the two banks of the Seine by the Tancarville bridge in 1965 and the Brotonne bridge in the 1990s, all contributed to these centres' revival.

To avoid creating a "two-speed" Normandy, new industries were established across the whole region. Economic advisers' aims were furthered when central government called for the industrial decentralisation of the Paris region. This led to the creation here and there of new, usually small, factories.

Animal feed and agricultural machinery were the two main industries, but local help was given to relaunch small traditional industries: iron-smelting at L'Aigle in the Orne, precision engineering and metallurgy in the Eure, and the giant Moulinex, manufacturers of electronics and electrical goods, all revitalised depleted areas. Normandy's proximity to Paris and improved communication systems enabled it to establish numerous businesses in the 1980s, although many employ unskilled labour.

Added to this was the central government decision in the 1960s to site three nuclear power stations in Normandy, two in Seine Mar-

itime and one in the Manche. In 1967 a nuclear waste reprocessing centre was set up at La Hague, near Cherbourg. In 1971 France's first nuclear submarine slipped out of the harbour at Cherbourg.

Tourists return

The last factor in Normandy's renaissance was tourism. Nearly the whole coast, as well as numerous picturesque inland sites, had suffered terrible damage; roads, railways and ports were mostly unusable. But, as we shall see in the next chapter, once rebuilding work was done, visitors returned to the region to enjoy the natural riches Normandy has to offer. ❏

LEFT: the decline of the agricultural sector was a severe economic blow.
RIGHT: Cherbourg rises from the rubble.

NORMANDY TODAY

Agriculture is still the most important economic sector in the region,
but industry and tourism also play vital roles

Europe today has a two-speed economy: one speed in the south, where agriculture is the main occupation, the population is widely dispersed and production centres are far from the markets they serve; another in the north, where most people live in cities well-placed for industry and agriculture, and where there are the vital communication systems needed to service a modern economy.

Normandy lies somewhere in between: an agricultural area in a well-populated region close to the French capital.

Malaise in farming

Compared with the rest of France Normandy has three times more people working on the land. However, agriculture holds little interest for young people, and service industries – in particular tourism – are gradually becoming the mainstay for the 21st century. Beyond that, the region wants to build preferential economic relations with its inland neighbour, the Île de France, as a natural extension of the lower Seine's industrial basin. It wants to see the ports of Cherbourg, Dieppe and Le Havre opened up to Europe and the rest of the world. And it wants better trade with northern Europe.

Post-war history of impoverishment and neglect has left the region with a poor reputation, and it needs to convince the rest of Europe of its strengths if it is going to achieve its aims. The basic belief that once the infrastructure is right, the rest will follow, keeps the public works programme pushing ahead on the road, rail, sea and air fronts. Recently achieved projects include the A29 and A28 autoroutes, the Pont de Normandie spanning the Seine estuary to link Le Havre with Honfleur, the electrification of the Paris–Cherbourg railway line in 1996 and the creation of a new Transmanche link to the Channel Tunnel.

PRECEDING PAGES: an eye on the future, a view from the past.
LEFT: Le Havre's port is the second busiest in France.
RIGHT: old and new blend together in La Havre.

Rural roots

Agriculture remains the main activity, covering 90 percent of the countryside and 10 percent of the working population. Altogether it comprises 7 percent of France's agricultural production. Traditional production (meat, dairy products and *cidricoles*), helped by the devel-

opment of tourism and consumers' return to natural foods, should see a rapid expansion in the years to come.

Normans are fond of the traditional landscape responsible for this produce, and though some old orchards have been grubbed up and smaller fruit-tree stocks introduced, many farms hang on to their huge, boughed trees, and practise mixed farming, with spotted Normandy cattle which still give good milk yields on the rich grass. Lower Normandy produces 15 percent of France's milk products. Since the 1980s this western region, made up of Calvados, the Orne and the Manche, has had the lowest decline in the number of farmers.

Gîtes, cereals and timber

In their endeavours to keep to small and mixed farming and the old ways of life, farmers have had some help from the EU and central government, a great deal of local sympathy, and the opportunity to turn old barns and out-houses into *gîtes*. But methods and crops have had to change. Cereal farming, for example, now occupies nearly 40 percent of Lower Normandy's farmlands.

With 350,000 hectares (865,000 acres) of forest, including beech and oak, the timber trade lies in a new type of long-range trawler, like those being used out of Dieppe and Fécamp, which have facilities to freeze fish on board.

CIDER CENTRE

Normandy produces nearly all of France's cider, over 50 million litres (11 million gallons) a year.

Industrial base

Some 400,000 people are employed in industry and building. The motor industry plays a dominant role in the region's economic life, employing around 30,000 people. The largest car manufacturers are Renault and Citroën, both based in eastern Normandy. These giants create work for a multitude of small fitting businesses and

and its allied industries represent a major activity in the region, but here, too, Normandy has lost numerous businesses and a corresponding number of employees.

Fishing

After agriculture, the fishing industry is Normandy's oldest and most traditional activity, with more than 1,000 boats and 3,500 fishermen. But while it remains an extremely active part of the economy, it has had to fight its corner, and to contend with territorial disputes in the waters around the nearby Channel Islands.

As elsewhere these days, traditional fishing yields little profit and the future of the industry

sub-contractors who swell the total employment figures in the motor industry.

Shipbuilding is no longer the great employer it was. Today it is mainly based in Lower Normandy, while an aeronautical industry has been set up in Upper Normandy. The electronics industry, scattered throughout the region, has had a hard time keeping up with the needs of modernisation.

Major port

Le Havre is still the second-largest port in France. Exports of cars, agricultural machinery and chemical products are principally destined for Spain and Germany, followed by Italy,

Great Britain and Benelux. A rather soulless, rebuilt town, Le Havre nevertheless thrives on being the entry point to the "River of Petrol". From the Côte de Grace above Honfleur you can see a skyline of green storage tanks which mark the first of the four most important refineries on the right bank of the lower Seine. Here 34 percent of France's petrol is treated and it is a leading area of petroleum research.

The chemical and petroleum industry, located in the same region, employs more than 26,000 people, of whom over half work in the base chemical and fertiliser sectors. Chemicals are now Normandy's leading export.

the largest of its kind in the world. Waste plutonium is sent here from Germany and Japan, provoking protests from international campaigners. Perhaps because people fear possible job losses, local opposition has been muted.

Funds for research and development have been released so that 21st-century Normandy can pursue its atomic evolution. Some of the most important research establishments and laboratories are located near Caen.

Research and promotion

Rouen is home to aerothermo-chemicals and, in the Seine Valley near Le Havre, private

Nuclear power

The refineries, representing 34 percent of French refining power, are just one part of Normandy's huge energy resources, which include three nuclear centres producing over 60 billion kw/h per year. Although nuclear power is an emotive subject, they have been seen, generally, as a welcome investment and employment provider in the region.

The La Hague nuclear reprocessing plant at Cherbourg is, along with Sellafield in Britain,

LEFT: a Greenpeace ship keeps a watchful eye on the Cherbourg plutonium plant.
ABOVE: tourism is an increasingly important industry.

research centres in the fields of petroleum, chemicals, pharmaceuticals and electronics have been opened. Alençon, in the Orne, is the centre for the promotion of work in the plastics industry.

Le Havre has been noted for its promotion of business outside the region, with its slow but sure increase in assisting exports. Consumables and equipment are the principal imports, mostly for the petroleum and chemical industries. They arrive in Le Havre mainly from Britain and Germany, North America and the Middle East.

New markets need to be conquered to end Normandy's reliance on the petroleum industry. A great deal is being done, through balanced economic development by experts who have been trying to ensure that the rural and stricken industrial zones may benefit from the best equipment and from industrial or artisanal materials adapted to their needs.

This action, although essentially political, has borne fruit: approximately 5,000 new businesses are started up in Normandy every year. Among the most interesting of the promotional organisations involved in this programme are the Agropole at St-Lô, which was initiated to encourage local food production, and Techno-Rice, the Anglo-French innovation centre based in Caen.

Getting the balance right

Of continuing major concern to those intent on developing the region is the lack of qualifications generally across the Norman workforce. There is an imbalance between the qualifications demanded by companies offering employment and those held by people seeking work. This imbalance has contributed significantly to the deterioration of the employment situation in Normandy, which today is one of the most badly affected regions in France.

However, the problem has been recognised and is being addressed. Training programmes are now being funded on both a national and a local level.

Tourism for tomorrow

The future for the region undoubtedly lies to a large extent in tourism. Normandy annually welcomes more than 10 million visitors, and the industry employs around 80,000 people. People from the United Kingdom and Ireland represent 70 percent of foreign visitors, either in transit or staying in Normandy.

For many years tourism has been essential to the coastal regions and since the late 1990s "green" tourism has developed. Cattle from the Camargue have been introduced to the Brotonne regional park; forest land has increased, and the beech forests of Upper Normandy and the oak forests of Lower Normandy are on the tourist maps, despite some destruction in the severe storms at the end of 1999.

The Seine, meanwhile, has seen its traditional barges, which link Normandy to Paris and the whole waterways system of Europe, in decline. In their wake have come pleasure boats whose owners are hoping to make the trip from Rouen to the sea, or even Paris to Honfleur or Le Havre, one of the great river trips of Europe.

The Normandy landing beaches continue to be a big draw for visitors; in fact, visitor numbers increased in the wake of the 50th anniversary celebrations in 1994, when many new museums and memorials were set up.

Parisian visitors

But a full third of the people who spend their holidays in Normandy are French, mostly from Paris, for the capital's citizens have long used the coast and the countryside as a place of easy escape. The fact that so many of them have second homes here accounts for a shortage of property for holidaymakers to rent.

The rich and famous have been coming to the region for years – the writer Françoise Sagan had a home in Normandy that was once owned by the celebrated actress Sarah Bernhardt (1844–1923) – and the new meritocracy have helped to preserve some of the old buildings from decay. These sophisticated Parisians know a good thing when they see one, and they are as keen as the Normans themselves to preserve the buildings and traditions of the region, to enjoy its incomparable food and help maintain its way of life.   ❑

LEFT: apples still rule the rural economy.
RIGHT: the dry dock at Granville.

THE NORMANS

Regional pride and commercial flair
are outstanding Norman characteristics

If you ask someone from Normandy what most readily sums up the Norman character, they may reply, *"Pt'être ben q'si, pt'être ben q'non"*. This rendering is approximate, but "Maybe yes, maybe no" is an accurate enough translation of an old country saying.

Normans are canny types who are happy to hesitate and to linger over a decision while they weigh up the pros and cons of the situation. They hate to make up their minds in a hurry. As they are also very stubborn – *têtu comme un Normand*, the rest of France calls it – this can be infuriating, but it is an extremely good bargaining technique. And the people of Normandy are nothing if not good negotiators. Like Monsieur Rouault, the shrewd but lazy father and a Norman *paysan* of the old school in Gustave Flaubert's *Madame Bovary*, they are "formidable bargainers on market-days, loving the tricks and haggling of the trade".

Best sellers

Normans enjoy the whole business of buying and selling. They say that if a Breton has four cows to sell, he will take them all to town on the first market day and do his best to get a good price for them. The idea is to get the unavoidable transaction over and done with as quickly and as painlessly as possible. Not so a Norman farmer. On the first market day, he will take one cow into town and have a good time selling her. He will ponder and plot until the next market day, when he will bring out the second cow and have another successful outing.

This native talent for commerce, combined with the rich resources of the region, made Normandy prosper earlier than other French provinces in the 19th century. The proximity of Paris via adequate roads and the waterway of the Seine was an important factor in the region's development. Fresh fish and seafood

---

PRECEDING PAGES: a spooky pageant in Bayeux;
a Dieppe fisherman sorting out his nets.
LEFT: two Norman farmers keep a close eye
on market-day negotiations.

packed in seaweed, fruit, vegetables, butter and cream were transported daily to the capital. The money earned was spent wisely, invested in building suitable houses and furnishing them in an appropriate manner.

Furnishing with confidence

Because of this early, enduring prosperity, the regional furniture of Normandy has a strikingly confident and solid quality. Cupboards, dressers and clocks tend to be handsome, in the spirit of Louis XV furniture and on the large side. The most typical piece of Norman furniture is the *armoire*, the cupboard that was tradition-

ing, with straight or triangular cornices and decorated with carved floral or rural motifs.

The Norman sitting-room is without fail impeccable and dominated by gleaming furniture shining with the patina that can only come from years of conscientious elbow grease. The Normans are a clean and tidy lot, and this is reflected in their small, neat towns and villages.

Traditional cupboards and case-clocks (the latter straight or sometimes with the pinched waist of the *horloge demoiselle*) are still very popular. Qualified cabinet-makers able to re-create to a high standard the old pieces of regional furniture can earn an honest living in

ally presented as a wedding gift to a couple by the bride's parents – the custom of giving a cupboard rather than money survived until recently.

The wedding cupboard is decorated with carved doves, flowers and fruit motifs – all suitable symbols of happiness, love and prosperity. It had pride of place in the living-room and was used to store a family's most precious possessions – linen, best clothes, souvenirs and relics. The woods vary, often oak, pine near Caen, mahogany in the Manche. As the family fortunes prospered over the years, other pieces of furniture appeared, perhaps a dresser *(un buffet)*, a chest of drawers *(une commode)*, or a clock *(une horloge)*, always substantial-look-

Normandy. Fellow Normans come to them to order *meubles* just like the ones they were brought up with, the reassuring dressers, cupboards and clocks they saw as children in their grandparents' homes. Once a Norman always a Norman: even those in exile and their descendants feel part of the old province. Furniture is one way of keeping up the link and they are excellent customers for the traditional artisans.

Enthusiastic hosts

For the visitor to Normandy, the local character manifests itself in a number of enjoyable ways. Tourism is all-important commercially in the region and treated with the utmost seriousness.

The Normans are very proud of their province and its history and prepared to work hard at communicating this passion to visitors. They want people to care and understand. Of course, it makes commercial sense, but there is more to it than that. The needs and interests of *les visiteurs* are more intelligently and sensitively catered for in Normandy than in many other parts of France. Caen's Peace Memorial is an unforgettable experience that will leave no one unmoved, whatever their knowledge or experience of World War II.

A small town like Bayeux, dominated as it is by its famous tapestry, has managed to set de l'Horloge to the people who run the half-closed hotels, everyone is willing and able to answer questions.

Le tourisme artisanal

Normandy specialises in what tends to be referred to in France as *le tourisme artisanal*. Artisans, shop-keepers and hoteliers have grouped together to open up specialist circuits which take you on *la route du verre* if glass-blowing interests you, *la route des métiers* if you prefer an all-round approach, *un circuit gourmand* for those who have an appetite for *dégustations*.

the scene for it in a way that makes a visit a fresh, exciting experience. A set-piece the tapestry may be, but it is not allowed to become fossilised. It is a long way from the guided visits where people shuffle their feet round a château and listen to a dull commentary.

In Bayeux off-season – late autumn or early spring – it is possible to spend a satisfying two or three days as well as absorbing the tapestry at leisure. From the lace-makers at the Atelier de Dentelle and the clock-makers at the Atelier

LEFT: an elegantly furnished salon in the Château Fontaine-Henry.
ABOVE: celebrating the Joan of Arc pageant in Rouen.

They have produced leaflets and opened up their workshops to visitors, a sound commercial ploy that almost invariably loosens the tightest purse-strings. You have to be very strong-willed to resist buying a copper pan in Villedieu-les-Poêles after seeing the informative film and watching copper being hand-crafted to a glittering smooth finish in the Atelier du Cuivre. And if you don't buy a pot in the Atelier, you will probably succumb in one of the dozens of copper shops that line the streets. Beware of cheap imitations, though: some of the stuff on sale in the shops is imported. But since you are in Normandy, you might as well emulate the natives and practise your bargaining skills. ❏

THE HIGH LIFE

Normandy's Côte Fleurie has been attracting the wealthy and the famous ever since Emperor Napoleon III came here in the mid-19th century

American writer F. Scott Fitzgerald believed that the rich are different from the rest of us. "That's right," retorted Ernest Hemingway, who was less deferential about these things, "they have more money." Fitzgerald never set a novel in Deauville but the creator of Gatsby and Daisy Buchanan and the Riviera settings of *Tender is the Night* would surely have appreciated the place.

It's overcrowded. It's overpriced. Some of its attractions are frankly vulgar rather than smart, kitsch rather than chic. But in spite of these objections, Deauville's combination of beach life and high life, of grand old seaside hotels and ultra-modern fashion, of racetrack and casino, retains a glamour and a romance that is impossible to deny.

On summer weekends in July and August the approach roads from other parts of the Côte Fleurie are jammed with the cars of the seriously rich and the merely profligate; with women in Chanel and shades, and bare-chested men in shorts, all in search of a space on the beach, or a seat at a café table.

Best address

Deauville's position as the premier social address on the Normandy coast was once held by the old fishing port of Dieppe further north. Dieppe always had a special attraction for visitors from the other side of the Channel, who could get there easily once the Newhaven packet boat began its daily service in the 1850s. Oscar Wilde went there after his imprisonment. Sickert went there to paint. A little colony of expatriate English aristocrats almost took over Dieppe society around 1900. At their head were Lord and Lady Cecil who lived in a villa at Puys. They imported English kippers and sausages for breakfast. They also imported snobbish ideas about how to treat the locals.

PRECEDING PAGES: the polo crowd on a cloudy day.
LEFT: poster advertising the Deauville Jazz Festival.
RIGHT: Régine and singer Gérard Lenorman try their hand at the casino's machines.

The incomers' favourite vice was the casino, once a splendid *fin-de-siècle* gaming hall that was flattened during the British-Canadian raid in 1942. One of its best patrons was Lady Blanche Hozier, mother of the future Clementine Churchill, who would queue patiently with a picnic basket waiting for the tables to open.

Queen Victoria, who twice passed through Dieppe on her way to visit King Louis-Philippe at the nearby château at Eu, probably didn't approve of the casino. Her son Bertie, Prince of Wales, almost certainly did, although he was not exactly welcomed by the stuffier expatriates when he came over to see one of his mistresses, the Duchess of Caracciola. The duchess later married a baron and became one of *Vogue*'s early fashion photographers.

Trouville

The turn of the century was also the high point of popularity for Trouville. It had grand hotels, a casino and a boardwalk when its neighbour

Deauville, was still little more than a gleam in a developer's eye. Then the Trouville authorities made the mistake of putting up the rent of their casino and the casino owners decided to move next door. Deauville's expansion began and didn't stop, while for many years Trouville drifted out of fashion and was allowed to slide downhill, a looked-down-upon, middle-class relative of the fast-money joint up the road.

Today Trouville is popular once again and deservedly so. Its atmospheric waterfront brasserie, Les Vapeurs, is renowned as a Normandy equivalent of the Brasserie Lipp on the Boulevard St-Germain in Paris. On warm sum-

Carlo and Cannes. But the central and most attractive focal point of the town remains Les Planches, the old wooden boardwalk that runs the full length of the beach. Les Planches may have been the backdrop for a hundred different fashion spreads over the years but it is still the "in" place for a spot of constructive posing. The unchanging spectacle of sand and sea and sky and of the red-and-blue umbrellas billowing in the wind is hard to beat – especially if savoured over a coffee and *calva* or a large glass of pastis while mingling with the beautiful people at an outside table at the Soleil Bar or the Bar de La Mer.

mer nights half the buskers in Deauville seem to turn up outside. Trouville's fishing boats, narrow back streets and small, family-owned shops give it a lively, year-round feel that persists even in mid-winter. Up above, the serene old Edwardian villas still look down on the town from the Corniche above the sea.

Deauville

Deauville has its own Edwardian villas and streets full of large, comfortable-looking, half-timbered houses built in 1930s mock-Tudor style. It also has a flash modern yacht marina and no shortage of the sort of luxury apartment blocks that have nearly overwhelmed Monte-

Les Planches is also the setting for Ciro's, the most fashionable and expensive restaurant in Deauville. The former pools tycoon and race-horse owner, Robert Sangster, keeps a permanent booking at Ciro's throughout the season and if you are in the same financial league then you too can enjoy lobster and asparagus tips at 290 francs a time while the paparazzi queue up at the entrance waiting for a famous face.

Film favourite

The old-fashioned bathing cabins further down Les Planches have the names of famous film stars emblazoned on their sides. This conjures up a kind of *Hollywood Boulevard* aura. The

French film-maker, Claude Lelouch, bestowed cinematic immortality on Deauville with his celebrated 1966 love story *Un Homme et une Femme*. Lelouch owns a house at Villers-sur-Mer and continues to use Deauville as a backdrop to his films, as do many other film-makers. Gérard Depardieu and Jeanne Moreau are other stars with places in the area.

The town continues to salute the movies with its annual Festival of American Film in early September, an event that pretty much brings Deauville's short but frenetic social season to a close. The festival may not quite be able to rival the shenanigans that go on down in Cannes ear-

The entire world of French horse-racing seems to move to Normandy for the *vacances*. Each morning the horses are exercised on the beach and allowed to paddle by the water's edge. The ambience may be a relaxing one but the action on the course at Deauville is competitive and highly prestigious. The principal races, such as the Prix Jacques le Marois and the Prix Morny for two-year-olds, are among the foremost events of their kind in Europe and the big English stables regularly challenge the top French trainers for the money.

Deauville's elderly, red-brick grandstand, its graceful, old, Norman-style weighing room and

lier in the summer but it has proved charismatic enough to lure stars of the lustre of Jack Nicholson, Michael Douglas and Sharon Stone to pose on the boardwalk in recent years.

At the track

Deauville's season begins at the end of July with the staging of the first two race meetings at its elegant flat-racing course and at the smaller but even prettier Clairefontaine course half a kilometre (⅓ mile) away.

LEFT: café society in Dieppe in the 1930s.
ABOVE: Robert Mitchum with Lucien and Martha Barrière, outside the suite named in his honour.

the profusion of horse chestnut trees that shade the paddock create a perfect setting and one in which enthusiastic tourists mingle freely with the *soigné* racing professionals. No bookmakers are permitted on French racecourses. Punters have to queue up, sometimes interminably, to place their bets with the French Tote (PMU). The good news is that it is remarkably cheap to get in, little more than 30 euros, even for the biggest Sunday programmes and less than that on weekdays.

Eating in the clubhouse restaurant, however, isn't so cheap. And many of those lunching in Le Brantôme at Deauville, whose glass walls are erected each season under a fabulous white canopied roof, show little interest in the events on the track as they enjoy their *sole normande* and *filet béarnaise*.

After the race

When the racing is over you can glance at the Grand Prix polo tournament in the centre of the course or wander down the road to the sales pavilion and catch a preview of the yearlings that will be on offer that evening. Or you can stroll back into town and enjoy a drink in the Hôtel Normandy, Deauville's largest and most sumptuous hostelry. This resplendent half-timbered fake was actually built in 1911 and inside

it feels as if it had been created by a combination of Scott Fitzgerald and Noël Coward. You keep expecting to see blazered lounge lizards on the look out for suitably rich widows whose fortunes they can tease away.

The Normandy's luxurious Bar Americain has an extremely long list of cocktails, and the head barman André Pallares can offer a choice of up to 80 Scotch whiskies. M. Pallares's drinks, all tall and refreshing, come with a sufficient kick to strangle your screams as you look down at the bill.

Bathing, posing, drinking, dining, racing: Deauville offers a menu of delights. (If it gets too much, there's a Thalassotherapy Centre in Trouville to clean you out, tone you up and calm you down.) But the climax to any visit to Deauville has to be an evening at the casino. This magnificent old white wedding cake of a building, fully floodlit at night, occupies a prime position looking out towards Les Planches and the sea. It was put up in 1911 like the Normandy and, like the hotel, and like just about everything else in the town that makes money, it is owned by the Barrière hotel group.

Casino Royale

Deauville was the model for Royale-les-Eaux in Ian Fleming's first and best James Bond novel, *Casino Royale*, with the unforgettable opening line about the nauseating "scent, smoke and sweat of a casino at three in the morning". These days, Bond might find himself diverted by Régine's nightclub and the casino's camp Las Vegas-style floor show with its mixture of tigers and former Folies Bergères dancers in what are still coyly referred to as "revealing costumes".

Fleming himself would no doubt be distressed to discover that the outside hall of the casino is now lined with slot machines and that the only night of the year when you still need to wear a dinner jacket is in August, on the occasion of the annual jockeys' black-tie ball. The late M. Lucien Barrière, who presided over much of Deauville's prosperity, hotly defended these changes on the grounds that they were financially unavoidable.

The chandeliers and the pile carpets are still there in the main salon along with the sleek aura of soft and velvety expense. And there is still something undeniably erotic about the spinning roulette wheel, the cries of "*Suivi*" and "*Banco*" and the feel of the crisp, clean playing cards and the gleamingly cold chips.

If you play and win, you can celebrate with a bottle of Roederer Cristal champagne up at the casino bar. If you lose, untie your imaginary black tie and stroll back nonchalantly through the night towards one of those stiff whiskies in the Normandy. As you go, lift your head and sniff the sea air. And smell the flowers and the ozone and the faint but discernible whiff of money drifting back towards you on the breeze. ❏

LEFT: the Aga Khan was well known in Deauville.
RIGHT: the casino as it looks today.

THE BIRTH OF IMPRESSIONISM

The new style that rocked the art world

had its origins in Normandy

Normandy was the great outdoor *atelier* of late 19th-century French artists. Dieppe, Étretat, Le Havre, Trouville, Deauville… each of its resorts could be represented in a weighty anthology of works by the greatest modern French painters. Here they set down their easels and tried to give a true impression of the bucolic farms, the cloud-soaked skies and the surf-spattered, grey-green sea. This is where Impressionism was born.

Some of the artists came from Paris, others were attracted from further afield: John Sell Cotman, J.M.W. Turner and Richard Parkes Bonington began a cross-Channel exchange of ideas from England; Johann Barthold Jongkind arrived from Holland; and James Whistler and John Singer Sargent were in the vanguard of Americans who later came in waves to find Claude Monet painting at his home in Giverny.

A wave of painters

Théodore Géricault was born in Rouen in 1791, and knew the young Eugène Delacroix, who went to school there. Jean-François Millet was born near Cherbourg in 1814, Eugène Boudin in Honfleur in 1824, Raoul Dufy in Le Havre in 1877 and Fernand Léger in Argentan in 1881. Georges Braque and Camille Pissarro ended their days here.

Boudin was born at 27 rue Bourdet in Honfleur, the pretty little port opposite Le Havre on the estuary of the Seine, which still has the air of a painter's paradise. He left us with enduring images of the bracing beaches of nearby Deauville and Trouville, of bonnets and ballooning dresses, petticoats and parasols, of blustery seas and great billowing skies. He also left us Claude Monet, Impressionist supreme, for it was Boudin who persuaded the young cartoonist from Le Havre to get out and paint.

PRECEDING PAGES: Monet's lovely water-lily pond.
RIGHT: the grand old man surrounded by paintings in his studio at Giverny.

Boudin's father was captain of a ferry boat that plied across the Seine estuary between Honfleur and Le Havre where the family moved when Eugène was 10. He left school at 12, and at 20, after being apprenticed to a paper-maker, he started up a stationer's and frame-makers in rue de la Communauté.

Among those he served and began to admire was Millet, the son of a peasant who was one of the first French painters to depict rural poverty. Ten years his senior, Millet had been trained by a local painter in Cherbourg, then in Paris where he continued to paint landscapes and peasant life. In 1849 he moved to Barbizon in

Claude Monet

Monet, who was born in Paris, the son of a grocer, grew up in Le Havre, where the family moved when he was five. In his teens he gained a minor local reputation as a caricaturist and he sold his drawings through various outlets, which is how, aged 18, he came knocking on Boudin's door. Monet did not, apparently, like Boudin's style of painting, but Boudin clearly thought Monet had potential. He took him under his wing and persuaded him to work out of doors, and to follow his example by studying the effects of daylight and the changing aspects of the shifting skies.

the forest of Fontainebleau just south of Paris where he spent much of his life in poverty quite equal to most of his subjects.

Surrounded by painters' paraphernalia, Boudin began to sketch. He was encouraged by Millet and other artists who came to his shop, including Constant Troyon, to whose paintings Boudin would later add the skies, and the landscape and marine painter Eugène-Gabriel Isabey. In 1844 Boudin visited Holland where he met Gustav Courbet and became impressed by Dutch 17th- and 18th-century landscape paintings. In 1851 he went to Paris to study informally, mostly by copying the works of the great masters.

"First Impressionist"

Boudin remained Monet's mentor, but both were also touched by the wild card of Johann Barthold Jongkind, one of several painters now referred to as "the first Impressionist". Born near Rotterdam, Jongkind had met and befriended the sociable Isabey in Paris in 1846 and they had travelled through Normandy painting together.

But even to Isabey, who made cider drinking fashionable as a result of his visits, the bouts of drunkenness and erratic behaviour of his protégé were excessive. They parted company and Jongkind returned, a lost cause, to Holland. Monet had not met Jongkind but his reputation was sufficient for him to write to Boudin: "Do you know that the only good marine painter we possess is dead as far as art is concerned? He is quite mad."

But by 1862 Jongkind had been taken in hand by various concerned parties and rehabilitated. As a result he revisited Le Havre where he made a lasting impression on both Boudin and Monet, who had just returned from military service in Algiers. He stayed on the coast for four consecutive summers, at Honfleur, Le Havre and Ste-Adresse, where Monet's parents had a summer home. The three painted together, and Jongkind exerted his influence

outside the town overlooking the Seine estuary. Over farm cider and Mme Toutain's excellent meals, art would be discussed with Corot, Courbet, Diaz and Daubigny whom he brought along. Sisley, Pissarro and Cézanne also found their way here, and the poet Baudelaire would add to the discussions.

There was never a real School of Honfleur, as there was at Barbizon, though the local artist Louis-Alexandre Dubourg suggested that there was when, in 1868, he presented the town hall with works by himself, Boudin and Jongkind.

These pictures became the basis for the art museum of Honfleur of which Dubourg was

through his sensitivity and lightness of touch, especially in his water-colours. Monet has referred to Jongkind as his "true master" who "completed the teaching I had already received from Boudin".

The hotbed of Honfleur

In 1864 Monet moved to Honfleur, which was becoming more of a hotbed than a haven. Isabey had taken to staying at the 17th-century Ferme St-Siméon in rue Adolphe-Marais just

the first curator. But the artists did form themselves into a group, calling themselves the Société Anonyme des Artistes-Peintres.

Salon sensation

One misty spring morning in 1872, Monet set up his easel in Le Havre and swiftly covered a 50 x 65-cm (20 x 25-inch) canvas with a mixture of blue and red paints. Before him the sun was rising, flicking its light across the water. The mauve of the brightening sea and sky was rubbed with darker marks of jetties and cranes and sailing ships, while a small rowing boat just in front of him darkened in the quiet water as it was silhouetted by the sun's warming rays.

LEFT: the stormy waters of the Channel at Étretat, as painted by Monet.
ABOVE: Boudin's figures on Trouville beach.

Monet called the picture *Impression: Soleil Levant* and exhibited it, together with the works of other members of the Société Anonyme des Artistes-Peintres, in the former premises of the photographer Nadar at 35 boulevard des Capucines in Paris, two weeks before the 1874 main Salon exhibition. One critic, Louis Leroy, writing in the magazine *Charivari*, contemptuously dismissed the work of what he called *Impressionnistes*.

The name stuck and the rest, of course, is history: eight Impressionist exhibitions were held between 1874 and 1886, after which the various members of the group continued to develop as

Trouville rather than peasants stooped in their daily grind. These were his "gold mine" pictures, the familiar seafront scenes peopled with what he called "little dolls", on canvases no bigger than large envelopes, called *pouchades*.

The Giverny years

Monet, between bouts of extreme depression, remained true to Impressionism and produced paintings of extraordinary vivacity, in particular his series of pictures of haystacks, of poplars and, in 20 different moods, the west front of the cathedral at Rouen, which no reproduction can fully convey.

artists in their own separate ways, but always returning again and again to the Normandy countryside.

The painters did not live off the fat as a result of their fame – or infamy. For years Boudin and Monet, like the rest of them, often begged and borrowed and starved. Monet was thrown out of a hotel in Falaise and Renoir, with whom he painted La Grenouillère, a favourite resort on the left bank of the Seine, stole bread for him.

It helped, of course, if the places the artists painted were fashionable. Boudin, who shared much of his outlook with the likes of Millet, nevertheless had as his subjects the Empress Eugénie and the bourgeoisie on the beach at

In 1890, two years before he began the series, he settled in the beautiful house and garden in Giverny in the Seine Valley, between Rouen and Argenteuil. Here Monet established his magnificent water garden which he went on painting, in all lights, up until his death, at the age of 86, in 1926.

The house and gardens are now restored and, however many visitors are crowded into them, it is still possible to feel the presence of the simple, single-minded, grand old man of Impressionism, a stocky figure, breathing heavily as he worked over his huge canvases, cigarette smoke curling up over his nicotine-stained whiskers.

Dieppe connection

By the time the Impressionist group broke up, the resorts were in full swing, stretching up the coast eastwards to Dieppe. Monet and Renoir were both familiar with this port. Pissarro, who had lived in Normandy since 1894, painted the town and harbour in 1901, just before his final project in Le Havre, his painting of St-Jacques.

Walter Sickert, a pupil of Whistler and leading light of the "London Impressionists", regarded Dieppe as his second home. He lived here from 1899 to 1905 and was indebted to the town's most charismatic figure, Jacques-Émile Blanche, a painter and collector with

Fauve, then Cubist, along with Léger, whom he met in 1910, Braque spent his last years at Varengeville-sur-Mer and has a lasting memorial in the *Tree of Jesse* window at the church of St-Valéry where he and his wife are buried.

Dufy, who also studied in Le Havre, became a friend of Braque. In Paris, Dufy followed the by-now fashionable Impressionist style for a while, until he discovered Matisse and the Fauves. It was impossible for him to have avoided the influence of Monet and Boudin, and there is a hint of them both in his 1904 painting *Beach at Sainte-Adresse*, but it is hard to imagine a painter more different from Monet

impeccable connections. In summer, his mother's house, Chalet du Bas Fort Blanc, echoed to the opinions of Aubrey Beardsley, André Gide, George Moore and Edgar Degas.

Le Havre revival

As the century turned, the scene was given a fresh impetus by two painters from Le Havre: Raoul Dufy and Georges Braque. Braque started out as a decorator, and was taught at the local art school, before going to Paris. First

and his circle. Dufy was a hedonist who sought trouble-free subject matter, but his images of Normandy are as enduring as Boudin's, and his fascination with boats and racehorses stayed with him throughout his life.

There is a fine collection of his work in the Musée des Beaux-Arts André Malraux in Le Havre, given to the town by his widow. The port's sailing boats have never looked breezier or the resorts more festive.

In the Musée des Beaux-Arts in Rouen a Dufy triptych of the Seine – an homage to the river as it flows from Paris to Le Havre – serves as a celebration of the river and coast that inspired so much remarkable talent. ❑

LEFT: festive yachts at Le Havre by Dufy, 1904.
ABOVE: Monet's *Impression: Soleil Levant*, which was to give a name to a whole artistic movement.

WRITERS

Some of the greatest names in 19th- and 20th-century French literature
either came from Normandy or chose to spend much of their time here

Normandy has produced more great writers, or inspired more great literature, than almost any other region of France. Some of the writers were non-Normans, such as Jean-Paul Sartre who lived for a while in Le Havre and made it the setting for his first novel, *La Nausée*; or Marcel Proust, who spent many sea-

side holidays in the Grand Hotel at Cabourg, which he transmuted into the "Balbec" of *À la recherche du temps perdu*. Others were Normans born and bred, such as Guy de Maupassant who acutely portrayed the stubborn peasantry of the Pays de Caux; or Gustave Flaubert, who dissected with sharp scepticism the middle-class snobberies of his native Rouen. The wild Cotentin country to the west has been luridly evoked by that strange Gothic-romantic novelist, Barbey d'Aurevilly.

Both Le Havre and Rouen have stronger literary associations than many much larger French towns. Maupassant, Sartre, Queneau and Salacrou all wrote vividly about the great

seaport of Le Havre. The dramatist Pierre Corneille was born in Rouen, where his house now holds a small museum of his work. He attended a Jesuit college whose glittering list of alumni includes Flaubert, Maupassant, the painter Eugène Delacroix, and André Maurois who was born at nearby Elbeuf and lived there for 30 years.

Parrots galore

Above all, Rouen belongs to Flaubert (1821–80), that walrus-moustached scourge of the local bourgeoisie. His father was head surgeon of the Hôtel-Dieu, still one of the city's main hospitals: here the family's former home, in one wing, is today a museum. You can visit Gustave's bedroom, from where he watched carts bearing corpses during a cholera epidemic. That famous green stuffed parrot stands here in its glass case. An attendant may assure you that this was *the* actual parrot that Flaubert borrowed to stick on his desk while writing *Un coeur simple*.

Five kilometres (3 miles) away beside the Seine is the village of Croisset where Flaubert lived for many years. His elegant mansion is no more, but the squat garden pavilion, where he would read or talk with friends, remains. Here are more Flaubert souvenirs, including another parrot (also claimed to be authentic).

In central Rouen, little remains of the bohemian quarter where Flaubert's Emma Bovary "walked amid a smell of absinthe, cigars and oysters". But the cathedral itself has been well restored, and with the novel in hand, you can retrace the famous scene where Emma uses the alibi of a guided visit to stave off the advances of her beloved Léon, "her tottering virtue clinging for support to the Virgin". This scene was found shockingly blasphemous, and helped lead to the book's prosecution.

Tragic saga

Just east of Rouen, the pretty village of Ry is probably the original *bourg* of Yonville where Emma lived with her dreary, doting husband.

And the true and tragic saga of the Delamare family of Ry lends a curious mystery to the question of what inspired Flaubert to write *Madame Bovary*. A Dr Eugène Delamare, former pupil of Flaubert's father, settled in Ry in the 1840s and married a local farmer's daughter. There are records to prove that she died in 1848, aged only 27, and he a year later. According to some accounts, he hanged himself, though his tomb today stands clearly in the village churchyard, where no suicide would have been buried. Ry now cashes in with an active Flaubert industry, including a museum of Bovary automata and an Emma Bovary trail.

Guy de Maupassant

De Maupassant (1850–93), Flaubert's disciple and close friend, also loved the Normandy coast. Born at the Château de Miromesnil, near Dieppe, he spent most of his childhood and parts of his later life in Étretat, a staid bathing-resort where he set the story of *Miss Harriet,* an English spinster who dies of thwarted love. Even sadder is *Une vie*, about a married woman's wasted life, set in the gentle country inland from Yport: the landscapes, altering with the seasons, reflect her varying moods.

Of Maupassant's two famous tales about prostitutes, *Boule de Suif* is set partly in Rouen

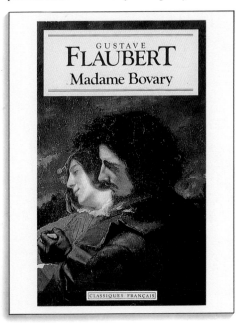

Un coeur simple

Flaubert chose Pont-l'Évêque, his mother's home town, as the setting for *Un coeur simple*, his sad tale about the noble Félicité, comforted in her old age by her *live* green parrot. The nearby coast also features evocatively in this story – the daily return of the fishing-boats to Trouville, the walks on the hills above. Flaubert was deeply attached to Normandy beaches, and to Trouville where he had met his first love, Elisa Schlesinger.

LEFT: Gustave Flaubert, scourge of the bourgeoisie.
ABOVE LEFT: one of Flaubert's parrots;
RIGHT: *Madame Bovary*, the book that rocked Rouen.

during the Prussian occupation, partly in nearby Tôtes at the Hôtel du Commerce (based on the Hôtel du Cygne, still there today). The joyful brothel in *La maison Tellier* was in Fécamp – "a homely looking house, quite small, with yellow walls". There actually was a *maison de passe* on that spot at that time: but the area has since been totally rebuilt. And the Fécamp that Maupassant describes, a great prosperous deep-sea fishing-port, has declined in recent decades.

An altered city

De Maupassant's novel *Pierre et Jean* paints a remarkable portrait of the busy prosperity of the mighty port of Le Havre in its heyday.

"Liners were expected from Brazil, the River Plate, Chile and Japan, also two Danish brigs, a Norwegian schooner and Turkish steamer... Above Sainte-Adresse, the two electric beacons on Cap de la Hève, like two gigantic twin Cyclops, threw their long powerful beams across the sea." The commercial harbour was "full of shipping which overflowed into other basins, in which the huge hulls, belly to belly, were touching each other four or five feet deep. All the numberless masts along several kilometres of quays, with their yards, mastheads and cordage, made this open space in the middle of the town look like a great dead forest."

evenings he spent in the low-life bars and bistros of the port area, notably the red-light St-François quarter now so tidy and dull. One biographer, Annie Cohen-Solal, has written: "In this city Sartre acquired daily habits he would never relinquish... he turned his patronage of cafés and hotels into a moral necessity."

His first novel, *La Nausée* (1938), is set in Le Havre, though he changed its name to "Bouville": here are its clanking trams (now no more), garish cafés, lecherous sailors, workers' marches and sea promenades. The book merges Sartre's fascination for low life with his hatred of industrial ugliness and human misery, along

A visitor today would not recognise that scene. Le Havre has changed utterly, due to severe war damage and subsequent changes in world shipping. It would be interesting to have de Maupassant's reaction to the modern city.

Sartre's port

Even the vivid portrait of Le Havre written by Sartre in the 1930s is unrecognisable. Jean-Paul Sartre spent five years there, teaching at the Lycée François-Premier, which still exists. He chose to live in a seedy hotel near the port. On his free days he would go to Rouen to be with feminist writer Simone de Beauvoir, who was teaching in a *lycée* there. But many free

with the central philosophical theme of the main character's disgust at all tangible matter.

Social contrasts

Something of the same desolate quality permeates *Un rude hiver*, a novel by Raymond Queneau (author of *Zazie dans le Métro*) who was born and brought up in Le Havre. Set in the 1914–18 war, it traces its bourgeois hero's mournful revulsion against "a world of work and horror" in a city of slums "bedecked with linen and crawling with urchins... the closest earthly image of hell". In different ways, Sartre and Queneau exemplified writers' reactions to Le Havre's sharp social contrasts of those days.

Queneau's hero visits the graves of his family in a hilltop cemetery, noting also the tombs of English soldiers who were wounded at the front in 1916–18, then died in hospitals here soon afterwards.

These were not the first Englishmen to have perished here on active service. Just east of the city is the old seaport of Harfleur, now a tangle of factories and refineries. Here in 1415, as related by William Shakespeare (who probably never visited France), the young Henry V summoned his dear friends once more unto the breach – "or close the wall up with our English dead!"

For all his bisexual, free-roaming nature, Gide's marriage was fairly happy and should not be seen as the original for the loving but tragic relationship in the novel. However, the physical setting at least is precisely true to life: a big white building with a score of large windows, "then, at the bottom of the kitchen garden, a little gate with a secret fastening". The lovers in the novel, like Gide and his cousin in real life, would go out by this highly symbolic *porte étroite* to sit on a bench in the beech-copse. The house and garden are still as he described them, though rather run-down. The famous little gate carries a picture of a dog with

André Gide

André Gide (1869–1951) and his wife Madeleine lie buried in the little village churchyard at Cuverville, northeast of Le Havre. His father came from the south, but his mother was from a wealthy Rouen family, with whom he spent part of his childhood. He married his first cousin, Madeleine, whose parents owned a hilltop manor house at Cuverville. This became the Gides' by inheritance, and he made it the setting for his sublime novel *La Porte Étroite*.

FAR LEFT: Guy de Maupassant, born in Château de Miromesnil; **LEFT:** Pierre Corneille's weathered statue. **ABOVE:** Victor Hugo's house at Villequier.

a Keep Out notice, *"Je garde ces lieux: vous y entrez à votre péril"* – a suitably Gidean spiritual warning.

Victor Hugo

Whereas Gide was half-Norman, an earlier writer, Victor Hugo, came to the region from outside (as did Sartre). His link was one of personal tragedy. He was friends with a wealthy family of Le Havre shipowners, the Vacquerie, who owned a handsome manor by the Seine near Caudebec, at Villequier; and in 1843 his daughter Léopoldine married Charles Vacquerie. Six months later, the young couple drowned in a sailing accident in the river. Hugo had idolised the girl, and for years he was shattered. Later he wrote about his feelings in one of his best-known poems.

The scene of the disaster is marked by a statue of Hugo on the river bank, with a line from the poem. The couple lie buried in the churchyard behind the manor, together with Hugo's wife and his younger daughter, Adèle, who died insane. The manor is now an elegant museum with interesting souvenirs.

Startling figure

A contemporary of Hugo's, Jules-Amédée Barbey d'Aurevilly, is the leading writer of western

Normandy (the Cotentin) and one of the most startling figures in French 19th-century literature – romantic Royalist, arrogant dandy, devotee of the macabre. It is odd that he is not better known outside France. He was born into the local gentry in the village of St-Sauveur-le-Vicomte, where his bust by Rodin stands by the castle and a tiny museum is devoted to him. In Paris he became a flamboyant Byronic figure, a leader of fashion and brilliant critic. Yet he remained deeply attached to the Cotentin peasantry and their traditions; and his best work deals with that rugged region, which in his day was still rife with witchcraft, superstition and bizarre legends.

Many of his stories and novels contain a Gothic element of mystery and terror, telling of morbid passions leading to strange crimes; but they also have a poetic resonance, and his feeling for the Cotentin's lonely landscapes is real and moving. The little port of Carteret is the setting for *Une vieille maîtresse*, about a young man ruined by his Spanish ex-mistress who writes him letters in her own blood. By the lighthouse on the headland, you can visit the ruined Roman lookout-post where they trysted, and the caves in the cliff where they made love.

Witches' tales

A more strange and powerful novel than this is *L'Ensorcelée*, ghoulishly steeped in blasphemy and witchcraft. Barbey sets it on the Lande de Lessay, a moorland today neatly cultivated but in those days more sinister, "the terrain of mysteries, the property of spirits, ever trodden by prowling shepherds and sorcerers". To this blasted heath there comes the awesome Abbé de la Croix-Jurgan, tall and proud, his face horribly scarred by tortures during the Chouan wars: "Never perhaps, since Niobe, had the sun lit up so poignant an image of despair."

As the tale unfolds, a squire's wife falls in love with this charismatic monster, but is then found drowned, bewitched by the *abbé* himself or by nomadic shepherds possessed of magic powers. Croix-Jurgan inhabits the sinister half-ruined Abbey of Blanchelande (northeast of La Haye-du-Puits), where as he prepares to serve Easter Mass he is shot dead at the altar by the vengeful squire. Ever after, travellers crossing the heath at night can hear a mournful bell tolling from the abbey whose windows are weirdly lit; inside, the *abbé*'s ghost is saying a Mass he can never finish. This beautiful abbey, nicely rebuilt, is set idyllically by a lake and has been taken over by a youthful group of religious hippies, who say they have heard no midnight bells, seen no phantom priest.

Marcel Proust

Last but far from least, we come to the still quite stylish bathing-resort of Cabourg, where a great white wedding-cake of a *belle époque* hotel, the Grand, stands on the promenade Marcel Proust: he stayed here many times between 1881 and 1914, and Cabourg in his novel became "Balbec", at once a terrain of precise sociology and a metaphoric dream-destination like the walks at "Combray". Proust came to the hotel first as a child, to seek relief from his asthma, then alone as an adult. So the "Balbec" parts of the book are a fusion of poetic childhood memories and mature social satire on the rich upper classes.

With his phobias against noise, draught and hot sun, Proust as an adult led an odd life in the hotel, often wearing a winter coat even in August; he might book three rooms and keep the two side ones empty, to ensure quiet. He both loved and hated the Grand, "this cruel and sumptuous hotel with its deafening and melancholy tumult", yet it was an ideal forum for his social curiosity: it was then very fashionable with Parisian society.

He also loved the shifting moods of the view from his bedroom, where the sun "pointed out to me far off, with a jovial finger, those blue peaks of the sea which bear no name on any map". He loved the hotel's dining-room, which in a famous phrase he compared to "an immense and wonderful aquarium" where the poorer people of Balbec would press their faces against the huge window from outside, to gaze in wonder at "the luxurious life of the occupants", as strange to the poor "as the life of strange fishes or molluscs".

Proust's legacy

Cabourg today is not as smart as it was, but it happily flaunts its Proustian connections. It serves all guests an obligatory *madeleine* for breakfast, its luxury restaurant is Le Balbec and its beach-club L'Aquarium, while its bar will serve a sea-green "cocktail Proust" (the bar of the adjacent casino is even called Du Côté de Chez Swann). The hotel has been well restored in *belle époque* style and the "Marcel Proust" bedroom has the right period fittings.

Proust's "Balbec so long desired" remains today much the same Cabourg of traditional villas. Some are the holiday homes of well-to-do Parisians, who today arrive by the *autoroute* and not on Proust's "beautiful, generous" train from the Gare St-Lazare.

Cabourg for him was also an erotic terrain. While he was staying at the Grand in 1907 he

began his romance with a cab-driver, Alfred Agostinelli. (When in the 1980s the newly-named Promenade Marcel Proust was formally inaugurated, the mayor proclaimed, "What a shining example Proust sets to the young men of today!")

Sublime tribute

Proust's love for the cab-driver was his inspiration in part for the unique and unforgettable Albertine of the novel – a homosexual writer's sublime tribute to heterosexual love. She is first glimpsed on the promenade, "a girl with brilliant, laughing eyes and plump matt cheeks, a

black polo-cap crammed on her head", as she and her "little band" of lively young friends "progress… like a luminous comet".

Later, as the narrator's love for Albertine intensifies, he comes to equate her in his mind with Balbec. As he watches her asleep, in the Paris flat where he is virtually holding her prisoner, "Her sleep… was to me a whole landscape. Her sleep brought within my reach something as serene, as sensually delicious as those nights of full moon on the bay of Balbec, calm as a lake over which the branches barely stir." Few sentences are more profoundly erotic than this, a high point of this most poetic of the world's great novels. ❏

LEFT: Marcel Proust immortalised *belle époque* Cabourg, and the town is proud of the connection.
RIGHT: Jean-Paul Sartre set *La Nausée* in Le Havre.

THE GREAT ABBEYS

Normandy has an astonishing collection of religious buildings,
some of them originally founded in the 7th century

The English writer, Patrick Leigh Fermor wrote an evocative description of his first meal at St-Wandrille de Fontenelle, published in *A Time to Keep Silence* in 1957: "Theplace had an aura of immense antiquity. Grey stone walls soared to a Gothic timber roof, and, above the Abbot's table, a giant crucifix was suspended. As the monks tucked their napkins into their collars with a simultaneous and uniform gesture, an unearthly voice began to speak in Latin from the shadows overhead."

This description could have applied at any time during its occupation over the past 500 years. The Benedictine abbey, in the Valley of the Saints in the lower reaches of the Seine, lives in perfect peace with itself, its guests and its congregation.

A simple canteloup tithe barn from Eure serves as its church, brought by the monks in 1969 and added to the beautiful and battered ancient buildings. Each morning devotees at Mass seated in its cool, clear silence, wait for the first murmurs of the distant Gregorian chant. It rises from the secret cells of history, calling clear across the stone colonnades of the 15th-century cloister, and as the brown-robed monks enter, the barn-church becomes spellbound by the simple plainsong.

Sunday choice

Although the land is soaked with the names of its saints, the Normans are not steeped in pilgrimages and tradition as, for example, their Breton neighbours are. The region's singular cult is of the young 19th-century nun, Ste Thérèse of Lisieux *(see page 258)*, who attracted a nationwide following. In general, Normans are conservative, church-going Catholics, but for daily Mass or Sunday worship they have a choice of churches from an astonishing collection of former abbeys.

PRECEDING PAGES: carved figures from the Abbaye St-Georges at St-Martin-de-Boscherville.
LEFT: Jumièges abbey became a centre of learning.
RIGHT: Abbot de Rancé, founder of the Trappist order.

The Church was always the keystone to administrative power and ecclesiastic impetus came in three waves. First under the Franks, who by the 9th century had founded episcopal sees in Bayeux, Coutances, Avranches, Sées, Lisieux, Évreux and Rouen plus 35 monasteries, one-third of them along the valley of the

Seine. The second wave was the greatest, the most splendid and enduring aspect of the Norman Achievement. In the 17th century, between the Wars of Religion, which saw off the Reformation, and the Revolution, which saw off the monasteries, there was a spirtual regeneration under the followers of St Maur.

Regeneration

Europe's monastery networks, established in 7th-century Italy by Ireland's St Columba in Bobbio and St Benedict at Monte Cassino, soon reached Normandy, though missionaries coming across the Channel had already begun forging links that have continued, in spite of the

Reformation, until this day. St Mellon, from Wales, is credited as founding the first bishopric in Rouen in AD 260, but it was not until the arrival in 640 of St Ouen, a high-ranking official at the Frankish court, that missionary zeal was backed by sufficient funds for large-scale building to begin.

His first task had been to oversee the building of a monastery at Rebais, east of Paris, after which he took holy orders and became bishop of Rouen, and set about converting all he could, starting at the local monastery of SS Peter and Paul which he enlarged into what would become the Benedictine Abbey of St Ouen.

Under the encouragement and influence of the saintly and politically ambitious Ouen, the monasteries of St-Wandrille and Jumièges were established 40 km (25 miles) down-river from Rouen on the right bank of the Seine. The monastery of St Wandrille, a man of such grace and beauty he was called "God's athlete" and a man so unspeakably saintly that he forsook the pleasures of his wedding night to join the order, was originally called Fontaenelle.

The first history of a western monastery, *Epic of the Abbots of Fontenelle,* was compiled here in AD 831, and so many saints followed in Wandrille's wake that the abbey celebrates, uniquely, its own All Saints' Day.

Jumièges

Jumièges, founded six years after St-Wandrille in 654, was put under St Ouen's Gascon protégé, St Philibert. Philibert was a court favourite and King Clovis II gave over the forests at Jumièges for his monastery, which was built around three sanctuaries. It became a great centre of learning and one of the largest monasteries in France.

These two monasteries only 16 km (10 miles) apart, were symbols of Frankish power and civilisation until the whirlwind violence of the Norsemen interrupted their progress – and before successive generations of the same Norsemen, with a vigour unprecedented in history, resurrected them and other abbeys and left Western Europe a far, far better place, architecturally, than they had found it.

Norman style

It was a 19th-century Norman historian, Arcisse de Caumont, who first put a name to the style that evolved out of the Carolingian period and was exemplified in France's first major abbey, at Cluny. He called it Romanesque. It was the style that, in 1066, William the Conqueror brought to Britain, where it is simply called Norman. It is characterised by rounded arches, stout round pillars, decorated capitals, sculpted tympanums and ornaments with zig-zags, chevrons, billets, nail-heads, cables and frets.

In Normandy it took on its own peculiar style. It favoured patterns rather than figurative decoration common to Romanesque elsewhere, and sometimes whole walls were ornamented, as in the nave at Bayeux. Without buttresses nave walls were so thick that the upper storey, the clerestory, could conceal a wall passage. Stone vaulting appeared in side aisles, though nave roofs still remained timbered.

Choice materials

There was plenty of material to choose from. Wood was abundant in the forests, although carving did not really take off until the Renaissance. (Normandy's exemplary wooden church is Ste-Catherine's, Honfleur, hurriedly hewn by local axe-masters after the Hundred Years' War.) There was flint in the chalk hills around the Seine valley and the Pays de Caux. In the west there was granite from which monumental buildings such as Mont-St-Michel seemed to grow; and the southern Perche region had iron-red sandstone known as *grison*. Most importantly, there was the easily-hewn light Caen stone, from which the great abbeys were built, as were many churches in southern England.

Fécamp

Normandy's first great Romanesque abbey was at its then capital, Fécamp, where a monastery had stood since the 7th century. Richard I, who had begun the building at Mont-St-Michel and he populated it with 50 monks from St-Wandrille, built Fécamp's Holy Trinity church and made his son, Richard the Good, promise to build a Benedictine abbey. Richard, impressed

as the "Heavenly Gate" and its fame was broadcast by troubadours, who were always made welcome.

Bayeaux and Caen

The Fécamp style was continued at Bayeux, built by William the Conqueror's half-brother Odo, and William and Matilda's churches in Caen. The Caen churches can be attributed to one of the most powerful ecclesiastic figures of the time, Lanfranc, who was born in Pavia in Italy in 1005 and educated as a lawyer. In 1039 he went to teach at Avranches, the episcopal see of Mont-St-Michel. Two years later he

with what he had seen of Cluny, brought Guglielmo da Volpiano, an abbot from Dijon, to Fécamp in 1003.

Today, Fécamp's huge and imposing abbey church, one of the largest in France, seems cold and lifeless, but in its heyday it was lively and rather exotic. Gilded and ornamented with silver and silk, it was the focus of pilgrims, some from England who would make it their first Continental stop on their way to Santiago de Compostela in Spain. It became known

became a monk at the newly established monastery at Bec-Hellouin, on the south side of the Seine beside the River Risle.

William the Conqueror came into contact with Lanfranc during his three-year siege of nearby Brionne and Lanfranc later negotiated with Pope Nicholas II the lifting of the excommunication of William and Matilda, distant cousins whose blood relationship should, according to Rome, have prohibited their marriage. The price extracted by the Pope was that they should build their two abbeys in Caen, the Abbaye aux Hommes dedicated to St Étienne (St Stephen) where William was eventually and unceremoniously buried, and, in a location 1.5 km (1 mile)

LEFT: St John, depicted in a manuscript from Alençon.
ABOVE: monks distilling Benedictine at Fécamp: the recipe is still a closely-guarded secret.

away, the beautiful, honey-stoned Abbaye aux Dames (La Trinité).

Bec-Hellouin

The abbey at Bec-Hellouin was begun in 1034 by a knight named Herluin who had hung up his sword and, the story goes, swapped his charger for a donkey and built a small cloister. Bec is Norse for small stream, and the setting of the abbey, in a broad valley where wood pigeons call, is still remarkably peaceful. There were 32 monks there when Lanfranc arrived, and it soon became one of the major monasteries in Europe with an impressive library. Lan-

franc continued to advise William and after the conquest of England he became the first archbishop of Canterbury, and *de facto* regent when William was away.

He was succeded both at Bec and Canterbury by the Italian theologian and philosopher, Anselm, and a plaque on the 15th-century St Nicholas Tower at Bec-Hellouin records the number of archbishops and bishops in England provided by the abbey over the years. (Canterbury's saintly Thomas Becket was abbot of the nearby monastery of Val Richer.)

In the Middle Ages Norman society was divided into the nobility, the clergy and the peasantry. The nobility defended the clergy who were not allowed to hold a sword: though William's half-brother, Odo, the bellicose bishop of Bayeux, is seen enthusiastically waving a club in the Bayeux Tapestry. When a knight grew tired of war and the hunt and when celibacy no longer meant sacrifice, he would retire to the abbey he had spent his life defending, bringing with him a gift of his best steed.

Monks had rights of tithe over the villages, and they created clearings in woodlands for farming. Vines were planted at St-Wandrille and by the 12th century there were some prosperous vineyards, but they did not last.

The famous Benedictine liqueur was made by a Venetian monk, Vincelli, who arrived at the monastery at Fécamp in 1510. He used 27 herbs and spices for the concoction, which he hoped would keep away the adverse affects of the Normandy weather.

Mont-St-Michel

Fécamp was eventually surpassed as a centre of pilgrimage by Mont-St-Michel *(see page 315)* whose clergy in time became some of the richest in France. Like all great vassals of the crown they had the rights of justice, of measuring and gauging, of sea fishing, of seaweed and treasure trove, and of collecting harbour dues. They owned the whole coast, had a lordship that stretched over hundreds of acres and nominated all local legal and administrative appointments.

The nobility had been the initial patrons of the abbeys, but changes of fortune meant changes of patronage and when, at the beginning of the 16th century, laws were passed to allow the unordained to be granted abbacies it was only a sign of how far things had slipped. Among new absentee landlords was Henri de Lorraine, who was appointed abbot of Mont-St-Michel at the age of five.

La Trappe

What Abbot de Rancé found when he arrived at the Cistercian monastery of La Trappe in 1664 was probably typical: just seven monks, who had long since abandoned their robes and their religion. Armand Jean le Bouthillier de Rancé was a godson of Richelieu and a womanising spendthrift who had a blinding conversion after the death of his lover, Marie de Bretagne, Duchesse de Montbazon. "I resolved to be God's as utterly as I had been the world's," he declared as he sacked the monks and devised the Trappist regime of anonymity, abstinence, manual labour and perpetual silence.

The Abbaye de La Trappe remains reclusive, but visitors can visit its shop and buy souvenirs. Only men are allowed to visit Normandy's other Trappist monastery, Notre-Dame-de-Grâce just outside Briquebec, though women may attend abbey church services.

Reform and Revolution

Rancé was a man of vision and influence but he was also a man of his time. He lived during the Counter-Reformation when Catholicism was

dents, was down to 15 monks in 1790 when it was turned into a stone quarry. Lord Stuart de Rothesy, British ambassador to Paris, took advantage of this: he bought the decorated arches over the main and cloister doorways to embellish his home in Highcliffe, Hampshire. Mont-St-Michel became a prison fortress and was initially used to hold 300 priests.

One by one, however, the monks began to return. But their lives would never be quite the same. Never again would there be the great riches of a powerful kingdom to lavish on their treasures, and today's communities often inhabit more convenient modern homes.

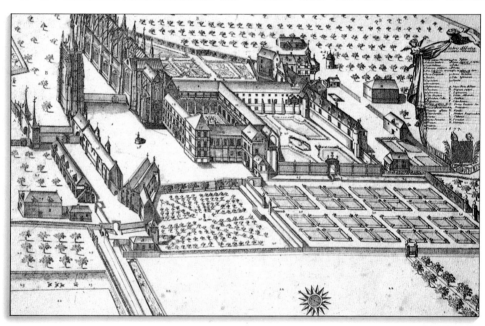

re-asserting itself. Its leading lights were the Maurists, followers of St Maur, a 6th-century monk brought up by St Benedict. They re-established the communities at Bec-Hellouin where Guillaume de la Trambaye, a brother architect and sculptor, designed the refectory, which has become the new abbey church.

The reform ended dramatically in 1789 with the French Revolution which devastated all the monasteries of France. Jumièges, which at its height had sustained 500 monks and depen-

Although the Revolution forced abbey buildings – dormitories, refectories, libraries and cloisters – to be put to other uses or closed down, many of their churches remained.

Today these outsized prayer houses tower over small communities, such as Beaumont-en-Auge or Lonlay, or are majestically cast adrift in the countryside, such as the beautiful church at Cérisy-la-Forêt. Even in towns such as Fécamp or St-Pierre-sur-Dives the abbey churches are too vast for their modern-day congregations, but they stand as monuments to a time when material and spritual greatness converged and the church was the symbol of the power in the land. ❏

LEFT: a monk at Bec-Hellouin.
ABOVE: a drawing shows Bec-Hellouin abbey before it was pulled apart during the Revolution.

FOOD

Normandy is the region of butter and cheese, cider and Calvados, seafood and salt-meadow lamb. It is not the place to go on a diet

For visitors to France intent not simply on enjoying the dishes that are placed in front of them but also on appreciating the culinary culture behind the *spécialités,* it always pays to consider the fat of the land – the butter, cream, olive oil, goose fat or pork dripping that flavour the food.

What could be more different than *marmite dieppoise* and *grand aioli* (poached fish and seafood prepared with a delicately rich cream and butter sauce or served with a gutsy garlic, and olive oil mayonnaise)? Or than *poulet Vallée d'Auge* and *cassoulet* (chicken with velvety cream, apples and Calvados, and a hearty casserole of pork, sausage, poultry and beans redolent of goose fat)? Or than those kings among French cheeses, Brillat-Savarin and Roquefort (sumptuously reduced cow's milk, and ewe's milk at its salty savoury best)?

France stretches from the dairy lands of northwest Europe to the sunny olive-oil shores of the Mediterranean and its regional cooking reflects the country's climatic differences. Normandy is the great northern dairy base for a whole spectrum of French cooking.

Land of bounty

A region of orchards and plenty, the province is also bordered by several hundred kilometres of coastline. The bounteous products of pastures and farms are complemented by gifts from the sea. Also endowed by the sea is the grass of the salt meadows. Rich in iodine and minerals, it delicately flavours the flesh of lambs and the milk of cows. It is as if a gastronomical deity or gourmet fairy godmother had favoured Normandy among all the regions of France.

Faced with such an abundance of riches, the Normans have always had the good sense to keep their cooking techniques simple. The traditional dishes of the region are unpretentious.

PRECEDING PAGES: gleaming copper ports in the kitchen of Château Lassay.
LEFT: the chef at Restaurant La Bourride.
RIGHT: tucking in to a seafood platter.

Top-quality ingredients need no embellishments, no disguises. Spices are used sparingly and the more pungent herbs are used in moderation – a little shallot, chives, chervil or sorrel.

The contribution of cream and butter – however luxurious – remains discreet. White wine is used rather than red in cooking, but less fre-

quently than cider or Calvados, which add a distinct but subtle flavour all of their own. Apples are a savoury garnish as well as the basis of innumerable tarts and desserts.

Seafood

Normandy is an ideal place to acquire a taste for seafood. Even the most reluctant shellfish eater will find it very hard to resist a bowl of tiny shrimps, served hot with the sweetest of creamy butters and close-textured *pain brié*, the traditional ridged bread of the region.

Take a small handful of minuscule cooked shrimps, snap off their heads, peel if you wish (only if you are a perfectionist – it takes a good

30 minutes to shell an average helping), place on a slice of buttered bread, season with pepper from the mill and eat. You should experience love at first bite. *Crevettes grises* are best eaten hot and by the seaside. Try them in the splendid brasserie Les Vapeurs on the main street near the market in Trouville.

From shrimps onwards and upwards, the true shellfish lover's progress will inevitably confront him or her with a *plateau de fruits de mer*. Seafood has to be absolutely fresh: when you order it in a restaurant, it is always reassuring to see plenty of other guests tucking into plates of crustaceans and molluscs served on beds of ice

While in Normandy, make the most of *moules marinières* or *moules à la crème*. They are ubiquitous on menus and seldom disappointing, even in very simple restaurants. A steaming bowl of mussels and a side-plate of crisp golden *frites* to toy with only requires a glass of sharp Muscadet-sur-Lie to make a perfect light meal.

The fish course

Mussels are used to flavour *sole normande*, the quintessential fish dish of Normandy. *Sole dieppoise* is probably the most celebrated version. Fillets of sole are poached in stock with mushrooms and the liquid is reduced to a fragrant

and seaweed (although this is messy eating however good your table manners).

A platter of Normandy seafood is a copious affair, involving a serious communal *dégustation* of oysters, mussels, clams, whelks, shrimps, prawns, crab, baby lobster (sometimes), limpets and winkles.

Plump and meaty, smooth, ridgy, long or oval, all manners of oysters are grown along the Cotentin peninsula, a fifth of France's total production, with the main parks in Isigny-sur-Mer, St-Vaast-la-Hougue and Blainville-sur-Mer. If you prefer your seafood cooked, firm sweet scallops are an expensive must in and around Dieppe. More affordable are mussels.

concentrate. In typical Norman cooking style, *crème fraîche* is added and the whole thing left to simmer before chilled *beurre doux* is briskly whisked in. Prawns are an optional extra. Sole is the favourite fish of the region. The larger the better; but Normandy cooking also excels at preparing small lemon soles, *limandes,* and delicate plaice, *carrelet*.

Crème de la crème

Probably ever since the original Normans brought with them their sturdy cattle from Scandinavia over a thousand years ago, milk, cream and butter (*le lait, la crème et le beurre*) have been the foundation of the cooking of the region. The modern pedigree Normandy breed of cattle (white, cream and cream-and-brown animals), produces more than a quarter of France's dairy needs and each gives up to 30 litres (6 gallons) of cream-rich milk a day.

The French are good at protecting their own and the Normans better than most: *crème fraîche d'Isigny*, pale, golden, with a *soupçon* of tartness under the sweetness, is the only *appellation contrôlée* cream in the country. An accolade it certainly deserves but which rankles with other cream producers.

In the old days cream was allowed to rise to the surface of the milk and *crème fraîche* was

Lent. Nowadays no fewer than five Normandy butters have *grand cru* status: Isigny, Ste-Mère-Église, Neufchâtel-en-Bray, Gournay and Valognes. Totally unsalted, these butters have a delicate, pure taste and fine texture. Sold in great slabs in the markets, they are worth sampling on their own – or on a piece of fresh bread if the idea of unadulterated butter brings out the puritan in you.

A full cheeseboard

The other famous *plateau* of Normandy is, of course, the cheeseboard, *le plateau de fromages*. Local cheeses tend to be soft and made

left to ripen naturally. There were always bowls of *crème* on the Norman table – the writer Gustave Flaubert included great quivering dishes of yellow cream in his memorable description of Emma and Charles Bovary's wedding feast.

Self-respecting Normans have always found life unendurably hard without a fair daily ration of butter, a fact witnessed by the Tour de Beurre in Rouen Cathedral. The story goes that this tower was built with money paid by the citizens for the dispensation to eat butter during

with rich cow's milk. Farm cheeses are produced all over the province, signs advertising *fromages fermiers* or *fromages artisanaux* beckoning enticingly at regular intervals, but the centre of traditional cheese production is really the Calvados region: five *appellation d'origine contrôlée* cheeses in a single *département* is very good going indeed and significantly above the French average.

A good Normandy cheeseboard will include at the very least three local cheeses. Many of these cheeses have a "bark" that is considerably worse than their "bite" – their smell tends to be much stronger than their taste. An honest selection will include a square Pont-l'Évêque,

LEFT: a butcher in Barfleur.
ABOVE: some of the region's many cheeses in La Fromagerie, in Eu.

Calvados

I n France a good meal always calls for a bottle of good wine, preferably local, *une bonne petite bouteille*. Normandy, however, is unusual in not having its own vineyards. The local drinks are apple-based.

Sweet and dry cider, *cidre doux* or *cidre sec* (also known as *brut*), or *demi sec*, in between, is made from carefully mixed different varieties of cider apples. With their rosy hues, their sharp greens or their russet tones, these apples look pretty enough to eat but they often taste much sourer than eating

apples. Although ordinary cider has lost ground to beer as an everyday drink, the better quality sparkling bottled ciders, *cidres bouchés*, are well-presented, well-marketed and gaining a new audience. An apéritif worth asking for is *kir normand*, cider (or sometimes *poire*, perry) with a spoonful or two of *crème de cassis*, blackcurrant liqueur.

Ordinary rough apple brandy is called *eau de vie de cidre*. It is much coarser than the celebrated spirit of Normandy, Calvados. High in alcohol, golden to amber in colour, fiery Calvados is made from distilled cider and slowly aged in oak casks. In times past, every self-respecting Normandy farmer distilled his own Calvados, often on the quiet, and to lethally potent alcoholic strengths.

Travelling stills were a common sight. Since the mid-1960s the French authorities have tightened up regulations in their fight against alcoholism. The Calvados industry is today strictly controlled and distilling permits are no longer automatically passed on from father to son.

There are two different grades of Calvados. *Calvados appellation réglementée* is made in 10 areas of Normandy using the single distillation method. Each *appellation* has its own distinctive flavour and characteristics. These 10 Calvados areas are Pays de la Risle, Vallée de l'Orne, Perche, Pays du Merlerault, Pays de Bray, Mortainais, Domfrontain, Cotentin, Avranchais and Calvados.

The finest of all Calvados, the only one to enjoy an *appellation d'origine contrôlée,* comes from the Pays d'Auge in the *département* of Calvados. Here it is made from local cider and twice distilled. Every spring there is a public tasting and grading in the town of Cambremer. This is at the heart of the *"route du cidre"*, and cider farms hope to be awarded the annual *cru de Cambremer* at the same tasting event. The winning farms can then display signs and may be visited.

All Calvados is then aged in oak barrels, moving from young casks where it acquires its warm toffee colourings to older casks where it matures in peace. Different years are blended to achieve a given Calvados's house style, with the most recent year determining the age under which the bottle will be labelled. Three-star Calvados has spent two years in the barrel, *vieux or reservé* three years. VSOP Calvados is five years old, including four years in cask. Calvados *hors d'âge* must be at least six years old, five of which are spent in the barrel.

A distinguished after-dinner drink, Calvados is also the secret taste behind traditional Normandy cooking, an ideal partner for *crème fraîche* and at home with fish, poultry, pork and desserts. It is also traditionally served chilled in the middle of a meal to revive flagging appetites – these days often in delectable sorbet form. This is rather bluntly known as *le trou normand,* the Norman hole. Calvados is added to coffee to make *café calva* (coffee in the old days was a luxury kept warm for several days on a corner of the stove and much in need of a little *je ne sais quoi* to improve it) and mixed with apple juice to make *pommeau*, a pleasant, born-again apéritif. ❑

LEFT: Pay d'Auge is the only region to have its own Calvados *appellation contrôlée.*

50 percent fat, with an orangey-yellow rind and a ripe, earthy aroma that is stronger than its tender flavour and texture. There will be a round Livarot with a shiny, reddish, washed rind, pungent aroma, elastic texture and sweet flavour. There might be a Brillat-Savarin, created in the 1930s by the great Monsieur Androuët, doyen of modern French cheesemakers. This round cheese with a pale, velvety crust is made with triple cream and has a 75 percent fat content. Not suprisingly, its taste is mild and buttery and its texture very smooth. There might be a square Pavé d'Auge with its spicy tang, a delicate Neufchâtel on its bed of straw. One of the

made of raw milk cured for at least three weeks in small dairies. It has a crust tinged with orange and its texture should be bouncy-firm rather than solid, chalk-like or runny. A good Camembert has a distinctive, rich, smooth taste that is slightly salty, and the taste lingers satisfyingly on the palate.

Should you want to buy one in a shop, do as the natives do. Take the cheese out of its little round wooden box, and press the centre with your thumbs to check that it gives a little. If the texture feels right, sniff discreetly – there should be a cheesey whiff but nothing too pronounced. You might see people testing half a

oldest cheeses in Normandy, Neufchâtel was probably already around before William and his men set sail for England. It has a soft, velvety texture and a somewhat salty taste.

Camembert

Naturally, there will be a genuine *Camembert de Normandie*. Ordinary supermarket *camembert pasteurisé* is produced practically everywhere in France but authentic Camembert has to come from one of the five *départements* which make up Normandy. The connoisseur's Camembert has a 45 percent fat content and is

dozen cheeses until they are satisfied they have the perfect Camembert. Like the rest of their compatriots, the Normans take their cheeses very seriously, and believe passionately that the cheeses of their *pays* are the best in France.

Meat for a feast

On the table at Emma Bovary's wedding feast were "four sirloins, six chicken *fricassées*, pot-roasted veal, three lamb gigots and a pretty roasted suckling pig surrounded by four *andouilles* [chitterling sausages] flavoured with sorrel". The meat-safe of prosperous Normandy has changed little since Flaubert described it in the middle of the 19th century. Veal is more

ABOVE: *andouilles* graced Madame Bovary's table.

popular than beef, but even more typical is the lamb bred on the salt marshes of the Manche near Mont-St-Michel, *l'agneau de pré-salé*. Young salt-meadow lamb is tender, lean and tasty and requires little accompaniment.

Succulent chickens, squabs and guinea fowl are bred in farmyards all over Normandy and still *fricasséed* with velvety cream sauces. Then there are *canetons*, the long-breasted ducklings from Yvetot and Duclair with a rich, gamey flavour, stuffed with liver, roasted, and served in a wine sauce. This is *canard rouennais*, one of the classic dishes of Normandy.

Tripe and sausages

The pigs of the region thrive on a diet of wind-fall orchard fruit. Normandy black pudding ranks among the most celebrated in France. Every year in March the town of Mortagne-au-Perche hosts an international black-pudding festival and competition, *la foire du boudin* and the *concours du meilleur boudin*.

Perhaps the most notable *charcuterie* of Normandy is beef tripe, *les tripes*. Best known of all are the slowly simmered *tripes à la mode de Caen*. These are cooked with plenty of vegetables and the flavourings include a little Calvados, and they are good and filling, as all workers' food should be. Also well worth trying are the aromatic skewered *tripes en brochette*, a speciality of La Ferté-Macé in the Orne.

Andouilles and *andouillettes*, smoked and uncooked chitterling sausages, respectively, are also popular with connoisseurs. *Andouilles* and *andouillettes de Vire* (from the town of Vire) are famous throughout France. An acquired taste they may be, but they deserve an experiment. Like many another *specialité de charcuterie*, they taste infinitely finer on the spot, very freshly made.

Traditional desserts

The traditional desserts of Normandy are dominated by the apples and pears that grow in profusion and which make superlative *tartes* with subtle fillings and excellent *confitures*, jams and jellies. Other sweet specialities worth a small detour are *brioches de Gournay*, freshly made *caramels d'Isigny* and, in Fécamp, *truffes* and *chocolats à la Bénédictine*. ❑

LEFT: the market on Trouville quay is always brimming with seafood fresh from the water.

HORSES

*Two national studs, a famous racecourse and prestigious yearling sales
mean that thoroughbred horses are a vital part of Norman life*

Horses are as quintessential a part of Norman life and the Normandy landscape as apple trees, Calvados and half-timbered barns. The vivid pictures in the Bayeux Tapestry provide a telling reminder of the use to which William the Conqueror put mounted horsepower in his battle against the Saxon foot soldiers at Hastings in 1066. These days the pride of Normandy horseflesh battle it out not on the battlefields but on the premier racecourses of western Europe.

The two French national studs, one at St-Lô in the Manche and one at Le Pin in the Orne, each have a complement of over 200 stallions. But the progeny of these sires will be predominantly trotting horses, cross-breeds and showjumpers. The two studs are also the breeding base of the Percherons, that distinctive strain of dappled grey or black dray horses. Both studs are open to the public: the Haras du Pin, which was planned around a château in a forest by Louis XIV's minister, Jean-Baptiste Colbert, is especially worth a visit.

Money and class

It is with the production of top-class thoroughbred racehorses, rather than cobs and hacks, that Normandy is most famously associated. The élite private stud farms like the Aga Khan's Haras de Bonneval near Mesnil Mauger, where rich Charolais cattle share the pasturelands, are not open to the public. Unless you are an insider you will have to be content with tantalising glimpses of these fairytale settings, seen over white paddock fencing as you journey through the lush green country.

There can be few other multinational industries in the world that are still conducted in such evocative surroundings as thoroughbred breeding. Elegantly cut lawns, immaculately maintained stallion boxes, old trees and even older

PRECEDING PAGES: going hell for leather
at the Deauville track.
LEFT: leading them back to the paddock.
RIGHT: a resident of Touques stud farm.

houses, blue blood, money and class – Normandy has all of these things.

Blue grass

What it also has, and what has made its fortune as a thoroughbred centre, is good-quality grass. The great Kentucky horsemen have always

attributed their phenomenal success in horse-breeding to the excellent grazing provided by Kentucky Blue Grass which is said to be more productive and less green than the Virginia Blue Grass further north.

In truth, the smooth-stalked meadow grass of Kentucky is little different from the extensive pasturelands of the great European breeding regions around Newmarket in England, in Tipperary and on the plain of Kildare in Ireland – and in Normandy. The big difference between the two sides of the Atlantic is that Normandy pasture is more watery than Kentucky Blue Grass and grows on a much thicker layer of soil.

American breeds, with such an abundance of fine grazing, tend to be bulkier and more forward-looking juveniles but they sometimes revert to a coarser, sprinting type later on. This is why American breeders continually return to the top European bloodlines to replenish their stock with those qualities of stamina, soundness and speed over middle distances that the best European-bred horses display.

The Aga Khan

The most dominant and influential owner-breeder in European racing during the 20th century was the third Aga Khan, who bought his first yearlings at Deauville in 1921 and summered there regularly in his own private villa. According to the colourful racing writer and *boulevardier* Quentin Gilbey, the Aga Khan was particularly fond of giving large quantities of rough Normandy cider to his guests at lunch and then sitting back to watch the effects on them throughout the afternoon.

era was the French textile millionaire, Marcel Boussac, who for nearly 60 years owned the Haras de Fresnay-le-Buffard at Neuvy-au-Houlme in the Orne.

After his death, this fabulous 260-hectare (650-acre) stud farm became the property of Stavros Niarchos, the Greek shipping tycoon and veteran racehorse owner, who died in 1996. It was subsequently purchased by a French company, Fresnay Agricole SA. Fresnay-le-Buffard sponsors the £100,000 Prix Jacques le Marois, one of the championship mile races of Europe and the highlight of Deauville's month-long August racing season.

The old Aga was very much a trader and not averse to selling some of his best stallions to the Americans when the price was right, but for the most part the plutocratic owners of the old school could afford simply to breed to race and to race predominantly among themselves. The old Aga's leading rival in the pre- and post-war

Strictly business

Thoroughbred breeding in France, as in every other first-division racing country, is strictly a business. And it is the players with the least insular outlook who have thrived. Of all the great Normandy stud farms none displays a more romantic exterior nor conceals a more business-like purpose than the Haras du Quesnay at Vauville, some 10 km (6 miles) south of Deauville. The château at Quesnay was built by the Count de Glanville in the 16th century; the stud farm was established in 1910 by the American millionaire William Vanderbilt, who had won the 1908 French Derby with a horse called *Sea Sick*.

Vanderbilt sold on his racing and breeding interests to his compatriot A.K. Macomber for 12 million francs in 1920. Macomber gradually lost interest in horses in later life and by the time the champion French trainer Alec Head took the stud over in 1958 there had been nothing much doing there for over 20 years.

Ahead of the game

Alec Head, who gave up training on his own account in the 1980s but whose family remains one of the most distinguished racing dynasties in Europe, is an exceptionally shrewd as well as a charming and charismatic man. During the

lion stations and stud farms of the world. Among the horses that have been bred there have been two Prix de l'Arc de Triomphe winners and two winners of the French Derby or Prix du Jockey Club. Le Quesnay stallions, some of them later exported to the US, have included *Riverman*, sire of two more Arc winners, and *Lyphard*, sire of the immortal *Dancing Brave*, and grand-sire of the 1993 Epsom Derby winner, *Commander-in-Chief*.

Alec Head's racecourse and sales ring successes were intimately bound up with his relationship with the late Count Roland de Chambure, the banker-cum-horse breeder who

1950s his foremost patron was the equally dashing Prince Aly Khan, son of the old Aga Khan and father of the present Aga Khan IV. On Prince Aly's death in a Paris car accident in 1960, Head's decision to continue his own horse-breeding business lost him the patronage of the new Aga, who feared a conflict of interests. Despite this, Head's skill at moving out of the tack-room and into the boardroom can be measured by the fact that he has since transformed Le Quesnay into one of the great stal-

died suddenly of a heart attack in 1988. Head and Chambure were one half of a quartet of French owner-breeders referred to enviously by their competitors as "Le Mafia". The count was only 19 years old when he inherited the 49-hectare (100-acre) Haras d'Étreham near Bayeux on the death of his father in 1953.

The old count was every inch the sporting aristocrat of yesteryear, a reckless gambler who would give away nominations to his best stallions whenever he had an irksome gaming debt to settle. His son recognised that if he wanted to hang on to his inheritance in the changed social and financial climate of the post-war era he would have to expand the stud on commercial

LEFT: preparing next season's winners.
ABOVE LEFT AND RIGHT: grooming and mucking out are tasks that never seem to end.

lines. He was helped out by a loan from his family's own merchant bank, but it was a sound investment. Today the stud farm that has passed on to his children runs to 240 hectares (600 acres), employs a permanent staff of 50 and has boxes for around 150 horses.

The Haras d'Étreham and the Haras du Quesnay each keep some 60 mares permanently on the farms, half of them owned by the stud and the rest belonging to patrons of the stud such as the international art dealer Daniel Wildenstein. The patrons pay to have their mares board at the farm and to have them covered by one of the resident stallions.

The Deauville sales

The count sold his first yearlings at Deauville in 1954 and each year the majority of the Étreham and Quesnay yearlings are sent to the sales with perhaps five or six out of 50 being kept back to race in the breeders' own colours.

Men like Marcel Boussac would never breed a mare to a stallion that they didn't own themselves, or sell a homebred foal at a public auction unless it was a cast-off for which they had no use. But to France's commercial breeders, the Deauville sales, which take place in the second half of August and which are the biggest European yearling sale outside Britain and Ireland, offer a premium opportunity to sell their wares to a large and captive audience at the height of the Deauville season.

The Deauville sales complex is a short stroll away from the racecourse and the main sessions are timed to begin in the early evenings just as the horse racing is finishing. You don't need a ticket or an invitation to attend. All you need to do is pick up a sales catalogue and then amble around the picturesque barns and paddocks with the requisite degree of self-confidence. Then you can watch the serious buyers scrutinising the lots that they may be considering making an offer for that night.

After that you can then wander through into the ultra-modern bidding theatre where bids are flashed up on an electronic screen in Euros, pounds, dollars and yen. Providing you don't scratch your nose at the wrong moment the spectacle of well-heeled wallets and powerful egos duelling for the choicest lots can provide engrossing free entertainment.

Producing winners

The Deauville record of winners produced is one of which any sales company would be proud, but the pedigrees of these star graduates have not always been fashionable enough to attract the game's biggest high rollers like the Maktoum brothers from Dubai. One effect of this trend has been to make Deauville excellent value for money for the purchaser.

The top lots in recent years have rarely gone for more than 300,000 euros (£250,000/ $375,000) whereas the top lots in Kentucky in July can still reach $1 million or $2 million a head. This may not be such good news for the smaller French breeders but, having been less dependent on Arab money during the bloodstock boom of the 1980s, the Deauville sale has caught less of a cold than its rivals now that the Arabs are breeding rather than buying the majority of their own stock.

Canny professionals like Alec Head remain quietly confident that the age-old allure of horse racing, coupled with the other attractions of Normandy and the glamour of Deauville in particular, will always be enough to entice wealthy punters to want to own, rather than simply to bet on, racehorses. ❏

LEFT: inside the stables at Le Haras du Pin, one of the two national studs.
RIGHT: exercising horses on the Deauville sands.

PLACES

A detailed guide to the whole of Normandy, with principal sites clearly cross-referenced by number to the maps

Normandy's name evokes a pastoral picture: mottled cattle munching in knee-high buttercup meadows beneath laden apple boughs; vast barns and farmhouses, their half-timbered walls infilled with earth-red brick or honey-coloured clay, creaking and weary with use and age; a seriously rich, green land that yields a bounty of cider, Calvados, butter, cream and cheese.

The ideal picture is also the real one, and it is exactly what a visitor can expect to see. But Normandy is by no means a uniform place. There are forests and flatlands, sandy shores and granite coasts, hidden valleys, old villages and the scars of war built over with memorials and modern towns. There are also the fishing ports and coastal resorts that inspired artists and writers in the late 19th century and are still attracting visitors today.

Most noticeable is the difference between the eastern and western halves of the region. Haute or Upper Normandy lies along the banks of the River Seine and stretches north and eastwards to neighbouring Picardy. To the west, bordering Brittany, is Basse (Lower) Normandy, where timber gives way to stone, the countryside is ensnared in the *bocage* and lanes sink between fields enclosed by ancient, flowering hedgerows. Rouen, France's fifth largest port, is Normandy's ancient capital and today it is a handsome provincial French town. It remains the capital of Haute Normandie and the Seine Maritime. Caen, home of the great twin abbeys of William and Matilda, is the capital of Basse Normandie.

Motorways make light of the whole region, which can easily be driven through at speed, but off the beaten track, where some of the greatest rewards lie, it is impossible to hurry. Following the coast road from Étretat to Le Tréport, there are stunning views to slow you down. As you wend your way through the Seine Valley, the abbeys of St-Wandrille, Jumiège and St-Georges will give you a sense of the region's timelessness; and the route through cider and Calvados country meanders through some of the most beautiful Pay d'Auge scenery. The chapters that follow will introduce you to these and to many of Normandy's other treasures and help you get the best out of your time in this varied region. ❏

PRECEDING PAGES: symmetrical fields in early summer; St-Germain-de-Livet in the Touques Valley; a rainbow over Trouville harbour.
LEFT: the cliffs and beach at Étretat.

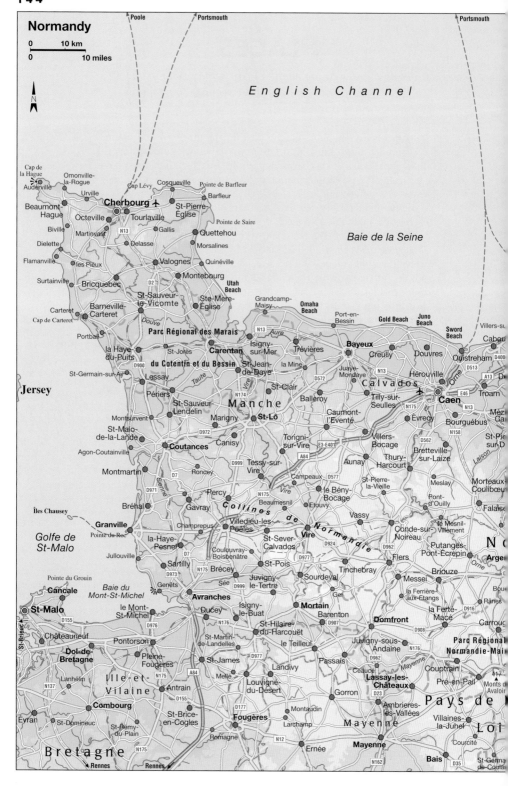

Normandy

0 — 10 km
0 — 10 miles

N

Poole   Portsmouth   Portsmouth

English Channel

Baie de la Seine

Cap de la Hague
Omonville-la-Rogue
Auderville
Cap Lévy   Cosqueville   Pointe de Barfleur
Urville   Barfleur
Cherbourg ✈   St-Pierre-Église
Beaumont-Hague   Octeville   Tourlaville   Pointe de Saire
Biville   N13   Gallis   Quettehou
Martinvast   Morsalines
Dielette   Delasse
Flamanville   Valognes   Quinéville
Surtainville   les Pieux
Bricquebec   Montebourg   Utah Beach
Carteret   D2   Ste-Mère-Église   Grandcamp-Maisy   Omaha Beach
Barneville-Carteret   St-Sauveur-le-Vicomte   Port-en-Bessin   Gold Beach   Juno Beach
Cap de Carteret   Douve   Sword Beach   Villers-su
Portbail   **Parc Régional des Marais**   N13   Aure   Creully   Douvres   Cabou
la Haye-du-Puits   St-Jores   Isigny-sur-Mer   Trévières   **Bayeux**   Ouistreham   D400
D900   du Cotentin et du Bessin   **Carentan**   la Mine   Hérouville   D513
St-Germain-sur-Ay   Lessay   Taute   St-Jean-de-Daye   D572   Juaye-Mondaye   N13   *Calvados*   A13   D
Jersey   Périers   Vire   St-Clair   Balleroy   Tilly-sur-Seulles   **Caen**   N13
St-Sauveur-Lendelin   **Manche**   Caumont-l'Eventé   N175   Evrecy   Bourguébus   Méz
Montsurvent   Marigny   **St-Lô**   Villers-Bocage   D562   St-Pie
St-Malo-de-la-Lande   D972   Torigni-sur-Vire   E3-E401   Bretteville-sur-Laize   sur-D
Agon-Coutainville   **Coutances**   Canisy   A84   Thury-Harcourt   Laison
Montmartin   D7   Roncey   Tessy-sur-Vire   Aunay   Morteaux-Coulibœu
Sienne   D999   Campeaux   D577   St-Pierre-la-Vieille   Meslay
Îles Chausey   D971   Percy   N175   Vire   le Bény-Bocage   Pont-d'Ouilly   Falai
Bréhal   Gavray   *Collines*   Beaumesnil   Vassy   le Mesnil-Villement
Granville   Champrepus   *de*   Etouvy   Condé-sur-Noireau   Putanges-Pont-Ecrepin   N
Golfe de   Pointe du Roc   Villedieu-les-Poêles   *Normandie*   D962   **Arge**
St-Malo   la-Haye-Pesnel   St-Sever-Calvados   *Vire*   D924   Flers   Orne
Jullouville   D7   Coulouvray-Boisbenâtre   D977   Tinchebray   Brïouze
Sartilly   Brécey   St-Pois   Sourdeval   Messei   Bou
D973   Juvigny-le-Tertre   Ger   la Ferrière-aux-Etangs   Rânes
Pointe du Grouin   Genêts   Sée   D999   la Ferté-Macé   D916
Cancale   *Baie du Mont-St-Michel*   **Avranches**   Isigny-le-Buat   **Mortain**   D908   Carrou
St-Malo   le Mont-St-Michel   Ducey   St-Hilaire-du-Harcouët   Barenton   **Domfront**   **Parc Régiona**
Châteauneuf   D155   N176   le Teilleul   Juvigny-sous-Andaine   N176   **Normandie-Mai**
Dol-de-Bretagne   Pontorson   St-Martin-de-Landelles   Ceauce   D962   Couptrain
Lanhélin   Pleine-Fougères   D977   Landivy   Passais   **Lassay-les-Châteaux**   Pré-en-Pail   Monts d'Avaloir
Ille-et-   A84   Mellé   Louvigné-du-Désert   Gorron   D23   **Pays de**
N137   *Vilaine*   Antrain   Montaudin   Ambrieres-les-Vallées   Villaines-la-Juhel
Combourg   D155   D177   **Fougères**   Larchamp   **Mayenne**   Courcité   **Loi**
Eyran   St-Dominuec   St-Brice-en-Cogles   Romagne   N12   Ernée   **Mayenne**   St-Germ
St-Rémy-du-Plain   **Bretagne**   N175   N162   **Bais**   D35   de-Couta
Rennes   Rennes

Map on page 150

ROUEN

Rouen is one of Normandy's most beautiful cities, equally delightful for visitors who want to roam the streets and eat in excellent restaurants as for those keen to trace the city's past through its historic buildings

The capital of Haute-Normandie and the region's largest city with a population of 380,000, Rouen lies on the River Seine between Paris and the sea. Forget the Romans. There is nothing of Rotomagus, their old trading place, to be seen above ground except in the Musée des Antiquités. Look ahead to where Normandy was baptised, with Rouen as capital, on a handshake between Rollo, head of the plundering Norsemen, and Charles the Simple, king of France. The year: 911. With the boundaries of the new duchy of Normandy agreed, Rollo changed his name to Robert and married the king's daughter, initiating three centuries of rule by Norman dukes with Rouen as their power base, and provoking the bitter struggle with England which Joan of Arc helped to resolve in the early 1400s.

Story in stone

Much of the city's history is in the open book of the **Cathédrale Notre-Dame Ⓐ** (open Mon–Sat 8am–7pm, Sun 8am–6pm), where the St Romanus and Butter towers of its Gothic façade look down over the heart of the old town. You can stand where Claude Monet put up his easel before these great towers of the west front for his series of paintings in 1894, and start reading bottom left.

The story begins here at the foot of the Tour St-Romain with 12th-century stones set on the foundations of a cathedral built by William the Conqueror, seventh in the line of Norman dukes, just three years before his forces invaded England. From the brutalism of the tower's lower stages, Gothic arches soar to the extravagances of the Flamboyant style that sets the character of the remainder of the west front.

By 1250 the cathedral we know today was complete, but in the succeeding centuries a fretwork of embellishments and the demands of restorers must have put it permanently under wraps. As the 19th-century English critic John Ruskin complained: "The beasts of workmen have scaffolding everywhere." St Jean-Baptiste porch on the left and St Étienne on the right, formed part of the old cathedral and survived a fire in 1200. Above them, in storeyed galleries, sculptured figures act out the life and martyrdom of St Jean and St Étienne.

Tour de Beurre

In the central porch, not completed till the 16th century, the Flamboyant style gives way to the Renaissance when Jacques Roux and his nephew Roland put the finishing touches to the right-hand tower, the **Tour de Beurre**. Roux would be relieved

to know that the tower is still standing, because it was built on a subterranean lake. Soon after construction began it started to lean, but the cracks were filled and building went on to its exquisite conclusion in the octagonal lantern in 1517.

The central tower completes and unites the composition, rising through the 13th to the 16th centuries to the lantern which so dramatically lights the space below and supports the tapering spire. In 1834, when Alavoine, the architect, died, he had been working on it for 11 years, but it was 40 more years before completion. The cathedral was badly damaged during World War II and restoration has been going on ever since. It suffered a serious setback as the result of the storms at the end of 1999. A pinnacle fell through the roof of the choir, damaging the interior, and the cathedral was temporarily shut to visitors.

Sculpted entrances

Opening from the rue St-Romain on the north side of the cathedral is the **Cour des Librairies**, once filled with booksellers' stalls, and beyond it the entrance to the north transept through the **Portail des Librairies**. Angels and monsters crowd the pages of this "encyclopaedia of the

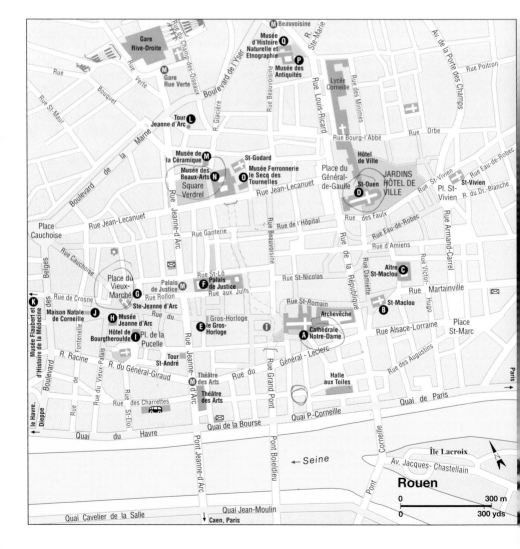

Map on page 150

Middle Ages". In a corresponding position on the south side is the **Portail de la Calende**, a 14th-century masterpiece, covered from top to bottom with sculptures inspired by French ivories.

After the rich display of the exterior, first steps inside bring something of an anticlimax. The soaring heights, the sheer magnitude of the enclosed space and absence of decoration reveal its creators' solemn intention. Its beauties must be sought out in such details as the slim, clustered columns that support the central tower; in the mighty organ above head-height, whose voice can make the whole edifice tremble; in the Escalier des Librairies (Booksellers' Staircase; 1480), by the Portail des Librairies; in the 13th-century windows in the ambulatory, and Chartres-blue glass in the rose windows; in misericords in the choir stalls, a mirror of life in the 15th century in which they were carved; in the chapel adjoining the south transept; in the tomb of Rollo, Normandy's first duke, who died in 933, "Founder and father of Normandy of which he was at first the terror and scourge, but afterwards the restorer".

Famous tombs

Among other tombs of the great and the formidable are those of William I, Duke of Normandy (died 942); the effigy of Richard the Lionheart, his heart in a casket in the stone beneath; Roland le Roux's Renaissance masterpiece of Cardinal Georges d'Amboise, Louis XII's minister and virtual ruler of France, who gave Rouen a fresh water supply and sanitation; Louis de Brézé, seneschal of Normandy (died 1544), a knight above, a naked corpse below, mourned by a kneeling Diane de Poitiers.

Archbishop's Palace

Rue St-Romain to the left of the cathedral skirts the **Archevêche** (Archbishop's Palace). In the forbidding wall only the ruined windows now survive from the **Chapelle d'Ordres** where the final act in the trial of Joan of Arc took place. The next day she was burned at the stake. In some of the houses opposite lodged the canons who condemned her to death. In this street, as elsewhere, the old wooden houses attract sympathetic businesses, such as dealers in antique furniture, books and prints.

Église St-Maclou

It is a delight to come to the **Église St-Maclou** ❸ (open Mon–Sat 10am–noon, 2–5.30pm, Sun 3–5.30pm), oppposite the Archbishop's Palace on the far side of the main rue de la République. This pyramid of pure Gothic is possibly the finest in the Flamboyant style in France; the burning zeal with which it was begun in 1437 persisted to its completion only 33 years later. The west front is an astonishing *tour de force*, its bow window of five great arches and gables carried up against flying buttresses "crowned by fretted niche and fair pediment – meshed like gossamer with inextricable tracery", said the English critic, John Ruskin.

Somewhere in that forest of pinnacles are two stone oil jars. The 6th-century

saint to whom the church was dedicated was a Scot who was canny enough to win the concession for supplying holy oil to the diocese. The carving on the entrance doors is attributed to the sculptor Jean Goujon, as are the black marble columns that support the organ in its loft, reached by a delicate spiral staircase.

Aître St-Maclou

Running along to the left of St-Maclou, rue Martainville is an attractive street of old, half-timbered bookshops which hides a ghostly secret: the **Aître St-Maclou ⓒ**. Inside a large wooden entrance, with only a tiny sign to identify it, is a quadrangle surrounded by timbered buildings, where young people stand chatting in groups. These are the studios of the **École Régionale des Beaux-Arts**. Regular exhibitions of the students work are held here (Mon–Sat 9am–noon, 2–6pm; free).

Look now at the carved wooden frieze above the ground floor on the timberwork gallery. Skulls, crossbones, coffins, hour-glasses, shovels, buckets, beds – all the gruesome paraphernalia of death are here, for this quiet retreat was a plague pit with bones heaped in the centre, under the once open cloister and in the space above as well. Rouen's victims of the Black Death are believed to have numbered 100,000 in the 14th century alone.

Two hundred years later the surrounding galleries were built. The bodies of the well-off were accommodated under the cloister, and the poor in the open centre space. Eventually the first floors received the overflow, as yet more and more were invited to this *dance macabre*.

Église St-Ouen

The view framed between the timbered house-fronts of the rue Damiette, north of St-Maclou, catches the breath with the beauty of the lantern tower of the **Église St-Ouen ⓓ** (open Wed–Mon 10am–12.30pm, 2–6pm). Unlike the cathedral, closely confined in a protective huddle of streets and houses, Rouen's second great

LEFT: the entrance to the Hôtel de Bourgtheroulde. **BELOW:** a tempting shop in the Vieux-Marché.

Map on page 150

church rises from lawns, trees and the wide open spaces of place du Général-de-Gaulle. These roughly cover the grounds and buildings of the Benedictine abbey founded in 1318, but still not completed 200 years later. The lantern towers on the west front of the church were demolished in the 19th century and insensitively replaced with the sham Gothic spires we see today.

The interior impresses by its great size, over 122 metres (400 ft) from end to end beneath an unbroken roof, and its great height, 33 metres (108 ft) to the nave ceiling. Light floods in from windows so vast it does not seem possible that their slender stone frames can support the enormous weight of the roof. In fact, the walls are propped by the flying buttresses.

Windows apart, there is little in the interior of interest beyond the organ in its gallery and the wrought-iron grilles barring approach to the high altar. There is too much evidence of the damage done by the Huguenots in the 16th century, and

revolutionaries in 1793, when shortage of weapons led them to set up a munitions factory inside. The smoke from the forges still blackens the stone.

Hôtel de Ville

After the Revolution the town hall that stood next to the Gros-Horloge was abandoned in favour of a new **Hôtel de Ville** built on abbey lands to the north of St-Ouen in place du Général-de-Gaulle. Where monks walked the cloister, civil servants now tread the corridors of power.

Just beyond the square is a former Jesuit College named the **Lycée Corneille** after its star pupil, though later students did not do so badly either – Flaubert, Maupassant, Delacroix and, later, writer and critic André Maurois also attended.

Gros-Horloge

Retrace your steps to the place de la Cathédrale, where, at No 25, the tourist office (tel: 33 2 32 08 32 40) is located in an ornate building. Ahead is the **rue du**

BELOW: the Gothic splendour of the Palais de Justice.

Gros-Horloge, which offers a natural (and traffic-free) introduction to the core of the old city. Once it was a main artery leading to the Vieux-Marché, and now, though bisected by a modern boulevard, is still rich in buildings of the Renaissance. The tall, timber-framed mansions nod overhead to their opposite neighbours, oblivious of the 21st century reflected in the shop windows below.

Spanning the street ahead is the **Gros-Horloge** , a delightful Renaissance pavilion set on an arch with the most splendidly embellished clock. It began life in 1389 in the belfry tower at its side, until Rouen, flushed with civic pride, gave it its present richly-gilded setting. One-handed, it tells the hour and week and moon's phases through a bull's eye above.

Two great bells, La Rouvel and Cache-Ribant, share the **Tour du Beffroi**, and from here the curfew is rung at 9 o'clock each evening. These bells rang for the people, calling them when decisions had to be made, when their rights were threat-ened, or when revolt was the only way to resist oppressive rule. Current renovation should result in better access to the clock, and a new museum is planned.

At the foot of the belfry tower is the **keeper's lodge**, a perfect house in miniature, and beside it a pleasing 18th-century **fountain** that tells how the nymph Arethusa was changed into this form by Artemis to save her from the attentions of the river-god Alpheus, who is the Seine. A fate worse than death?

Palais de Justice

Near the Gros-Horloge, and glimpsed up a side-street in the rue aux Juifs, is the **Palais de Justice** (Law Courts; not open to the public). Built near the end of the 15th century by Roland le Roux, architect of the cathedral, it is one of the world's richest examples of Gothic architecture. And it has survived not only restorers, war and desecration, but also restorers restoring the work of restorers. Here was the seat of Normandy's parlia-

BELOW: a splash of colour in Rouen's market.

Map on page 150

ment, a private place, hidden behind towering walls, its beauty not for the public eye. Now, only railings interrupt the view, and we can marvel at the artistry with which the façade ascends through the comparatively plain lower storeys to the glorious profusion of flying buttresses, lantern windows, turrets, tracery and crockets rising like champagne bubbles against the steeply sloping roof.

Hidden treasures

The wing on the left, the **Salle des Pas Perdus**, has a theatrical connection – although we are not allowed access to the interior. When the old court, the Vicomté de l'Eau, was shifted here from its temporary home in the cathedral, a table of white marble came with it. The great Corneille, Rouen's dramatist son, must often have thumped it when addressing the court as advocate.

In the central block are the handsomely decorated staircase, the great hall, and the judges' retiring room which so tastefully interrupts the main front. It was once the king's private room. Restoration of the courtyard cobbles in 1976 produced surprising and hitherto unknown evidence of Rouen's history: a 12th-century Jewish building in the Romanesque style.

The old market

The rue du Gros-Horloge leads to the **place du Vieux-Marché** ⑥. This was a market-place nearly 1,000 years ago, and still is today. Every morning, except Monday, it comes alive, filled with stalls full of fresh produce and flowers. The tall, timber-framed houses that surround it were yet to be built. There was no hint that it was to be the theatre of judicial murder and the catalyst of France's heroic and ultimately successful struggle to throw the English out of Normandy. It was here that Joan of Arc was burned alive on 30 May 1431, and her ashes thrown into the Seine.

On the spot where the flames were lit, only a few stones remain from the church of **St-Sauveur**. Nearby, marked

BELOW: carved intimations of mortality in the Aître St-Maclou.

by a 20-metre (65-ft) cross, is the 1979 church of **Ste-Jeanne d'Arc**. Like a beached ship, this modern building sits uneasily under a ski-slope slate roof and pyramid gables, but glows warmly inside with the brilliant lustre of old stained glass. The church is surrounded by cafés with bright umbrellas over their pavement tables.

Musée Jeanne d'Arc

In a strange echo of the beginnings of Joan of Arc's crusade, you too can hear voices in the **Musée Jeanne d'Arc**  (open mid-Apr–mid-Sept daily 9.30am–7pm; mid-Sept–mid-Apr 9.30am–noon, 1.30–7pm; admission charge) on the south side of the square. From the outside, the museum looks like a souvenir shop, so could easily be missed, which is unusually discreet for such a popular place.

A taped commentary in four languages complements the waxwork figures that bring nearly to life the characters in her story, from childhood in Domrémy to her death at the stake. A manuscript in the museum has the only existing drawing of Joan, a doodle scribbled in the margin by a bored clerk at her trial.

Hôtel de Bourgtheroulde

Turn right where rue de Gros-Horloge meets the square, and you will come to the place de la Pucelle (named after The Maid, once again) and discover the **Hôtel de Bourgtheroulde**  (pronounced *Boortrood*) the mansion that Guillaume de Roux built for himself in the early 16th century. He was counsellor to the Exchequer at the time.

Thanks to the bank that now occupies it (in whose hands could it be safer?) we can enter the courtyard and admire the octagonal staircase tower, the surviving Flamboyant Gothic end building and the fine Renaissance gallery along the south side. In its six arches is the sculpted frieze of the *Triumphs of Petrarch*, his triumphs somewhat dimmed by the passage of time, and on the stone below the celebrations of the Field of the Cloth of Gold, again

LEFT: a café near St-Maclou. **BELOW:** St-Ouen towers over the pedestrian-only rue Damiette.

Map
on page
150

somewhat tarnished by weathering. Guillaume de Roux's son, the abbot, was on the field near Calais at the meeting between England's Henry VIII and the king of France in 1520. Each tried to outdo the other in lavish entertainment to cement an alliance which ended three years later in the English invasion of France

Corneille's home

Nearby in the rue de la Pie is the **Maison Natale de Corneille ❶** (open Thur–Mon 10am–noon, 2pm–6pm, Wed 2–6pm; admission charge) where the playwright Pierre Corneille was born in 1606. Had Corneille been more successful in his intention of setting up as a barrister, drama's loss might have been the Law Courts' gain.

Luckily, the reception given to his comedy *Mélite* took him to Paris, where his genius won him the sponsorship of Cardinal Richelieu, until the popularity of *Le Cid* led the cardinal to try to have it panned by the critics.

BELOW: the vast interior of St-Ouen.

At 40, the acclaimed master of French comedy and tragedy married and returned here to the rue de la Pie, seldom leaving except to stay in his country house at Petit Couronne. In 1662 he returned to Paris to live, giving way in public esteem to an up-and-coming young verse-maker, Racine. Drama, off-stage, links Corneille with the Revolution through his descendant, Charlotte Corday. Her hatred of the Jacobins led her to seek out Jean-Paul Marat in his bath and plunge a knife into his heart *(see page 46)*.

Musée Flaubert

From the Vieux-Marché rue de Crosne and avenue Gustave Flaubert lead to the vast complex of the **Hôtel-Dieu**, Rouen's old hospital. Behind high walls in a wing of the hospital lived Achille-Cléophas Flaubert, the resident surgeon, and here Gustave was born in 1821. What effect his early life within the surroundings of the hospital had on his upbringing may perhaps be measured in the morbidity and

pessimism of his works and his hatred of bourgeois values.

His undeniable achievement is celebrated in the **Musée Flaubert et d'Histoire de la Médecine** (open Wed–Sat 10am–noon, 2–6pm, Tues 10am–6pm; admission charge), the family home.

The poster outside says it all through the images of a brace and bit in a case of surgeon's tools. Inside there is some original family furniture and paintings and Flaubert's famous parrot under a glass dome. But the surgeon's manuals may make your hair curl.

Tour Jeanne d'Arc

Make your way to the place Cauchoise and up the broad boulevard de la Marne. Off to the right, on rue du Donjon, the conical roof of **Tour Jeanne d'Arc** (open Mon, Wed–Sat, 10am–12.30pm, 2–6pm, Sun 2–6.30pm; admission charge), thrusts like a rocket's nose cone above the surrounding modern buildings. This tower is all that remains of the splendid castle Philippe-Auguste, king of France, built in the early 13th century.

The castle was allowed to fall into disrepair and suffered the indignity of being used as a quarry. Then, after a spell as a convent, it became a cotton mill. Its failure brought back the nuns, this time running a girls' school, and there were more demolitions to make a garden. The tower itself was threatened. At this point the conscience of France was roused, the tower saved, and the scene of Joan of Arc's humiliation was preserved.

She had been brought here from her prison cell in the **Tour de la Pucelle** (Maid's Tower) and confronted with the most gruesome instruments of torture. Had she not given the right answers under interrogation, they would undoubtedly have been used. It is said that English soldiers looked on, unable to understand a word of the proceedings. Inside the tower, an exhibition guides visitors through the history of the original castle and the principal events that have taken place here.

BELOW: graceful statue outside the Musée des Beaux-Arts.

Rouen *faïence*

France's reputation for the manufacture and decoration of china and earthenware stands high here. The gracious rooms of the **Hôtel d'Hocqueville** overflow with the finest examples of *faïence*, such as the horn of plenty that is so conspicuous a motif of its decoration. This 17th-century mansion in rue Faucon is the **Musée de la Céramique**  (open daily 10am–1pm, 2–6pm; admission charge), tracing the history of the potter's art from the earliest civilisation to its flowering in the 17th and 18th centuries.

Faïence is most typical of the local ceramics, and modern copies are on sale throughout the city. Rouen plates – made of a mixture of local clays covered with a white tin-based enamel and decorated with colourful designs, maxims, plays on words and expressions of love – speak volumes, revealing an intimate glimpse of the humanity of their owners.

Aside from the Sèvres porcelain, the museum's collection has such oddities as the terrestrial globe painted by Pierre Chapel in 1775 and a violin made by some Delft Stradivarius.

Musée des Beaux-Arts

At the foot of rue Faucon in square Verdrel, crossing rue du Bailliage, is the **Musée des Beaux-Arts**  (open Thur–Mon 10am–6pm; admission charge). which has been extensively renovated with a smart new reception area and more than 60 different galleries.

One of France's finest art galleries, it thinks of itself as "*fraîche*" and invites a new, fresh look at the work of the great artists from the Spanish, Italian, French and Flemish schools. Velásquez, Veronese, Caravaggio, Rubens, La Tour, Ruysdael, Ingres, Géricault, Delacroix – all are represented here by important canvases. Closer to our own time, you can renew acquaintance with Sisley's sensitive Impressionism, with Monet's superb west front of Rouen cathedral, and with Dufy's *joie de vivre*.

In the sculpture garden, classic figures pose in frozen immobility under the glass

BELOW: one of the exhibits in the Musée Le Secq des Tournelles.
RIGHT: the ceramic violin in the Musée de la Céramique.

Map on page 150

Map
on page
150

roof. Can it be true that there was a model of the church of St-Maclou made of bread-crumbs once displayed here?

And if you're interested in knowing what Pierre Corneille looked like, there he is in terracotta, and, looking rather fierce, in oils.

A passion for iron

Henri Le Secq des Tournelles was a clerk in a lawyer's office and flights of fancy were reserved for his leisure hours. Then Henri developed a passion for the black-smith's art and began collecting wrought-iron. When he died in 1920 he bequeathed the collection to Rouen, and an appropriate home was found in the redundant church of St-Laurent in rue Jacques Villon.

This is now the **Musée Ferronnerie Le Secq des Tournelles** ⓞ (open Thur–Mon 10am–1pm, 2–6pm; admission charge). Henri's taste embraced an astonishing va-riety of objects, from keys to corkscrews, flat-irons to jewellery, household tools, even a chastity belt – all commonplace articles (except for the latter, perhaps) ele-vated by the metalworker's art.

Musée des Antiquités

From the museum, head up rue Beauvoi-sine to the **Musée des Antiquités** ⓟ (open Mon and Wed–Sat 10am–12.15pm, 1.30–5.30pm, Sun 2–6pm; admission charge). The antiquities are housed in the glazed cloister and buildings of a former convent. Here are the plaster casts that show just what the Field of the Cloth of Gold was like. Plenty of evidence, too, of the Romans in Rouen. A mosaic Orpheus charms the animals and Apollo pursues a reluctant Daphne, rescued from the Roman baths in Lillebonne. Locks, chimney-pieces, tapes-tries, ivories and carved woodwork fill the gaps in Rouen's history.

The nearby **Musée d'Histoire Naturelle et Etnographie** ⓠ has an interesting col-lection devoted to Central Africa and the South Sea islands. It is temporarily closed but exhibitions are often held in the grounds (tel: 33 2 35 71 41 50). ❑

RIGHT: Rouen's beam-and-plaster façades.

Map on page 166

LE HAVRE

Le Havre rose like a phoenix from the ashes of war and now celebrates its rebirth as a modern city with a rich past, as a flourishing port and a centre of art and culture

In the league table of French ports, **Le Havre** ranks second only to Marseille, yet it didn't exist until the 16th century, and both port and town were almost destroyed in World War II. That it rose, phoenix-like, from the ashes to develop into today's thriving port and industrial centre (pop. 250,000) shows remarkable resilience and formidable courage.

François I began the harbour in the silted-up mouth of the Seine in 1517, thinking it would make a good base for an assault on England. François-Ville, as he called it, was not an immediate success. Ships ran aground on sandbanks until beacons were lit to guide them in.

All at sea

Tides played havoc with the town, carrying the fishing fleet into the flooded streets. Then the English under the Earl of Warwick sailed in and took possession for 10 months. Hoping for better fortune, the town's name was changed to Havre de Grâce, and Richelieu, Louis XIII's Minister of State, took it in hand, deepening the harbour and joining it to neighbouring Harfleur by canal.

The English were back again in 1694 after bombarding Dieppe, and destroyed much of the port and hundreds of houses. The Havrais responded by building a new harbour of stone. In 1759 the persistent English returned with similar effect, but peace and an alliance with the American colonies brought stability and prosperity.

Louis XVI built new docks and put walls round the town, happily resisting the temptation to call it Louisville. With Napoleon's ambition to invade England the town grew in status and importance. Following Le Havre's support for the "rebels", ties with the United States grew stronger and in 1864 their first steamship, the *Washington*, arrived, initiating a lucrative exchange of trade.

Devastation and rebirth

During the 20th century, Le Havre was to suffer from friends and enemies alike in the devastation of World War II, from German bombs in 1940 and as the target of Allied bombing in 1944. Though Paris had been liberated, Le Havre was still occupied. Given the extent of the devastation, the Havrais could have been excused for abandoning the task of renewal.

That they did not do so is due largely to the vision of one man, the Parisian architect Auguste Perret, and his pioneering use of one material: reinforced concrete. Perret retained the 16th-century chessboard pattern of streets, but gave his new town space and wide boulevards opening onto the port.

PRECEDING PAGES: eating by the beach. **LEFT:** triathlon competitors in the town centre. **RIGHT:** Le Havre thrives on industry and shipping.

Central features

Central to the city's design is the **Hôtel de Ville A**, superbly sited on one of Europe's largest squares, liberally decorated with flowers, trees and fountains. From here the long, elegant avenue Foch points west to the sea and the rue de Paris, south to the docks. In these apartment- and office-lined boulevards Perret brought rainbow hues to his concrete, varying the colour according to the situation, light and character of his buildings.

Two contrasting churches

Of the original rue de Paris, nothing remains except for one building, the restored **Église Notre-Dame B** (open daily 10am–5pm). It has a 16th-century Gothic tower from which the English, invited in by French Protestants in 1562, mounted their guns and fired on the French camp.

Cardinal Richelieu (1585–1642) presented the church with the great organs (restored in 1980) and the carved oak organ case. In 1974 the church became a cathedral for the new diocese of Le Havre.

There is a nice contrast between Notre-Dame and Perret's **Église St-Joseph C** (open daily 10am–5pm; tel: 02 35 46 34 57). The concrete tower, which has affinity of outline with the Empire State Building, rises 106 metres (348 ft) to its belfry above the boulevard François.

Clustered pillars support the tower above the central altar, and the whole interior is speckled with constellations of coloured light from stained glass set in the walls and ablaze with sunshine.

Brazilian contribution

Walking east along rue Louis Brindeau, you come to Brazilian architect Oscar Niemeyer's **Maison de la Culture du Havre/Espace Niemeyer D**. This arts and recreation centre, completed in 1982, hosts a varied programme of classical concerts, theatre and cinema. Its distinctive white outline has earned it the nickname "the elephant's foot".

LEFT: memorial outside Oscar Niemeyer's "elephant's foot".

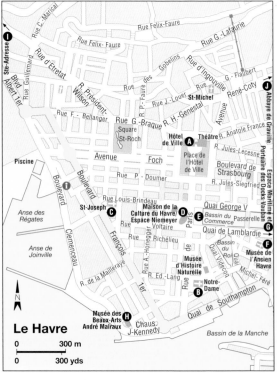

Le Havre

Map on page 166

Beyond, the **Bassin du Commerce** Ⓔ, now filled with leisure craft. The elegant new **Passerelle** footbridge, supported by steel cables, crosses it, giving a good view of the impressive Espace Niemeyer.

The old city

The **Musée de l'Ancien Havre** Ⓕ (open Wed–Sun 10am–noon, 2–6pm; admission charge) in rue Jérôme Bellarmato, south of the Bassin du Commerce, is housed in a restored 17th-century lodge belonging originally to an old Le Havre family.

The city's history from 1517, through its great days as a transatlantic port on to modern times is brought vividly to life through maps and engravings, photographs, models and paintings. It leaves you with enormous admiration for Le Havre's formidable powers of renewal and achievement.

Maritime museum

The port is too important not to have a museum devoted to itself. The **Espace** Maritime et Portuaire des Docks Vauban Ⓖ (open Tues–Wed, Sat–Sun 2.30–6pm; admission charge) on the quai Frissard is a celebration of the maritime past. Worldwide links in the days of the multi-funelled transatlantic liners are recalled, merchant ships and the cargoes they carried – cotton, wool, coffee and oil – the men who sailed in them, the perils of the sea and the threat of fire. Hoses at the ready, the fireship *Le Havre III* is moored at the quay outside.

From Easter to September you can take a trip round the docks and harbour from the quai de la Marine on the pleasure boat, *La Salamandre*. From this viewpoint, the immensity of the port operations and the size of the docks, can be seen in comfort (tel: 02 35 42 01 31 for details).

Malraux's museum

Heading back along Quai Colbert to the *centre ville*, you will pass the **ferry terminal** in the Bassin de la Citadelle, from where vessels cross to Portsmouth. If you

BELOW: an exhibition in the André Malraux museum.

continue along quai de Southampton, you will come to the city's most distinguished building, the **Musée des Beaux-Arts André Malraux** ⒣ (open Mon, Wed–Fri 11am–6pm, Sat–Sun 11am–7pm; admission charge).

Named after novelist and critic André Malraux (1901–76), the museum opened in 1961. It has a modern feel to it and impressively displays its collection of pictures and sculpture, regardless of period, in the best possible conditions. The glass-and-steel gallery, with a moated entrance, is simple in construction and layout.

Inside there are no walls. Screens can be shuffled into place to give the interior new spaces, new volumes, new shapes. Aluminium blinds in the laminated glass roof filter the natural light as required.

The paintings richly deserve their setting, progressing through the European schools to outstanding works by Impressionist Eugène Boudin (1824–98) and Fauvist Raoul Dufy (1877–1953) and his contemporaries.

Fashionable resort

Boulevard Clemenceau lures us away to Le Havre's other role, as a seaside resort. The *plage* stretches for some 2 km (1½ miles) to the attractive garden suburb of **Ste-Adresse** ❶, where villas crowd the slopes above the Seine estuary, nudging each other for a share of the magnificent view. In 1841 the proprietor of *Le Figaro* bought a house here, surrounded by farmland. Writers, painters and musicians followed, and by World War I the last farm had disappeared. Sarah Bernhardt, Alexandre Dumas *fils*, Gabriel Fauré, Raoul Dufy and Claude Monet all had villas here. Monet said: "I have everything here that pleases me – light and water."

The Dufayel Palace on the slopes became the seat of the Belgian government in exile during World War I.

From the terrace of the **Fort de Ste-Adresse** there is a wonderful panorama over the port and across the estuary to the Côte de Grâce. Visitors like to linger over meals in the Nice-Havrais restaurant, one of the best fish restaurants in town with a grand view. A favourite Le Havre excursion skirts the hill past the "Pain du Sucre", the sugar loaf-shaped mariners' monument, takes in the nearby Bernhardt villa with its mosaics, and continues to the lighthouse on **La Hève** headland.

Abbaye de Graville

Another popular excursion leads inland to a hilltop above the Rouen road – the **Abbaye de Graville** ❶ (open Wed–Sun 10am–noon, 2–6pm; admission charge). The shrine was built to protect the relics of 6th-century St Honorine, but fear of marauding Normans led to her remains being spirited away to Conflans, near Pontoise, for safe keeping. Happily, her tomb is now back in the priory.

The museum, in surviving monastic buildings, has a remarkable collection of church sculpture in stone, alabaster and wood, intriguing relics of the Black Madonna and documents revealing the chequered history of the priory.

From the wooded setting of the old cloister there is a spellbinding prospect of the Seine on its way to the sea.   ❏

Map on page 166

LEFT: giving the boat a lick of paint. **RIGHT:** securing a space in the yacht marina.

Map
on page
174

THE SEINE VALLEY

*A journey along a stretch of the great river, starting at the ports of
Le Havre and Harfleur and ending at Monet's garden in Giverny,
taking in châteaux, abbeys and forests en route*

Born in Burgundy, brought up in Champagne and reaching maturity in the cider orchards of Normandy, the 771-km (479-mile) Seine shows a marked reluctance to reach the sea. The Celts named it the Seine from their word for "bend" – an apt epithet for this snake-like river.

For France the Seine has been a mixed blessing. A highway for trade in tin with Cornwall in England, for the expanding culture of Rome and the founders of the great abbeys, it was also the open door for invaders from Scandinavia, the Vikings. The Normans, predators and pillagers of abbeys and churches, struck a deal that gave them control over the occupied territory north of the river. Poachers turned gamekeepers, they restored the abbeys, rebuilt the churches, and brought the region prosperity and stability.

Commercial history

The rest is commercial history: embanking to improve the passage of large vessels to Rouen and Paris; the reclamation of the flood plain to extend docking facilities at Le Havre and Rouen; and the construction of the Tancarville Canal so that barges could reach Le Havre from the river without braving the estuary. The most dramatic recent development is the Pont de Normandie, which connects **Le Havre ❶** *(see page 165)* and Honfleur at the mouth of the Seine. Opened in 1995, and at the time the largest cable-stayed bridge in the world, it is just over 2 km (1¼ miles) long and able to withstand winds of up to 440 kph (275 mph). Vehicles and pedestrians cross the bridge 50 metres (165 ft) above the water.

River traffic

The barges that ply the river can go on to connect up with the vast network of waterways which stretch throughout Europe, though the number of traditional barge operators has been in sharp decline. Now the waterway is looking for tourists to climb aboard sparkling luxury passenger boats that ply from Paris to Honfleur. Depending on the tide, the journey from Rouen to the sea takes up to four hours.

Harfleur

Leaving Le Havre by the Tancarville road does little to reassure you that you are about to embark on the most fascinating excursion this side of the Rhine. The first port of call is one no longer. **Harfleur ❷**, swallowed in the city suburbs, has a surprisingly attractive heart. This was once the chief port of Normandy until it was choked by sand. Where navies once

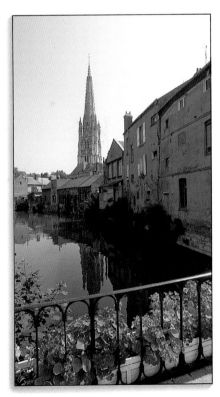

anchored, there are now roads, wharves, waste and pipelines. The 15th-century church with its stone spire alone holds up its head against the indignity of it all, keeping for itself the fine view from the bridge over the sluggish stream of the Lézarde.

In 1415 England's Henry V with 30,000 men besieged the old port, and, taking it, threw out the inhabitants and installed his soldiers. A local hero, Jean de Crouchy, rallied the remaining residents and ousted the attackers. A month later came Henry's triumph at Agincourt, and soon Normandy was back under the English crown.

With white chalk cliffs dominating the river road east it is an almost surreal experience to drive below, like being in an amphibious vehicle. In the distance is the thin, spider's web outline of the Tancarville bridge, and at the cliff foot the wooden chalet rural retreats cling like washed-up debris on a shore.

On the heights above, and best reached from Harfleur through Gonfreville, is the **Château d'Orcher** (open Jul–mid-Aug, daily 2–6pm; grounds Fri–Wed 2–6pm; admission charge) with a cliff-top terrace, the view from which the *seigneur* is gracious enough to share. From this eyrie, 90 metres (295 ft) above the river, framed by oil installations on reclaimed land below and Le Havre's enormous presence on the estuary, is the misted vision of Honfleur under the Côte de Grâce on the far bank.

Tancarville bridge

Modern French engineers certainly have a light touch. For a bridge the size of **Tancarville ❸**, 1.6 km (1 mile) with its approaches, the lightness of the concrete and the slightness of the filaments supporting the latticed steel highway are a nice contrast to the work of their medieval predecessors in the massive remains of the castle that overlooks it.

The impact the bridge has made on the economic life of the region has been tremendous. Before 1959 the Seine effectively isolated Upper from Lower Nor-

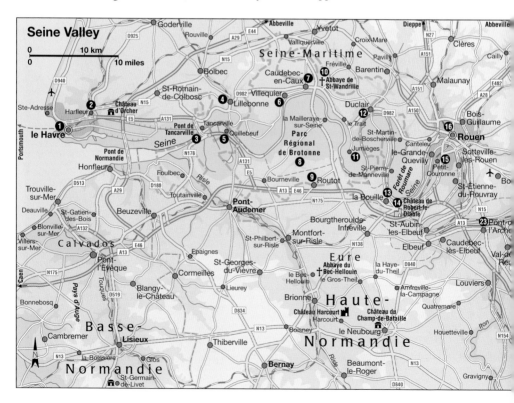

Map
on page
174

mandy, forcing long detours through the first bridging point at Rouen, or acceptance of the uncertainties of the numerous ferries. Now the even more ambitious **Pont de Normandie**, linking Le Havre with Honfleur, has altered the pattern of life in the estuary once again.

Local legends

It would be a great pity if our quest for improved communications was allowed to interfere with a legend. Where the Tancarville bridge joins the other side of the gorge is the cliff called Pierre du Géant. This is where the giant Gargantua used to sit on the rock while he washed his feet in the Seine below. Legends galore mingle with fact in the history of the **Château de Tancarville** (free access to exterior; guided tours of the interior by appointment; tel: 02 35 96 00 21).

The château's spectacular situation on the cliff, once even more formidable when the Seine flowed at its foot, was chosen by Tancred, a 10th-century Norman *sei-*

gneur, for his stronghold. Not till the early 1300s, when the last Tancarville fell in battle, did it leave the family, one member of which was William the Conqueror's tutor. Subsequent owners extended the castle, but later wars and the Revolution reduced it to today's still impressive ruins. Round, restored, and oddly triangular inside, the Tour de l'Aigle once stored the archives. It introduces the cliff terrace and the broken walls and towers cradling the modern château, begun in 1710.

The Tour Carrée has the longest history, surviving intact until the Revolution, but it is overshadowed by the great Tour Conquesart, some 300 years its junior. Between them are the remains of the chapel and banqueting hall. The Tour du Griffon was reserved for important offenders against authority, though making the walls nearly 3 metres (10 ft) thick seems like overkill.

The devil appears to have reserved the Tour de Lion for himself, since it is always referred to as the Tour du Diable.

RIGHT: the Tancarville bridge.

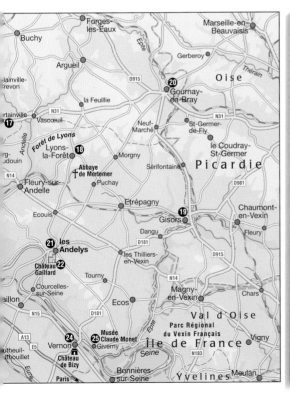

However, the awful hole he inhabited is empty. The local priest, alerted by the people, evicted him with a dash of holy water and a few well-chosen words. Exit the devil, grimacing horribly.

What of the occasion when three kings prevented a duel between Robert de Tancarville and the Sire de Harcourt over a mill at Lillebonne? Thinking, for reasons unknown, that they could not afford to lose either man, the kings of France, England and Navarre stopped the fight. Less testing times prevail in Tancred's castle. Customers of the terrace restaurant named after the giant's rock can leave their swords at home.

Roman roots

As the road from Tancarville turns inland across the flat plain of the Marais (marshlands) that separates **Lillebonne** ❹ from the Seine, it is difficult to believe it was once a port. Yet, covered by the river silt are the traces of dock installations to prove it. The Gauls knew a good site when they saw one. Here, at the junction of the River Bolbec with the Seine, the Calètes tribe from Belgium established their capital. Julius Caesar must have had the same idea. Following his conquest of Gaul in 51 BC he selected Lillebonne as an administrative centre, guarding the Seine Valley and the highway to the coast. So Juliobona was born and named in honour of Caesar's daughter, Julia. Lillebonne is its modern survival. Evidence that this new town became a settled community is there, plumb in the middle of the main street, the **Roman amphiheatre** (tel: 02 35 38 53 72 for opening hours; free).

A small amphitheatre of the 1st century was transformed in the next into a stone-built theatre for a population of around 25,000 people. The 10,000 spectators, Gauls and Romans, sat on the stone terraces, now mostly grass-covered, reaching their seats and leaving after the performance through seven exits to the vaulted passages at the top. The Romans had an expressive word for them – *vomitorii*. The

BELOW: the Roman theatre at Lillebonne.

Map on page 174

site of the proscenium lies under the feet and the wheels of people in the place Félix Fauré; precisely what was performed on the stage, nobody knows.

The Roman city under Lillebonne's modern shopping streets sleeps on, waiting for foundations to be dug or sewers laid to be brought unexpectedly back to life. A café proprietor uncovered a mosaic of hunting scenes in his back garden, the site of a temple to Diana and Apollo. To Lillebonne's loss it is now in the Musée d'Antiquités in Rouen. However, there are many other archaeological treasures to be seen in the municipal museum, including a Gallo-Roman tomb. Only one wall remains of the great hall in the hilltop fortress opposite. This is where Duke William called a meeting of his supporters to discuss invading England.

Golden valley

The circular tower built by the Harcourts in the 13th century seems to have had a charmed life. Henri V captured it, but left it unscathed; it was also spared by the nouveau riche cotton-spinner who acquired the castle in the 19th century and built himself a château among the ruins. The valley between Lillebonne and Bolbec was humming with the mills of spinners and weavers, and it was known as the **Vallée d'Or**, the Golden Valley. After World War II they had all disappeared.

Quillebeauf

If Lillebonne lost a port to the silted river, it gained one in **Port-Jérôme**, though Napoleon III would have been surprised to learn that his uncle Jérôme had given his name to petro-chemical installations. Certainly he would have been proud of the obvious prosperity they have brought to Lillebonne.

Car ferries cross to the Viking port of **Quillebeuf ❺**, which seems abandoned to its long quays on the opposite shore. Modern bustle passed by this wide stretch of river on the other side. It was rescued from the ravages of war by Henri IV in

BELOW: the intricate detail of Caudebec's Notre-Dame.

gratitude for being the first Norman town to recognise his sovereignty, though renaming it Henricopolis can't have been too acceptable. The fortifications have gone, but the fine Romanesque church and old houses with carved timbers, including Henri's, recall former glories.

Drowning tragedy

Eastward from Lillebonne the roads divide and part company with the river, the more inviting D81 hugging the high ground for 15 km (10 miles) till the forest sweeps down to take the little town of **Villequier** ❻ in its green embrace. Where the Seine curves gently into a bay the beauty of the place is almost an invitation to tragedy, and it is indelibly associated with a tragic event. The well-to-do local family of Vacquerie, with a flourishing boat-building business, were overjoyed when their son Charles married Victor Hugo's daughter Léopoldine in 1843. Six months later they were both dead, drowned while boating on the river.

In *À Villequier* from Victor Hugo's collection of poems, *Les Contemplations*, he expressed his grief. In the church, his beloved "Didine" and her husband lie together along with the writer's wife Adèle, and the whole tragic affair is laid out in the **Musée Victor Hugo** (open Wed–Sat, Mon 10am–12.30pm, 2–6pm, Sun 2–6pm; admission charge), in the Vacquerie house. The family might almost still be there so sensitively is the atmosphere of the period evoked by the original furniture, paintings, books, letters and photographs. Outside, flower gardens slope down to the river, and ships change pilots for the journey upstream.

Caudebec

Caudebec ❼, 1.6 km (1 mile) further on, is a shadow of its former self, but enough of its old buildings remain for the imagination to flesh out the bones of the skeleton and see it again as a town built of wood, the tall jettied houses huddled together like nowhere else in France.

BELOW: the ancient La Haye de Routot yew tree.

Map
on page
174

Caudebec's fate had always been tied to the nearby abbey of St-Wandrille, and the transfer of the market from there in 1130 began its slow growth to become the chief port and market town of the Caux region. When the town's plea for independence from the abbey was refused, several monks were murdered. Justice seems to have been satisfied, however, with the gruesome hanging of two of the ringleaders.

For 30 years the English occupied Caudebec. Two years after their departure the kings of France and Sicily dropped in with assorted nobles and an army of thousands, which must have stretched the town's hospitality a little. Henri IV came in 1592 and charmed everybody by calling the church the "most beautiful chapel in the kingdom", and then dashed their pride by adding "but the jewel is badly mounted".

The town's fortunes began to slide when the Edict of Nantes was revoked in 1685, sending half the population into exile, taking their weaving skills with them, but the final straw came with the Revolution; Yvetot was made capital of Caux in its place.

The beauty of Notre-Dame

With nothing left to do but die, the town fell back on its natural virtues – a wonderful situation in the green hills against the ever-changing backdrop of the river, the Saturday market, the enduring attraction of the church of **Notre-Dame** (open 9am–noon, 2–7pm) and the surviving cluster of old Norman houses.

Emerging unscathed from the fires of the last war, the church faces its most serious threat from water, as the corrosive elements blur the intricate detail of the carved limestone. Nothing, however, can obscure the beauty of that tower, the triple-crowned spire, the triple porch and the rose window above.

Guillaume Letellier, the 15th-century master mason who conceived it all, lies buried in the Lady Chapel. Pointing down

BELOW:
leisure time
on the river.

from the arched ceiling a stone of immense weight provides ample evidence of his skill.

Happily, much of the flavour of Caudebec's past is proudly displayed in its oldest house, the stone-built, 13th-century **Maison des Templiers**. The Biochet-Bréchot collection it contains links the primitive artefacts of pre-history with the achievements in art and culture in more recent times. The little River Gertrude, on whose banks the old house was built, was once almost arched over by the upper storeys of wooden houses.

Wildlife haven

The **Parc Régional de Brotonne** ❽ was once a ferry trip away from Caudebec, but the new toll-bridge, the Pont de Brotonne, has brought the hidden pleasures of this great beech forest within easy reach. The French take their forests seriously, with the aim of protecting and enhancing them as wildlife habitats, while at the same time allowing complete freedom of access and encouraging appreciation of the many associated crafts and activities that sustain rural life. Aberdeen Angus and Camargue cattle have been introduced and bird hides set up for the public.

For information about the park, contact the visitors' centre: Maison du Parc Naturel Régional des Bouche de la Seine Normande, tel: 02 32 70 46 32.

The flat valley has a most distinctive character, which can be seen in the architecture on the **Route de Chaumières**, the Cottage Route, which skirts the park to the north. Scattered round the fringes of the wooded area are a clog-maker's workshop, an old bakery, a flax and linen centre and a gaily decorated windmill, all close to **Routot** ❾.

At **La Haye de Routot** the ancient yew trees in the churchyard, said to be 2,000 years old, are so enormous that shrines have been carved out of their trunks. There is an apple centre here as well as an operational blacksmith's forge at **Ste-Opportune-la-Mare**.

BELOW: Abbaye St-Georges at St-Martin-de-Boscherville.

Map
on page
174

St-Wandrille

A short walk upstream from Caudebec is the **Abbaye de St-Wandrille** ❿ (church open daily; free; guided tours Tues–Sat 3.30pm, Sun and festivals 11.30am; admission charge; Gregorian Mass/Vespers: Mon–Sat 9.45, 5.30pm, Sun/festivals 10am, 5pm). It is situated in the village of the same name in a lovely valley running down to the Seine. Theft and pillage, fire and massacre dogged this place from the moment Wandrille, deserting his bride on their wedding night to devote himself to the service of God, set his monastery here in AD 648. He reckoned without the Norsemen, who burned the abbey in the 8th century, and came back to do the same two years after it was rebuilt.

The monks fled, not to return till 960. A new abbey, consecrated in 1033, was burned down, then rebuilt; then the spire collapsed and demolished most of the building. The monks conceded defeat: in the Revolution the ruins were sold by the State, and a spinning mill was established.

Monks' return

An English nobleman, the Marquis of Stackpole, rescued the abbey, and on his death in 1894 the monks bought it back, only to be evicted seven years later. Maurice Maeterlinck, the Belgian dramatist, was the next owner, until the Benedictines returned to stay in 1931, converting a 15th-century barn they brought from the Eure as the monastery church.

The only voices that are raised today at St-Wandrille are in the Gregorian chant – a beautiful experience if you are able to time your visit to coincide with a Mass.

On the wooded hill behind the abbey is the little chapel of **St-Saturnin**, mute witness for over 1,000 years to its neighbour's vicissitudes.

Jumiège

Jumièges ⓫ lies 16 km (10 miles) above the shipyards of Le Trait, where the river doubles back on itself. Above the trees rise the ruined towers of one of France's erstwhile most influential monastic insti-

BELOW:
a wedding
picture at
Jumiège.

tutions – the **Abbaye Notre-Dame de Jumiège** (open mid-Apr–mid-Sept, daily 9.30am–7pm, winter, daily 9.30am–1pm, 2.30–5.30pm; admission charge), served by 900 monks and 1,500 lay brethren.

St Philibert seems to have left the royal court at the same time as St Wandrille to found his abbey here in 654. Like St-Wandrille's abbey it was destroyed by the Norsemen two centuries later and the monks were all massacred. The consecration of the new abbey church of Notre-Dame in 1067 was witnessed by William the Conqueror on his triumphant return from England.

The 14th century saw extensive additions in the choir and chapels, and successive abbots added new building and increased the abbey's material wealth. The dispersal of the monks at the Revolution heralded change and decay, unfortunately connived at by the parishioners of Jumièges who refused to swop church for abbey. Soon it was being looted for building material, even dynamited by an impa-tient timber merchant, until rescue came in the shape of the Lepel-Cointet family.

Recreated glory

Sympathetic reconstruction and stabilisa-tion of threatened structures ensure that the pleasure of ruins at Jumièges will be with us for a long time to come. Below the great ivory towers the remaining walls trace out the vast dimensions of the orig-inal building, and exercise the imagina-tion to re-create its former glory. A doorway in the south wall leads through a passage to the **Église St-Pierre**, the abbey's modest predecessor.

The former abbot's lodge is now the museum, filled, not surprisingly, with fragments salvaged from the abbey, tombs, gargoyles and statues, but nothing more moving than the black marble slab that covered the heart of Agnès Sorel, Charles VII's mistress. On her death in 1449 it was presented to the abbey.

St-Valentine's, the parish church which roused such local pride, has an unfinished

BELOW: inside the Château-Musée at Martainville.

Map
on page
174

air, though it was started in the 11th century, and suffered over-sized additions in the 16th century.

Sailing scenes

Back to river business, and **Duclair** ⑫ on the D982 towards Rouen. From the stalls of the quay or the gallery of the **promenade du Catel** on the cliffs above, the Seine offers an ever-changing picture show. From the stars of the big, Rouen-bound cargo vessels to the sail-on parts played by the weekender, it is a continuous performance framed prettily in the lime trees of Liberation Quay. The name recalls the wartime devastation Duclair suffered, invisibly mended since.

Serenely untroubled, the belfry of the church of **St-Denis** still springs from 12th-century arches and has some 16th-century stained glass.

From the clifftop cemetery, where tombstones stand amid the wild flowers that tolerate the chalk, the promenade du Catel looks over the sweeping curve of

the river downstream. The riverside drive below the cliff leads to the abbey that escaped the fate of most abbeys during the Revolution by being adopted as a rather over-endowed parish church.

Abbaye St-Georges

One of the most perfect examples of Romanesque architecture in France is the **Abbaye St-Georges** at **St-Martin-de-Boscherville** (open Jun–Sept 9am–7pm; Oct–Mar 2–5pm, Apr–May 9.30am–noon, 2–7pm; admission charge). Unchanged and undamaged, with only its west turrets added since it was completed in 1125, it replaced a church founded in 1050 by Robert de Tancarville, William the Conqueror's chamberlain.

The abbey church has an impressive nave of eight arcades, a beautiful apse, delicately carved capitals, and in the Chapter House a unique room, the Salle Capitulaire, the architecture of which is a reminder that the Normans once had a kingdom in Sicily.

BELOW:
dappled shade
in the Forêt
de Lyons.

Painters and picnics

The river takes another plunge southward here round the Roumare forest. The only escape is via the ferry to the left bank at **La Bouille** , where the inhabitants of Rouen love to picnic and Monet loved to paint. On a hill overlooking the river is the **Château de Robert-le-Diable** ⑭, more intriguing for its name than the remnant of a fortress that looks real only at a distance. Robert the Devil enjoys in legend a Jekyll-and-Hyde personality, since he is more probably Robert the Magnificent, Duke of Normandy and father of the Conqueror. He was a highly estimable character who would never, as legend claims, have poisoned his way to dukedom, let alone haunt the place as a wolf.

Corneille's country retreat

Views of the Seine apart – and those from the **Qui Vive Monument** and the **Roches d'Orival** are splendid – the less elevated road between the Forêt de Rouvray and the river leads 8 km (5 miles) through

paper mills and oil refineries to "the house in the fields", the country retreat at **Petit-Couronne** ⑮ (open Apr–Sep, Wed–Mon 10am–noon, 2–6pm, or by appointment; admission charge) that Corneille inherited from his father in 1639.

In the timber-framed, 16th-century cottage the atmosphere and character of the family's occupation for nearly a century have been wonderfully re-created. Standing by his original writing desk it seems more than possible that the author of *Le Cid* could come through the door from his garden bakehouse, hands white with flour.

Canteleu, on the opposite, right-hand bank upstream, is poised above Rouen's port area, its chimneys mirroring the spires of the city. At its feet is **Croisset** and the surviving wing of the **Maison Flaubert** (open Thur–Mon 10am–noon, 2–6pm, Wed 2–6pm; admission charge). *Madame Bovary* first scandalised society here in 1857.

Away from the water

Above Croisset, stands the great port of **Rouen** ⑯ *(see page 149)*. Negotiate the city to make a detour away from the river, going east on the N31 to **Martainville** ⑰ where an early 16th-century château contains one of the best folk museums in Upper Normandy, the **Château-Musée Départemental des Traditions et Arts Normands** (open Apr–Sept, Mon, Wed–Sat, Mon 10am–12.30pm, 2–6pm, Sun 2–6pm; Oct–Mar, until 5pm; admission charge). The exhibits, from furniture to garden implements and costumes, are displayed according to region.

Château de Vascoeuil

Beyond it is the **Château de Vascoeuil** (open Jul–Aug, daily 11am–7pm; mid-Apr–Jun and Sept–mid-Oct 2.30–6.30pm; admission charge) where a delightful waterfall, literally a water staircase, tumbles through the grounds. You can almost tell from the proud bearing of the restored 12th-century building that it has won a "Masterpieces in Peril" award. One end is modestly half-timbered but the building progresses storey on storey in golden

LEFT: grassy ruins of the Abbaye de Mortemer

Map on page 174

coloured stone to the soaring heights of the rocket-like look-out tower.

In the garden below, the baronial dovecote has found a new purpose in life as a gallery, but its chief attraction is permanent: a massive wooden ladder that revolves on a central pivot to give easy access to the nesting places. The château itself, as a lively regional arts and history centre, hosts exhibitions of painting and sculpture, some of which spills over into the garden. There is a room in the tower devoted to Michelet, the French historian who wrote many of his books in his study there. When you consider that his *Histoire de France* alone ran to 24 volumes, you can understand how the place could have become a little neglected.

Fôret de Lyons

The château is on the north edge of the **Forêt de Lyons**, a former hunting ground of the dukes of Normandy, and a regular place for dropping supplies for resistance workers in World War II. Like many of France's forests, this one was badly damaged in the storms of late 1999, but it is regenerating. The forest is accessible all year round, the **arboretum** from May to October, 9am–7pm; tel: 02 32 49 61 07.

Musician's retreat

At the very heart of the 10,700-hectare (26,430-acre) forest is the popular, tranquil town of **Lyons-la-Forêt** ⑱. Off the main road, amid massive beech trees, it was chosen as a retreat by the composer Maurice Ravel, and in his half-timbered house in rue de la République he wrote *Le Tombeau de Couperin* in 1917.

Eight kilometres (5 miles) away in a glade in the woods are the remains of the splendid **Abbaye de Mortemer**, the first Cistercian monastery in Normandy. It was destroyed in the French Revolution, though its 17th-century convent building remains, and there is a museum of monastic life. The 15th-century dovecote in the grounds was rebuilt in the 17th century and used as a prison.

BELOW: the view from Gisors' castle.

Fortified border towns

On the southern side of the forest lies **Gisors** , one of a number of fortified towns along the border, following the valley of the Epte. It was designed by the early Norman dukes to keep out the French.

Dominating the town is its **château**, begun in 1097 by William Rufus and expanded by Philippe-Auguste, who occupied it in 1193 when its owner, Richard Lionheart, was held captive in Germany. During the 15th and 16th centuries prisoners here elaborately decorated the walls of the **Tour de Prisonnier** (open Feb–Nov, Wed–Mon 10am–noon, 2–5pm; admission charge). The **Église Sts-Gervais-et-Protais** dates from the time of Rufus, but is mainly 13th to 16th century.

Rural invention

The D915 border road continues to the north, past **St-Germer-de-Fly**, which is in fact just the wrong side of the border in the *département* of Oise, but the abbey church which dominates the small town is the grandest in what can still be called the Bray region. Entrance to the church is through the town hall in the 14th-century fortified gate.

Heading up the D915 a short way you come to **Gournay-en-Bray** ⑳, the next border town. Here lived one of those inventive Norman farmers' wives who mixed fresh cream with curds to produce Petit-Suisse. The capitals of the **Église St-Hildevert** have some wonderful, primitive figurative carvings.

Back to the river

The best way to get back to the river is to return to Gisors and take the D181; where it crosses the N14, follow signs to the attractive, half-timbered twin towns of **Les Andelys** ㉑ that hug the river under chalk cliffs that look like broken teeth.

In 1593 the court painter Nicolas Poussin was born near Les Andelys and the **Musée Nicolas Poussin** (open Wed–Mon 2–6pm; admission charge),

BELOW: the château that Richard the Lionheart built.

Map
on page
174

with 19th-century paintings and displays on local history, is in rue St-Clotilde.

The Lionheart's castle

The cliffs here are echoed in the ravaged, ivory castle of **Château Gaillard** ㉒ (open mid-Mar–mid-Nov, Thur–Mon 10am–noon, 2–6pm, Wed 2–6pm; admission charge). There was a trade-off involved in its history: Richard the Lionheart got the site in exchange for releasing Dieppe to Philippe-Auguste, but it was a deal that went wrong.

Legend says Richard promptly built his massive fortress in just a year. In reality, however, it took three years. Philippe besieged and eventually took the castle, but the state it is in now is due to Henri IV, who allowed two religious houses to take away stone for building. In the haggling that followed the château lost out.

BELOW: the lily pond that Monet created and painted.

Beautifully sited, it remained good material for artists such as the celebrated English painter J.M.W. Turner, who came here in the 19th century.

Pont-de-l'Arche

The château is perched on a rocky outcrop above the Seine. From here, you could follow the D313 a short distance to where it meets the N15, then head north, in the direction of Rouen, to visit **Pont-de-l'Arche** ㉓, just below the junction of the River Eure with the Seine. It was given its first bridge by Charles the Bold to deter Vikings from sailing upstream. Its effectiveness can be judged in the stained-glass window in **Notre-Dame des Arts**, which shows a boat being hauled with difficulty through an arch of the bridge.

Vernon

From here, you can either go back down the N15, or take the E5 Autoroute de Normandie, to **Vernon** ㉔. Of its wilder days as Henri I's frontier stronghold, only a few walls and the **Tour des Archives** remain. A number of old, timber-framed houses invite a pleasant exploration of the town. The **Musée Municipal Poulain** (open Tues–Sun 10am–noon, 2–6pm), has

some good Impressionist works, and the Collegiate Church of **Notre-Dame**, which is locally known as the cathedral, is well worth a visit.

To the west of the town, along an avenue of clipped lime trees, is the classical **Château de Bizy** (open Apr–Oct, Tues–Sun 10am–noon, 2–6pm; Nov, Feb–Mar, Sat–Sun 2–5pm; admission charge) still in the hands of a family connected to Napoleon Bonaparte as well as to his marshals Suchet and Massena. It has some fine tapestries and pieces of furniture. The formal garden, which has an impressive collection of cars in its stables, was laid out by Louis-Philippe, and modelled on Versailles.

Monet's home

On the east side of Vernon, a handsome stone bridge links the town with Vernonnet on the right bank. A right turn here leads shortly to the village of **Giverny**, close to which lies the world's most famous lily-pond, the model for some of the best-known Impressionist painting. The house that is now the **Musée Claude Monet** ㉕ (open Apr–Oct, Tues–Sun 10am–6pm; admission charge) was home to Claude Monet from 1883 until his death in 1926. Today, it is one of the most visited sites in Normandy.

In spite of the crowds disgorging from coaches, it is a wholly delightful place, beautifully renovated. The bright and colourful interior of the house is set off by Monet's collection of Japanese prints and ceramics. His large studio, hung with huge copies of his works, is now a souvenir shop, where staff deal efficiently with long queues of customers and comfortable sofas provide a place to rest.

There are two separate gardens: the Clos Normand in front of the house is a cottage-style garden, a riot of seasonally changing Monet-type colours that manages to look pleasantly wild while being carefully tended; and the famous water garden, reached through a tunnel under the road. You can become part of the picture here, crossing the Japanese bridge and looking down on the cluster of lily-pads in the pond.

American influence

The modern **Musée Américain** (open Apr–Oct, Tues–Sun 10am–6pm; admission charge) in the lane behind Monet's house, demonstrates the influence that Monet and French Impressionism had on American painting. It was founded by Daniel J. Terra, a former US Ambassador at Large for Cultural Affairs, and was opened in 1992. Among the interesting works of art here are paintings by Mary Cassatt, (1844–1926) and Winslow Homer (1836–1910).

A little further up this lane, where every garden looks as if it is proudly aware of being on show, is the Hôtel Baudy, where Monet's American disciples used to stay. In the garden behind (accessible if you stop off for a drink or lunch) their small studio is retained in its original state.

Five minutes' walk brings you to the little church on a hill where piped music plays softly, and the Monet family grave receives bouquets of wild flowers. ❑

Map on page 174

LEFT: Monet's house at Giverny. **RIGHT:** a quiet afternoon in Vernon.

Map
on page
195

DIEPPE

*Although ferry travel to Dieppe diminished with the opening of the
Channel Tunnel, it is still a lively place, attracting visitors as it has ever
since the daring craze for sea bathing first became fashionable*

Dieppe means "deep". That was the Vikings word for it, and as Dieppe it has stayed. Carved from the estuary of the River Arques, the safe harbour that gave protection to the longships has been enlarged and extended to today's great port system to satisfy the demands of the fishing fleet, worldwide seaborne trade and the cross-Channel ferries.

Growing importance

The town's importance grew following the Norman conquest of England, which effectively made both sides of the Channel one country, but exposed it to the depredations of both sides. Captured by Richard the Lionheart in 1188, sacked by Philippe-Auguste in 1195, its prosperity ruined during 15 years of English occupation in the 15th century and recovered in the next, Dieppe's fortunes rose on the performance of its navigators, who discovered Guinea, Cape Verde, Brazil and the bay of New York.

Trade with the new-found land brought lucrative cargoes of spices and ivory through the port. One of the merchant princes, Jean Ango, became a key figure in Dieppe's history and powerful enough to conduct wars on his own account. It was left to the combined fleets of England and Holland to destroy virtually all the town's timber-framed buildings in bombardment from the sea in 1694, but the rebuilding gave the town its distinctive and elegant arcaded brick terraces.

Tourism starts here

At the beginning of the 19th century, the popularity of sea-bathing under the patronage of the Duchesse de Berry *(see page 48)*, and the birth of tourism through passenger traffic from England, gradually introduced the resort as we know it. Dieppe was later to play a crucial part in World War II, and is still adjusting to the changes brought about by the Channel Tunnel, which drastically reduced the ferry business.

This route starts at the castle on the hill, giving you a grand overview of the town and the beach. However, if you arrive by sea, as a foot passenger, the bus from the ferry terminal will drop you close to the tourist office on the Pont Ango, opposite the quai Duquesne *(see page 199)* so you may wish to visit the quayside sites first before making your way up to the castle.

Château on the hill

In the streets of the old town or on the *plage* one constantly feels the benevolent surveillance of the **Vieux Château et Musée du Château**  (open Jun–Sept,

PRECEDING
PAGES: a ferry
arriving in
Dieppe harbour.
LEFT: the Café
des Tribunaux
in the place du
Puits-Salé.
RIGHT: the
Porte des
Tourelles.

daily 10am–noon, 2–6pm; Oct–May Wed–Mon 10am–noon, 2–5pm; admission charge) which stands on the western cliff. Four pepperpot towers (now only three) and flanking walls were raised against the English in the 15th century. A prison in the Revolution, a barracks until 1906, it escaped demolition to become a museum in 1923.

The château is a movable feast of the arts, mounting fine exhibitions in a new gallery against the background of the Musée de Dieppe's main collection. Its strength is in ivory. The raw ivory came into the port from the 17th century on, and was fashioned by sailors into keepsakes. In the hands of artists it was made into objects of great delicacy. Your very presence in the same room as the model ship, *La Ville de Dieppe,* makes the shrouds tremble and sails strain against spars.

An inspiration to artists

The paintings by Pissarro, Sisley, Renoir, Courbet and Sickert interpreting, with love, the magnetic attraction of the town, will make you catch your breath. The mystery is why Pierre Graillon's fame for his work in wood and terracotta is only local. Georges Braque – another local resident, who came to live and die in nearby Varengeville – is represented by a remarkable series of prints.

Leaving the château by the bridge over the moat, you can share the view with Delacroix, though he was hardly bowled over by it. He wrote in his *Journal* on 30 August 1854: "A heavenly morning; I went out alone and climbed the hill behind the castle. I sat down in a field where corn had been reaped, and made a sketch of the castle and the view – not that it was particularly interesting, but so as to retain the memory of this exquisite moment."

St-Rémy

The great **Église St-Rémy B** (opening hours vary; tel: 02 35 84 21 65) is the third of that name, and a refugee from the confines of the château, where the surviving

BELOW: the view from the old castle.

Map
on page
195

tower threatens players on the tennis courts below with falling stones. Work on the church began in 1522, the choir and side chapels being completed by 1545, then, the Wars of Religion intervening, work was not resumed until 50 years later.

Progress in the 17th century was slow. The Anglo-Dutch bombardment of 1694 and the vandalism of the revolutionaries in 1789 were further setbacks. Not until the 19th century was this Gothic building completed, because Gothic it had started and Gothic it had to finish. Only the façade on the little square and the side doors acknowledge the change in style to the Renaissance. The second of the two towers was never built.

Inside, the panelling in the choir, the beautiful Renaissance decoration of the sacristy and the rococo organ defy the passage of years, but outside it is another story. Wind and weather have smudged the detail, and masons strive to make crockets curl just as they did some 400 years ago.

RIGHT:
eagle lectern
in St-Jacques
church.

Porte des Tourelles

From the church head down rue des Bains where, keeping close company with the Casino, you'll find the **Porte des Tourelles** fortifications, the only survivors of the walls and gates that once surrounded the town. Properly known as the **Porte du Port Ouest**, they have outlived five casinos and two generations of hotels, served as a prison during the Revolution, and suffered the indifference of an ungrateful state that sold them to a private buyer in 1850.

The old gate gives on to the quiet backwater of the place Camille-St-Saëns, where a large car park is a reminder that this area was once filled with carriages of the rich and favoured on their way to the theatre. The theatre is still there, buried in the grey, anonymous building behind the Tourelles. Beneath a painted ceiling, barebreasted nymphs stretch their arms invitingly from the boxes in gilded abandon, trailing the fruits and flowers of a long-forgotten Elysium.

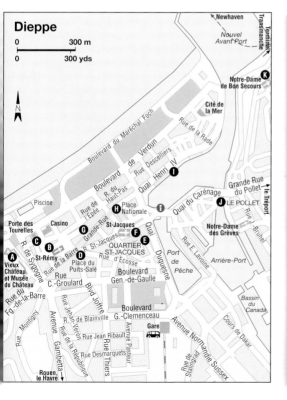

Dieppe map

The Casino

Close to the old town gateway stands Dieppe's **Casino**, which has a long history. "Les Bains Caroline" was the first casino here, named after the Duchesse de Berry, who came here from 1824 to 1830 to "take the waters", demonstrating that the new habit of sea-bathing must be good for you, because it was patronised by the aristocracy. Hot-water baths followed, gardens were laid out, concerts were given. The *plage* had arrived.

Attention turned to the rest of the seafront; Empress Eugénie even sketched a plan for the lawns. By 1857 the elegant Regency building of the first casino had given place to a new glass-and-iron casino that had obvious affinities with London's Crystal Palace.

Thirty years later, the dilapidated building was replaced with yet another casino in the then popular Moorish style, its domes and minarets complementing the twin chimneys of the tobacco factory further along the *plage*. In the gardens and on the terrace, Dieppe's English colony met to exchange views on art, music and literature with the French, or listened to the 60-strong casino orchestra, unaware that the ballrooms would later become bedrooms for wounded soldiers.

War and recovery

After World War I the fourth casino was built in a less flamboyant style. The era of nightclubs, jazz bands and cocktails had arrived. "Operation Jubilee" of World War II put an end to all that (*see page 56*). The *plage* was the focal point of the 1942 reconnaissance, and the prime objective on "White Beach" was the casino. After the attack had been repulsed the ruined building was levelled by the Germans.

Alongside the present building there is a thalassotherapy centre, a huge public swimming pool, tennis courts, a mini-golf range, a large car park and a tourist information centre.

The casino and these other, more 21st-century, attractions stand near the end of

BELOW:
a working
fishing trawler.

Map on page 195

the boulevard de Verdun. Parallel to this, beyond broad, green swathes of lawn, the boulevard du Maréchal Foch runs beside the great sweep of beach – Dieppe's famous *plage*.

Café des Tribunaux

Unless you are tempted by a day on the beach, you should retrace your steps past St-Rémy to the **place du Puits-Salé** (Square of the Salt Wells), a reminder that until the 16th century salt water at high tide often mixed with fresh water in the well. Here at the heart of Dieppe is the **Café des Tribunaux**, an impressive old inn of uncertain age, that has always been the social centre of the town. The clock gave it its former name in 1736 of the Cabaret de l'Horloge.

The café has often posed for artists, Sickert and Blanche among them, and at a table on the terrace the content of *The Savoy*, the influential English magazine of the 1890s was thrashed out between Aubrey Beardsley and his editor.

Quartier St-Jacques

Beside the Tribunaux, the vista is closed by the tower of St-Jacques in an area developed as a whole after 1694, the **Quartier St-Jacques** **E**. From the window of his room at the Hôtel du Commerce in the place Nationale, Camille Pissarro had an Impressionist's-eye view of the church. He painted eight variations on St-Jacques, including a scene in the rain, with a market in full swing below, and the swings and roundabouts of a visiting fair.

Pissarro wrote to his son, Lucien: "The fair is here just now. Wooden horses, music by Gounod and other classics on the steam organ. I can't sleep!"

New flats replacing run-down tenements edge into the place Louis Vitet, once a meat market. Framed by the arches of the old school is Dieppe's finest timber-framed building; built in 1621 as a residence, it survived the fires of 1694 to become a warehouse for the tobacco factory on the *plage*.

BELOW: seafood of every kind is for sale.

Most prominent in that view is the tower of the **Église St-Jacques**  (tel: 02 35 84 21 65 for opening times), Dieppe's only high-rise building, dominating the market-place and filling every street in the surrounding quarter with the riotous detail of its Gothic tracery. An earlier church on this site was burned down (a good old Normandy custom it would appear), and St-Jacques today survives as the rebuilding of 1282. However, the work was to be painfully extended in the 15th and 16th centuries and by serious restorations in the 19th century.

On Saturday morning a huge, lively market takes place in the streets around the church, selling fresh fish and local produce of all kinds.

King of the sea

Overhead, gargoyles grimace, buttresses fly, rose windows bloom and statues shelter in niches. Inside, 20 chapels march the length of the 13th-century nave, each one with its own dedication, altar, rights and privileges. Treasures abound: the carved relief on the oratory of Jean Ango with his coat of arms; Adam and Eve and a cat-headed snake; the sacristy built at his own expense by the "king of the sea", Jean Ango, its frieze peopled with natives of Brazil, and visual proof of the discovery of America by Dieppois; the superbly carved oak staircase inside; near the floor, graffiti of a 15th-century galleon cut with great accuracy by a Dieppe sailor on his knees. Presiding over all from below the rose window is the Louis XIV organ with the voice of 2,800 tubes and the mute support of two carved figures with trumpets.

Grande-Rue

The **Grande-Rue** , which begins in the place du Puits-Salé, is a street of contrasts. Couture shops sit happily beside *charcutiers*, bookshops, boutiques, antique shops and grocers. Chocolate sardines in a tin or a set of *boules*, they are all there in a street that would not be out of place in one of the smarter quarters of Paris.

BELOW: Église St-Jacques.

Map
on page
195

On Saturday, market day, it becomes part of a country market town overflowing with all the produce of the Normandy countryside. From elderly farm wives with a basket's contents of beans or spring onions to enormous vans with more varieties of cheese than you ever knew existed, the tide of this most animated, most colourful, most mouth-watering display flows on into rue de la Barre, rue St-Jacques and the **place Nationale H**.

Presiding over all is the spirited statue of Duquesne, Dieppe's honoured admiral, a specialist in bombardments. The title of admiral was posthumous. Louis XIV could not confer the title on him in his lifetime because he belonged to the reformed church. Even his ashes could not be returned from Switzerland until 1894.

Fresh fish

On the **quai Duquesne**, opposite the tourist office (where the ferry bus drops passengers and from where a mini tourist train begins its journey) Dieppe's fish-wives sprinkle water on the heaped mussels and glittering fish on the stalls they set up from 8am to noon every day except Sunday. In the **Café Suisse**, under the **Arcade de la Bourse** nearby, steaming bowls of *moules marinière* are served. Diners under the Arcades get double protection – from the elements and for the buildings. Built after the bombardment in 1696, they are listed ancient monuments.

Quai Henri IV

The **quai Henri IV I** runs from the head of the harbour, the Avant Port, alongside the marina, and holds several surprises, if the eye can be diverted from the menus of the restaurants along its length. No. 33 is a place to look out for: Wwhere there is now a school building, Jean Ango built himself a palace in the 16th century called "La Pensée" (Pansy), appropriately set in a fabulous garden. From his windows, nothing escaped him – his fleet at sea, his cargoes being unloaded in the port and the wagons on the road to

BELOW:
Dieppe's
busy quayside.

Arques. He magnificently entertained François I here, and Henri IV used it as a hotel. In 1694 it went up in flames.

No. 49 was the Hôtel d'Anvers, and on the reverse of the entrance archway is a relief sculpture of the city of Antwerp. When Delacroix first came to Dieppe he stayed at the Hôtel de Londres at Nos 5 and 7, wrestling with boredom most of the time. His friends bored him, people he disliked bored him, and he was bored with walking on the pier. There was a deeper cause of his unhappiness – the failed search for his lost youth. Twenty years after his celebrated *Liberty Guiding the People* he was within a year or two of his last showing at the Salon.

Cité de la Mer

Between quai Henri IV and the boulevard de Verdun is an attractive quarter of narrow streets and what were once fishermen's cottages. Here, in rue de l'Asile Thomas, is the **Cité de la Mer** (open daily 10am–6pm; admission charge), a scientific centre and a lively museum devoted to ship building, local geology and marine life, with two large aquariums and radio-controlled boats for kids.

Italian link

There is another Dieppe. Cross the bridge by the tourist office to **Le Pollet** ❶ to discover a different world. As "foreign" in speech and appearance as in manners, the Polletais are the lingering evidence of an Italian connection that began when ships called in here from Venice on the way to Flanders.

Above the houses the cliff rises honeycombed with caves that provided homes for fishermen's families and hovels for yesterday's drop-outs, and was once the platform for heroic endeavour.

From here, the fortified hill of La Bastille, the English in 1442 threatened the town. Nothing the French could do would dislodge them until the young Dauphin, the future Louis XI, flung himself on the walls in an attack his officers felt obliged to follow. The successful though costly exercise was to be echoed in the Normandy landings on the beaches below 500 years later.

Two more Notre-Dames

From the rue du Petit-Fort with its well-preserved brick and flint fishermen's cottages, steps climb to the Semaphore and the church of **Notre-Dame de Bon Secours** ❹ (open daily 10am–5pm), with magnificent views from the cliff, but it's a stiff walk on a warm day.

Down on the quay, **Notre-Dame des Grèves** (open daily 10am–6pm) suffers a façade nibbled to Swiss cheese by the greedy elements, but the Abbé Cochet's description of it as a *bâtard et hermaphrodite* seems a little strong. It overlooks a marine graveyard where the hulks of old ships are beached to die.

Up beyond Notre-Dame de Bon Secours is the new ferry terminal, the **Terminal Transmanche**, from where ships and the faster, thrice-daily Seacat cross the channel to Newhaven. Once here, you will find no refreshments or facilities, and it's a long hike back into town. ❏

LEFT: local café in Le Pollet. **RIGHT:** the château looms over the town.

Map on page 195

Map on page 214

RURAL ROUTES FROM DIEPPE

Running inland from Dieppe, country lanes follow gentle streams,
while sleepy villages and small towns conceal idiosyncratic
local museums and attractive gardens

Get on your bicycle in Dieppe and join Oscar Wilde for breakfast at the Clos Normand. "Do you remember," he wrote, "the pretty girl at the little café by the river at **Martin-Église** where we drove together with Robbie and More on bicycles behind us?"

Dieppe's favoured rural excursion is a short pedal up the road beside the River Arques, and the mellow red-brick building, once a farm, has tables set out in an apple orchard through which a trout stream runs. Water music is the perpetual accompaniment to a meal. Nearby a statue of the Virgin keeps sentry duty from her box on a bridge, and there is a strong local tradition that Joan of Arc crossed it on the way to her death in Rouen.

Arques-la-Bataille

Arques, or as it came to be known after the event, **Arques-la-Bataille ❶**, lies beside the D1 a few bungalows and a forest further on, with an obelisk on the hillside to remind us that here in 1589 the Protestant Henri IV with a handful of men fought and won a resounding victory over the overwhelming forces of the Catholic League. A bas-relief over an archway in the château pays a belated tribute, since it was put there only in 1845. It shows Henri, now worn nearly bodiless, on horse-back and approached by a figure offering the crown of France.

The **château** (free access) is reached up a steep road through a gap in the outer wall. Built by William the Conqueror's uncle, it became a pawn in the aspirations of assorted kings till the invention of gunpowder made its possession a liability rather than a military asset. Even in its romantic decay, broken walls crumbling into grassy earthworks and a fallen stair rendering the great keep unassailable, it remains a most impressive ruin and a vaguely threatening place.

Kissing fields

Mermaids, creatures with pointed ears and the recumbent figure of a "chevalier" with his feet above ground invite a visit to the church at **Envermeu ❷**. From here to the River Bresle and the Picardy border are the kissing fields, old apple orchards heavy with mistletoe, and only the shock-horror of **Foucarmont** between. Three bells in a hooped frame, sub-Corbusier columns, and a bunker pierced with holes signal the church – a 1959 firework display of coloured glass and concrete ugliness inside.

South of Dieppe the Scie Valley's apple orchards promise, and deliver from the presses at the **Cidrerie Duche de Longueville**, Normandy's answer to the

PRECEDING PAGES: a sleepy Sunday morning.
LEFT: time for a trim.
RIGHT: a young farmer starts work.

produce of the grape. Longueville lies 16 km (10 miles) south of Dieppe.

Château de Miromesnil

Between the two towns, on the N27, cornfields and beech avenues lead to the **Château de Miromesnil** ❸ (open for guided tours May–mid-Oct, Wed–Mon 2–6pm; admission charge; tel: 02 35 80 02 80). This delightful and inventive building was begun in 1589 and completed 40 years later.

Top left is the window of the room from which Guy de Maupassant first announced his existence, although something of a mystery surrounds his birth. It seems that his parents, determined to give their child the best start in life, chose the silver spoon of a good address by taking a short lease on the château.

Gustave Flaubert was present as godfather when he was baptised in the private chapel of St-Antoine in the grounds in 1850. Among the souvenirs of the writer who was to achieve international fame, is a cup lettered with the word "Amitié", the natural friendliness that inspired his interest in all classes and conditions of men.

Miromesnil has a delightful *potager*, a walled kitchen garden where vegetables and flowers grow harmoniously together, tended lovingly by the present incumbent of the château and his wife.

Social hub

Fields away, **Offranville** ❹ bears the imprint of a painter and writer who had a profound and benevolent influence on art and letters in the early part of the 20th century – Jacques-Émile Blanche. Among his visitors, during the 40 years he lived here (from 1902–42) were Jean Cocteau, André Gide, Walter Sickert and James Whistler.

Today, the **Musée Jacques-Émile Blanche** (open Easter–Sept, Sun and festivals 2.30–6pm; other times by appointment; tel: 02 35 85 40 42) in the Maison du Parc du Colombier is devoted to his life, his paintings and literary works.

BELOW: grey slates and bright poppies.

Map
on page
214

Offranville also has attractive gardens, the **Parc Floral William Farcy** (open May–Aug, Wed–Mon 10am–7pm; Apr and Sept, Sat–Sun 10am–7pm; admission charge). Here, 2.5 hectares (6 acres) of gardens have been well planted to ensure colour throughout the spring and summer.

Le Bourg-Dun

On the River Dun 13 km (8 miles) west, **Le Bourg-Dun ❺** has a magnificent 16th-century house, gable-ended to the road, in flint, brick, stone and wood, and a church, **Notre-Dame**, of extravagant proportions, part 11th and 12th centuries.

The little River Dun is accompanied to the east by the Saâne, joined at Gueures by the Vienne before reaching the sea at Quiberville. Fortunately, the rivers are closely followed by roads inland, and it is a rewarding experience to pursue a leisurely exploration of this little-known countryside. One of the delights of the small hamlets is the number of thatched cottages with irises growing on the roofs.

BELOW: irises on thatched roofs are a typical sight in this region.

Flainville ❻ is a case in point; it is just up the road towards the coastal resort of St-Aubin, but centuries further away in time. The road that serves it stops abruptly at a 16th-century calvary and becomes a cart track across fields of flax. The farmyard of the old manor with its still-surviving barns and sheds hides the most remarkable and, unfortunately, most neglected monument of Normandy's Middle Ages: the **Chapelle de Flainville** (it is often closed, but you may be lucky enough to find it open). Built in 1324 by the *seigneur* Estout de Gruchet, its walls and ceilings once exquisitely decorated, the chapel retains a beauty from which not even damp and decay can detract.

Caux capital

Return to Le Bourg-Dun and follow the D925 until it meets the D142, then head south. On the N29/N15, halfway between Rouen and Le Havre, is **Yvetot**. It is the capital of the Caux region and, because of extensive damage, is largely a post-war

re-creation. The church of **St-Pierre** has stained-glass windows that can be measured in square metres.

A natural break

A few kilometres west on the N15, where a road branches north for Fécamp and Le Havre, turn south onto the D33. Here you will find **Allouville-Bellefosse** , a place which, unlike Yvetot, had no history to lose, but it does have one very elderly inhabitant – a 1,200-year-old oak tree. It is 16 metres (52 ft) in circumference at the base, and in its hollow heart there are two chapels which were the inspiration of a parish priest in 1696. The old tree has recently had to undergo heart surgery.

Hidden down lanes nearby, in an ancient barn, is the **Musée de la Nature** (open daily 9am–noon, 2–6pm; admission charge), whose environmental objectives are difficult to resist. Local fauna and flora get supportive treatment here, and injured wild animals and oiled seabirds are rehabilitated in their natural environment.

Among temporary and permanent exhibits is one display room that concentrates on marine mammals.

Clères

To the east, and 16 km (10 miles) due north of Rouen, is **Clères** ❽, which has its feet in the waters of the Clérette, the river that runs the length of the main street under little bridges, past the market hall and the Auberge du Cheval Noir, which has tables beneath a canopy, looking for all the world as if captured on canvas by an Impressionist.

Across the road the **Musée d'Automobiles et Militaire** (open Easter–Sept, daily 10am–6pm; Oct–Mar, Wed–Sat 1–6pm, Sun 10am–7pm; admission charge), solicits interest outside with a 1942 vintage torpedo and inside with motorbikes, bicycles and old racing cars.

Next door the **Parc Zoologique** (open Easter–Sept, daily 9.30am–6.30pm, Mar, Oct, Nov, daily 9.30am–noon, 1.30–5pm; admission charge) offers sanctuary and

BELOW: water wheel in Pays de Bray.

Map
on page
214

freedom to 2,000 birds of more than 250 species and beasts like antelopes, deer, kangaroos and monkeys, all in the garden of a Renaissance château.

Royalty and Resistance

Forges-les-Eaux ❾ lies 34 km (20 miles) to the east of Clères (cut across country on the D6/D919). It was an iron-working centre in the Middle Ages, but the discovery of the spring waters' beneficial qualities in 1573 brought prosperity and royal patronage. Anne of Austria took the waters here, hoping that she would be able to provide her husband with an heir, but not until six years later was the future Louis XIV born.

Cardinal Richelieu joined their majesties here in the lovely wooded park below the spa building, now a casino. A grotto and the façades only of 17th- and 18th-century buildings contribute to the wistful appeal of this haunted place, which the **Musée de la Résistance** (open Apr–Sept, daily 2–6pm; admission

charge; tel: 02 35 90 64 07) in the grounds of the Hôtel de Ville serves to reinforce.

Neufchâtel-en-Bray

Our circuitous route ends in the heart of the Bray region, **Neufchâtel-en-Bray ❿**, renowned for its production of the heart-shaped Coeur de Neufchatel, the oldest type of cheese in Normandy.

In 1940 the town's heart was almost completely destroyed, but one building, a Norman manor house in the Grande Rue St-Pierre, survived to become the **Musée du Pay de Bray Mathon-Durand** (open by appointment; tel: 02 35 93 06 55; admission charge).

The tools of rural arts and crafts, such as cheese- and clog-making, pottery and earthenware, cooperage and saddlery, share elegant rooms, and in the garden there is an ancient market hall with apple presses and a well. In another garden, in the rebuilt Civic Centre, a massive female head with nostrils flaring flashes cartwheel eyes outside the Palais de Justice.   ❑

BELOW: the Forge-les-Eaux casino.

Map on page 214

THE ALABASTER COAST

*Travel this dramatic stretch of coast from the resort of Le Tréport
in the east to the town of Fécamp in the west, visiting
villages that inspired artists and architects*

In choosing a popular name for this fine stretch of the Normandy seaboard – 120 km (75 miles) from Le Tréport to Le Havre – the French, as usual, erred on the side of sophistication. Streaked with sand and crusted with soil these jagged, white chalk cliffs suddenly drop sheer from the platform of the Pays de Caux to the sea below, making the drive along the winding and picturesque roads a dramatic and exhilarating experience.

LeTréport

Le Tréport ⓫, 32 km (20 miles) east of Dieppe, is poised above its harbour at the mouth of the Bresle. It has a personality happily split between commercial shipping and fishing and the seaside resort sheltered snugly below the last and highest cliff this side of Picardy. The two worlds meet on the quays, which are always crowded, lively and colourful, but a few steps up the hill, reached through a gate by the old Hôtel de Ville, are the quiet streets of the old town.

The 16th-century **Église St-Jacques**, still smarting at never having had the spire it was promised, dominates the harbour. There are good views from the garden behind the church, and even better from Les Terrasses at the top of a punishing flight of steps up the west cliff.

Secure in the old prison is the **Musée des Enfants du Vieux Tréport** (open Easter–Sept, daily 10am–noon 2.30–6pm; admission charge), the "children" in question being objects associated with Le Tréport's cultural heritage.

Royal retreat

There are two places linked closely with the town: the little bathing resort of **Mers**, across the Bresle in Picardy, with its hotels and villas, was a Parisian's fantasy of a rural retreat by the sea in the late 19th-century.

The other is **Eu ⓬**, 4 km (2½ miles) upstream. Always connected with the royal families of Normandy and France, Eu possesses a faded glory. The château, now shared between the Hôtel de Ville and the **Château Musée Louis-Philippe** (open mid-Mar–Oct, Wed–Mon 10am–noon, 2–6pm; free), was begun in 1578, but the unfortunate red-brick building we see today is of indeterminate age, like the service lift between the floors. It was intended for Napoleon, but Louis-Philippe fell in love with it, and during his occupancy twice entertained Queen Victoria here.

The Chapelle du Collège was built in 1620 by Catherine of Cleves, widow of Henri Guise, nicknamed Scarface, who

PRECEDING PAGES: the white cliffs of Étretat.
LEFT: Le Tréport, seen from above.
RIGHT: Ferdinand, Duke of Orleans, sits on his horse in Eu.

was murdered on the orders of Henri III. In their marble mausoleums they lie on either side of the altar.

The medieval **Église Notre-Dame et St-Laurent** contains some fine 13th-century tombs. It is dedicated to Irish archbishop, Lawrence O'Toole, who came here in 1181 to make peace between the king of Ireland and Henri II.

Valley views

By-roads hug the cliff westwards through **Mesnil-Val** to **Criel-Plage** at the mouth of the Yères and **Criel-sur-Mer** in the green valley inland, where the 17th-century **Château Chantereine** stands on the banks of a trout stream. If you care to climb the 104 metres (340 ft) of Mont Jolibois on the cliff, the views from the belvedere of the Yères Valley and up the coast to the River Somme are glorious.

South and west the coast road sends out lanes to farms and villages scattered among the patterned fields. The difference with Penly is that its output is measured not in bushels or tonnes, but in MWes, 2,600 of them in fact. Penly Nuclear Power Station makes a dramatic interruption in the cliffscape, carving a deep scar of roads behind, and thrusting a platform of space-age buildings and industrial development into the sea in front.*

Wilde's hideaway

The breach in the cliff at **Berneval** ⑬ is a natural one and the beach itself perfect for bathing. The resort, at the top of the steps cut in the rocks known as the Giant's Staircase, is the sort of place in which a stranger could lose himself, especially if he had just left prison, as Oscar Wilde had when he booked into the Hôtel de la Plage under the assumed name of Sebastian Melmoth. The next year, 1897, he was celebrating Queen Victoria's Diamond Jubilee with a fête for the local children, presenting them with toy trumpets and accordions. The charm of the rustic idyll soon faded, and Wilde left for Naples and Alfred Douglas.

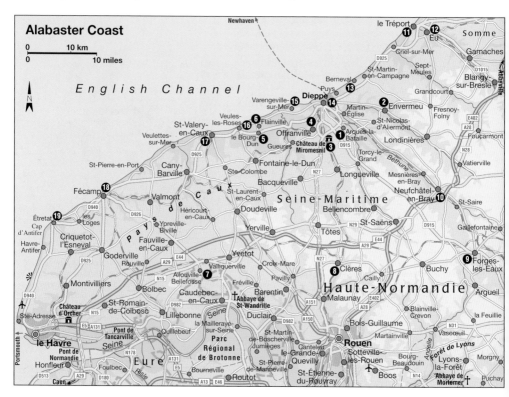

Map on page 214

Centuries of struggle

Wilde's personal tragedy is completely eclipsed by Berneval's part in the horror of 19 August 1942. The success of the Allied raid on Dieppe depended on silencing the huge coastal batteries *(see page 56)*. That of Berneval was assigned to Canada's No. 3 Commando, whose men were landed, scaled the cliff and engaged the battery. None got away.

Earlier struggles are recalled in **Caesar's Camp** in the fields by the sea, the hill-fortress of a tribe of Gauls captured by the Romans.

There is a sharp descent into **Puys** on the outskirts of Dieppe, the scene of another disastrous assault in 1942, ending in the massacre of the Royal Regiment of Canada. Alexander Dumas *fils* built a house here in 1870 in which his father died, and in Villa Cecil Lord Salisbury spent his holidays, until a zealous customs officer demanded duty on whisky he had sent from England. In a huff he sold his house and never returned.

Varengeville

West of **Dieppe** ⑭ *(see page 193)* the coast road,drops down hairpin bends to Pourville, crosses the Scie by a bridge bitterly fought over in World War II, and wanders through the delightful hamlet of **Varengeville-sur-Mer** ⑮. The Cubist painter Georges Braque (1882–1963) made his home here, and created a rural Chartres in the tiny barn-like chapel of **St-Dominique**, his big oriel window glowing golden with *galets*, stones from the beach.

Almost opposite, an avenue of trees leads to the **Manoir d'Ango** (open Apr–Oct, daily 10am–12.30pm, 2–6.30pm; admission charge), the Renaissance palace Jean Ango, Dieppe's merchant prince, built on the spoils his ships brought from India, Brazil and the New World.

In the courtyard is the finest *colombier* to be found in the region, providing Ango with fresh meat in the winter from 600 pairs of pigeons.

The sailors' church on the cliff top, from where there are tremendous views,

BELOW: the Manoir d'Ango in Varengeville-sur-Mer.

has been recorded in innumerable canvases by Monet. It has Braque's *Tree of Jesse* window, and in the cemetery a white bird spreads its wings over his grave.

Bois de Moutier

Of Varengeville's **Parc du Bois des Moutiers** (gardens open mid-Mar–mid-Nov daily, 10am–noon, 2–6pm; admission charge), the architect Sir Edwin Lutyens wrote: "It is so lovely here, so quiet and delicious". The house he built for banker Guillaume Mallet in 1898, one of the few he designed outside England, is a delight in itself, although usually only open to pre-arranged groups (tel: 02 35 85 10 02). It has the most beautiful situation at the head of a wooded valley with gardens running down to the sea and much of the planting was inspired by Gertrude Jekyll.

Walk through the pine forests that hide the elusive lighthouse of **Phare d'Ailly** and discover the twisted columns and high altar in the church of **Ste-Marguerite-sur-Mer**, dating from 1160.

Veules-les-Roses

The road then dips to watering places, climbs again and skirts the watercress beds at **Veules-les-Roses** ⓰. Here rises France's shortest river, reaching the *plage* just 1,194 metres (1,300 yds) away, providing a delightful footpath walk along its banks, over bridges, past thatched cottages, flower gardens and old watermills. Not surprisingly the path begins as the chemin des Champs Élysées. *

The church of **St-Martin** is a gallery of sculpture in wood and stone. Ships, mermaids, beasts and angels climb the columns to the wooden-vaulted roof. A beggar on a crutch asks for alms of a man on a horse flourishing a sword. The colouring and the carving is crude, but the effect is immediate. Victor Hugo loved Veules, often visiting the house of his friend Paul Meurice where an elaborate memorial stands by the *plage*. The ruins of another church, **St-Nicolas**, on the hill behind, were in Meurice's garden. Time seems to stand still at Veules.

BELOW: Bois de Moutier is an inspiration to artists.

Map on page 214

St-Valery-en-Caux

"How many sailors, how many captains, have blithely left for far-off journeys?" Victor Hugo wrote in appreciation of the brave men of **St-Valery-en-Caux** ⑰. The little port, hemmed in by the steep cliffs of the Caux, now owes more to *boules* and baccarat, sailing and sun-bathing than fishing. It mounts a programme of events every year in which almost everything from Henri IV to herrings has its festival. Henri stayed there, so they say, in a grand, timber-framed house on the west quay. The **Maison Henri IV**, built in 1540, preserved and restored, doubles as Tourist Information and exhibition centre.

Penitents' Cloister

Up a steep street behind the old house is the **Penitents' Cloister**, now a hospital, but founded in 1623 as a monastery. Before the Revolution the garden was lovingly tended by Friar Antoine. When the monastery was seized, the convent became the headquarters of a Jacobin club, later a barracks and military prison. Friar Antoine, however, refused to leave his garden, and finished his days there in 1816, aged 66. The last of the penitents is recorded simply as "Antoine Dubourg, gardener, formerly Friar Antoine".

On the western cliff is a memorial to the French Cavalry Division, which, together with the Scottish Highlanders, fought a desperate rearguard action in the port after France's collapse in 1940. The Scottish monument on the east cliff overlooks a town risen from the rubble.

Inland detour

Pleasant little seaside villages fill gaps in the cliffs between St-Valery and Fécamp, except for **Paluel** which has a nuclear power station that supplies 10 percent of France's needs.

To reach Fécamp, you can take the winding coast road, the D79, which runs through **Veulettes-sur-Mer**. Here, it might be difficult to resist an excursion through the lush water-meadows of the

BELOW: idyllic scene in Veules-les-Roses.

Durdent. Alternatively, you can strike inland a short distance towards **Cany-Barville**, where the château built by the uncle of the architect of Versailles managed to keep its furniture safe from the revolutionaries in the 1790s.

The artefacts of a rural tradition are looked after here by the **Ecomusée Moulin St-Martin**, which is set in a 15th-century mill (open Mar–Nov, daily 2–7pm; admission charge).

A left turn off the D925 just before it reaches Fécamp brings you to **Valmont**, which has a certain prestige, due to the 12th-century Benedictine abbey, its church now a haunting ruin; and to the gaunt, 15th-century château, built by the Estouteville family, where François I used to stay.

Fécamp

In **Fécamp** ⑱ they worship cod and the rich, amber liquid we call Benedictine. The latter is produced in a building you might be forgiven for confusing with the abbey, if the remnant of that great institution, the church of **La Trinité** (open daily till dusk), did not dominate the big fishing port. Legend determined its siting – in the centre of town – at the spot where, it is said, the trunk of a fig tree was washed ashore with a vessel containing blood from the wounds of Christ concealed inside it.

By 1220 a church of cathedral-like proportions with a central lantern-tower had been erected. It is a treasure-house of stained glass, carved screens, tombs, altar pieces, and a tabernacle containing relics of the Precious Blood. Each July and August the church hosts an important classical music festival which attracts international singers and players.

Benedictine Palace

In rue Alexandre Le Grand, a busy city street, the **Musée Centre des Arts** (open Wed–Mon 10am–noon, 2–6.30pm; admission charge), is housed in some splendour in a former private mansion. Apart from

BELOW: seafood is sold straight off the boats at St-Valéry-en-Caux.

Map on page 214

the Rouen ware and ivory on display, a typical interior of the Caux region has been reconstructed in the attics.

The **Palais Bénédictine** (open for guided tours mid-Mar–mid-May and Sept, daily 10am–noon, 2–5.30pm; mid-May–Aug, daily 9.30am–6pm, limited visits in winter; admission charge) was built in 1892 in a regrettably florid style, but it does exhibit priceless collections from the old abbey.

A tour takes in the distillery and cellars and offers a tasting of the liqueur first produced here by a monk, Dom Vincelli, in 1510; its recipe of herbs and spices is still a closely guarded secret. Few visitors come away without buying a botttle to take home.

Étretat

The cliffs put on a spectacular performance at **Étretat** ⑲, embracing the curved beach and esplanade in the arms of the **Porte d'Amont** on the right, and the **Porte d'Aval** on the left, both pierced by

openings worn through the chalk by the sea. Near the latter is the needle-pointed **Aiguille d'Étretat**.

Although Marie-Antoinette had a private oyster bed here, it was artists and composers such as Corot (1796–1875) and Offenbach (1819–80) who popularised the resort. The white beaches are a favourite destination now, whenever the weather is fine. The thatched boats once used as stores by the fishermen are now appealing restaurants.

On the Amont cliff a small chapel, **Notre-Dame de la Garde**, stands sentinel. Close by, a small museum is devoted to two little-known aviators, Nungesser and Coli, who set off from here with high hopes in 1927 and died attempting a first crossing of the Atlantic.

At the nearby point called **Cap d'Antifer**, a lighthouse flashes its warning out into the Channel. Beyond, the cliffs march on, to be broken at last by the Seine's abrasive flood and by the neat villas of Ste-Adresse. ❑

BELOW:
the Palais
Bénédictine
in Fécamp.

BAR *LE* **WELCOME** BRASSERIE

RESTAURANT

BRASSERIE

Map on page 224

CAEN

The favourite residence of William and Mathilda, reduced to rubble by Allied bombing in World War II, Caen is now an agreeable modern city with some of its greatest ecclesiastical buildings still standing

Visitors penetrating the mesh of ring-roads, industrial estates and post-war housing areas that surround modern-day Caen may find it instructive, even therapeutic, to while away the wait at the traffic lights with sustained fantasies about the city's earliest incarnations. Try Catumagos, the fledging Celtic settlement that grew up here on an island at the confluence of the Orne and Odon rivers. Or the Gallo-Roman port of Cadomus, with its neighbouring villages scattered across fields and marshland now covered with concrete and tarmac.

Twin abbeys

Better still, return to the mid-11th century, when this walled town became William and Matilda's favoured residence and their major power base in western Normandy. These monarchs put Caen on the map, and bequeathed the city its two great abbeys, the Abbaye-aux-Hommes and Abbaye-aux-Dames, both founded on the north bank of the Orne in response to the lifting, in 1059, of the papal excommunication imposed following their cousinly marriage nine years earlier.

Today the abbeys act as towering book-ends between which everything of historic interest in Caen can be found. Midway between them stands the hilltop Château de Caen, a castle founded by William and much enlarged by his son, Henri I. It is still the city's hub, although no longer its heart – World War II ended that, when the "Battle for Caen" reduced three-quarters of the city to rubble.

The modern town

From the ensuing decades of hasty reconstruction and utilitarian town-planning, Caen has emerged as a functional and busy city, its industries benefiting from the 1855 Caen canal that links it to the Channel 12 km (7½ miles) to the north.

As the capital of Basse-Normandie and Préfecture of Calvados, this city of 120,000 inhabitants has worked hard to regain its cultural stature.

A lengthy process of restoration has preserved numerous monuments, and a good spread of lawns, parks and gardens, planted courtesy of Allied bombers, have been incorporated into the city centre. This can easily be toured on foot, along streets lined by interesting shops and restaurants, and kept lively by a university to the north of the castle.

Place Courtonne

For many visitors Caen begins with the **place Courtonne ◯**, and the best way to arrive is by water, sailing up to join the

PRECEDING PAGES: café owners open up for business. **LEFT:** flags fly above Caen's castle. **RIGHT** stop here for a bilingual breakfast.

serried yachts and pleasure boats that moor in the adjacent **Bassin St-Pierre ❸**. In the week the square functions as a car park and bus junction, but on Sunday mornings is given over to an antiques market. At its northern end is the **Tour Guillaume-le-Roy**, a remnant of the town's ramparts that once looked out over the Odon, but which is now a chess-piece castle stranded in traffic.

A short walk north, along rue Buquet, is the **Vieux Quartier de Vaugueux**. This is a pleasantly pedestrianised fraction of old Caen centred on the rue du Vaugueux. Its timbered buildings are home to restaurants offering everything from fast-food to Madagascan cuisine and the gourmet dishes of one of Caen's best-known restaurants, **La Bourride**.

Abbaye-aux-Dames

At the south of rue du Vaugueux, rue des Chanoines leads eastwards up to the **Abbaye-aux-Dames ❻** (open for guided tours daily 2.30pm, 4pm; free), the first of William and Matilda's twin abbeys to be built. Nine centuries ago it would have stood amid meadows sloping down to the Orne, with its own attendant village, known simply as Le Bourg-l'Abbesse. A few remnants of St-Gilles, its parish church, can be seen standing in a garden opposite the west front of the abbey's church, **La Trinité**.

Begun in 1060 and consecrated six years later, only a few months before William invaded England, Matilda's church is a monument to both the grace of the Romanesque style and the creamy sensuality of Caen stone. Despite the loss of its spires in the Hundred Years' War, a zealous revamping of the west front in the 1850s and the well-scrubbed homogeneity that has resulted from the recent restoration of the interior, there is much to enjoy. The nine bays of the nave, roofed with pointed vaulting in the 12th century, are textbook Romanesque, while the crypt, forested with columns, has hardly changed since the day it was built. Direct-

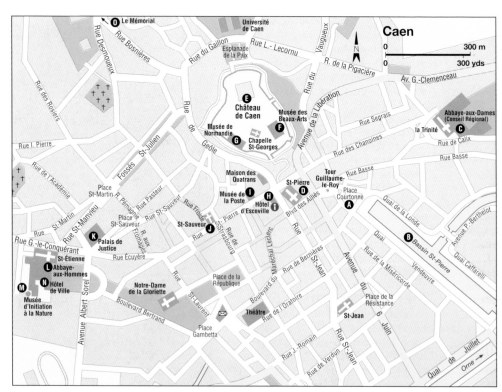

Map
on page
224

ly above this, in the choir, a black marble slab marks the tomb of Queen Matilda, who died in 1083.

The crypt is often locked, but can be viewed on one of the guided tours around the adjacent **conventual buildings**. These were laid out in 1704 by Guillaume de la Tremblaye, who designed a similar ensemble for the Abbaye-aux-Hommes. The Revolution prevented the completion of the fourth wall of the cloisters, but the abbey's classical buildings and formal gardens have since been restored to make an harmonious residence for the Conseil Régional de Basse-Normandie.

Spiritual heart

William and Matilda's abbeys may be the most venerable buildings in Caen, but the church closest to the hearts of its citizens is the **Église St-Pierre ❶**. Just west of the Tour Guillaume-le-Roy it is under restoration, and archaeologists are now excavating the adjoining cemetery. Begun in the late 13th century, St-Pierre's orderly Gothic nave contrasts with the richness of its Renaissance eastern end, the dripping decorations paid for by wealthy Caennais. The spire and roof were destroyed in the war, and their impressive reconstruction is easily appreciated when you climb the steps that lead up to the château further north. The church now houses a stunning modern organ.

The château

The **Château de Caen ❺** is today a grassy ghost town, with the few buildings that survived the war now used as museums. The ruins at its northern end are the most tangibly feudal, where thick, massive walls emerge from the surrounding lawns like the teeth of a badly-buried giant. Here you can see the outline of the castle's Donjon, a moated keep raised in 1123 by Henri I but felled by the Convention in 1793. To its west is a lonely survivor from the 12th century, the Salle de l'Échiquier (Exchequer's Hall), the great hall of Henri's palace.

Pause on the castle's western ramparts, though, and you can still contemplate a skyline punctuated with spires and bel-

fries, a poignant hint of what Caen must have been like before bombs rained down.

Visiting the museums

In the south of the castle precincts two museums lie on either side of the small **Chapelle St-Georges**, dating from the 12th to 15th centuries and now an exhibition space. To the east, the renovated **Musée des Beaux-Arts ❻** (open Wed–Mon 9.30am–6pm; admission charge) has a wide-ranging collection of fine paintings and prints, with some of its choicest works acquired by Napoleonic pillage. It is particularly strong on 17th-century French and Italian painting, though the artists represented stretch from Van der Weyden and Dürer to Courbet and Dufy. It was extensively modernised in 1994, and houses an especially nice café.

To the west of St-Georges, the **Musée de Normandie ❼** (open Wed–Mon 9.30am–12.30pm, 2–6pm; admission charge) occupies the former residence of the city's governor, with a medieval

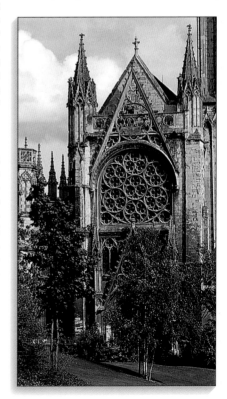

RIGHT: St-Pierre, the spiritual heart.

Jardin des Simples (Medicinal Garden) laid out alongside. Its rooms are a résumé of life in Normandy down the centuries, with informative exhibits on the region's diverse styles of agriculture and architecture, displays of cider- and cheese-making, lace and copper work, and an esoteric collection of liturgical candle-making equipment from a factory in Cherbourg.

Shopping centre

The western side of Caen, from the château to the Abbaye-aux-Hommes, is the city's most active and energetic. Its main artery is rue St-Pierre, while boulevard du Maréchal Leclerc, which follows the Odon's old course, winds south past large department stores such as Nouvelles Galeries and Monoprix. Within this compact grid of shop-lined streets – which include a good supply of bars, *salons de thé* and heartlifting *patisseries* – are a scattering of historic buildings.

On the west side of Église St-Pierre, Caen's **Tourist Office** is located in the

Hôtel d'Escoville ⓗ in place St-Pierre, an Italianate mansion built in the 1530s. A short walk north at 31 rue de Geôle, and easily seen from the château, is the 15th-century timber-latticed **Maison des Quatrans**. Going down rue St-Jean in the opposite direction, you can see the gnawed towers of the **Église St-Jean**. Begun in the 14th century, it was never completed as it was built on marshland. Despite the noticeable slant of its west front and internal pillars, it is still in use.

Wandering the streets

West along rue St-Pierre, at Nos 52 and 54, stand two half-timbered buildings. Inside the first, the **Musée de la Poste** ⓘ (Postal Museum; open Wed–Mon 10am–12.30pm, 2–6pm; admission charge), boldly romanticises the delivery of mail, from the galloping messengers of the Bayeux Tapestry to the brightly-anoraked heroes of today.

A short walk further west is the curiously attractive **Église St-Sauveur** ⓙ,

BELOW: the crypt of La Trinité.

Map on page 224

known as Notre-Dame de Froide-Rue, which consists of two naves built side by side, one 14th century and the other 15th.

From here, rue St-Pierre continues west into the rue Écuyère and an area known for its antiques shops, beyond which is Place Fontette, dominated by the octagonal hulk of Caen's **Palais de Justice** Ⓚ. This is the most direct route to the Abbaye-aux-Hommes, but a preferable detour is to take one of the narrow streets, such as rue Froide (next to the church) or rue aux Fromages (off rue Écuyère) that lead north to spacious place St-Sauveur.

Lined with 18th-century houses, the square is the scene of Caen's principal **market**, held every Friday. In its centre is a statue of Louis XIV masquerading as a Roman emperor.

Abbaye-aux-Hommes

From here there are views west to the spires of the **Abbaye-aux-Hommes** Ⓛ (open for guided tours daily 9.30am–4pm; free/donation), which can be reached by

walking down rue St-Manvieu. William's abbey is a mixture of styles. It consists of an abbey church, **St-Étienne**, abutted to a grandiose ensemble of 18th-century monastic buildings. The imposing west front of the church is reached via rue Guillaume-le-Conquérant, where a small cul-de-sac square to the left gives visitors the chance to gaze up at its 82-metre (269-ft) towers.

Uneasy history

The harmony of this façade belies St-Étienne's battered history. Work on the church began in 1067 and was virtually complete by the time of William's death 20 years later. The Conqueror's funeral turned out to be a farcical affair, with the route of the cortège disrupted by a fire in the town and the burial service interrupted by a man claiming his father owned the land where the grave was dug. He left only after being paid compensation.

When the coffin was eventually lowered into its vault William's decomposed

BELOW: the Hôtel des Quatrans.

corpse burst, creating such a stench that the congregation fled. His tomb was desecrated by the Huguenots in 1562, and again in the Revolution, and it is said that only a solitary femur now rests beneath the inscribed slab set in front of the altar.

Despite such indignities, St-Étienne has remained William's triumphal mausoleum. The west front and nave are remarkable for their restrained décor and exquisite sense of proportion, while the the early 12th-century sexpartite vaulting that roofs the latter is one of the earliest examples in Europe. In the next century Gothic spires were added to the towers and the choir and east end built.

Natural history museum

The abbey buildings to the south of St-Étienne now house Caen's Hôtel de Ville and the small but diverting **Musée d'Initiation à la Nature**  (open Mon–Fri 9.30am–12.30pm, 2–5.30pm; admission charge), housed in the abbey's old bakery. This offers a concise guide to the Normandy countryside, with aromatic gardens, a *chemin géologique* and displays of stuffed birds and animals.

The entrance, and the most prestigious façade, are in the Esplanade Louvel, reached by turning left along rue Duc Rollon after leaving the church.

Hôtel de Ville

Guided tours of the **Hôtel de Ville** (daily, 9.30, 11am, 2.30pm and 4pm) allow a limited inspection of its monastic chambers and cloister. Designed in 1704 and completed 60 years later, the abbey buildings were turned into a school by Napoleon in 1802.

Most of the rooms, which have splendid wood-panelling and furnishings, serve civic purposes: the chapter house is a registry office, the refectory a reception hall. In the former sacristy is a small display of the enormous lace head-dresses *(coiffes)* women wore in the last century.

In a separate building, the 14th-century **Salle des Gardes**, the abbot received his guests. After its restoration in 1974, the results of the excavations were set under glass. Here you can gaze on the walls of the Gallo-Roman port of Cadomus, and at the 3,000-year-old skeleton of a young woman, one of Caen's earliest citizens.

Expatriate community

In the north of the city is the **Université de Caen**. Founded in 1432 by the Duke of Bedford, regent of England's Henry VI, the present campus is a serene pool of 1950s tower blocks and parkland sprawling across 33 hectares (82 acres). On the western edge of its grounds is the small and overgrown **Protestant cemetery**.

In the mid-19th century the city hosted an English expatriate community of over 1,000. Among them was England's best known dandy, George "Beau" Brummel, who was consul here from 1830 to 1832. He had inherited a fortune that enabled him to live with impeccable flamboyance until gambling debts forced him to flee to France. A tragic decline into penury, prison and paralysis culminated in his death in 1840, and the inelegant headstone that now marks his grave here. ❏

LEFT: the great Abbaye-aux-Hommes.

Map on page 224

The Caen Memorial

On the northwestern outskirts of Caen stands a smooth, monolithic building, split in two by a rough-hewn fissure marking its entrance. Surrounded by well-trimmed lawns and fluttering flags, it might be the flashy HQ of a multinational software company – until you read the uncompromising text carved in its façade. *La Douleur m'a brisée, la Fraternité m'a relevée, de ma blessure a jailli un fleuve de Liberté.* (Pain broke me, Brotherhood lifted me up, from my wounds sprang a river of Liberty.)

Composed by a citizen of Caen in tribute to the Allied forces that liberated the city, these words herald **Le Mémorial ❶** (open daily except first two weeks of Jan, 9am–7pm; Jul–Aug till 9pm; admission charge), a war museum dedicated to the pursuit of peace. Opened by François Mitterrand on 6 June 1988, it differs spectacularly from the D-Day museums found elsewhere in Normandy.

Built on three levels, Le Mémorial uses a barrage of audio-visual techniques to set the Battle of Normandy in the context of World War II, with thematic links to previous and subsequent international conflicts. Its centrepiece is a walk-down spiral gallery chronicling the 20th century's descent into war. Darkened rooms evoke the dark years of Occupation, wide spaces mirror the world-widening of the conflict in 1942.

Three "spectacles" supplement this historical expedition (if you are pushed for time, see these first). First a film montage, using both real and fictional footage, vividly recounts the events of D-Day as simultaneously experienced by both the Allied and German forces. A series of illuminated maps then outlines the subsequent progress of the war. A second film, *Hope*, concludes with images of continuing conflict and idealistic calls for world peace. This enduring aspiration is picked up in a separate gallery, housed in a former German bunker, that honours Nobel Peace Prize winners.

The Mémorial has its critics: some see it as narcissistically hi-tech, a slickly-marketed piece of civic aggrandisement engineered by Caen's mayor, Jean-Marie Girault. How can a museum promote peace without sensationalising the achievements of war? Is it *"Un Musée pour la Paix"*, or just a hypermarket selling history to clipboard-wielding schoolchildren who come only to test its efficacy as an echo chamber?

Whatever its failings, the Mémorial's chosen subject is too serious to be ignored, and its displays undoubtedly prick the emotions. You may not become a pacifist, but something will linger – a photograph of Russian Jews being hung, a child's boot from Auschwitz, film from Stalingrad. And D-Day is never quite the same – particularly if your visit coincides with one of the groups of veterans that frequently tour the museum. Sporting berets and regimental ties, and inevitably grown frail and grey, their presence twists the experience. Some are moved to tears, others to jingoism. "We come every year," they patiently explain to a generation fortunate enough to have never known war. "Those that can. It's a pilgrimage."

Le Mémorial is on the esplanade du Général Eisenhower. If going by bus, take No. 17 from place Courtonne. ❑

RIGHT: nations united in peace.

Map on page 233

BAYEUX AND THE D-DAY BEACHES

Bayeux is an historic town and its tapestry is one of Normandy's great treasures, but many people come to this area in search of more recent history, to be found on the D-Day beaches

To the men in marketing, the coast of Calvados between the mouths of the Orne and Vire rivers is known as the **Côte de Nacre**, the Mother-of-Pearl Coast. For most visitors it is, and always will be, the **D-Day Beaches**. The events of 5–6 June 1944, when 135,000 troops landed here as part of Operation Overlord, have irrepressibly dented what would otherwise be an undemanding string of seaside resorts and quiet ports devoted to harvesting excellent shellfish.

More than half a century later, the Côte de Nacre bristles with a legacy of fortifications, memorials, museums and military cemeteries that stand amid the beach hotels, aquaria and mini-golf courses of this popular summer holiday destination.

With the development of **Ouistreham** as a cross-Channel ferry port in 1986, roads, hotels and hypermarkets sprang up around the Orne estuary. The Caen canal, constructed in the mid-19th century to link the city to the sea, runs parallel to this river. Now deepened to take ships of up to 30,000 tonnes, it is spanned by the Pegasus Bridge.

Tour of the beaches

Many people start this tour from a base in **Caen ❶**, and take the D515 north. The D-Day landing beaches stretch along Calvados's great sandy shoreline as far east as Cabourg and the Côte Fleurie. To the west they spill into the Cotentin where the American forces landed on Utah Beach (*see page 234*). Inland at St-Mère-Église is **Milestone 0**, the start of the **Liberty Highway**, which runs, via the zero-km marker on Utah Beach, 1,145 km (711 miles) to Bartogne in Belgium, with markers every kilometre.

Finding your way around the beaches is made easy because of the enormous

continued interest in the events of D-Day, helped by popular museums and well-kept monuments. Since the 50th anniversary celebrations in 1994, almost every village here seems to have established a museum or memorial in rememberance of the part it played in the conflict.

Pegasus Bridge

Near the town of **Bénouville** you will come to the **Pegasus Bridge ❷**. Situated at the eastern end of the beaches, it was an early objective in the campaign to establish an eastern foothold on French soil. Just after midnight on 6 June 1944, gliders and paratroopers of the British 6th Air-

LEFT: Gold Beach near Arromanches.
RIGHT: the zero-km marker on the Liberty Highway.

borne Division (whose insignia is a fly-ing horse, hence Pegasus) landed in the nearby fields and quickly secured the bridge. Despite protests by veterans, the original bridge was replaced in 1994 to facilitate traffic along the canal. But in 2000 the old bridge, lying in a nearby marsh with its bullet holes still visible, was dragged and re-erected next to the new bridge, as part of the Pegasus Bridge memorial, where there is now a large park and museum, **Site de Pegasus Bridge** (open May–Sept, daily 9.30am–6.30pm; Oct–Nov, Feb–Apr, 10am–1pm, 2–5pm; admission charge).

A memorable detour

On the east bank of the Orne two associ-ated sights are worth a detour (D514). In the village of **Ranville ❸** the **British and Commonwealth War Cemetery** contains 2,536 dead, including Lt Den Brotheridge, the first Allied soldier killed in the invasion. Neat lawns, rows of white headstones and a parish church built in the Romanesque style from soft-toned Caen stone paint a very English scene.

Just beyond **Sallenelles ❹** are the rem-nants of the **Merville Battery**, a heavily armed brick in the Atlantic Wall. Captur-ing it proved a costly affair – 70 men were lost, and its guns turned out to be less powerful than believed. Today, cows and horses graze nonchalantly beside its case-ments, while the small **Musée de la Bat-terie de Merville** (open Apr–Sept, daily 10am–1pm, 2–7pm; admission charge) struggles to be an aide-mémoire.

Following the shore

To the west of Pegasus Bridge, the D514 follows the shore for the length of the Côte de Nacre, with the well-signposted **Circuit de Débarquement** indicating the beaches, memorials and museums associ-ated with what the French call, J-Jour and most of us know as D-Day. The first three landing beaches that lie between Ouistre-ham and Port-en-Bessin were given the code-names **Sword**, **Juno** and **Gold**, and

BELOW:
Pegasus Bridge at Bénouville.

Map on page 233

it is here that the British and Canadian troops disembarked. Many of the resorts along the coast were re-built after the war, paying homage to their liberators with street names such as avenue de Amiral Mountbatten, while the village of Colleville re-named itself **Colleville-Montgomery**. Memorials are still being added to town centres, and new museums opened to honour a particular troop division or action.

At the same time seaside life goes on: some visitors come to **Courseulles-sur-Mer ❺**, a busy yachting port, to see the Sherman tank dragged out of the sea in 1971 to decorate its seafront; others come to enjoy some of the best oysters in Normandy. Near the harbour entrance is the **Maison de la Mer** (open May–Jun, daily 9am–1pm, 2–7pm; Jul–Aug, daily 9am–7pm; Sept–Apr, Tues–Sun 10am–noon, 2–6pm; admission charge), which has an aquarium with a tunnel running through it and an extraordinary collection of seashells.

Washed-up port

West of this resort, villas and casinos give way to campsites and wheatfields, as the land rises to a coastline indented with cliffs and bays. Not far from the village of **St-Côme** a windy viewpoint overlooks **Arromanches-les-Bains ❻** a small resort that is the best place to survey the startling remains of the ingenious artificial port towed across the Channel as part of the invasion force. Arromanches now has a **360° Cinema** (open Jun–Aug, daily 9.40am–6.40pm; Apr–May, Sept–Oct, daily 10.10am–5.40pm; Feb–Mar, Nov–Dec, daily 10.10am–4.40pm; admission charge), where you can see dramatic footage of the landing and the war.

The **Mulberry Harbour**, one of the pioneering achievements of D-Day, was built by sinking 146 *caissons* – hollow rectangular concrete boxes – to form a semi-circular harbour wall, with further protection from a breakwater of scuttled ships behind. Floating piers and pontoons, which could rise and fall with the tide,

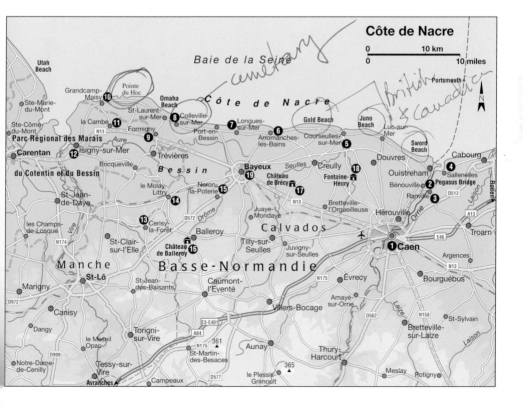

were used to create 16 km (10 miles) of waterborne roads over which vehicles and equipment could be driven ashore. The **Musée du Débarquement** (open May–Sept, daily 9am–7pm; Feb–Apr, Oct–Dec, daily 9.30am–12.30pm, 1.30–5.30pm; admission charge) right behind the small beach in Arromanches has photographs and Admiralty film of "Port Winston" in action, complete with barrage balloons, battleships and tanks rolling ashore. There are also models of the Mulberry Harbour, the remains of which are clearly visible through the huge, sea-facing window.

American landing beaches

A short drive westwards, at **Longues-sur-Mer ❼**, the D104 leads seaward to the remains of the **Longues Battery**. Here, four well-preserved casemates, some still armed with guns, crown the cliffs. West of the pleasant fishing port of **Port-en-Bessin** lies **Omaha Beach**, which, along with **Utah Beach** on the eastern Cotentin

Peninsula (*see page 297*), was where the US troops made their landings. Another Mulberry Harbour was established here but destroyed on 19 June 1944 by storms.

The heaviest D-Day casualties were incurred at Omaha, and the **American Cemetery** at **Colleville-sur-Mer ❽** overlooks the cliffs and beach where much of the fighting took place. The Americans repatriated many of their dead, but the cemetery, which is spread over a 70-hectare (172-acre) site, nevertheless contains 9,386 graves. At the entrance a time capsule dedicated to General Eisenhower, containing reports of D-Day landings, has been buried. It will be opened on 6 June 2044. Within the cemetery, a semi-circular memorial is decorated with maps detailing the developments of the war and a soaring bronze statue representing the Spirit of American Youth.

Behind this memorial a Garden of the Missing records the names of those whose bodies were unidentified or lost at sea. Towards the sea a viewpoint looks down

BELOW: the German cemetery at La Cambe.

Map on page 233

on the sands where the fighting occurred, while to the west grids of white crosses and Stars of David are laid out with tight-lipped precision on an immaculate carpet of grass, a visual correlative of infinity.

Centuries of battle

A short way inland (D517) the village of **Formigny** ❾ was the scene of another famous battle: the final conflict of the Hundred Years' War. Here, in April 1450, the French finally ousted the English. While the early English triumphs were won by devastatingly acurate use of the long-bow, it was the French cannon that finally expelled the occupiers.

The most telling memorial to the fighting that took place on D-Day can be found at **Pointe du Hoc**, a headland 12 km (7 miles) further west. The ground remains emphatically pockmarked with bomb craters, and the ruined bunkers have been left much as they were after US 2nd Rangers stormed the cliffs to destroy a six-gun battery positioned here.

The **Musée des Ranger**s (open Jun–Aug, Tues–Sun 10am–7pm; Apr–May, Sept–Oct, 10am–1pm, 3–6pm; admission charge) in the nearby fishing port of **Grandcamp-Maisy** ❿ commemorates their achievement.

A short drive south at **La Cambe** ⓫ (D113), you can see the quite different way with which the Germans, with restrictions imposed by the French, buried their dead. Here 21,160 soldiers lie beneath rows of horizontal headstones, grouped around a central funereal mound. The graves are shadowed by oak trees and sets of symbolic black stone crosses. The Teutonic melancholy of La Cambe is a marked contrast to the stiff-lipped formality of the American cemetery at Colleville-sur-Mer, or the chin-up epitaphs that distinguish the British graves.

The inland Bessin

Inland from the Côte de Nacre lies an undulating plateau of land known as the **Bessin**. Its clay soil gives rise to a lush

BELOW: Omaha Beach American cemetery.

The Bayeux Tapestry

In 1476 an inventory of Bayeux cathedral noted that amongst its possessions was "a very long and very narrow strip of linen, embroidered with figures and inscriptions representing the Conquest of England, which is hung round the nave of the church on the Feast of Relics and throughout the Octave".

Often referred to in France as the "Tapisserie de la Reine Mathilde" (Queen Matilda's Tapestry), this 70-metre (230-ft) church hanging should, strictly speaking, be called "Bishop Odo's Woollen Embroidery". If the historians have got it right, then it was Odo, Bishop of Bayeux and half-brother of William, who, perhaps as early as 1067, commissioned English women from Kent to embroider a length of linen with scenes recounting the story of 1066 and all that.

Odo is a prominent character in this narrative, and it may be that the tapestry was

specifically created for the consecration of his cathedral in 1077. The pivotal act in the story, where England's King Harold swears allegiance to William's cause, is set in Bayeux. Guillaume de Poitiers' chronicle says it took place in Bonneville-sur-Touques.

Later we see Episcopus Odo supervising the building of the invasion fleet, and blessing the troops' food and wine. Forbidden by the scriptures to draw blood with a sword, he charged through the Battle of Hastings wielding a club. The bellicose bishop was well rewarded – created Duke of Kent, and given the port of Dover. By 1086, as the Domesday Book records, he was the largest landowner in England after William.

Was Odo merely the tapestry's patron, or the creative genius behind its story, so coolly didactic, so subtly woven with economies of truth? Of the many pleasures offered by this 11th-century comic strip, one of the most engaging is the spectacle of seeing history in the making – literally being fabricated.

Its creators omit to tell us, for example, how William's fleet was forced east by storms from the mouth of the Dives to the Somme estuary; or of Harold's victory in Scotland, and how his battle-weary troops marched 402 km (250 miles) south in 12 days. Instead, everything is directed towards the big moral lesson that justifies the Conquest – Harold broke his oath, and suffered the consequences.

The value of this cartoon as propaganda was not lost on Napoleon, who in 1803 had it put on display in Paris in an attempt to drum up support for a repeat invasion of England. Most likely its viewers were, as we are today, captivated more by its minutiae than its message. We marvel at a *petit* Mont-St-Michel and Halley's Comet, note the stubble on the chin of Edward's doctor, watch the jackal-like corpse-robbers, and wonder how they knew about shish-kebabs.

Though seen as an historical document, the tapestry is also a great work of art, with an inherent universality. Scene 47, where a woman and child stand by as William's troops torch their home, provides an emblematic portrait of the refugee. And somehow, although he is not on their Bayeux Trail questionnaires, schoolkids always find the man in the margin with the sword-sized penis.

LEFT: Harold is knighted by Duke William.

Map
on page
233

pastureland famous for its dairy products, and the name of **Isigny-sur-Mer** ⓬, an otherwise insignificant market town at its western end, is now a familiar sight in Europe's fridges. This is also, according to the Disneyland Paris publicity machine, where the family of its founder comes from: the Disneys were "d'Isigny".

The Bessin countryside is peaceful, with enough woodland, châteaux and idiosyncratic museums to provide a refuge from the noise of war. The **Forêt de Cerisy**, straddling the border with the Manche *département*, is a remnant of the ancient beech forest that once surrounded the village of **Cerisy-la-Forêt** ⓭. A Benedictine abbey was founded here in the 11th century by William the Conqueror's father, Robert the Magnificent. Though the abbey is no longer there, its huge restored church is one of the finest in Normandy, standing out like a beacon in the quiet countryside.

To the northeast three traditional Bessin industries are celebrated: in the village of

Le Molay-Littry ⓮, the **Musée de la Mine** (open Feb–Dec, daily; free). is devoted to a coal mine that operated here for two centuries following the discovery of the fuel in 1741.

Nearby the **Moulin de Marcy** (open Feb–Dec, daily; free) is a restored 19th-century flour mill and farm. Further east, **Noron-la-Poterie** ⓯ (open Mon–Fri 9am–noon, 2–6pm; free) has been producing *grès au sel* (salt-glaze pottery) since the 13th century. Modern examples are sold in local shops and studios.

Château de Balleroy

At the eastern end of the Forêt de Cerisy, the **Château de Balleroy** ⓰ is the first recorded extravagance designed, in 1626, by François Mansart, the architect who later worked on the Château de Blois. Balleroy and its attendant village is best approached along the road from Castillon (D73). Behind the château's stately exterior lie richly decorated salons that have survived since the late 17th century.

BELOW:
the steep roofs of Fontaine-Henry.

In the 1970s the château was bought by the late Malcolm Forbes, a millionaire publishing magnate and thrill-seeker who created a **Musée des Ballons** (Hot Air Balloon Museum) (open Jul–Aug, daily 10am–6pm; Mar–mid-Oct, Wed–Mon, 9am–noon, 2–6pm; admission charge) in its outbuildings.

Visiting the châteaux

Mansart is also thought to be responsible for the 17th-century formal gardens that adjoin the **Château de Brécy**  (for opening hours contact the tourist office, Pont St-Jean, Bayeux, tel: 02 31 51 28 28), to the east of Bayeux. The nearby **St-Gabriel-Brécy** priory is a cultural centre and has attractive gardens. The château lies just off the D82 that runs southwest from Creully, an attractive town built above the Seulles valley.

Five kilometres (3 miles) to the east, the **Château de Fontaine-Henry** (mid-Jun–Sept, Wed–Mon 11.30am–6.30pm; Easter–mid-Jun, Sat–Sun 2.30–3.30pm;

admission charge) is well worth visiting. Here, the remains of a 15th-century castle have been capped with splendid Renaissance buildings that are notorious for their steep, sloping roofs, which in the northern wing rise higher than the walls that support them.

Popular centre

The capital of the Bessin is **Bayeux** , a city that attracts hordes of visitors but somehow maintains its sanity. Perhaps it has grown used to occupation, having been variously overrun by Romans, Bretons and Saxons before becoming one of the first towns to be colonised by the Vikings – Norse was spoken here as late as the 11th century.

In the 20th century Bayeux was occupied by German forces, but as it was the first French city to be liberated by the Allies it was spared the destruction wrought elsewhere, and has an agreeable nucleus of historic buildings to the south of its central thoroughfare, rue St-Martin. This runs into pedestrianised rue St-Jean further east, from where waterside paths follow the course of the Aure.

The **Bayeaux Tapestry** *(see page 236)* is displayed in the **Centre Guillaume-le-Conquéran**t (open May–Aug, daily 9am–7pm; Sept–Oct, mid-Mar–Apr, daily 9am–6.30pm; Nov–mid-Mar, daily 9.30am–12.30pm, 2–6pm; admission charge), which occupies a former seminary, built in 1693, in the rue Nesmond. *La tapisserie* resides in a dimly-lit, bullet-proof, glassed gallery. There is an audio-guided tour, but this rather races along and it is advisable to first visit the centre's upper floors, where a cinema and excellent displays set out the background to the tapestry.

The cathedral

To the northwest of the seminary rises Bayeux's **Cathédrale Notre-Dame** (open Jul–Aug, daily 9am–7pm; Sept–Jun, daily 9am–6pm; free). Of the original church begun in the 1040s and completed by Bishop Odo in 1077, only the crypt and parts of its west towers survive. The bulk of the stonework is Gothic, but the central

LEFT: Bayeux cathedral is mostly Gothic.

Map on page 233

tower was added in the 15th century and capped with a 19th-century dome that has attracted phenomenal disapproval.

Look out, too, for the small house that a hermit built on the roof. The work of successive centuries is clearly visible in the interior, too, where the decorated arches of the Romanesque nave are surmounted by a 13th-century clerestory and vaulting – though the eye is inevitably caught first by the pulpit, installed in 1787 and inspired by an *île flottante*. The crypt is decorated with delightful Gothic frescoes.

Lace-making centre

On the north side of the cathedral, its entrance shaded by a magnificent 200-year-old plane tree in the place de la Liberté, is the **Musée Baron-Gérard** (open June–mid-Sept, daily 9am–7pm; mid-Sept–May, daily 10am–12.30pm, 2–6pm; admission charge). Cool, dark and soothingly crowd-free, this former Bishop's Palace houses a collection of fine art, lace, porcelain and furniture gathered in the 19th century by Baron Henri-Alexandre Gérard, whose undiscriminating tastes led him to acquire anything from local porcelain and lace, to a portrait of romping nymphs and a still-life of fried eggs.

Between the 17th and 19th centuries Bayeux became a centre of lacemaking – by 1860 there were 10,000 workers in the area. The Musée Baron-Gérard has a room devoted to lace bonnets, while on the south side of the cathedral an **Atelier de Dentelle** (Lacemaking School) currently teaches the craft to 25 students.

The school is part of the 18th-century Hôtel du Doyen, which also houses the **Musée d'Art Religieux** (open daily 10am–12.30pm, 2–6pm; admission charge), containing religious treasures from the cathedral.

Memorials

A short walk southwest, along rue des Chanoines, is **Le Mémorial du Général de Gaulle** (open mid-Mar–mid-Jan, daily 9.30am–12.30pm, 2–6.30pm; admission charge). This museum celebrates the life of the man who was rapturously welcomed into the city on 14 June 1944. To the west, in the tree-lined place Charles-de-Gaulle, a column celebrates the event.

Further south, rue St-Loup leads into boulevard Fabian Ware, part of the city's ring-road, with the **Musée Mémorial de la Bataille de Normandie** (open May–mid-Sept, daily 9.30am–6.30pm; mid-Sept–Apr, 10am–12.30pm, 2–6pm; admission charge) to the right. It gives a thorough account of the conflict with the aid of maps, photos, newspaper articles and enough weapons, vehicles and military equipment to mount a *coup d'état*. Its introductory film compilation, using newsreels of the day, is one of the best of its kind to be found anywhere.

A little further along is the largest World War II **British and Commonwealth War Cemetery** in France, containing 4,648 graves. Across the road a **Memorial to the Missing** bears a Latin epitaph uniting the two great events that collide here: *Nos a Guilielmo Victi Victoris Patriam Liberavimus* (We, once conquered by William, have set free the Conqueror's land). ❑

RIGHT: a medieval figure on stilts in a local pageant.

Map
on page
256

DEAUVILLE AND THE CÔTE FLEURIE

The Côte Fleurie has been attracting artists and writers as well as high rollers since the mid-19th century. Today's visitors find it easy to understand the region's appeal

The Côte Fleurie is the high spot of Normandy's seaside. Here are huge beaches, vast villas and apartments and the dazzling lights of casino and grand-hotel chandeliers – even though some may have seen more glorious days.

As well as the poodles, poseurs, gourmands and smart yachts, there are campsites and sand yachts and shops selling large shrimp nets to trawl the shallow shore. Between sunshine and showers is a brief glittering social season in Deauville, while Honfleur, pretty as a jigsaw picture, cannot help attracting weekend visitors all the year round.

Outlining the coast

The coast proper, in the *département* of Calvados, lies between Cabourg and Honfleur, a 40-km (25-mile) stretch of the D513. At two points it rises up from the shore into unexpectedly rustic corniches, above the Falaise des Vaches Noires rocks between Houlgate and Villers-sur-Mer, and along the Côte de Grâce above Honfleur, once a thriving port, which still has the makings of an old maritime town.

On the other hand Dives-sur-Mer and Touques, the other two medieval ports on the coast named after the rivers on which they stand, have silted up and been left high and dry behind the resorts which grew up on their extended estuaries.

Rivers also provide the coast's western and eastern boundaries: to the west, the Orne arrives from Caen and the Suisse Normande through the marshland beside the Route du Marais; to the east the Seine's last meanders are contained inside the Parc Régional de Brotonne. Now the Pont de Normandie spans the river connecting the coast to Le Havre and the Alabaster Coast beyond. Inland are the rolling green hills of the Pays d'Auge.

The approach from Caen

The coast is shadowed by the A13/E46 Rouen–Caen motorway, and from the east, the new Pont de Normandie brings visitors from Le Havre. Coming from Caen's ferry port of Ouistreham the D514 slips across the Orne and passes through **Sallenelles** *(see page 232)*. Inland the lanes wander through the marshes and the Route du Marais, a pleasant backwater with *gîtes* and manor farms selling their produce. The centre for this district is **Troarn**, on the high ground behind, and just the other side of the motorway, where a small, boarded-up Gothic priory sits on the edge of a modern estate.

PRECEDING PAGES: gaily painted houses beside Deauville's marina.
LEFT: the Vieux Bassin in Honfleur.
RIGHT: Sunday market in Dives-sur-Mer.

On the coast **Merville-Franceville** heralds the Côte Fleurie. Its modern buildings and camp sites are strung out along a great desert of a beach on which there are a couple of military sites. On the west end of its seafront is an 18th-century redoubt built in the style of the great French military architect Vauban. Just inland, among the fields, is the 16-hectare (40-acre) German Merville battery (*see page 232*).

In search of lost writers

Past modern-day bunkers in the sand dunes of the local golf course, the road continues to **L'Hôme** where a promenade leads towards the promenade Marcel Proust at **Cabourg** ❶. From 1907 the writer spent his summer holidays at the resort's house of hedonism, the Grand Hotel, a great, cream mansion which dominates the main square.

Its marbled, pillared hall and chandelier-dripping lounges should be visited even if only for a cup of coffee, while serious gastronomers may head for the hotel's Balbec restaurant looking over the sea, which Proust called "the aquarium".

Proust's association with the place, which is now run by Pullman International Hotels, is further milked in the Marcel Proust suite, where guests are charged a high rate for the privilege. During the season the resort awards an annual Marcel Proust literary prize.

Cabourg, a one-shopping-street town, has fine examples of late 19th- and early 20th-century châteaux-on-sea architecture, incorporating steep gables, slate roofs, tall chimneys and the fanciest finials you can find. But efforts to restore the glamour are under way, including the completely renovated Casino, glittering once again after years of being dulled by sea salt, and flaking in the wind.

Conqueror's port

Behind Cabourg, on the far side of the River Dives, is **Dives-sur-Mer** ❷, which is now *sur terre* with no sign that it ever was a port, let alone the spot where

BELOW: girls on the beach at Deauville.

Map on page 256

William the Conqueror with his barons and prelates and soldiers set sail, via St-Valery-sur-Somme, on 12 September 1066. For a month the fleet of open boats were fitted out in the port, among them *Mora*, Matilda's gift to William. In 1861 Arcisse de Caumont, the well-known archaeologist from Caen, had the names of William's heroic fellow knights inscribed on a plaque and placed in the church of **Notre-Dame**, which was built in thanksgiving by William in 1067.

The history of Dives's large church is familiar on this coast where religious relics were washed ashore with miraculous regularity in the 10th and 11th centuries. Sixty-six years before William arrived a crucifix appeared on the beach and a shrine was made in a chapel under the eye of the abbey at Troarn. It became a centre of pilgrimage until the crucifix was destroyed in 1562 during the Wars of Religion. Today, with flying gargoyles characteristic of the local Gothic churches, it has a tumbledown air, and sparrows call from its fan-vaulted aisles.

Chocolate and crabs

Opposite the church is the Michel Dupont *chocolatier* with a *salon de thé*. The road to the right leads to the old market square and a fine wooden market hall, **Les Halles**. It dates from 155, and was entirely rebuilt after World War II. The square's other old building is the **Lieutenance**, residency of the Duke of Falaise, restored in 1920 when the rest of the buildings in the square were torn down.

A further collection of ancient buildings is the **Village d'Art de Guillaume le Conquérant**, a tourist trap which for three centuries served as the Auberge de l'Epée Royale, the *relais de poste* on the coast road from Rouen to Caen. This coaching inn was renamed in the 19th century, statuary was imported for its courtyards and it is now a pleasant spot to stroll through.

Dives's port today lies around a collection of small fishing boats on the quay beside the river, roped to the wall when the tide goes out. On sale are live pink crabs and grey shrimps and mussels by the litre, freshly caught the previous night.

Houlgate

Within 2 km (1 mile) the River Dives reaches the sea at **Houlgate ❸**. The chemin de la Cascade leads through a pretty little valley of thatched houses topped by irises, pigeon lofts and a watermill. Otherwise, Houlgate is another resort of classic Norman château architecture, of timber balconies, rafters and balustrades, concave roofs, dormers, domes and witches'-hat towers.

The Grand Hotel, a mammoth Second-Empire building in railway-station style (complete with clock) has now been converted into apartments, although the casino on the beach in front of it still operates a bar, cinema and disco.

Villers-sur-Mer

The resort is sited against a hillside, which drops down to the sea over a pile of rocks called **Les Vaches Noires** because they look like a herd of black cows. It is possible to walk over these rocks to the town of **Villers-sur-Mer ❹**, but only, be warned,

at low tide. Otherwise the road climbs back over the hills, reaching a panorama point with a *table d'orientation* that signposts the land visible westwards (Arromanches) and north (Cap de l'Havre).

There have been good fossil finds on this part of the beach, a UNESCO Site of Special Scientific Interest. The **Musée de Paléontologie** (opening times vary, check with tourist office, tel: 02 31 87 01 18), in the Maison des Jeunes, behind the market houses a small collection of them.

This is another family resort, which feels more like a real town. Activity is centred around Mermoz, a popular seafood restaurant on the seafront. The casino is modern, ugly, functional, and open until the small hours every weekend.

Resorts in the hills

Beyond Villers are a couple of resorts tucked into the hills, **Blonville-sur-Mer** and **Bénerville-sur-Mer**. Up behind the latter is **Tourgeville**, in the middle of a short but scenic route. This small town

has a cluster of thatched, half-timbered houses and there is a wonderful view down across the bright lights of Deauville. British and German fallen lie side by side in the cemetery here.

Touques

Although he set sail from Dives, William the Conqueror had his principal residence on this coast near **Touques** ❺ on the parallel river of the same name. Above the port, at **Bonneville**, he had a better command of the coast. There is not much left of the chalk-white walls and towers: just part of the outer wall, the *donjon* and the stumps of five towers. An underground passage leads from the old gate to the river. It is privately owned, with limited opening hours, but even if you can't get in you can enjoy the fine view over the Touques valley.

Touques itself is a plain little town, and many young people move here from the coast because property is cheaper. It has two good churches: **St-Pierre**, from the

LEFT: colourful beach brollies.
BELOW: beach huts named after the stars.

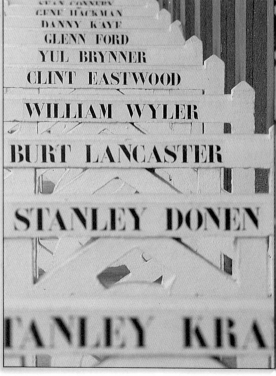

SEAN CONNERY
GENE HACKMAN
DANNY KAYE
GLENN FORD
YUL BRYNNER
CLINT EASTWOOD
WILLIAM WYLER
BURT LANCASTER
STANLEY DONEN
TANLEY KRA

Map
on page
256

11th century and now deconsecrated, and 12th-century **St-Thomas**, named after its founder, the then Archbishop of Canterbury. There is a statue of him with mitre and crosier, but the interior is rather empty and dull. On the short road between here and Trouville is a large pottery making traditional Normandy glazed earthenware.

The high life

The Côte Fleurie's two best-known resorts of Deauville and Trouville lie either side of the Touques estuary; each has a different flavour, which is easy to detect after only a few hours. **Deauville ❻**, with its two marinas, is the showcase: its casino the most glittering, its hotels the most grand, its restaurants and cafés the most expensive, and its racecourse still a great attraction. In Deauville, people are on parade, walking along the famous boardwalk, **Les Planches**, or cruising the streets in their spotless cars. In Trouville real life enters in.

Trouville started it all. The small oyster-fishing village on the estuary of the silted-

up Touques attracted artists in the 1830s, and the fashionable soon followed, as did the habit of bathing and the railway from Paris. On the west bank, under a consortium headed by the Duke de Mornay and advised by Dr Oliffe, the British Ambassador to Paris, the marshes were drained and an entirely new town, Deauville, was put in place. As in contemporary England, where the Prince of Wales took his court and camp followers down to Brighton, so in France Emperor Napoleon III and the Empress Eugénie greatly favoured these ritzy Channel resorts.

Just back from the beach is the **casino** where dinner is expensively served in the pink, knicker-rouched boudoir of **Ciro's** by immaculate, silent waiters. At night the casino's sumptuous halls and spangled chandeliers are a beacon to hedonistic human moths. A government tax is levied for anyone entering the gaming rooms, but there is action to be seen among the one-armed bandits, and in the bar where a roulette wheel spins. Check out, too, the

BELOW:
Deauville
races, the
highlight of
the summer
season.

exquisite little theatre, venue for weekend and summer shows, where champagne can be served at the tables in the gods.

Also worth seeing is the Villa Strassburger, now owned by the town council and preserved in the style of its wealthy late 19th-century American owner, who bought it from Baron Rothschild.

Trouville-sur-Mer

Deauville may be smarter, but geography gives **Trouville** ❼ its trump card. Its liveliest street, boulevard Fernand Mourneaux, which runs beside the river, faces south: when the sun is shining, it shines on it all day. Life can be lived *en plein air* all the year round and many restaurants have gas-heaters beside their pavement tables so that even in January people can sit outside.

Regulars from Deauville will usually cross the Pont des Belges to Trouville when they want to go out to eat. This is the place to have a bowl of *moules frites* at **Les Vapeurs** or the **Central** after the casinos

are closed: as long as there is a light on, the restaurants boast, you will be served.

Activity centres on the **fish market**, built in 1935. It takes place daily, and on Wednesday and Sunday a general market stretches the length of the quay.

Two landmarks are unmissable: the 1912 **Hôtel de Ville** (Town Hall) and the **casino**, at the start of the boardwalk along the shore to the north, towards the aquarium and the yacht club. The older streets and shopping lanes are down around this end of the town.

Among many mansions on the way out to Honfleur, is **Villa Montebello** (1865), which houses the town **museum** (open Apr–Sept, Wed–Mon 2–6pm; admission charge). Paintings by Isabey, Huet and Charles Mozin, the first French painter to come here, show what they saw, and reveal how it has changed.

Though not as grand as its neighbour's, Trouville's 1912 casino is enormous. It contains a water therapy centre, a gala room and conference halls, cinema, restaurant and of course the gaming

BELOW: Trouville's elegant beachside houses.

Map
on page
256

rooms, done out in the style of a Louisiana paddle steamer. And still no more than 10 percent of the building is occupied.

Honfleur

The bright lights fade as you take the rural corniche heading for **Honfleur ❽**. Here there is typical Pays d'Auge country, of cows in buttercup fields beneath old orchard boughs, with the addition of the Channel waters beneath. En route is **Villerville**, a small town that tips down precipitous streets to the sea.

Shortly beyond it is a high spot worth visiting even if you are only in Honfleur for half a day. This is the 17th-century chapel of **Notre-Dame-de-Grâce** (open daylight hours), 1 km (½ mile) from the centre of town, which gave its name to this coast. This is a delightfully idiosyncratic little building, which still attracts pilgrims and votive offerings.

People also come for the view. From this rural setting, in a glade on high ground, there is a grand panorama of Le Havre and the Seine estuary which the **Pont de Normandie** spans impressively. There is also a good view from the terrace of the **Ferme St-Siméon**. It is very expensive to eat here, but should the temptation arise to have a look around the flower-draped buildings and to take coffee on the terrace, it should not be resisted.

Honfleur is, without doubt, the jewel of Normandy's coast. Its maritime credentials are impressive, too: it came to prominence in the Hundred Years' War when Charles V fortified it and installed the Admiral of the Fleet, Jeanne de Vienne, as the town governor.

From 1419 to 1450, when the church of **St-Étienne**, was built, it was occupied by the English. Their departure was celebrated with the construction of the wonderful wooden church of **Ste-Catherine** at the heart of the old town. St-Étienne now houses two museums, the **Musée de la Marine** and the **Musée d'Ethnographie et d'Art Populaire Normand** (open Apr–Jun, Sept, Tues–Sun 10am–noon,

BELOW:
you can see the sights of Honfleur while riding in a calèche.

Map on page 256

2–6pm; Jul–Aug, daily 10am–1pm, 2–6pm; mid-Feb–end Mar, Oct–mid-Nov, Tues–Fri 2–5.30pm, Sat–Sun 10am–noon, 2pm–5.30pm; admission charge). The former has a large collection of model ships and engravings, the latter consists of nine rooms reconstructed and furnished in the traditional Norman style.

Maritime heritage

Among the South Sea island traders and discoverers who set sail from Honfleur, was Samuel de Champlain who founded Quebec, and Rabelais' fictitious giant who went in search of Utopia. Shipbuilding flourished and the surrounding salt marshes gave the town a commodity in which to trade.

Two salt stores with oak roof timbers can be seen in rue de la Ville. These were erected under Louis XIV's chief minister, Jean-Baptiste Colbert, who greatly improved the port, adding the **Vieux Bassin** around which the old town is now centred. The **Lieutenance** on the river side of the dock is the former Caen gate and the only surviving part of the old town wall.

Boudin and Satie

From the old dock and attractive quay with tall, slate-fronted, 16th-century buildings, nothing is hard to find. The **Musée Eugène Boudin** (open mid-Mar–Sept, Wed–Mon 10am–noon, 2–6pm; Oct–mid-Mar, Wed–Mon 2.30–5pm; admission charge), housed in the chapel of a former convent, is essential. It contains a fine collection of paintings, including Corots and Monets, and a number by Boudin himself.

The town has many plaques commemorating the famous, among them the composer Erik Satie, born in rue Haute in 1866, who has his own museum, **Maison Satie** (open May–Sept, Wed–Mon 10am–7pm; mid-Feb–Mar, Oct–Dec, Wed–Mon 10.30am–6pm; admission charge). This is an unusual place in which, clad in high-tech, infra-red helmets, visitors are guided from room to room by Satie's music. ❑

RIGHT: boats are blessed in Honfleur on Ascension Sunday.

CAMEMBERT AND CALVADOS COUNTRY

A gentle journey through valleys, hills and orchards where you can taste some of the region's best-known products and visit some splendid châteaux and religious buildings en route

Map on page 256

B etween the Caen Plain and the lower Seine is a secretive land, hidden among hills, valleys and forests. It is a rich countryside of old orchards and dappled cows, of manor houses and châteaux and half-timbered farms.

It is also the heart of the production area of Normandy's three particular delights – cider, Calvados and cheese. To help you find your way around the country lanes to the places where local drinks can be sampled and bought, the local authorities have mapped out a *Route du Cidre*.

Joining two regions

Two rather separate regions, based on the main stretches of two parallel rivers, are included in this chapter. To the east is the **River Risle** which flows through the *département* of the Eure in a broad valley of meadowlands. Its two largest towns are Pont-Audemer and, on a tributary further inland, Bernay. Both make good bases for touring.

To the west, in the Calvados *département*, the distinctive **Pays d'Auge** region is centred on Lisieux and riven by the Touques which flows into the sea between Deauville and Trouville. Rural *gîtes* and *chambres d'hôtes* are seldom far away.

Calvados country

Between Lisieux and the sea, where the A13 autoroute whistles from Rouen to Caen, is **Pont-l'Évêque** ❾ which gives its name to one of three Pays d'Auge cheeses, a square, soft cheese with a full flavour. The town was badly damaged during World War II, but some old houses remain on the busy main street, rue St-Michel and its continuation, rue de Vaucelles. Its grand church, St-Michel, has been well restored and has dramatic and effective modern stained-glass windows.

On the N177 just north of town is the distillery and museum of **Père Magloire Calvados** (open daily 10am–noon, 2–6pm; admission charge), where you can discover all there is to know about apple brandy and its associated crafts during regular 45-minute tours, which include a film show. There is also a model of the *El Calvador*, the Spanish galleon washed ashore in 1588 which gave its name to the *département* and the drink.

Just beyond the museum, at **Canapville**, is the **Manoir des Évêques** (open Mon–Sun by appointment only; tel: 02 31 65 24 75; admission charge), which until recently was thought to have been one of

PRECEDING PAGES: Manoir des Évêques at Canapville.
LEFT: bishop's head carved on the manor's door.
RIGHT: dairy herds are well cared for.

the original homes of the bishops (*évêques*) of Lisieux. It is certainly grand enough. The guided afternoon visits in summer take visitors around its two 15th-century half-timbered buildings and 13th-century core.

To the south of Pont-l'Évêque on the same road, opposite a leisure lake, is the imposing Château de Betteville and in an ancient barn beside it is the **Musée de la Belle Époque de l'Automobile** (open Easter–11 Nov, daily 10am–12.30pm, 1.30–7pm; admission charge). Among a collection of 100 cars is a stunning blue-and-black Bugatti Petite Royale from 1932 which must have wowed people on the seafront at Deauville.

Hills of the Pay d'Auge

The next turning south on the right, the D580, leads up into the hills of the Pays d'Auge at **Pierrefitte-en-Auge**. This village is approached through a collection of old farm buildings leading to a little bistro, Les Deux Tourneux. Its church has excellent 17th-century paintings.

Next on the D580 is **St-Hymer**, made up of only a handful of buildings including a pleasant restaurant and a huge abbey church. There is still a retreat in the

Map on page 256

grounds of the abbey, which dates back to 1067 when it was a dependent of Bec-Hellouin. In the early 18th century it became a centre of Jansenism, a severe discipline which was outlawed in Paris by Louis XIV.

Rather than submit to Jansenism, the abbey at **Beaumont-en-Auge** ⑩ just to the northwest, gave itself over to a military academy. Among its pupils was Pierre Simon, a local farmer's son, who became one of France's most distinguished astronomers and scientists, president of the French Academy and Marquis de Laplace (1749–1827). A plaque marks his birthplace in place du Verdun.

Picturesque villages

Ten kilometres (7 miles) west on the N175 is the roadside town of **Dozulé** and just beyond it the D49 picks up the Route du Marais, through marshlands that slip down to the sea. Turn left to **Putot-en-Auge**; it has a small church with a fine Romanesque portal and a graveyard for Allied soldiers who did not live long after D-Day.

About 5km (3 miles) to the south is **Beuvron-en-Auge**, the most touristy place in the Pays d'Auge. This pretty village, centred around an intimate oval *place*, has a collection of pristine, half-timbered buildings that house restaurants and shops selling gifts and local produce.

Above it, at **Clermont-en-Auge**, park the car and walk down to the delightful little chapel founded in the 11th century and containing a fine 15th-century wood crucifix. From here, 100 metres (325 ft) up, there is a view over the Touques Valley, and across the Caen Plain.

Famous connections

From Beuvron-en-Auge you can follow the well-signed **Route du Cidre** (Cider Route), which wanders happily through some of the most attractive scenery in the Pays d'Auge. It passes a number of manors and châteaux, most of which are private and remain closed: **Val de Richer**, home of the great 19th-century statesman François Guizot, built on the Val de Richer abbey where Thomas Becket was first abbot; **lLa Roque Beynard** where

André Gide was mayor; **Manoir du Champ Versant** at Bonnebosq, now a *gîte*, occasionally open to the public.

A score of farms in this area have a signpost outside advertising Cru de Cambremer, where cider and Calvados can be sampled and bought, and a tour is offered.

Cambremer

Cambremer ⑪, in unbelievably beautiful countryside, claims particular importance for it is to this small town, in May each year, that producers bring their cider, Calvados, and *pommeau* (a sherry-strength apéritif made of Calvados and apple juice) to an old barn for tasting. Those that make the grade are accorded a sign outside their establishments. Pays d'Auge *appellation contrôlée* Calvados differs from other Normandy Calvados in that it is made by a double distillation process, rather than by single, continuous distillation. A good place to see the huge copper stills in action, and to taste the final product, is **Calvados Pierre Huet** (Manoir la Brière

Ste Thérèse of Lisieux

A round 100,000 pilgrims a year climb a hill in Lisieux to the basilica of Ste-Thérèse of the Child Jesus. As a place of pilgrimage, it ranks second in France only to Lourdes, with which it shares not only a reputation for working miracles but also a degree of commercialisation.

Ste Thérèse was born in Alençon on 2 January 1873 as Marie-Françoise-Thérèse Martin, the daughter of Louis Martin, a successful watchmaker, and Zelie Guerin, who married after each had been turned down for conventual life. M. Martin informed his bride on their wedding night that he did not intend then or ever to consummate the union, but resolve weakened and the couple in due course had nine children, of whom Thérèse was the youngest. "Nine flowers bloomed in this garden," wrote one of her biographers in the kind of prose characteristic of everything written about Thérèse, "of which four were transplanted to Paradise before their buds had quite unfolded."

The survival of the frail infant Thérèse is the first of the many miracles associated with her. Her mother died when she was four, and the family moved to Lisieux to a house called Les Buissonnets (The Shrubbery). It was an exceptionally pious household. Thérèse had her own altar, where she prayed daily, and the first word she recognised in print was "heaven", probably because when the family circle read together, the text was either the *Lives of the Saints* or the *Liturgical Year*.

Outings with her father were visits to the Blessed Sacrament in various churches, especially the chapel of the Convent of the Carmel. At nine, Thérèse again nearly died, but a vision of Our Lady smiling at the young girl effected an immediate and complete cure. She then wished to enter the convent as a postulant, only to be told she was much too young.

A larger-than-life marble group in the garden at Les Buissonnets immortalises the day in 1887 when Thérèse, then 13, won her father's backing for what had been a ceaseless but till then unproductive campaign to enter the Carmel convent before she was 16. He took her on a pilgrimage to Rome, where Pope Leo XIII told her: "You will enter if God wills it." Thérèse accordingly entered the convent as Thérèse de l'Enfant Jesus on 9 April 1888. She was 15. In the normal course of events, the world would have heard no more of Thérèse after the convent gates closed behind her. The happenstance destined to bring millions of pilgrims to Lisieux was an order by the Mother Superior that she try her hand at writing. The result was her *Story of a Soul*, subtitled *The Springtide Story of a Little White Flower*.

The autobiography strikes a universal chord, despite its relentless diminutives – the "little" flower, the "little ball for the Child Jesus to play with", and so on. Her most famous passage is fusion with Jesus in the form of a wedding invitation.

Racked by consumption, Thérèse died at the age of 25. Normandy led a canonisation campaign which came to fruition in 1925. In 1997 she was again honoured by being made a Doctor of the Church by Pope John-Paul II. ❏

LEFT: Ste Thérèse, canonised in 1925.

Map on page 256

des Fontaines, Cambremer; open daily for sales except Sun pm in season and Sat out of season; tel 02 31 63 01 09), where you can also buy cider and *pommeau*, as well as home-made jams and jellies.

An alternative is **Espace Boulard** at **Coquainvilliers** (open by appointment, tel: 02 31 48 24 01) on the D48 on the eastern side of the Cider Route .

South of Cambremer the road falls away to **Crèvecoeur** ⑫ where **Le Château de Crèvecoeur** consists of old buildings, including a fine pigeon loft, assembled by the Schlumberger brothers from Alsace. They were successful mining engineers and there is an exhibition of their work, as well as a flock of black mop-headed Crève-coeur chickens saved from extinction.

Pilgrims' rest

Some 17 km (10 miles) due east of Crève-coeur is **Lisieux** ⑬, a former Roman provincial capital and the main town of the region, with a population of 26,000. Beside the old Episcopal Palace is the fine former cathedral of **St-Pierre**, the earliest Gothic church in Normandy. During the war, the town, a German base, was flattened.

Signs of its former architectural attractiveness are few, but some can be seen in the **Musée d'Art et d'Histoire** (open Wed–Mon 2–6pm; admission charge), at 38 boulevard Louis Pasteur, on the opposite bank of the Touques where several timber-framed houses remain.

The main reason many people come here today is to trace the story and see the shrine of Ste Thérèse *(see facing page)*. A tape in various languages guides visitors through the rooms of her middle-class home, **Les Buissonnets**, and a room of memorabilia can be visited beside the **Carmelite convent** where she lived from the age of 15 until her death at 25 in 1897.

Above and beyond these, and quite unmissable is the vast **Basilique Ste-Thérèse** (open daily 9am–6pm; free), topping 93 metres (305 ft) and reminiscent of Paris's Sacré Coeur. It was begun a year after her canonisation in 1925 and

BELOW: monks outside the Basilique Ste-Thérèse.

completed in 1954. The neo-Byzantine interior is aesthetically valueless, but it attracts thousands of pilgrims.

Moated manors

From Lisieux the D64 through the Touques valley provides a picturesque route south towards Vimoutiers, through peaceful pastoral countryside typical of the region. Overlooking the valley, on the D579 5 miles (8km) south of Lisieux, is the **Château de St-Germain-de-Livet** ⓮ (open Apr–Sept, Wed–Mon 10am–noon, 2–7pm; Oct–Nov, Feb–Mar 10am–noon, 2–5pm; admission charge).

This delightful moated manor with chequerboard walls dates from the 15th century. Guided tours begin in the guard room, which has 16th-century wall paintings and continues to the first floor where there are typical Pays d'Auge tiles.

To the west of the D579 is **Coupesarte**, a beautiful timbered and moated manor farm. It is privately owned; the grounds are open to the public on special days.

A few kilometres beyond, near the Aga Khan's stud farm at St-Crespin, is the grand 16th-century **Grandchamp-le-Château** (not open to the public). Just outside the modern little town of Mézidon-Canon, 15 km (10 miles) west on the D47, is the **Château de Canon**, approached down an avenue of lime trees. The château's magnificent gardens are laid out with an ornamental pool, statuary and various follies. Outdoor events, including "nature weekends", are staged during the summer.

The largest hall of all

The main town on this western side of the Auge is **St-Pierre-sur-Dives** ⓯, to the south. It is a market town that has France's largest medieval hall (Les Halles). Built in the 11th century it measures 85 metres (280 ft) long and 21 metres (70 ft) wide. People travel from miles around to visit the vast Monday market, when, in addition to the small local producers in the old hall, there are countless stalls spread over acres of adjacent wasteland.

BELOW: calvados distillery in Pont-l'Évêque.

Map on page 256

The hall was built in the 13th century by monks of the **Abbaye de St-Pierre-sur-Dives**, whose church, consecrated under William the Conqueror, survives to dominate the town. Crossing its nave is a sundial rod with zodiac signs embedded in the floor.

The best way to see its cloisters and part of the former abbey is to visit the **Musée du Conservatoire des Techniques Fromagères Traditionnelles de Normandie** (open May–Oct, daily 9am–noon, 2–6pm; Nov–Apr, Tues–Fri 9am–noon, 2–6pm, Sat and Mon 9am–noon; admission charge), in the adjacent convent building. Though not the best cheese museum, it gives a picture of the local business in which St-Pierre plays its part.

Churches and miniatures

BELOW:
tiny objects
in the Musée
du Mobilier
Miniature.

Before seeking out the cheeses, make a brief detour 12 km (8 miles) south down the D90 past **Barou-en-Auge** and **Norrey-en-Auge**. The sandstone farms in this part of the Auge take on a creamy, golden, colour. At Barou-en-Auge the church has lost half its nave, and a side chapel has a primitive black skull-and-crossbone frieze.

The church at Norrey-en-Auge is also primitive, with wall paintings in need of restoration. The *opus spicatum* (herring-bone stone-work pattern dates the church to around the 10th century.

Just beyond the D90 turning to these churches is **Vendeuvre** where the chateau houses the **Musée du Mobilier Miniature** (open May–Sept, daily 10am–6pm; admission charge). The miniature pieces of furniture in this fascinating collection are models made by craftsmen prior to building the real things. The collection is usually a big hit with children, who will also enjoy the water gardens.

Cheese greats

Livarot ⑯, a sleepy, rather run-down town, has a **Musée du Fromage** (open Apr–Oct, Mon–Sun, 10am–noon, 2–6pm; Nov–Mar, Tues–Sat 2–5pm; admission charge) in a small château on the west side

of the town where the traditional way of making this circular, pink-crusted local treat is explained in great detail.

Heading south along the D579, you reach Ste-Foy-de-Montgommery where Field-Marshal Rommel was driving in June 1944 when he was caught by aircraft fire, and can make a short diversion east to **Lisores**, a hamlet put on the map by Fernand Léger (1881–1955). The Cubist painter of bright solid shapes was born nearby in Argentan. He had an isolated farm down a lane from Lisores; in a barn with an outside wall showing one of his pictures in coloured tiles is an exhibition of his work.

Vimoutiers , a short distance further south, was virtually destroyed in 1944 and is essentially a modern town. It has set itself up as the capital of one of France's most famous cheeses, Camembert, though the village of Camembert itself lies just to the southwest. The town has the best cheese museum in the region, the **Musée du Camembert** (open May–Oct daily 9am–noon, 2–6pm; Nov–Apr, Tues–Fri 9am–noon, 2–6pm, Sat, Mon 9am–noon; admission charge), and a statue of farmer's wife Marie Harell, credited as having brought this cheese to the attention of a grateful world after getting the recipe from a priest from Brie whom she sheltered during the Revolution.

Marie Harel worked on a farm, the Manoir de Beaumoncel, overlooking **Camembert**, a pretty hamlet some 6 km (4 miles) southwest of Vimoutiers. The small Camembert museum here is a disappointment, and is overshadowed by the newer and larger-scale **Ferme Président** (open daily; tel: 02 33 36 06 60; admission fee) which covers the history and production of the cheese in a much more engaging way, and offers tastings, too.

The Camembert *appellation* is now strictly controlled and the only farm in Camembert still making the cheese by the traditional method fails to qualify. But it is worth seeking out the farm of François Durand (Ferme de la Heronnière, tel: 02 33 39 08 08), a mile or so west along the D246. The shop is open most of the day and tours of the production process are available Monday to Saturday, at 3.30pm.

The Risle Valley

The solitude of the countryside continues over to the east, in truly rural towns such as **Orbec** , one of the more attractive Pays d'Auge towns. The exemplary Norman Renaissance **Vieux-Manoir** in the main street has 1563 carved on a lintel. On the right, heading towards the gigantic 16th-century north tower of the church of **Notre-Dame**, where bright dragons grip the nave's hammer beams in their teeth, is the stone façade of the 17th-century **Hôtel de Croissy** where Claude Debussy composed *Jardin sous la Pluie* in 1895.

Eighteen kilometres (11 miles) northeast of Orbec, is **Bernay** , a small town that seems full of bustle, with its lively cafés and bars. Rue Gaston-Follope is a street of old timbered buildings, antiques shops and the small **Musée Normand** (open Wed–Mon 10am–noon, 2–5.30pm; admission charge). Bernay's abbey church was begun by Guglielmo da Volpiano in

LEFT: external exhibit at the Léger exhibition in Lisores.

Map on page 256

1013, but more lively is Ste-Croix, dating from the 14th century and containing statues and tombstones from Bec-Hellouin, a sign that the great abbey is within reach.

The D133 follows the Charentonne, a tributary of the Risle, and crosses the Risle at Beaumont-le-Roger. From the edges of the Forêt de Beaumont, the D133 continues east, rising onto the fertile plain of **Le Neubourg**. The town of that name is an airy place with a wide main street.

Field of battle

Just outside it is **Château du Champ-de-Bataille ㉑** (open daily by appointment; tel: 02 32 34 84 34; admission charge), a curious place. The battle it commemorates was between Rollo and a rival Norman, who slugged it out for supremacy over these lands. It was not until after World War II that the 17th-century château was given to the Harcourt family, descendants of one of Rollo's knights, in recompense for their Thury-Harcourt home, destroyed in the war. Today it is owned by a successful interior

designer who has filled it with antiques and spent a large sum restoring the place.

Château Harcourt

The Harcourts did have another ancestral pile nearby, **Château Harcourt ㉑** (open Mar–mid-Nov, Wed–Mon 10am–6pm; admission charge), built by Robert II of Harcourt in the late 11th century and in family hands until it was taken over by the French Agricultural Academy in 1828. With half-hearted displays of flora and fauna, it is a mix of institutional poverty and feudal grandeur, emanating from the medieval flavour of its 20-metre (66-ft) wide moat and fortified walls. There is also a large **arboretum**, with 200 species, mainly conifers, from around the world.

Bec-Hellouin

From Harcourt it is just 6 km (4 miles) up the D137 to **Brionne**. This small town has statuary from Bec-Hellouin in its otherwise plain church and a large Sunday market beside it. Above the town is a fine,

BELOW: the Camembert museum in Vimoutiers.
RIGHT: growing up fit and strong.

Map on page 256

square 11th-century keep; it was while besieging the duke of Burgundy here in 1047 that William the Conqueror came in contact with Bec-Hellouin and its Italian abbot Lanfranc, who was to become such a help to him in later life.

The **Abbaye du Bec-Hellouin** ㉒ (guided tours, tel: 02 32 44 86 09; admission charge), lies 6 km (4 miles) north, in the small flat valley of the Bec. Tours are conducted by urbane and witty white-robed monks. All that remains of the original building destroyed after the Revolution is the belfry of St Nicolas. The tomb of Hellouin, the knight who founded the abbey in 1034, is in the centre of the newer church which has taken over the 17th-century refectory.

The attractive village beside the abbey centres on a small green and a church brimming with statuary the abbey lacks. From Bec, the D137 crosses the Risle and heads for the wooded hills and **St-Georges-du-Vièvre** 9 km (5 miles) distant. Just before it, on the left-hand side, is the **Château du Launay**. It is privately owned, but a walk in the grounds is rewarded by the sight of one of the most imaginatively carved dovecotes in Normandy.

Pont-Audemer

The D130 now follows the Risle through **Montfort-sur-Risle**, squeezed under a cliff beside a ruined 13th-century castle, before crossing to **Pont-Audemer** ㉓ on the left bank. This is a lively place, with half-timbered houses looking especially attractive beside a bridge over a backwater of the Risle at the southern end of the rue de la République. This main street also has the unfinished façade of St-Ouen, a church with Renaissance stained-glass windows.

The town's grandest hotel-restaurant is the half-timbered **Auberge de Vieux Puits**, but there are also inexpensive places, making it a good base for the Pays d'Auge, the Parc Regional de Brotonne, and for Honfleur and the pricy Côte Fleurie.   ❑

RIGHT: a scene of tranquillity – the moated manor farm of Coupesarte.

Map on page 256

HILLS AND PLATEAUX OF THE EURE

The character of Normandy changes in the Eure region. It's worth getting off the beaten track to discover hilltop villages, giant dovecotes and some splendid Romanesque architecture

The landscape of the Eure is not what one expects of Normandy. Instead of small meadows, hedges, orchards, sunken roads, woods and glades, there are vast fields of cereal crops stretching in all directions to the horizon, only occasionally interrupted by a copse of trees or farm buildings. Driving along the main roads through the *département* is a bit monotonous, but anyone prepared to wander away from the beaten track will soon discover there is much to be enjoyed.

Departmental capital

Évreux ❷ is the capital of the Eure *département*. It is an attractive city, in spite of having suffered frequent fires and violent destruction from the 5th century, when the Vandals sacked the old Roman town, up to World War II when German and Allied air raids razed many buildings.

Standing high amid the modern buildings, however, the **Cathédrale Notre-Dame** (open daily 8am–noon, 2–7pm) is the city's pride and joy. Founded in the 6th century, it was rebuilt in the 12th century and again in the 13th and has been restored several times since, giving the building a rich mixture of styles. Especially worth seeing are the stained-glass windows, the carved wooden screens of the side chapels and the intricately sculpted north porch.

Next to the cathedral **L'Ancien Évêché**, the former bishop's palace, built in 16th-century Renaissance style, houses the **Musée Municipal** (open Tues–Sun 10am–noon, 2–6pm; admission charge), which has a particularly fine archaeological room incorporating part of the town's Gallo-Roman ramparts as one of its walls. Among the exhibits can be found Paleolithic jewellery, Roman bronzes of Jupiter and Apollo, medieval tombs, Aubusson tapestries, Nevers and Rouen china, and 17th to 18th-century paintings.

Often passed unnoticed because of the draw of the cathedral, **Église St-Taurin** is another church worth seeking out. Just off rue Josephine, it is part Romanesque, part Renaissance, and houses the magnificent shrine of Évreux's first bishop, St Taurinus, a 13th-century masterpiece.

Friendly bells

Contributing to the pleasures of the city is the River Iton which winds past the cathedral. A riverside walk which follows the old ramparts, and is named after Robert de Flocques, who liberated Évreux

PRECEDING PAGES: haymaking at Beaumesnil.
LEFT: Évreux's cathedral.
RIGHT: the golden shrine in St-Taurin.

from the English in 1441, ends up at a colourful floral square, la place Général-de-Gaulle. Here you'll find an ensemble comprising the splendid Hôtel de Ville, an Italianate theatre and the **Tour de l'Horloge**. The latter, an elegant tower built in the 1490s, has a two-tonne bell known as La Louyse.

Some 13 km (8 miles) east of Évreux, the river that gives the Eure *département* its name flows parallel with the Seine for a while before joining it near **Louviers**. Like the other rivers of the *département*, it has some outstanding stretches.

Pacy and Cocherel

One such stretch can be found 8 km (5 miles) northwest of **Pacy-sur-Eure** at **Cocherel**, a pretty, straggling village of half-timbered houses beside the tree-shaded river, and the site of a famous battle in 1365, early in the Hundred Years' War when the brilliant, brutal Bertrand du Guesclin defeated the combined forces of England and Navarre.

Aristide Briand, several times premier of France between 1909 and 1929, lived in Cocherel for some years before his death in 1932 and is buried in the village churchyard. There is a fine statue of him in an ivy-draped alcove near the river. Close by, a memorial marks the spot where 15 French soldiers were killed in June 1940 attempting to defend a bridge.

Pacy, too, has a statue of Briand. He became known as the "apostle of peace" and won the Nobel Peace Prize in 1926 in recognition of his efforts to bring about Franco-German reconciliation.

Embattled town

Ivry-la-Bataille ㉕, 17 km (10 miles) south of Pacy on the D836, gets its name from a battle in 1590, when Henri IV defeated the forces of the Catholic League. The site is marked by an obelisk, erected in 1804 near the village of **Epieds**.

Ivry itself is a quiet place that has taken to heart its link with the victorious king. In rue Henri IV you will find the Patisserie

BELOW: the imposing rooftops of a half-timbered château in Louviers.

Map
on page
256

Henri lV as well as the Hostellerie du Roi Henri lV, while in a fine old half-timbered building at 5 rue de Garennes stands the Boucherie Henri lV. The latter probably has the most legitimate claim to the name, since Henri is supposed to have lodged at the house at the time of the battle.

Though on the wrong side of Normandy's border, the **Château Anet**  (open Apr–Oct, Mon–Sat 2.30–6.30pm, Sun 10–11.30am, 2.30–6.30pm; Nov–Mar, weekends only; admission charge), just south of Ivry, should not be passed by. Built by the beautiful Diane of Poitiers, who bewitched Henri II, it was in its day the most lavish Renaissance palace in all France and enough of it remains to give an idea of those gilded days.

Valley towns

Along the Avre Valley west of Dreux, three fortified towns, Nonacourt, Tillières and Verneuil-sur-Avre, built by Henry I of England as a line of defence between Normandy and France, saw a great deal of bloody action towards the end of the Hundred Years' War.

Of the three **Tillières** is the least interesting, but **Nonancourt** has a number of well-restored half-timbered houses around the Place Aristide Briand, including one housing the tourist office that leans so much it seems on the verge of falling over. Around the church, some of the alleys have a medieval flavour.

Verneuil-sur-Avre

Verneuil-sur-Avre ㉗ has the most appeal of the trio, and it is a good place to stay, too, with a fine selection of hotels and shops. The place de la Madeleine is its centre, the giant tiered and multi-styled tower of the **Église Ste-Madeleine** (open May–Sept, daily 9am–7pm; Oct–Mar 9am–5pm) casting a long shadow over the square. There is some superb stained glass, and a larger-than-life nativity.

The 12th-century Romanesque church of **Notre-Dame** (open May–Sept, daily 9am–7pm; Oct–Mar 9am–5pm) is also

BELOW: the tomb of Diane of Poitiers.
RIGHT: figures on the façade of St-Madeleine.

worth seeing for its remarkable collection of 16th-century statues, the work of local sculptors. This church is built of *grison*, a distinctive red agglomerate stone found in the area. Part of the town's fortifications are made of this material, notably the **Tour Grise**. Alongside stands a section of the old wall; behind, a pretty, half-timbered house looks across the Avre to the delightful **Parc André Fourgère**.

Preserving the past

The town's ancient houses have been lovingly restored, especially the 15th- and 16th-century buildings distinguished by chequered walls and corner turrets in the rue de la Madeleine and rue Notre-Dame and the 18th-century Bournonville Hotel, an aristocratic townhouse.

Verneuil also has one of the few abbeys to have survived on its original site, the **Abbaye St-Nicolas** (chapel only open daily 10.30–11.30am, 3–4.30pm). Gregorian chant is still used in some of the services (tel: 02 32 32 02 94 for details).

Stolen relics

Breteuil ㉘, 12 km (8 miles) north of Verneuil, has some pretty little waterways and an unusual Hôtel de Ville in the place Lafitte, built in ornate Gothic style but on a strangely small scale. There are a number of half-timbered houses round the square, but more impressive is the church with its 12 massive red *grison* pillars in the nave and decorated panel ceiling.

Conches-en-Ouche ㉙, another 12 km (8 miles) north, was founded in the 11th century and given its name by Roger de Tosny, who stole some relics of Ste Foy from Conques, a holy place in Aquitaine on the pilgrim route from Le Puy to Santiago de Compostela in Spain. Hence the three *coquilles St-Jacques* (symbols of the pilgrims) in the town's coat-of-arms.

Standing on a hill almost enclosed by the River Rouloir, Conches proved a valuable defensive site, especially in the 15th-century Hundred Years' War when it was occupied on two occasions by the English. Its castle was finally dismantled

BELOW: a Percheron dray horse.

Map on page 256

in 1591, but its ruined keep, overgrown with greenery, remains an attractive sight.

The **Église St-Foy**, dedicated to the saint, originated in the 11th century but was almost entirely rebuilt 500 years later. The 16th-century stained-glass windows, depicting the lives of Christ, the Virgin and Ste-Foy, are remarkable.

On Saturdays in July and August there are guided walking tours of the town-starting at 10.30am (tel: 02 32 30 76 42 for details).

Northwest of Conche-en-Ouche, towards Bernay (*see page 262*), is the **Château de Beaumesnil** ㉚ (open Easter–Sept, Wed–Mon 10am–noon, 2–6pm; admission charge), built in 1640 with a fine baroque façade. The garden, which was laid out by 17th-century landscape designer, André Le Nôtre, can be enjoyed even when the building is closed.

The rugged Perche

To the southwest of Breteuil lies a part of the Orne *département* called the **Perche**, a rugged area of wooded hills and valleys in marked contrast to the gentle scenery of the southern Eure. **L'Aigle** ㉛, 23 km (15 miles) west of Verneuil, is the gateway to the region as well as serving as its main market centre.

L'Aigle has the largest market in Normandy (the third largest in France) and every Tuesday morning farmers descend on the town to trade their livestock. There's a general market too, which centres on the huge place Boislandry and spills through several streets linking the place St-Martin and the place de la Halle, where the Renaissance café is a reminder of *belle époque* society life.

Overlooking a section of the market, the impressive **Hôtel de Ville** was formerly a château, built in 1690. Inside, there's an interesting **museum** (open Mon–Fri 9am–noon, 2.30–5pm; free) of musical instruments. In an outbuilding which also houses the tourist office, another museum uses wax figures and recorded voices to illustrate the Battle of Normandy.

BELOW: village children.

Horses and sausages

The Perche itself is a beautiful part of Normandy, yet feels separate from it. Its largest town is **Mortagne-au-Perche** ㉜, famous as the home of the Percheron horse and for its black pudding fair, which is held every year in March. Over a weekend, 5 km (3 miles) of sausage are sold.

The Percheron, a strong beast bred to carry knights in armour and now subject to renewed interest among Japanese horse breeders, is commemorated in statue form in the public gardens. The horse carries Cupid, who in turn carries Neptune's trident and the goddess Ceres, and symbolises Neptune's love for Ceres, as a result of which the two become horses.

During the 17th century, many people from the Perche emigrated to Canada; one of them, Pierre Boucher, the "patriarch" of French Canada, came from Mortagne. A stained-glass window in Notre-Dame church recalls his exploits.

At **Tourouvre**, 8 km (5 miles) to the northeast, is the **Musée de l'Émigration**

Percheronne au Canada (open Jun–Sept, Tues–Sun 9am–noon, 2–5pm; admission charge), which explains how 250 emigrants from the region are responsible for 1.5 million descendants today.

Behind the church can be seen the remains of Mortagne's former fortifications, the **Porte St-Denis**, originating from the 15th century. Alongside, the 17th-century, turreted Maison des Comtes du Perche is set around an inner courtyard.

Hilltop towns of the Perche

Sixteen kilometres (10 miles) south is **Bellême** ㉝, regarded as the capital of the Perche, though visitors may wonder why this quiet hilltop town is preferred to Mortagne. Like Mortagne it was once walled but all that remains is a gateway flanked by towers. The church, dating from the late 17th century, has an ornate interior, especially the baptismal font. More recently, the town has become known for its golf course.

Elsewhere in the Perche, the communities are much smaller, villages and occasional manor houses hidden among the folds of the hills and between the forests. Few of the manor houses are open to the public, but several of them, with their turrets and towers, add a touch of the medieval to the general scene.

Among the villages, **Longny-au-Perche**, lying in the Jambée Valley, is noted mainly for its pretty Notre-Dame de Pitié chapel on the hill above. West of Bellême, **La Perrière** ㉞, a hilltop village with some fine old buildings, has one of the best views in the whole of the Perche and an interesting exhibition on lace and textiles in the **Maison du Filet** (open Apr–Sept, Wed–Mon 2.30–6pm; admission charge).

The **Abbaye de la Trappe** is located at the edge of the Perche forest, a lovely area of lakes, some of which are equipped for boating and family activities. The Trappist order was founded here in 1664. The monastery can't be visited but the monks have a shop selling produce from various French abbeys. To show that this strict, silent order is geared to the modern world, credit cards are accepted. ❑

Map on page 256

LEFT: a fountain outside the Abbaye de la Trappe.

Dovecotes

According to an old joke, the fertility of the Norman soil comes from the *fieffe*, the droppings of the pigeons flying over the countryside. Pigeons have had an important part to play in both the diet and the architecture of Normandy. The attractive *colombiers*, grain silo-sized dovecotes they were kept in, are still evident all over the region. Some were so grand that decrees were passed and duels fought to preserve the status and privileges they conferred.

Pigeon-rearing started as a quest for a more varied diet in winter, and in the Middle Ages it was fashionable to eat both their flesh and their eggs. But by the early 16th century the economic rewards for selling the droppings became so great that the landed gentry worked to exclude all but themselves from being enriched. In 1583 a royal decree was issued to regulate the number that could be owned and authorising punishment for anyone not returning a ringed pigeon and for anyone caught eating a bird that was not their own. Pigeons became such a valuable source of income that pairs were used to settle debts and given as wedding presents. Racing pigeons were introduced and fast birds fetched high prices. Dovecotes became increasingly valued works of art.

There were two kinds of dovecotes, the *colombier à pied,* a single-purpose building which the wealthier preferred, and the *colombier bi-fonctionnel* where the ground floor might be used as a stable, while the middle level was used for poultry and pigeons were kept at the top. Their height would depend on the wealth of the owner, and they rose to around 18 metres (60 ft). They could be square, polygonal or round and were built in the variety of materials that Normandy has to offer, with roofs originally made of thatch.

Although their materials and exterior shapes differed, they all followed a similar design. The roof was conical or pepperpot shaped, topped with a *lanteron,* a small opening for the birds to enter or leave. One or two *lucarnes* (dormer windows) gave air and additional access. Other small openings were strategically placed in the walls to match the building's design. Families' coats of arms decorated the doors and a stone ledge, known as the "rat bar" encircled the building about a third of the way up the outside wall to keep out rodents.

Interior walls were filled with *boulins*, small niches for nests made of brick or clay. A rotating pole set in a stone base in the centre of the building formed the pivot for the revolving ladders which were used for keeping an eye on the nests. To gather eggs, a keeper would climb the ladder, check the *boulins*, climb down again, move the ladder round, and go up once more, and so on all the way round.

Like many fine buildings, a number of Norman dovecotes were destroyed in the Revolution of 1789, as they were viewed as an aristocratic excess. But the Revolution also decreed that pigeon-owning should henceforth be available to everyone. It is still possible to see the old dovecotes. Two *Routes de Colombiers* are offered by the Seine Maritime and Eure tourist boards, but be warned that the excellent brochures are not followed up with road signs to help visitors on the maze of country roads. ❑

RIGHT:
Renaissance-style dovecote.

Map
on page
290

ORNE

*The National Stud is the pride of the Orne, but the region also has
several splendid châteaux, a lace-making centre, a spa and
lots of opportunities for varied outdoor activities*

The Orne is the only *département* in Normandy not to have a seaboard, but it makes up for this deficiency by having a greater share of delightful wooded valleys and lush green hills. The fact that it lacks a Mont-St-Michel or a Rouen or a Bayeux Tapestry to draw in the visitors does not appear to worry it much, and in recent years it has been making the most of its wonderful potential to attract those who prefer to expend energy on sports.

Lace centre

The *département* has no great cities, but its largest town and capital, **Alençon ❶**, was once capital of all Normandy. The dukes' castle, built in the 14th and 15th centuries and dominated by a crowned tower, is now a prison. The town survived World War II remarkably well. After its liberation General Leclerc established his headquarters here beside the River Sarthe, in what is now the **Musée de la Dentelle** (Lace Museum) (open Mon–Sat 10am– noon, 2–6pm; admission charge).

Alençon is famous for its lacework, which became renowned throughout Europe in the mid-17th century, after Louis XlV's chief minister Jean-Baptiste Colbert established a lace-making centre specialising in Venetian-style needle-point (*see page 285*). In great demand, it became known as both the "queen of lace" and the "lace of queens".

There is another lace collection in the **Musée des Beaux Arts et de la Dentelle** (open Tues–Sun 10am–noon, 2–6pm; admission charge), alongside paintings by French artists and a display of Cambodian curios collected by Adhemard Leclère, governor of the former French protectorate in the early 20th century.

Alençon's centre, lively during the day, is a delight to wander around. The impressive church of **Notre-Dame**, dom-inating the semi-pedestrianised Grande Rue, has a particularly fine porch, its delicate tracery a match for any of the lace produced in the town. Most notable among Alençon's many old houses are the 15th-century **Maison d'Ozé** next to the church and the birthplace of Ste Thérèse of Lisieux, opposite the 17th-century prefecture in rue St-Blaise.

Fine countryside

Hard against Normandy's southern border, Alençon lies amid some very fine countryside. A 10-minute drive to the southwest is one of Normandy's prettiest villages, **St-Ceneri-le-Gerei ❷**, built on a granite spur dominating a loop of the Sarthe in the **Alpes-Mancelles**. Inside the

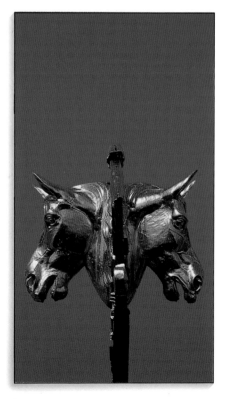

Romanesque church are some faded 14th-century frescoes, while in a nearby field close to the river a tiny 14th-century chapel contains a statue of the saint after whom the village is named.

Just north of Alençon the oaks, beeches and conifers spread their branches to form one of the largest forests in Normandy, the magnificent **Forêt d'Écouves**. The joint highest point in western France is here, at the Écouves signal station at 417 metres (1,368 ft), a height it shares with the Mont des Avaloirs across the border in the *département* of Maine. During the final days of the Battle of Normandy the forest provided excellent cover for the retreating Germans, and a tank stands in the heart of the forest as a lasting memorial to the French army's success in flushing them out.

Son-et-lumière

At the edge of the forest, **Sées** ❸ possesses the Orne's only **cathedral**, a beautiful Gothic building with twin towers, rising 60 metres (197 ft) above the fields – an inspirational landmark for travellers for over 600 years. At night, superbly floodlit, it is even more outstanding. *Son-et-lumière* shows telling the cathedral's history are a feature of summer evenings and there are regular classical concerts. Just across the Orne, which flows through the town, stands the old market hall, built in the form of a rotunda, with an intricate timber-framed roof supported on stone columns.

Three great châteaux

The N158 from Sées to Argentan passes close to three of the Orne's lovely châteaux. The **Château de Médavy** (open mid-Jul–mid-Sept, daily 10am–noon, 2–6.30pm; admission charge; park free) is a stately home built by the Grancey family in the early 17th century, replacing an earlier fortress, two towers of which can still be seen in the grounds.

Château de Sassy (open Easter–Oct, daily 3–6pm; grounds open all year;

BELOW: Alençon is a working town.

Map on page 290

admission charge) is even grander, a red-brick and white-stone building on a hill-side overlooking formal terraced gardens. Although building started in 1760, it was not completed until after the Revolution. Inside are some fine Aubusson tapestries and a magnificent library. A small chapel in the grounds contains a 15th-century altarpiece carved from oak.

The *pièce de résistance* of the Orne's châteaux lies between these two: the simply named **Château d'O** ❹ (open Apr–Jun, Sept, Wed–Mon 2.30–6pm; Jul–Aug, Wed–Mon 10.30am–noon, 2.30–6pm; Oct–Mar, Wed–Mon 2.30–5pm; admission charge), near **Mortrée**.

Set in an extensive wooded park and surrounded by the still waters of its moat, it has distinctive pepperpot towers and steep, pointed roofs. Built in Renaissance style in the 15th-century by Jean d'O, chamberlain to Charles VIII, it reached its zenith and was lost under François d'O, finance minister to Henri III, a hedonist and an incompetent, who died bankrupt.

The château was sold to pay off his debts. Especially worth seeing inside are 17th-century frescoes in the drawing-rooms. An 800-year-old farm in the grounds has been turned into one of the region's finest restaurants.

Along the road from Sassy, the little village of **St-Christophe-le-Jajolet** is a place of pilgrimage for followers of the patron saint of travellers, St Christopher. On feast days in July and October, pilgrims drive cars around a large statue of the saint outside the church.

Argentan

Argentan ❺, like Alençon, is a centre of lace and its *point d'Argentan* is made exclusively by the nuns of the Benedictine abbey on the southern outskirts of the town. Almost everything else of interest centres around the place St-Germain, where a busy market is held on Tuesday.

Towering above the stalls is the **Église St-Germain** (open Apr–Jun, Sept, Wed–Mon 2.30–6pm; Jul–Aug, Wed–Mon

BELOW: the Renaissance Château d'O, near Mortrée.

10.30am–noon, 2.30–6pm; Oct–Mar, Wed–Mon 2.30–5pm; admission charge). It was seriously damaged during the war but some interesting features survived, including its Flamboyant porch, a domed belfry and some excellent 16th-century glass.

The chapel of St Thomas is a reminder that it was from Argentan that the four knights set out, in the wake of Henry II of England's ill-chosen words, to murder archbishop Thomas Becket before the altar at Canterbury Cathedral.

Across the square is the **château**, an imposing building with square towers, built in 1372 by Pierre II, Count of Alençon. It now serves as the Palace of Justice. The chapel next to it was built around the same time and now houses the library and tourist office.

"A horse's Versailles"

As the trotting-horse and carriage symbol for the Orne indicates, this part of Normandy is proud of its equine traditions.

The area around Argentan is the heart of the region's horse-breeding country and 14 km (9 miles) east of the town, amid the forests along the N26, is the most famous stud-farm *(haras)* of them all, the **Haras du Pin** ❻ (National Stud; open Apr–mid-Oct, daily 9.30am–6pm; mid-Oct–Mar, daily 2–5pm; admission charge).

Created in the late 17th century through another initiative by Louis IV's minister Colbert, the stud's magnificent château and stables, at the end of a broad, grassy avenue and grouped round a horse-shoe shaped courtyard, are known as "the horses' Versailles". In the season, it is home to around 80 stallions, a mixture of Arab and English thoroughbreds, French trotters, cobs and giant Percherons.

A tour of the stud takes in the stables, and collections of 19th-century carriages, saddles and harnesses. There is always plenty of activity to watch, with horses being exercised, annual horse-shows and dressage events and, in September and

BELOW: muted reflection of an Orne castle.

October, racing at the *hippodrome* at the nearby village of **Le Pin-au-Haras**.

The Falaise Pocket

Nine kilometres (5 miles) north of the Haras, horse-power of another sort made its mark in the arena of world history. The countryside around **Chambois ❼**, a quiet village with the remains of a 12th-century fortress, is today a peaceful picture of rustic life: dappled cows graze the lush meadows beneath apple trees and country people go about their daily life on small, half-timbered farms.

In August 1944, however, this area, known at the time as the **Falaise Pocket**, was where the Nazis' formidable panzer divisions were cornered and smashed as they tried to escape along the Dives Valley, in what General Eisenhower described as one of the biggest slaughterfields of the war. The victory brought the Battle of Normandy to an end after 77 days of conflict. A monument to the armoured divisions involved overlooks the site on **Mont-Ormel**, just north of Chambois, on the D16.

Nature parks

Occupying the southern part of the Orne is one of France's largest regional nature parks, the **Parc Régional Normandie-Maine ❽**. There are several towns within its boundaries, but the honour of "capital" falls on the little village of **Carrouges ❾** on the D2 between Argentan and Alençon. Here the **Maison du Parc**, the park's visitor centre, is housed in a restored chapterhouse, an outbuilding of the 16th-century château. The centre has information about flora and fauna, walking, cycling and horse-riding.

The **Château** (open Apr–mid-Jun, Sept, daily 10am–noon, 2–6pm; mid-Jun–Aug, daily 9.30am–noon, 2–6.30pm; Oct–Mar, daily 10am–noon, 2–5pm; admission charge) is unusual, being built of red brick. A magnificent gatehouse leads to its impressive leafy park, at the centre of which the castle stands, square towers at

BELOW: taking out a pedalo at Bagnoles-sur-l'Orne.

each corner and surrounded by a moat. Not to be missed is a tour of the interior, entered by a drawbridge and inner court-yard and famous for its sumptuous fur-nishings, décor and paintings.

Taking the waters

Carrouges lies between the forests of Écouves and Andaines. At the heart of the latter lie the spa towns of **Bagnoles-de-l'Orne** ➓ and Tessé-la-Madeleine, the Orne's main holiday resorts. Bag-noles's heyday was in the Edwardian era and while it still has chic shops, smart hotels, *salons de thé* and lakeside casino, it looks a little faded, despite recent efforts to update its image.

The 25°C (77°F) waters of the **spa**, which is the largest in western France, attract thousands to the **Établissement Thermal** each year. There are also plenty of outdoor activities on hand – tennis, golf, swimming, walking, riding, boating and climbing rocks in the nearby gorge (details from the Maison de Tourisme).

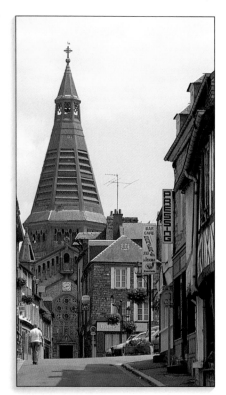

La Ferté-Macé

La Ferté-Macé ➑, 6 km (4 miles) to the northeast of Bagnoles, is a market centre and industrial town. Its church has an un-usual patterned façade of coloured bricks and stone. Its **museum** (open Apr–Jun, Sept–Oct, Sat–Sun 3–6pm; Jul–Aug, daily 3–6pm; admission charge) has a display of old and precious ecclesiastical curios.

A lakeside leisure centre, created in the 1990s on the edge of the town, has *gîte* accommodation and a full range of activities, including swimming, wind-surfing, fishing, riding and golf. But La Ferté-Macé's greatest claim to fame is its contribution to Normandy's culinary arts: *tripe-en-brochette*, strips of tripe cooked on skewers.

Lofty pear town

Due west of here is one of the Orne's most attractive towns. **Domfront** ➓, dating from the 11th century, stands on a rocky spur high above the *bocage* countryside of the **Passais**, an area of pear orchards. In spring it becomes a mass of white blossom which from a distance, in hazy sunshine creates the appearance of a frost-covered landscape. *Poiré*, a pear cider, is a popular local drink.

On a lofty perch are the crumbling towers, ramparts and casemates of a fortress that was dismantled in 1608. Some sections of the old town walls can still be seen along rue des Fosses Plisson, where old houses blend into the walls and towers. Within the walls, the medieval character of the old town has been well preserved. An unexpected sight in the centre of town is the **Église St-Julien**, which was constructed in 1924 of con-crete in neo-Byzantine style and full of lavish gilt decoration.

Approximately 8 km (5 miles) north-west of Domfront, in a picturesque val-ley, is **Lonlay-l'Abbaye**, which was founded in the 11th century. Only the church remains, but the village is still worth a visit, for its setting as well as for the church, and for the chance to sample the delicious *sablé de l'Abbaye* biscuits, a type of shortbread that is still made to a traditional recipe.

Map on page 290

LEFT: St-Julien at Domfront.

Royal Lace

Alençon is the home of Normandy's lacemakers, craftworkers dedicated to textile's most complex and dedicated endeavour. The visitor will find them in the museums and for sale in shops at a high price which reflects the extraordinary amount of work required to produce these intricate examples: it takes 32 hours to make 6.5 sq. cm (1 sq. inch).

The industry grew up on the back of the textile industry, spurred on by a national economic interest. The court of Louis XIV, the Sun King, was the most elaborate in all Europe, and its foppish courtiers created a demand for lace. The extravagant lifestyle of the monarchy sailed the State close to bankruptcy and it needed all the guile of Louis's imaginative chief minister, Jean-Baptiste Colbert, to keep the country solvent.

Lace at the time was manufactured almost exclusively in Venice, and Colbert decided the money would be better spent at home, so he set up a royal school of lacemaking at Alençon to provide the king and the court with the trimming they needed. Venetian imports were subsequently banned and the Alençon lace became *de rigueur*. The museum and school in rue Pont Neuf has a fine veil made for Marie-Antoinette. Napoleon I and the Empress Eugénie also wore the lace.

Point d'Alençon, involving a geometric pattern, was already established when Colbert came along in 1655: he merely added funds and royal approval. In the early 17th-century Alençon was making *vélin,* an antique cutwork made on parchment. After Colbert, *point de France* was introduced. This was adapted from the Venetian lace which, at its most intricate, involved 6,000 buttonhole stitches to 6.5 sq. cm (1 sq. inch). Its decorative stitches were characterised by circles known as "O". Later the designs incorporated small bunches of flowers.

Nunneries throughout Normandy used to produce lace, each providing a particular style which could immediately identify its place of origin. In the mid-19th century, women's headdresses, which had grown into the tall and elaborate concoctions now seen as part of the traditional folk costumes, were replaced by small frilled bonnets. But whatever the style of headwear, the lace distinguished which part of Normandy the wearer came from.

Today, this industry is still state-run in Alençon and grants go towards a handful of workers who ensure the craft survives. It is arduous, eye-straining work and a single piece may take many years to complete.

It is possible to find lace in other parts of Normandy that is still made by nuns. In Argentan, for example, *point d'Argentan* is made by nuns who occupy the Benedictine abbey to the south of the town. Its history is as honourable as Alençon's, and it was also a centre for *point de France.* It was popular at court until the late 18th century, when the lighter Alençon lace came more into vogue, Today the nuns work to a pattern rediscovered and popularised in the 19th century.

In the Augustine convent in Bayeux nuns show visitors examples of the establishment's craft. The convent's most famous daughter, Marie-Catherine, founded Canada's first hospital, the Hôtel-Dieu in Quebec. ❏

RIGHT: lace in the Musée de la Dentelle.

Map on page 290

SUISSE NORMANDE

You won't climb many mountains in "Swiss Normandy" but you will be delighted by the lush, peaceful countryside and enjoy a vivid history lesson in Falaise, William the Conqueror's birthplace

Despite its name, this rural backwater south of Caen has no mountains, no lakes (except where a dam has been thrown across the River Orne) and only the occasional exposed rocky height among the otherwise heavily wooded hills. Nevertheless, this small area has great natural beauty, and much of it is barely touched by tourism.

The core of the region

At the core of the Suisse Normande is the **River Orne**, a river of varying moods, in turn lazy, flighty or turbulent, which cuts a winding path from Putanges-Pont-Écrepin in the south through the green hills straddling the border between the Orne and Calvados *départements*, to Thury-Harcourt 40 km (25 miles) to the north. Falaise, William the Conqueror's birthplace, lies to the east.

The area saw a great deal of action during World War II, and most of the towns and villages have been rebuilt. As a result they tend to lack inspiration, and must rely on the backcloth of greenery for their attraction. But they do all make good bases, with shops for essentials, comfortable hotels and a selection of camp sites.

Thury-Harcourt ⓭ is a case in point. It has an excellent tourist office and is a popular spot for canoeing. The less sporty may find its chief attraction lies in the grounds of the ruined **Château d'Harcourt**. Built in the reign of Louis XIII for the illustrious Harcourt family *(see page 263)*, it was used during World War II by the Germans, who burned it to the ground on their retreat in 1944. The overgrown ruins are evocative, but more appealing still are the grounds where grassy meadows give way to banks of cultivated flowers in the formal gardens. There are also quite lengthy walks along the river bank. A chapel in the grounds contains items salvaged from the château after the war.

Activity centre

Because major roads are few and far between in this region, people travel slowly and appreciate their surroundings. One of the few main roads is the D562 which runs 19 km (12 miles) south of Thury-Harcourt to Condé-sur-Noireau by way of **Clécy** ⓮. Known as the capital of Suisse Normande, Clécy is the liveliest and most attractive of the valley villages and it offers a wide range of activities.

Canoeing comes high on the list, but some of the finest climbing faces in Normandy are here, too, and the **Rochers des Parcs**, towering above the Orne, are often swarming with roped-up climbers. It is a good centre for walking, with several *grandes randonnées* (long-distance foot-

PRECEDING PAGES: cyclists' view over Clécy.
LEFT: kayaking on the Orne.
RIGHT: pedalling off to the hills.

paths) and for horse-riding, fishing and hang-gliding. Hang-gliders launch themselves from the **Rochers de la Houle**, reached by way of the Route des Crêtes, a road (D133B) running along the ridge of the hills. The panoramas are exceptional, especially from the **Pain de Sucre** and the rocks themselves.

The village is the most tourist-oriented in the Suisse Normande. Cafés and restaurants, including the much-photographed Moulin de Vey, line the tree-shaded riverside walks near the **Pont du Vey**. Brightly-coloured pedalos and water tricycles splash between the banks.

One of Clécy's attractions is the **Musée du Chemin de Fer Miniature** (open Easter–Sept, daily 10am–noon, 2pm–6pm; Mar–Easter, Oct–Nov, Sun 2–5pm; admission charge). This is one of the largest model railways in Europe, with more than 430 metres (1,410 ft) of track and 14 trains on the go at any one time.

The Suisse Normande is an area that shouldn't be rushed: in fact the nature of the roads won't allow it. East of the Orne en route from Clécy to Pont-d'Ouilly, 11 km (7 miles) to the south, a maze of narrow, winding lanes invites visitors to lose themselves among the hills, isolated farms and orchards.

Pont-d'Ouilly ⓑ, both crossroads and border town (between Calvados and the Orne *départements*), lies at the centre of the Suisse Normande and is one of its main resorts. The valley broadens out here and the town is centred around the river, with its willow-shaded banks. Although rebuilt and modernised after the war, there is evidence of an earlier age when spinning and tanning were the local industries: granite and red-brick mills stand neglected at St-Christophe and Le Bateau.

Rocks and gorges

From Pont-d'Ouilly the D167 south keeps close to the Orne for 4 km (2 miles) until it reaches **Pont-des-Vers**, then, by way of the Rouvrou Meander, where the river all but loops back on itself, climbs to the

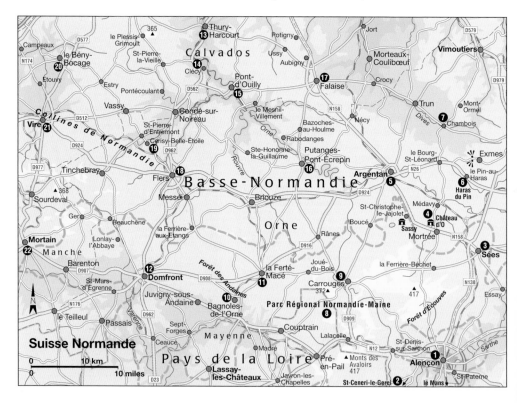

Map on page 290

Roche d'Oëtre, a rocky outcrop that gives a hint of what those marketing men were getting at. It stands at the top of a 118-metre (387-ft) precipice, overlooking not the Orne but a tributary called the **Rouvre**, its valley slopes covered in trees and yellow broom. Nearby, a cave called the Fairies' Room was a hiding place for brigands and fugitives of the Revolution.

To the south, the Orne passes through the **Gorges de St-Aubert**, a gentle gorge with only the occasional glimpse of a craggy rock face through wooded slopes, before reaching **Rabodanges**, where the grey 17th-century **château** appears at the end of an ornamental drive.

The village also gives its name to a dam built across the Orne to the south. Primarily there to create electricity, it forms a long, narrow lake which has become a popular leisure centre with water-skiing, jet-skiing, windsurfing and fishing.

At the upper end of the dam is **Putanges-Pont-Écrepin ⑯**, the region's southern gateway. Quietly attractive, it lies on either side of the Orne, which drifts lazily past small boats tied at their moorings and beneath drooping willows.

The Conqueror's town

While the Suisse Normande may be a fairly confined area, its landscape of rolling, wooded hills, farms, orchards and hidden hamlets extends somewhat further and brings within its domain much larger centres of interest. **Falaise ⑰**, just 18 km (11 miles) east of Pont-d'Ouilly, is one – a town that simply shouldn't be missed.

Falaise had more influence on the history of England than any other town in France, for it was here in 1027 that William, son of Robert the Magnificent, Duke of Normandy, and Arlette, daughter of a local tanner, was born. William was born in the château, and at the age of 39 became the Conqueror of England.

William's castle

The massive walls of the **Château Guillaume-le-Conquérant** (open daily 10am–6pm; admission charge) and the keep still stand today, dominated by the 35-metre (115-ft) **Tour de Talbot**, built in the 13th century by Philippe-Auguste. Extant, too, is the room where William was born. A chapel houses the list of 300 knights who accompanied him to Britain. The heavy restoration may upset purists but the amazing concrete gatehouse and the use of modern furnishings inside is undeniably imaginative, and the sophisticated audio-guide brings the place to life.

Carved mementoes

Beside the spring near the castle keep, where Arlette was washing clothes when she met Robert, a modern sculpture depicts the fateful moment. The town's most dramatic statue is near the castle's main gate in cobbled place Guillaume-le-Conquérant. This splendid bronze statue of William on a rearing horse rises above a plinth depicting six of his forebears, from Rollo, first duke of Normandy.

Looming over the square is the **Église de la Trinité**, with ornate flying buttresses and curious gargoyles and carved figures on the south side.

Flers

Flers , 25 km (15 miles) to the west of Putanges on the D962, is more concerned with commerce and light industry than tourism, but it makes a good base for excursions. It also has an attractive 16th-century **château**, renovated and enlarged in the 18th century, which during the Revolution became the headquarters of the Chouans, a group of Norman royalists led by Count Louis de Frotté who took up arms again against the republicans.

The partly-moated château stands in beautiful grounds, now a public park. It contains a **museum** (open Easter–mid-Oct, Mon–Fri, Sun 10am–noon, 2–6pm, Sat 2–6pm; admission charge) with some paintings by Daubigny, Boudin and Corot, and a section on the town's once-important cloth-weaving industry.

Floral hill

Some 8 km (5 miles) northwest of Flers on the D18, is the village of **Cerisy-Belle-Étoile** ⑲ which lies at the foot of Mont de Cerisy, a modest height of 260 metres (870 ft) with superb views over the surrounding *bocage*. Access is via a bosky toll road, which winds up the hillside to a ruined **château** at the top. Built by an English aristocrat, Lord Burkinyoung, around 1870, it was bombed in 1944.

Waymarked walks and mountain-bike trails wind through the woods, which rhododendrons turn to a mass of colour in spring. There is a terraced bar and restaurant, and an open-air theatre which is used regularly for traditional music and dancing. At the end of May, the hill is the venue for the Fête des Rhodos.

Pleasant surprises

A short drive away lie the remains of the 13th-century **Abbaye de Belle-Étoile** at the head of a peaceful valley, its arches and cloisters now incorporated into an apple orchard. There is little to see but it makes a delightful spot on a sunny day and it is easy to imagine why it attracted monks in the Middle Ages.

LEFT: William in conquering mode. **BELOW:** the Falaise castle where he was born.

Map on page 290

The *bocage* countryside that is such a lovely characteristic of this part of Normandy occasionally throws up some unexpected sights and one of them lies just north of Condé-sur-Noireau. **Château Pontécoulant** (open mid-Apr–Sept, Wed–Mon 10am–noon, 2.30–6pm; mid-Nov–mid-Apr, Wed–Sun 2.30–6.30pm; admission charge) distinguished by its small round towers and row of tall arched windows, dates from the 16th century and comes into view round a bend at the end of a landscaped park hidden in a wooded valley. The château contains some fine pieces of antique furniture.

Another surprise is found in the valleys near **Le Bény-Bocage 20** on the D577 north of Vire, which is 26 km (16 miles) west of Condé-sur-Noireau. In 1889, Gustave Eiffel, the man responsible for Paris's most famous landmark, built a railway viaduct over the Souleuvre Valley. After the railway ceased running, in 1990, Europe's first **bungee-jumping centre** was set up here, using a platform fixed to the top of one of the viaduct's stone pillars. Now thousands of visitors go to watch (or participate), as dare-devils dive off head first, nothing more than a rubber band preventing them from slamming into the ground 60 metres (200 ft) below.

Vire

The best of what remains of the medieval sights of **Vire 21** is the **Tour de l'Horloge**, a 15th-century belfry on top of a 13th-century gateway, once part of the town's ramparts. Beyond the church, the place du Château looks down on the River Vire which loops round the town. In the Middle Ages this rural valley, the Vaux de Vire, was the town's industrial zone, producing textiles. It became associated with a collection of bawdy workers' songs published under the name *Vaux de Vire*, which is said to have led to the word "vaudeville".

Of the **château**, all that remains is a ruined keep standing amid the trees, the rest having been demolished in 1630.

Down below, the **Musée Municipal** (open Wed–Mon 10am–noon, 2–6pm; admission charge), installed in the

medieval **Hôtel-Dieu** close to the river, is dedicated to local arts and crafts. The town is famous for its contribution to Norman cuisine, the *andouille*, a chitterling sausage, something of an acquired taste.

Going south

South of Vire, the D577 runs through rich countryside of rolling farmland, woods and orchards towards **Sourdeval**. Continue on to **Mortain 22**, a pleasant town where a small waterfall tumbles 25 metres (82 ft) alongside a woodland walk.

Mortain stands at the corner of the Parc Régional Normandie-Maine, where the landscape of Normandy is protected and museums pay tribute to local crafts. One worth seeking out is the **Maison de la Pomme et de la Poire** (Apple and Pear House; open Apr–Sept, daily; admission charge), south of the village of Barenton. Part of the pleasure of the quest is that the surrounding countryside, towards St-Cyr-du-Bailleul, is full of tiny lanes and unrestored half-timbered farm buildings. ❑

RIGHT: bungee jumping from an old viaduct.

Map
on page
298

CHERBOURG AND THE COTENTIN

For many visitors, the port of Cherbourg is their introduction to Normandy. Beyond it lie stunning sandy beaches and some quiet rural landscapes that time has overlooked

I n the north of the Manche *département*, the Cotentin Peninsula juts stubbornly out into the English Channel, a severely eroded remnant of the great mountains of the Armorican Massif that underpin France's northwest corner. Maritime traditions come to the fore in this isolated corner of Normandy, with its western seaboard blessed with rugged cliffs and magnificent beaches swept clean by strong tides. A weatherbeaten coastline of lighthouses, headlands and fortified harbours is tempered by the presence of old-fashioned seaside resorts and stretches of refreshingly undeveloped shore.

The Cotentin feels thoroughly Norman – as brusque and solid as the belaboured figures painted in the 19th century by Jean-François Millet, born in a small village to the west of Cherbourg. It was sons of the Cotentin who ventured south to establish lucrative kingdoms in Sicily and southern Italy during the 11th and 12th centuries. They were the descendants of the Vikings who settled here in great numbers, and whose presence is still remembered in its Norse place-names, such as at St-Vaast-la-*Hougue* (hill) and Bricque-*bec* (stream).

Cherbourg

Some visitors may have driven to the Cotentin Peninsula from one of the Channel ports further to the east, but many arrive at the port of **Cherbourg ❶** on a ferry from Poole or Portsmouth.

They will find little sign of the illustrious port where Napoleon resolved "to re-create the wonders of Egypt". Although the idea of transforming this exposed fishing village into a naval base was considered in 1686, the fortified breakwater now linking its offshore islands was not completed until 1853. Cherbourg developed

a rôle as a transatlantic port, with grand terminals built to receive the prestigious liners that docked here between the two world wars.

In 1944 the port was a key objective in the first phase of Operation Overlord, and fell three weeks after D-Day to the US 7th Corps. Hitler had ordered that the harbour be left "a field of ruins", and photographs of its devastation can be seen in the **Musée de la Guerre et de la Libération** (open summer, daily 10am–6pm; winter, Tues–Sun 9.30am–noon, 2–5.30pm; admission charge), housed in the 19th-century hilltop Fort du Roule, which enjoys a commanding view of the port.

PRECEDING PAGES: oyster beds at St-Vaast.
LEFT: Barfleur harbour.
RIGHT: a baby gull contemplates the world.

City of the sea

From the Fort du Roule you'll be able to see Cherbourg's newest museum complex, **La Cité de la Mer**, situated in the Transatlantic Harbour Terminal and devoted to the undersea world (opens spring 2002, tel: 02 33 23 31 60 for details or visit www.citedelamer.com). The star attraction is the French nuclear-powered submarine, *Le Redoubtable*. The 45-minute tour (aided and abetted by the latest high-tech gimmickry) will provide a fascinating insight into the daily life of the modern submariner. The supporting cast includes a state-of-the-art aquarium and pavilions with exhibitions on technological advances in deep-sea exploration, oceanography and related topics.

The historic part of Cherbourg is located in the streets west of the **Bassin du Commerce**, where the place Général-de-Gaulle serves as a central square and market venue. For shopping and exploring, head for the pedestrian precincts and narrow streets to its north, such as rue Tour-Carrée and rue de la Paix.

Visitors with time to spare may like to head south of the place Général-de-Gaulle to rue Vastel, to visit the **Musée Thomas-Henry** (open Tues–Sun 9am–noon, 2–6pm; admission charge). It exhibits a miscellany of fine art, including some lively 17th-century Flemish painting, a haunting *Pietà* by Nicolas Poussin and portraits by Millet.

Ports and forts

From Cherbourg, take the D901 east towards the spacious fishing port of **Barfleur ❷**, which has an easy-going atmosphere that belies the strong seas just offshore. It was here in 1120 that the *White Ship* carrying Henry I's son was blown on to the reefs, drowning the English heir and 300 others.

Today, Normandy's tallest lighthouse stands at the **Pointe de Barfleur**, a short drive north. The climb to the top will appeal to numerologists, as it has 12 storeys, 52 windows and 365 steps.

Driving south, you discover that the northeastern corner of the Cotentin Peninsula conceals a scenic surprise. Get

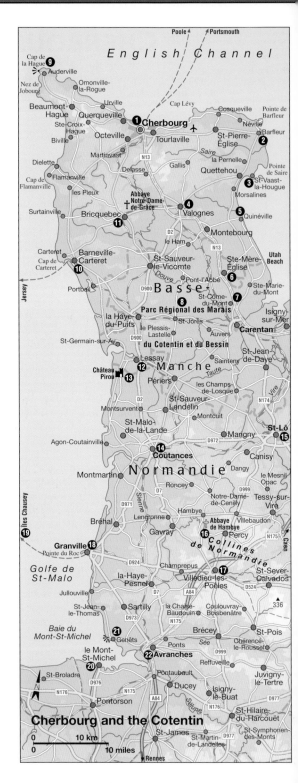

Cherbourg and the Cotentin

Map on page 298

off the main D902 road and take the D25, through a triangular pocket of rolling countryside, known as the Val de Saire, adorned with narrow lanes, thick hedges, gorse and wild flowers, with a viewpoint at La Pernelle offering extensive views along the east coast.

Back on the D902, take a left turn to the sprawling oyster port of **St-Vaast-la-Hougue ❸**, guarded by the Fort de la Hougue. This is a survivor of the coastal defences erected by military architect Sébastien Vauban following the destruction of the French fleet by Anglo-Dutch ships in 1692. The fort is still in use, but a similar one can be visited on the nearby **Île de Tatihou**. This flat island, which has a small **Musée Maritime**, can be reached by a short boat trip from quai Vauban and is ideal for a leisurely walk.

In the market town of **Valognes ❹**, some 16 km (10 miles) southwest once you get back on the D902, you can visit the **Musée Régional du Cidre et Calvados** and its companion **Musée de l'Eau de Vie** (open Apr–Sept, daily 10am–noon, 2–6pm; admission charge). Both pay homage to the Norman zeal for extracting liquid from the apple.

Wartime memories

Almost due east of Valognes, on the coast, lies **Quinéville ❺**. The **Musée de Liberté** (open mid-Mar–May, Oct–mid-Nov, daily 10am–6pm; Jun–Sept, daily 9.30–7.30pm; admission charge) in the town claims to be the first European war museum without weapons and is dedicated to the lives of ordinary French people under German occupation.

By the end of 6 June 1944, 23,000 men and 17,000 vehicles had been brought ashore at Utah Beach, and within three weeks the Cotentin Peninsula was in Allied hands. As at the eastern flank of the D-Day beaches, airborne troops were used to secure inland positions in advance of the seaborne landings.

Among the 13,000 men dropped from the skies, one paratrooper gained lasting fame by getting caught on the steeple of **Ste-Mère-Église ❻**, 10 km (6 miles) inland. For two hours John Steele hung in the air feigning dead before being taken prisoner. His ordeal was re-told in the film, *The Longest Day*.

In the town a dummy paratrooper still hangs from the church's spire, and the landings are commemorated in its stained glass. Nearby the **Musée des Troupes Aéroportées** (open Apr–Sept, daily 10am–6pm; Feb–Mar, Oct–Nov, daily 10am–noon, 2–6pm; admission charge) works hard to convey, to a growing audience that has never known war, the reality of D-Day. It has a C47 dropping plane and a fearfully-flimsy WACO glider with shop dummies as passengers. Once you have read Jim's poignant "Tonight's the night" letter to his parents, posthumously posted home, their use does not seem so out of place.

Rural traditions

On the outskirts of Ste-Mère-Église, the **Musée de la Ferme du Cotentin** (open Mar, Sun 1–6pm; Apr–May, Oct–Nov, daily 1–6pm; Jun–Sept, daily 11am–7pm; admission charge) offers a useful chance

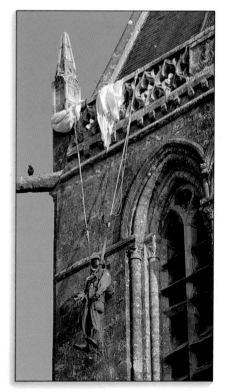

to get inside one of the covetable ensembles of stone-and-slate farmhouse buildings that are typical of western Normandy.

Built around a courtyard and well, the farm dates from the late 16th century but recreates rural life at the start of the 20th. Its collections of farming tools include a plethora of woodcutters' axes.

Branching northeast at **St-Côme-du-Mont ❼** (on the D913, known as the Voie de la Liberté), you will quickly reach the stunning expanses of **Utah Beach**, where the US forces landed on D-Day.

Alternatively, you could have chosen to drive from Quinéville down a relentless, haunting stretch of sand, one of the best coastal drives in Normandy, to reach Utah Beach, and then gone inland to visit Ste-Mère-Église.

Marshes and water meadows

The Cotentin Peninsula was once an island, and a southern band of low-lying land and marshes, the **Cotentin Pass**, now stretches between Lessay and Carentan.

Watered by the Douve, Sèves, Taute and Vire rivers, this area forms the heart of the recently created **Parc Régional des Marais du Cotentin et du Bessin ❽**. Among its extensive patchwork of marshes and water-meadows is the Canal des Espagnols, constructed in 1809 by 400 Spanish prisoners-of-war shipped in as part of an ambitious project of Napoleon's to link the peninsula's east and west coasts.

In the centre of the Parc Régional is the cattle town of **Carentan**, the eastern gateway to the northern Cotentin. It's best to pass straight through the gate – a golden rule for enjoying this corner of Normandy is to avoid the N13, where huge lorries pound to and from the port of Cherbourg. Instead, take the most minor roads you dare – with sea on three sides you're likely to find golden sands at the end.

The land's end

We shall save the southern part of the peninsula for the next chapter, and con-

BELOW: a beach picnic of fresh oysters.

Map on page 298

tinue our tour by going west of Cherbourg, where civilisation peters out as you approach **Cap de la Hague ❾**, Normandy's Land's End. If you have the time, take the D45 which trickles along the coast via the village of **Gréville-Hague**, where a bust of Jean-François Millet celebrates the 19th-century painter's involvement with the region.

The road then continues to the minimalist harbour of **Port Racine**, which claims, with obvious justification, to be *le plus petit port de France*; and eventually concludes at Goury, where a lighthouse rising from the rocks punctuates the end of the road like an exclamation mark.

This area north of **Beaumont**, was once defended by a dyke cut by the Celts and consolidated with walls by the Romans. It is not hard to imagine these early settlers appreciating the majestic sweep of the **Baie d'Écalgrain**, to the south of **Auderville**. Today it is skirted by a scenic route (D401) which virtually passes through the living-rooms of **Dannery**,

where a right-turn leads out to the cliffs at **Nez de Jobourg**.

Powerful plants

Here the blustery sea-views are complemented by an agreeable restaurant, the Auberge des Grottes. After gazing out to sea, it is something of a shock to look southward and find the landscape blighted by the blocks and chimneys of La Hague nuclear reprocessing plant. This vast plant employs 8,000 workers and has an Information Centre by its main entrance. Further south, at the opposite end of the spectacular *plages* along the **Anse de Vauville**, is another nuclear installation, the **Cap de Flamanville** power station.

The best beaches

South of here the coast is characterised by windswept beaches bordered by banks of sand dunes, which are among the best beaches in Normandy. The northern stretches of the Cotentin also have the most appealing and relaxed resorts on the

BELOW: cottages overlook the bay at Vauville.

Map
on page
298

peninsula, among them the twin communities of **Barneville-Carteret** ➓. Carteret is focused around its fishing port, also a departure point for ferries to the Channel Islands, but it has a small and beautiful beach in the shadow of a rocky headland.

A much longer and broader beach lies across the estuary in **Barneville-Plage**, the beach community attached to Barneville town, which lies about a mile inland. The small town of Portbail, 6 km (4 miles) further south, occupies an attractive spot overlooking the sands and marshes in the adjacent estuary. This is one of the prettiest villages in the Cotentin, with a leafy *place* and a couple of pleasing churches, and would make a good base.

About 16 km (10 miles) inland lies **Bricquebec** ⓫, another appealing town. Dominated by a castle with a 23-metre (75-ft) keep and clock tower, now occupied by a hotel, the town retains more old buildings than average. It is worth timing your visit to coincide with the Monday market.

Benedictines and Vikings

Lessay ⓬, 27 km (17 miles) south of Barneville, is renowned for its exquisite, Romanesque abbey church, restored after the war. An influential Benedictine abbey was founded here in 1056. The church has impressive stained glass inspired by Celtic designs, with adjacent conventual buildings dating from the mid-18th century.

A somewhat sleepy place, Lessay comes alive in mid-September when it is the venue for the three-day Ste-Croix horse fair that has been held here since at least the 12th century and attracts up to 400,000 visitors a year.

On the coast, 14 km (9 miles) southwest of Lessay is **Château Pirou** ⓭, a fine feudal castle which puts on *son-et-lumière* displays celebrating its Viking past. South of Lessay the D2 crosses the austere **Lande de Lessay** moorland to reach the Cotentin's ancient capital, **Coutances** (*see next chapter*). ❏

RIGHT: Écalgrain Bay lies on the wilder shores of the Cotentin peninsula.

Map
on page
298

SOUTHERN COTENTIN

*The attractive port of Granville, a fine Norman-Gothic cathedral in
Coutances, and a town that specialises in copper pots and pans are a few
of the finds as you wend your way through gentle* bocage *countryside*

The Cotentin gets its name from the diocese of Pagus Constantinus, founded by the 3rd-century Roman emperor Constantius Chlorus. His capital was at Constantia, today the hilltop cathedral town of **Coutances** ⓮.

Not much of old Coutances survives, but it possesses one magnificent treasure. Approach it from the west (D44), via its extremely popular companion resort of **Agon-Coutainville**, and you will have a good view of both the cathedral and the remnants of the medieval aqueduct that once spanned the Bulsard, one of three rivers that meet to the south of the town. At the top of rue Tancrède, the place du Parvis is a modern market square that squats in front of the cathedral like an irreverent offering.

The great cathedral

The **Cathédrale Notre-Dame** (open all year, daily 9am–7pm; Jul–Sept, Mon–Fri guided tours of the upper storeys at 10.30am, 3.30pm and 5pm, Sat–Sun 3.30pm and 5pm; tel: 02 33 19 08 10) is a rocketship in stone, launched in the 1040s by the local de Hauteville family who had recently acquired their kingdoms in southern Italy and Sicily. By 1274, their Romanesque church had been surmounted by Gothic additions that scaled new heights – a thundering 41-metre (135-ft) lantern tower and twin spires that soar to 78 metres (256 ft).

The cathedral is a fine example of the Norman Gothic style: in the west front the pursuit of slenderness verges on the anorexic, while double flying buttresses dance around the east end. These elegant strains continue inside with vertical lines and ambitious vaulting, lightened by the octagonal lantern tower and delicate stained glass – among which you can see, high in the north transept, a depiction of Thomas Becket sailing to England.

Herbal gifts

South of the cathedral, in rue Geoffrey de Montbray, stands the 15th to 16th-century **Église St-Pierre**, with its own rival lantern tower. Now that it has lost its stained glass, the unusually light interior resembles the inside of a sumptuously decorated eggshell.

A short walk east of the place du Parvis is Coutances' **Jardin des Plantes**. Once the grounds of a splendid 17th-century hotel, the gardens were bequeathed to the town in 1850 on the condition that its herbs be made available to its citizens free of charge.

The house is now the **Musée Quesnel-Morinière** (open Mon, Wed–Sat, 10am–noon, 2–5pm, Sun 2–5pm; admission

PRECEDING PAGES: typical *bocage* countryside near Villedieu-les-Poêles.
LEFT: haymaking is still done in the traditional way.
RIGHT: a stained-glass window in Coutances cathedral.

charge), guarded by a giant cider press with a good collection of art and antiques indoors. The most notable piece is Rubens' *Lions and Dogs Fighting*.

Within striking distance of Coutances is **Château de Gratot** (open daily 10am–12.30, 2–7pm; admission charge) with an 18th-century pavilion and 15th-century Tour à la Fée (Fairy Tower). To the south is Orval church, the remnants of an important 12th-century priory where St Omer was born.

St-Lô

In 1796 Coutances' position as capital of the Cotentin was usurped by **St-Lô** , lying 27 km (17 miles) to the east and now the Préfecture of the Manche *département*. The city was all but obliterated in June 1944, then blitzed again by modern architecture. It is worth visiting for the uncompromising manner in which the church of Notre-Dame was rebuilt: the war left a hole between the two towers of its west front, which was simply filled

with a contrasting wall of green stone. On the north side of the church you can see an unexploded shell lodged in its walls.

In the town centre a modern **Musée des Beaux Arts** (open Easter–Oct, Wed–Mon 10am–noon, 2–6pm; admission charge). successfully intermingles treasures ranging from an ancient Ethiopian Bible and a Tiepolo drawing to a set of 16th-century Bruges tapestries and works by Corot, Boudin and Millet.

Abbaye de Hambye

South of Coutances and St-Lô, the Cotentin lapses into the characteristic, relaxing *bocage* countryside of small fields bordered by raised hedges. Through this landscape the River Sienne meanders gently north towards Coutances, while further inland the Vire aims for St-Lô.

Ten kilometres (6 miles) north of Villedieu-les-Poêles, a strand of the Sienne wanders past the ruins of the Benedictine **Abbaye de Hambye** (open Apr–Oct, Wed–Mon 10am–noon, 2–6pm;

LEFT: the ramparts of St-Lô. **BELOW:** ruins of the Abbaye de Hambye.

Map on page 298

Jul–Aug, 10am–6pm; Nov–Mar, Sat–Sun 1–6pm; monastic buildings can only be seen as part of a guided tour; admission charge). These atmospheric 13th-century ruins provide a worthy excuse to potter through the Sienne Valley – take the D198 east of Gavray – and are complemented by an idyllic set of farm buildings, orchards and munching cows that make a convincing commercial for the monastic way of life.

Lots of pots

Villedieu-les-Poêles ⑰ means "God's Town of the Frying Pans", a name derived from the pots and pans that coppersmiths have been making here for centuries. It is undoubtedly the shiniest town in Normandy, its high street bedecked with copper, brass and pewter goods. In the 12th century it was the headquarters of the Knights of St John and a staging post on the pilgrimage route to Mont-St-Michel.

The town still has a medieval feel, with narrow alleys branching off from its streets into small *cours* (courtyards), such as those along the central rue Général Huard and the pedestrianised rue Docteur Havard.

One legacy of its metalworking traditions is the **Fonderie de Cloches** (Bell Foundry) (open mid-Feb–May, Sept–Nov, Tues–Sat 10am–noon, 1.30–5.30pm; Jun–mid-Jul, daily 10am–noon, 1.30–5.30pm; mid-Jul–Aug, daily 9.30am–6.30pm; admission charge), close to the river in rue du Pont-Chignon. Bells are still made here, and a guided tour reveals the skills behind this sonorous art.

Similar enlightenment is available at the **Atelier du Cuivre** (Copper Workshop), while other museums are devoted to pewter, copperware, clocks, lace and Normandy furniture.

Granville

The port of **Granville** ⑱ lies 28 km (17 miles) due west at the northern end of the vast **Baie du Mont-St-Michel** that bites into the Cotentin's southwestern corner.

BELOW: pots and pans for sale in the copper capita

Its prominence owes a lot to the English, who built fortifications on a rocky spur here in 1439 as part of their assaults on Mont-St-Michel. Within three years the Normans had captured this fortress, and the walled town that grew up on Le Roc is now referred to as the **Haute Ville**.

During the 18th century Granville, like St-Malo in Brittany, prospered both from the labours of its cod fishing fleet off Newfoundland and the exploits of its state-sponsored pirates. During the 19th century it developed as a fashionable seaside resort. As the most attractive town on the Cotentin Peninsula, Granville still attracts a lot of visitors. However, it is easy to lose them wandering around the quiet streets and alleys of the Haute Ville.

In the main entrance to the Haute Ville, known as La Grande Porte, the **Musée du Vieux Granville** (open Oct–Mar, Wed, Sat–Sun 2–6pm; Apr–Jun, Wed–Sun 10am–noon, 2–6pm; Jul–Sept, Wed–Mon 10am–noon, 2–6pm; admission charge), recalls the town's seafaring past and makes a useful prelude to a tour of the adjacent ramparts. These provide excellent views, and a walk can be extended right around Pointe du Roc, where you can see the remains of concrete defences built by the Germans during the war.

The upper town's western end is filled by the weatherbeaten church of **Notre-Dame**, its chapel walls decorated with marble plaques giving thanks to the fishermen's patroness. At the eastern end, below the panoramic **place de l'Isthme**, a walkway crosses the Trenche Anglais, cut by the English to separate Le Roc from the mainland. Steps lead down to the casino and promenade du Plat-Gousset.

A string of fish restaurants overlook the port in the lower town (**Basse Ville**), which is also where you will find most shops, cafés and attractions, including the Féerie du Coquillage (Shell Wonderland), the Palais Mineral and Le Roc Marine Aquarium.

From the port, boats cross to the Channel Islands or the nearer **Îles Chausey** ⓳,

BELOW: Granville's port has a romantic history.

Map
on page
298

a splash of low-lying granite islands where stone was quarried for the construction of Mont-St-Michel.

High tides and good views

South of Granville the D911 follows the curve of the Baie du Mont-St-Michel, along a notably scenic route signposted "Avranches par la Côte". At **Bec d'Andaine** there is a good view across the sands to the island of **Tombelaine** and **Mont-St-Michel** ⓴ beyond *(see page 315)*, as well as signs warning of the danger posed by the strong tides. If you want to walk across the bay, visit the Maison de la Baie in **Genêts** ㉑, where guides can provide safe passage – just as their predecessors did for medieval pilgrims.

If the mists permit, there are more good views of Mont-St-Michel to be had from the **Jardin des Plantes** in **Avranches** ㉒. Despite damage caused by the war the town has a welcoming atmosphere. If you can't face the claustrophobia of Mont-St-Michel, you might consider staying here.

BELOW:
sacred relics in
the Avranches
museum.

Avranches history

Avranches once had a cathedral, and you can see a model of it in the **Musée Municipal** (open Jun–Sept, daily 9.30am–noon, 2–6pm; admission charge) to the north of place Littré. Its displays provide a good introduction to life in the Southern Cotentin, with exhibits ranging from decorative tiles rescued from the Abbaye de Hambye to lovingly-made furniture and costumes of the 19th century.

A stupendous collection of illuminated manuscripts brought from Mont-St-Michel in the wake of the Revolution is exhibited in the **Hôtel de Ville** (open Jul–Aug, daily 10am–6pm; Jun and Sept, 10am–noon, 2–6pm; admission charge).

The position of the old cathedral can be gauged from a lonely stone in a corner of La Plate-Forme, a grassy terrace reached by an arch north of the Palais de Justice. Here a memorial commemorates the place in front of the cathedral where, in 1172, Henry II publicly atoned for the murder of Thomas Becket.   ❑

Map on page 316

MONT-ST-MICHEL

The narrow streets where pilgims once trod are now filled with tourists, but despite the commercialisation of this once holy place, the sight of Mont-St-Michel, rising from the mist, is stunning

The story of **Mont-St-Michel** begins in 708, when the Archangel Michael appeared before Aubert, Bishop of Avranches. He issued instructions for a church to be built on top of Monte-Tombe, a rocky island at the mouth of the River Couesnon. Aubert obeyed, and managed to construct a small oratory dedicated to St Michael, thus laying the foundations for what was later to become the top tourist attraction in France outside Paris. Once part of the Forest of Scissy, this 78-metre (258-ft) high rock is now an island crowned by a fortified abbey nearly as high again.

Perilous place

Mont-St-Michel's phenomenal development can be explained by its strategic position on the frontier between Brittany and Normandy. It stands aloof in the **Baie du Mont-St-Michel**, where treacherous mists, tides and quicksands serve as natural defences. The threat posed by these sands is borne out by Scene 17 of the Bayeux Tapestry, which shows two trapped Norman soldiers being rescued by the noble Harold.

In AD 966 Duke Richard I installed Benedictine monks from St-Wandrille on the island, with work on an enlarged abbey starting in the early 11th century. By then Mont-St-Michel was already an established place of pilgrimage that attracted Michael-worshippers, known as *miquelots*, from afar. They continued to arrive despite the ducal and Anglo-French wars that raged through the Middle Ages, with the opposing armies simply demanding a safe conduct payment.

By the end of the 13th century Mont-St-Michel had acquired a three-storey Gothic abbey, with a garrison installed in the lower town. During the Hundred Years' War new defensive walls were constructed that defied repeated English

attacks. Two bombards, left behind by the English after their final attempt in 1434, stand beside the **Porte de l'Avancée** . This gateway was the only break in the medieval ramparts and, as visitors are surprised to discover, is flooded at high tide.

Change of ownership

Following the defeat of the English at Formigny in 1450, Mont-St-Michel enjoyed a new popularity. In subsequent centuries it suffered from rule by absentee abbots, a decline partially checked by the arrival of monks from a new Benedictine Order, the Maurists, in 1622. After the French Revolution the abbey became a prison, which only closed in 1863, following a lengthy campaign initiated by

PRECEDING PAGES: Mont-St-Michel at low tide.
LEFT: the great church on the rock.
RIGHT: an 11th-century wall painting of St Michel.

Victor Hugo. Eleven years later the abbey was declared a national monument. In 1966, 1,000 years after the Benedictines first arrived on Mont-St-Michel, a small community of monks from Bec-Hellouin returned.

Today Mont-St-Michel is a textbook definition of a tourist trap. It is at its most impressive when seen from afar, with its famous silhouette rising above the hazy sands and salt marshes. As you travel down the **causeway** that has linked the mount to the mainland since 1880, its aura of enchanted isolation disappears.

Pilgrim hordes

Every year 850,000 people visit Mont-St-Michel, piling on to an island only 1 km (⅔ mile) in circumference like angels crowding on to a pin-head. As you join the throng, think of the medieval pilgrims who came before you, sporting cockle-shells and lead badges depicting the Archangel. Pilgrims still arrive today, carrying flags and singing hymns as they

climb up to the abbey along **La Grande Rue B**. This street is the town's principal artery, and at any time of the year it is liable to be blocked with fellow visitors. When faced with such congestion, the only successful means of progress may be to buy an enormous ice cream and carry it before you like a crucifix warding off evil.

Unless you are in urgent need of a fluorescent plastic sword or some Mont-St-Michel dominoes, you can avoid La Grande Rue and its thrusting souvenir shops (wait for the abbey's own shop, which is spacious and well-stocked) by taking the flight of steps opposite the Post Office. These ascend to the town's 13th- to 15th-century ramparts, which, turning left, lead via a series of defensive towers to the **abbey entrance** (open May–Sept, daily 9am–6.30pm; Oct–Apr, daily 9am–5.30pm; obligatory guided tour; admission charge).

On the way you can admire the silvery sands of Mont-St-Michel Bay, with the **Tour du Nord C** offering good views of

LEFT: souvenir shops in a busy street.

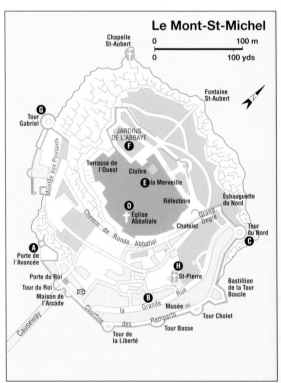

Le Mont-St-Michel

Map
on page
316

the nearby island of Tombelaine. In the 12th century there was a priory here, and English forces erected a castle on the island during the Hundred Years' War.

With more than 80 chapels, cells, towers and public chambers, a guided tour of the abbey complex is necessarily a complicated progress through the succession of buildings and social hierarchies that have been stacked up on the island over the past 1,000 years.

The tour begins

Visits normally begin on a wide terrace to the west of the abbey, near a point called **Gautier's Leap** after a prisoner who jumped to his death from its heights. This is reached by climbing a grand inner staircase – the adjacent buildings are where the eight members of today's religious community live.

Work on the **Église Abbatiale** (Abbey Church) **D** began in 1017, with the transept built over what was once the island's highest point. The architects made use of an earlier 10th-century church to form its crypts and supports; a remnant of this original building lies directly below the terrace, now known as the chapel of **Notre-Dame Sous Terre** (not always included in tours). The terrace itself was once covered by the three westernmost bays of the abbey's nave, removed in 1776 after falling into disrepair.

Inside the church four bays of the Romanesque nave survive to face the chancel, rebuilt in 1446–1521 in the Flamboyant Gothic style. The transept crossing and lantern date from the 1890s, when the famous skyline of neo-Romanesque belfry, neo-Gothic spire and golden statue of St Michel was created.

La Merveille

La Merveille **E** is the name given to the early 13th-century Gothic masterpiece added to the north side of the church. This marvel of the medieval world stands in ghostly tribute to the island's monks and the society that once revolved around

BELOW:
13th-century
abbey cloister.

them. Built on three levels, each divided into two rectangular rooms, it reflects the social strata of its day.

On the top floor is the enclosed world of the monastic order. Here you find the cloister, open to the skies, where the monks could meet and meditate. Next to this is the refectory, where rows of narrow windows filter the sunlight, and a pulpit where holy words would have been read aloud in Latin during meal times.

Beneath the cloister is the **calefactory** and **scriptorium** (misleadingly named the Salle des Chevaliers in the 18th century), where huge fireplaces enabled the monks to get some warmth, and large windows allowed them to work on the abbey's illuminated manuscripts. Adjacent to this is the **Salle des Hôtes**, formerly reception rooms for the rich and powerful guests visiting the abbot. On the lowest floor were storage cellars and the **almonry**, where pilgrims were received and alms dispensed to the poor. This is now, appropriately, a bookshop and souvenir hall.

Gothic horror

If the great granite carcass of the abbey now seems more like a horror-film set than a place of devotion, it is partly because it has been denuded of the stained glass, religious statuary, tapestries and hangings that would once have adorned its walls. Furthermore, the years the abbey served as a prison have left a grim stain. The delicate columns and arches of the cloister were made into cell walls, and you can still see the hoist which was used to haul up supplies, powered by prisoners walking like hamsters in a treadwheel.

Today visitors can escape to the fresh air of the **Jardins de l'Abbaye ❺**, reached through a door at the western end of the almonry. This allows access to the steep and wooded north side of the island, with interesting views back up to La Merveille. Below the gardens' western corner is the 15th-century Chapelle St-Aubert.

Beyond the abbey

After leaving the abbey, you can explore the higher reaches of the town by walking south past the **Musée Grévin** (open mid-Feb–mid-Nov, daily 9am–5pm; admission charge), the best of a trio of museums that suck visitors in from the crowded streets. All three offer "abbey experiences": the Grévin favours waxworks, while the **Musée Historique et Maritime** and the **Archéoscope**, both in La Grande Rue, prefer dusty model ships and audiovisuals, respectively.

West of the museum, the chemin de Ronde Abbatial curls round the island to a series of terraces and paths that descend to the **Tour Gabriel ❼**, constructed in 1524 and later crowned with a windmill.

An alternative descent is to take the steps below the Grévin, a route that passes the cemetery of the island's parish church, **Église St-Pierre ❽**. The entrance to this 15th-century church is in La Grande Rue. The interior walls are covered with plaques, banners and *ex-votos* brought here by pilgrims. In a chapel, surrounded by flickering candles, a large, silver statue of the Archangel stands with his sword raised high, demonstrating that the cult of St Michel is alive and well. ❑

LEFT: fortified tower. **RIGHT:** Mont-St Michel from the air.

Map on page 316

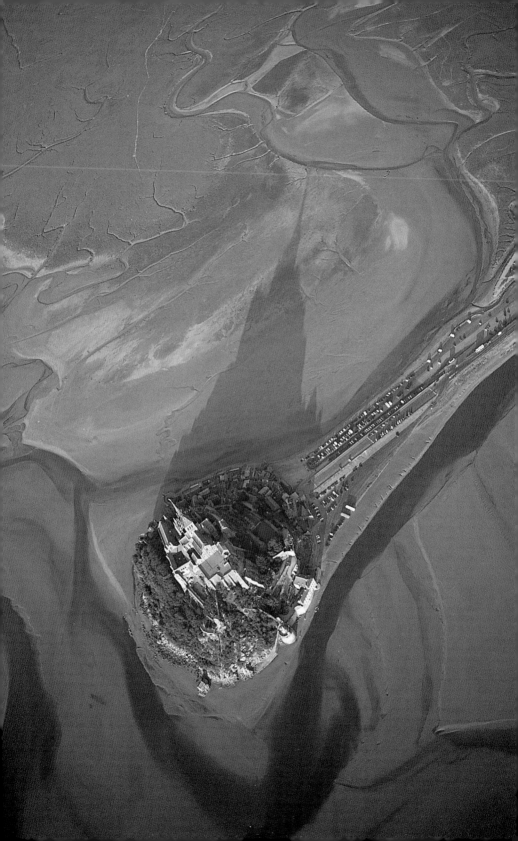

INSIGHT GUIDES

TRAVEL TIPS

New Insight Maps

Maps in Insight Guides are tailored to complement the text. But when you're on the road you sometimes need the big picture that only a large-scale map can provide. This new range of durable Insight Fleximaps has been designed to meet just that need.

Detailed, clear cartography
makes the comprehensive route and city maps easy to follow, highlights all the major tourist sites and provides valuable motoring information plus a full index.

Informative and easy to use
with additional text and photographs covering a destination's top 10 essential sites, plus useful addresses, facts about the destination and handy tips on getting around.

Laminated finish
allows you to mark your route on the map using a non-permanent marker pen, and wipe it off. It makes the maps more durable and easier to fold than traditional maps.

The first titles
cover many popular destinations. They include Algarve, Amsterdam, Bangkok, California, Cyprus, Dominican Republic, Florence, Hong Kong, Ireland, London, Mallorca, Paris, Prague, Rome, San Francisco, Sydney, Thailand, Tuscany, USA Southwest, Venice, and Vienna.

✕ INSIGHT GUIDES

The world's largest collection of visual travel guides

CONTENTS

Getting Acquainted

The Place

Normandy is an ancient province of 30,627 sq. km (11,825 sq. miles), about the size of Belgium, with 600 km (375 miles) of coastline. It is divided into an upper and a lower region. Upper (Haute) Normandy lies to the east around the basin of the River Seine. The relatively recent geology of the area's chalk, clay and limestone has created a flat landscape, which rises to a plateau of around 122 metres (400 ft) in the Perche region towards the south, where the Neubourg Plain is particularly featureless. To the north is the Normandy Vexin, a chalk plain that continues into the Caux region and the Alabaster Coast with its dramatic white cliffs. The north east Bray region is a depression between the two. The Seine cuts its way through chalk cliffs and then through reclaimed marshland around the estuary. In the west of the region bordering Lower Normandy is the Auge, an undulating land of small hills and valleys with flourishing orchards.

Geologically, Lower (Basse) Normandy is much older than Upper Normandy. Its main feature, rising to the west of the Caen Plain, is the Armorican Massif of shale and granite rocks, which form the Cotentin peninsula and the highest hills in western France – Mount Alavoirs and the Ecouves Forest Beacon both rise to 417 metres (1,368 ft). This region is typical *bocage,* a wooded landscape of small fields, which are enclosed by ancient hedgerows.

Woodlands were once a great feature of the whole of Normandy and two large tracts of forested land come under the protection of the Parcs Naturels de France: the Parc Régional Normandie-Maine in the centre and south of the region and the Parc Régional de Brotonne, northwest of Rouen. A third protected region, this one largely of marshland cut by rivers and ditches, is the Parc Naturel Régional des Marais du Contentín et du Bessin in the Cotentin pensinsula.

Heavy clay soil has resulted in the local architectural feature of *colombage* – half-timbered walls infilled with clay. The other major building material is the cream-coloured Caen stone and, in the Perche region, *grison,* a red-coloured sandstone.

Population

Normandy has a population of just over 3 million. The main centres of population are in three principal cities, which form an industrial triangle based along the River Seine. The largest city of the three, and the former capital of Normandy, is Rouen, which has a population of 380,000. Le Havre, the second largest port in France after Marseilles, has a population of 198,000. Caen, capital of Lower Normandy and seat of the Normandy regional council, has a population of 117,000.

Culture & Customs

Normans have long had a reputation for being conservative, Catholic, courteous, country people. They are said to like their traditions and have a pride in the countryside and in their homes. Their history is celebrated on such occasions as the William the Conqueror festival in Cabourg and the Joan of Arc festival in Rouen. Pilgrimages tend to be more popular in the Cotentin area, where they have more in common with neighbouring Brittany.

Normans are renowned for being very proud of their cuisine, and family meals are something of an occasion. Annual festivals celebrate the harvests of cider, flowers and fish, and there are seasonal markets for cherries, apples and plums.

Time Zone

For most of the year, France is one hour ahead of Greenwich Mean Time (GMT). There is sometimes a week or two in March and October when there is no time difference, if summer time (daylight saving time) begins and ends on different dates in France and the UK.

Electricity

Electric current is generally 220/230 volts. It alternates at 50 cycles, not 60 as in the US, so North Americans will need a transformer for shavers, travel irons, hairdryers, etc., which also takes care of the fact that outlet prongs are different. Visitors from the UK will just need adapters for two-point plugs.

Weights & Measures

The metric system is used in France for all weights and measures, although you may encounter old-fashioned terms such as *livre* (about 1 pound or 500 grammes in weight) still used in smaller shops and markets.

For quick and easy conversion remember that 1 inch is approximately 2.5 centimetres, 1 metre is roughly equivalent to a yard, 4 ounces is just over 100 grammes and a kilogram is just over 2 lbs. As a kilometre is five-eighths of a mile, a handy reckoning while travelling is to remember that 80 kilometres = 50 miles.

Weight:

3.5 ounces (oz) = 100 grammes (g)
1.1 pound (lb) = 500 grammes (g)
2.2 lb = 1 kilogram (kg)

Length:

0.39 inches = 1 centimetre (cm)
1.094 yard = 1 metre (m)
0.62 mile = 1 kilometre (km)

Liquid:

2.113 pints = 1 litre (l)
0.22 Imp gallons = 1 litre
0.26 US gallons = 1 litre
2.2 Imp gallons = 10 litres
2.6 US gallons = 10 litres

Temperature:

Temperatures are always given in celsius (centigrade). Here are some fahrenheit equivalents:
0°C = 32°F;
10°C = 50°F;
15°C = 59°F;
20°C = 68°F;
25°C = 77°F;
30°C = 86°F;
35°C = 95°F

Climate

The Cotentin peninsula benefits from the warming effect of the Atlantic Gulf Stream. The countryside inland is verdant, as there is plenty of rain here, most of which falls in the autumn. Much of the countryside is given over to pasture and orchards – a visit during blossom time (roughly mid-April to mid-May) is very rewarding. It is often said that the climate of Normandy is similar to that of Southern England and it is true that it is quite variable. However, it is generally a few degrees warmer, whatever the season. Winters are fairly mild (average temperature in January is 7.6°C/46°F) and it rarely gets stiflingly hot in summer (average temperature in August is 22°C/72°F).

Government & Economy

The name Normandy derives from the Northmen, or Vikings, who invaded and settled in the region from AD 820. William the Conqueror, 6th Duke of Normandy, was a direct descendant of the Vikings. Even prior to this time, however – around AD 280 – the

Normandy & the Arts

Some of France's most celebrated citizens, particularly in the realms of literature and art, were either natives of Normandy, or chose to live here. The playwright Pierre Corneille (1606–84) was born in Rouen, as was the writer Gustave Flaubert (1821–80); Guy de Maupassant (1850–93) was born near Dieppe and spent many years in Étretat.

In the art world, the region is especially noted for the development of the Impressionists, who were inspired by the coastal region around Dieppe, Le Havre, Deauville and Trouville. Nicolas Poussin (1594–1665), Jean François Millet (1814–75), Eugène Boudin (1824–98) and Raoul Dufy (1877–1953) were all born in the region. Claude Monet (1840–1926) had a house in Giverny, now open to the public.

In music, the composer Erik Satie (1886–1925) was born in Honfleur, and both Maurice Ravel (1875–1937) and Claude Debussy (1862–1918) were greatly inspired by the region.

Romans established a peaceful rule in the region, which lasted many years; during this time they founded a large number of the towns that are still in existence, such as Rouen, Bayeux and Avranches.

There are signs that Normandy was initially settled around the Stone Age, but it is for its connections with England, conquered by William in 1066 and the scene of the great Allied beach landing of World War II, that many British people are acquainted with the region.

Upper Normandie comprises the *départements* of Seine-Maritime and Eure, and Lower Normandie covers the *départements* of Orne, Manche and Calvados.

Each *département* – roughly comparable to an English county – is divided into a number of disparately sized *communes* whose district councils control a town, village or group of villages under the direction of the local mayor. Until recently, France was ruled largely by central government, but the Paris-appointed *préfets* lost much of their power in the 1980s, when the individual *départements* gained their own directly elected assemblies; this in turn gave them far more financial and administrative autonomy.

Each *département* still has a *préfet*, but the role is now more advisory than executive; the *préfecture* is based in the principal town of each *département*. *Communes* are now responsible for most local planning and environmental matters; decisions relating to tourism and culture are mostly dealt with at regional level, while the state controls such matters as education, the health service and social security.

French *départements* are identified by an individual number, which is used as a convenient reference for administrative purposes, for example it forms the first two digits of the postcode in any address and the last two figures on vehicle licence plates. The *département* numbers follow an alphabetical order, i.e. Calvados–14, Eure–27, Manche–50, Orne–61, Seine-Maritime–76.

Normandy's economy is still largely based on agriculture, primarily dairy farming, and also the production of apples, together giving rise to the three 'Cs' of Normandy: cream, cider and Calvados. Although some small traditional farms still survive, much of the farming is now more commercial. A sizeable proportion of the population works in agricultural-related industries such as food processing. Heavy industry is mostly confined to the Seine Valley, with the river being accessible to ocean-going vessels as far as Rouen, and the ports, particularly Le Havre, which is second only to Marseille in the importation of petrol products. Dieppe and Cherbourg, also still have active shipyards.

Business Hours

Office workers normally start early – 8.30am is not uncommon – and often stay at their desks until 6pm or later. This is partly to make up for the long lunch hours (typically from noon or 12.30pm for two hours) that are still traditional in banks, shops and other public offices. Many companies, however, are beginning to change to shorter lunch breaks, in line with other parts of northern Europe. Banks are normally open Monday–Friday 9am–noon and 2pm–4 or 5pm, but these hours may vary slightly.

Public Holidays

The following is a list of major public holidays. It is common practice, if a public holiday falls on a Thursday or Tuesday, for French business to *faire le pont* (literally "bridge the gap") and take the Friday or Monday as a holiday as well.

Details of closures should be posted outside banks, etc. a few days before the event but it is easy to be caught out, especially on Assumption Day in August, when everything closes down.
● **New Year's Day**, 1 January
● **Easter Monday** (but not Good Friday)
● **Labour Day**, Monday closest to 1 May
● **VE Day**, 8 May
● **Ascension Day**, May
● **Whit Monday/Pentecost**, late May (date dependent on Easter)
● **Bastille Day**, 14 July
● **Assumption Day**, 15 August
● **All Saints' Day**, 1 November
● **Armistice Day**, 11 November
● **Christmas Day**, 25 December (but not Boxing Day, 26 December)

Planning the Trip

Visas & Passports

To visit France, all visitors need a valid passport. Citizens of EU countries, Andorra, Monaco, the US, Canada and Switzerland do not require a visa. If in any doubt as to which documents you need, check with the French consulate in your own country. If you intend to stay in France for more than 90 days – and this includes EU citizens – you will need a *carte de séjour*, which should be available from the French consulate.

Customs

All personal effects may be imported into France without formality (including bicycles and sports equipment). It is illegal to bring into the country any narcotics, pirated books, weapons and alcoholic liquors which do not conform to French legislation.

Although duty-free allowances ceased on 30 June 30 1999, there are still recommended allowances, which we have listed below. These allowances can, however, be exceeded, provided that proof can

Recommended Customs Allowances

The recommended customs allowance, for each person over 18 years of age, is as follows:
● 10 litres spirits or strong liqueurs over 22 percent vol.
● 20 litres fortified wine
● 90 litres wine (of which no more than 60 litres may be sparkling)
● 200 cigars
● 400 cigarillos
● 800 cigarettes
● 110 litres beer
● 1 kilo tobacco
If you are in any doubt about what you are allowed to bring back from France, you can always check with your local customs office. In the UK, contact HM Customs and Excise, Dorset House, Stamford Street, London SE1 9NG (tel: 020 7928 3344) or any other Excise enquiry office.

be given that the goods bought are for personal consumption (e.g. for a family wedding) and not for resale.

Health Care

The International Association for Medical Assistance to Travelers (IAMAT) is a non profit-making organisation, based in the US (417 Center Street, Lewiston NY 14092, tel: 716-754 4883). Anyone can join, free of charge, although a donation is requested. Benefits include a membership card, entitling the bearer to services at fixed IAMAT rates by participating physicians, and a Traveller Clinical Record, a passport-sized record completed by the member's own doctor prior to travel. A directory of English-speaking doctors belonging to IAMAT and on call 24 hours a day, is published for members' use.

EU nationals should check before leaving for France that they qualify for subsidised treatment under the EU agreement – most British nationals do: check with the Department of Health and acquire from them an E111 form. Note, however, that the E111 does not cover the full cost of any treatment, and it advisable to take out private insurance as well.

Note: For minor ailments you can consult a pharmacy (recognisable by its green cross sign). Pharmacists in France have wider powers than chemists in the UK or the US and many types of medicine may be available over the counter that are only obtainable on prescription at home. If you need to see a doctor, expect to pay around FF110 for a simple consultation, plus a pharmacist's fee for whatever prescription is issued. The doctor will provide a *feuille des soins*, which you need to keep to claim back the majority of the cost (about 75 percent) under the EU agreement. You have to attach to the *feuille* the sticker *(vignette)* from any medicine prescribed to enable you to claim for that too. Refunds are obtained from the local *Caisse Primaire* (ask the doctor or pharmacist for the address).

In cases of medical emergency, either dial 15 for an ambulance or call the *Service d'Aide Médicale d'Urgence* (SAMU) which can be found in most large towns and cities – numbers are given at the front of telephone directories.

The standard of treatment in French hospitals is generally high, and you should be able to find someone who speaks English to help you. You may prefer to try to be admitted either to the American Hospital at 63 boulevard Victor-Hugo, 92202 Neuilly, tel: 01 46 41 25 25, or the British Hospital Hertford at 3 rue Barbes, 92300 Levallois-Perret, tel: 01 46 39 22 22, both of which are just outside Paris. Show the hospital doctor or the authorities your E111 and you will be billed for around 25 percent of the cost of the treatment. If you have private medical insurance you will need to pay the fee while in France then reclaim it from your insurance company.

Money Matters

In January 1999 the Euro was introduced as the new monetary system throughout France, and in January 2002 the Euro replaced the franc, as it did the individual currencies of most EU member countries. Visitors from the UK can purchase Euros, or Euro travellers' cheques, from banks or travel agents before leaving home in the same way that they would previously have purchased francs.

In Normandy, banks displaying the "Change" sign will change foreign currency and, in general, at the best rates; note that you will need to produce your passport for any transaction. If you can, avoid hotel or other independent bureaux, as these usually charge a high commission.

Credit cards are widely accepted with Visa being by far the most common; Visa can now be used in many hyper- and supermarkets. Access (MasterCard/Eurocard) and American Express are also accepted in some establishments. Credit cards and cash cards from many European banks can now be used in French cashpoint machines outside banks. Check the validity of your cashcard with your home bank before departure. You will need a four figure pin number.

French bank cards have chips *(puces)* containing their ID details, whereas UK cards have this information on a magnetic strip; the latter is not always easily readable by French card-reading machines, which may cause cards to be rejected or other problems.

Travellers' cheques are also widely accepted.

Travel with Pets

Animal quarantine laws have now been revised and it is possible to re-enter Britain with your pet without quarantine. Conditions are stringent, however, with tough health requirements and restricted points of entry. For further information you are advised to contact the Ministry of Agriculture, or the French consulate if you are abroad. Note that you will need a valid vaccination certificate for your pet if you travel between countries in continental Europe.

Getting There

By Air
Air France: tel: 0845 0845 111, www.airfrance.co.uk is the principal agent for all flights to France and in addition to handling their own

Useful Numbers

The following number in Paris may be useful:
● **Air France:** 119 Champs Elysées, 75384 Paris Cedex 08, tel: 08 02 80 28 02
American airlines:
● **American Airlines:** tel: 00 33 142 99 99 01
● **Continental,:** tel: 00 33 142 99 09 15
● **Delta:** tel: 00 33 493 21 34 86

services they also deal with bookings for smaller operators.

Travellers from the US can get direct flights to Paris but it may work out cheaper to catch a charter flight to London and then take another flight from there. **Nouvelles Frontières** offer some of the most competitive fares on scheduled and charter flights to Paris and London from the US and Canada.

Other low-price charter flights can be obtained through bucket shops, although France is not as well served by these as many other European destinations; watch out for bargains and special offers in the national press.

Students and young people can normally obtain discounted charter fares through specialist travel agencies in their own countries or from USIT **Campus European Reservations**, Terminal House, 52, Grosvenor Gardens, London SW1W 0AG, tel: 08702 401010. The main USIT office in New York is **Council Travel** at New York Student Centre, 895 Amsterdam Avenue, New York, NY 10025, tel: 212 663 5435.

In France, students should try USIT **Connect**, 12 rue Vivienne, 75002 Paris, tel: 01 42 44 14 00, fax: 01 42 44 14 01.

Discounts on internal flights in France are available from **Air Inter** under their *Grands Bleus* tariff, which gives young people under 25, and students under 27 up to 65 percent reduction on off-peak flights. For information and booking, contact Air France *(see above)*.

By Sea

Since the opening of the Channel Tunnel, ferry services have become increasingly competitive, so shop around for discounts and special offers. Five-day trips often offer the best value. The following companies operate across the English Channel to Normandy ports. All of them carry cars and foot passengers.

Brittany Ferries offer sailings from Portsmouth to Caen, and Poole to Cherbourg (summer only). They also sail to St Malo, just west of the region from Portsmouth and Poole. For details contact The Brittany Centre, Wharf Road, Portsmouth PO2 8RU, tel: 08705 360360; www.brittany-ferries.com).

P&O Portsmouth sail from Portsmouth to Cherbourg and Le Havre. For fares and schedules contact P&O Portsmouth, Peninsula House, Wharf Road, Portsmouth PO2 8TA, tel: 0870 242 4999 or 0803 013 013, fax: 01705 864211.

P&O Stena also operate the short sea route from Dover to Calais. Contact them at, Channel House, Channel View Road, Dover CT17 9TJ, tel: 087 0600 9009. The sailings are extremely frequent and some visitors prefer a shorter sea crossing and a longer drive to Normandy at the other end.

Hoverspeed Fast Ferries operate a new Superseacat service from Newhaven to Dieppe, crossing in just over 2 hours. For details contact the International Hoverport, Dover CT17 9TG, tel: 08705 240241; fax: 01304 240 088; www.hoverspeed.com.

By Rail

Eurostar services from London Waterloo to Paris offer a quick connection onto the French rail network, although this generally involves changing stations in Paris as the Eurostar comes into the Gare du Nord. There are direct connections to the main cities of the region from Paris St-Lazare and Montparnasse stations. Paris to Rouen takes 1 hour 20 minutes, Paris to Caen 2 hours 10 minutes.

Le Shuttle

With a journey time of only 35 minutes, **Le Shuttle** carries cars and their passengers from Folkestone to Calais on a simple drive-on-drive-off system. Payment is made at toll booths, which accept cash, cheques or credit cards. Prepaid tickets and booked spaces are available. Booking is not strictly necessary as you can just turn up and take the next available service, although at busy times you may have to wait. Le Shuttle runs 24 hours a day, all year round, with a service at least once an hour through the night.

The toll-free motorway link between Rouen and Abbeville makes this a good alternative to the longer ferry crossings. Information and bookings from: Le Shuttle Customer Services Centre, PO Box 300, Folkestone, Kent CT19 4QW, tel: 08705 353 535.

From the Gare St-Lazare, there are through trains to Bayeux, Caen, Carenten, Evreux, Gisors, Le Havre, Liseux, Rouen, Vernon and Yvetot. In season, there are also through trains to Houlgate and Dives-Cabourg.

From Montparnasse station there are through trains to L'Aigle, Argenton, Briouze, Flers, Granville and Vire. Trains from the Gare du Nord, Paris, travel to Eu and Le Tréport. For other destinations, change at Caen, Lisieux or Rouen. For bookings and information, tel 0870 584 8848 or visit Rail Europe's Travel Shop, 179 Piccadilly, London W1 (www.raileurope.co.uk). The Travel Shop service includes ferry bookings, discounted tickets for young people, a *Carte Vermeil* for senior citizens, which gives a generous discount on tickets, and Eurodomino rail passes *(see below)*.

The SNCF (Société Nationale des Chemins de Fer de France) is the French rail service. Tel: 08 36 35 35 35 or visit their website on www.sncf.fr for reservations and further information. French railway stations will accept Visa and most credit cards.

Rail Passes: There are several rail-only and rail combination passes available to foreign visitors. These must always be bought before departing for France. In the UK a Eurodomino Pass offers unlimited rail travel on any 3, 5 or 10 days within a month. This can also be purchased in conjunction with an Air France-Rail ticket.

Reductions in France: for those aged between 12 and 25 years, a reduction of 25 percent is available on proof of age. For senior citizens, proof of over 60 gives a 25 percent reduction in fares. There are various other reductions available for families travelling together where there are children under 12 or 16 years of age. Ask at railway stations for details.

Visitors from North America have a wide choice of passes, including Eurailpass, Flexipass and Saver Pass, which can be bought in the US, tel: (212) 308 3103 (details) or 800 223 636 (reservations).

Similar passes are available to travellers from other countries, although the names of the tickets and conditions may vary slightly.

Ticket Validation

Rail tickets bought in France must be validated using the orange automatic date-stamping machine at the entrance to the platform. Failure to do so may incur a surcharge. Note that reservation is essential for travel on TGVs.

By Bus

Eurolines is a consortium of almost 30 coach companies, operating in France and throughout Europe. One of the cheapest ways of reaching France (with services to Caen, Le Havre and St Malo), discounts are available for young people and senior citizens. The ticket includes the ferry crossing. **National Express** coaches have connections with the London departures from most major towns in the UK – for details, contact: Eurolines, 52 Grosvenor Gardens, Victoria, London SW1W 0AU, tel: 0207 730 8235, or the main reservations office at 23 Crawley Road, Luton, tel: 01582 404511.

By Road

There is a good motorway from Paris – the A13 to Evreux, Caen, and Rouen – and from the Belgian border – the A28. North of Rouen, the road links with the new A29 to Le Havre, which improves access from that port to the coastal resorts of Deauville, Trouville, etc. This makes Normandy well suited to travel by car. The roads in the region are good and reasonably uncrowded, except on the main routes to and from Paris during peak holiday times such as public holidays and the first and last weekends in August.

Almost all the motorways in France are privately owned and subject to **tolls** (credit cards are usually acceptable). Tolls are also payable on the Brotonne bridge (cash only) and the Tancarville bridge over the Seine and the Pont de Normandie, which connects Le Havre to Honfleur, and the A29 autoroute.

The centre of Caen is less than 30 minutes from the port of Ouistreham, and Rouen is only approximately one hour away from the ports of Le Havre or Dieppe.

Useful Addresses

International Tourist Offices
UK
French Government Tourist Office
178 Piccadilly, London W1V 0AL
Tel: 0906 824 4123 (calls charged at 60p a minute)
e-mail: piccadilly@mdlf.demon.co.uk
www.franceguide.com
A French Travel Centre for information, books and guides is now open at the above address.

Normandy Regional Tourist Board
The Old Bakery, Bath Hill, Keynsham, Bristol BS31 1HG
Tel: 0117 986 0386
Fax: 0117 986 0379
e-mail: stephenrodgers@compuserve.com
USA
French Government Tourist Office
444 Madison Ave, 16th Floor, New York NY 10020
Tel: 212 838 7800
Fax: 212 838 7855
Los Angeles
9454 Wilshire Boulevard, Suite 715
Beverly Hills, Los Angeles CA 90212-2967
Tel: 310 271 6665
Fax: 310 276 2835
Paris
Maison de la France
20 avenue de l'Opéra, 75001 Paris
Tel: 01 42 96 10 23
Fax: 01 42 86 80 52

Tourist Offices in Normandy
Regional
Comité Régional de Tourisme de Normandie, Le Doyenné, 14 rue Charles-Corbeau, 27000 Évreux
Tel: 02 32 33 79 00
Fax: 02 32 31 19 0
e-mail: normandy@imaginet.fr
Departmental
Seine-Maritime, 6 rue Couronné, BP 60, 76420 Bihorel-les-Rouen
Tel: 02 35 12 10 10
Fax: 02 35 59 86 04.
Calvados, Place du Canada, 14000 Caen
Tel: 02 31 27 90 30
Fax: 02 31 27 90 35
e-mail: cdt@cg14.fr
L'Eure, Hôtel du Département, Boulevard Georges Chauvin, BP 367, 27003 Évreux
Tel: 02 32 62 04 27
Fax: 02 32 31 05 98.
L'Orne, 88 rue St-Blaise, BP 50, 61002 Alençon Cédex
Tel: 02 33 28 88 71
Fax: 02 33 29 81 60.
La Manche, Maison du Départment, Route de Villedieu, 50008 Saint-Lô Cédex
Tel: 02 33 05 98 70, freephone from the UK: 0800 028 6572

Websites

The internet is a great place to find out more information on hotels, methods of transport, places to visit, restaurants and cafes, and even such specifics as what the weather will be like when you get there. Here is a selection of useful sites to start you off:
General
www.normandy-tourism.org
www.normandieweb.org
www.normandienet.tm.fr
Transport
www.sncf.fr
www.britrail.co.uk
www.eurostar.co.uk
www.raileurope.com
Accommodation
www.chatotel.com (chateaux & independent hotels)
www.fuaj.org (youth hostels)
www.relaischateaux.fr
www.campingfrance.com
www.gites-de-france.fr
Restaurants
www.bottin-gourmand.com
www.calvacom.fr/savoy
Weather
www.meteo.fr

Fax: 02 33 56 07 03
e-mail: manche-tourisme@cg50.fr
Major towns
Caen
Place St-Pierre, F-14000 Caen
Tel: 02 31 27 14 14
Fax: 02 31 27 14 18
Dieppe
Pont Jehan Ango, BP 152, 76204 Dieppe Cédex
Tel: 02 32 14 40 60.
Fécamp
Maison du Tourisme BP 112, 113 rue Alexandre le Grand, 76403 Fécamp Cédex
Tel: 02 35 28 51 01.
Le Havre
186 Bd Clemenceau, BP 649, 76059 Le Havre Cédex
Tel: 02 32 74 04 04.
Lisieux
11 rue d'Alençon, BP 7197, 14107 Lisieux Cédex
Tel: 02 31 62 08 41
Fax: 02 31 62 35 22.

Rouen
25 Place de la Cathédrale, BP 666,
76008 Rouen Cédex
Tel: 02 32 08 32 40

Embassies & Consulates
The nearest consular services are
all located in Paris.
USA Embassy
2 avenue Gabriel
75008 Paris
Tel: 01 43 12 22 22
Australian Embassy
4 Rue Jean Rey
75724 Paris
Tel: 01 40 59 33 10
British Embassy
35 rue du Faubourg St-Honoré,
75008 Paris
Tel: 01 42 66 91 42
Canadian Embassy
35 avenue Montaigne
75008 Paris
Tel: 01 44 43 29 00
Eire Embassy
12 avenue Foch
75116 Paris
Tel: 01 44 17 67 00

Practical Tips

Emergencies

To report a crime or loss of
belongings, visit the local
gendarmerie or *commissariat de
police*. Telephone numbers are given
at the front of local directories. In the
event of an emergency, dial 17 for
the police. If you lose something on a
bus or a train, first try the terminus
to see if it has been handed in. (Go
to the Objets Trouvés office.)

If you lose a passport, report it
first to the police, then to the
nearest consulate. If, for any
reason, you are detained by the
police, ask to telephone the nearest
consulate for a member of the staff
to come to your assistance.

If you lose your credit card, notify
the authorities immediately on the
following UK numbers:
American Express: 00 44 273 696
933
Visa: 00 44 151 472 1141
Diner's Club: 0800 460 800
MasterCard: contact your own bank.

Emergency Numbers

Ambulance 15
Police 17
Fire brigade *(pompiers)* 18
(all freephone)

Security & Crime

Sensible precaution regarding
personal possessions is all that
should really be necessary when
visiting France. Theft and other
crime exists here as elsewhere
but it should not be a serious
problem as far as tourists are
concerned.

Drivers should follow the rules of
the road and always drive sensibly.

Heavy on-the-spot fines are given
for traffic offences, such as
speeding, and drivers can be
stopped and breathalysed during
spot checks. The minimum fine for
speeding is €150, and immediate
fines of up to €3,200 can be levied
for drink-driving offences. If you do
not have enough cash to pay your
fine, you will be required to pay a
deposit. Police are fairly visible on
the main roads of France during the
summer months.

Media

Regional newspapers contain
national and international as well
as local news. They have a far
higher standing in France than their
counterparts in the UK and are
often read in preference to the
national press. The principal
regional paper in Normandy is
Ouest France. The main **national
dailies** are *Le Monde* (good for a
liberal overview of political and
economic news), the more
conservative *Le Figaro* and the very
left-wing *Libération* and
L'Humanité. Le Point and *L'Express*
are the major weekly news
publications. British and American
dailies, notably *The Times, The
Guardian,* the *Daily Telegraph* and
the *International Herald Tribune* are
widely available in major towns and
cities. *Normandy,* a glossy, bilingual magazine on the life and
culture of the region, is published
every two weeks and widely
available.

Television viewers can receive
the two main national channels,
TF1 (commercial) and Antenne 2
(state-owned but largely financed
by advertising), as well as FR3,
which offers regional programmes.
Cable TV gives access to BBC
channels.

France Inter is the main national
radio station (1892m long wave)
and it broadcasts English-language
news twice a day in summer
(generally 9am and 4pm). BBC
Radio 4 can be received fairly well
in parts of the region on long wave
(198 khz), as can the World
Service.

Post Offices

Postes or PTTs are generally open Monday to Friday 9am–noon and 2–5pm as well as Saturday 9am–noon (opening hours are posted outside). Inside major post offices, individual counters are marked for different requirements – if you just need stamps, go to the window marked *Timbres*. If you need to send an urgent letter overseas, ask for it to be sent *par exprès*, or through the Chronopost system, which is even faster but very expensive.

For a small fee, you can arrange for mail to be kept *poste restante* at any post office, addressed to Poste Restante, Poste Centrale (for a main post office), then the town post code and name. A passport is required when collecting mail.

Stamps are often available at tobacconists *(bureaux de tabacs)* and other shops selling postcards and greetings cards.

Telegrams can be sent during post-office hours or by telephone (24-hours); to send a telegram abroad, dial 0800 33 44 11.

Fax and photocopying facilities are often available at major post offices and *maisons de la presse* (newsagents), and many supermarkets also now have coin-in-the-slot photocopiers.

Telecommunications

The French telephone system is now one of the best in the world. That is not to say that you can be guaranteed that telephone boxes *(cabines publiques)* are always operational, but most are.

Telephone numbers in France are of ten figures, given in sets of two, e.g. 01 23 45 67 89.

International calls can be made from most public booths, but it is often easier to use a booth in a post office – ask at the counter to use the phone, then go back to settle the bill – but you have no record of the cost of the call until the end.

Coin-operated phones take most coins and card phones are now very common and simple to use. It is worth purchasing a phone card *(une télécarte)* if you are likely to need to use a public call box, as most have now been converted to cards. Cards are available from post offices, stationers, railway stations, some cafés and *bureaux de tabacs*. If you use a phone (not a public call box) in a café, shop or restaurant, you are likely to be surcharged.

If using a US credit phone card, dial the company's access number: Sprint, tel: 00 00 87; AT&T, tel: 00 00 11; MCI, tel: 00 00 19.

International Calls

To make an international call, lift the receiver, insert the money (if necessary), dial 00, then dial the country code *(see below)*, followed by the area code (omitting any initial 0) and the number.

International dialling codes:

Australia	61
Canada	1
Ireland	353
UK	44
US	1

Useful numbers:

Operator services	13
Directory enquiries	12

If you need to make a phone call in rural areas, or small villages with no public phone, look out for the blue plaque saying *téléphone publique* on private houses. This means that the owner is officially required to allow you to use the phone and charge the normal amount for the call.

You cannot reverse charges (call collect) within France but you can to countries that will accept such calls. Go through the operator and ask to make a PCV *(pay-say-vay)* call. Telephone calls can only be received at call boxes displaying the blue bell sign.

The cheapest times to telephone are weekdays between 7.30pm and 8am, Saturdays after 1.30pm and all day Sunday.

Children

In France generally, children are treated as individuals, not just appendages. It is pleasant to be able to take them to **restaurants** (even in the evening) without heads being turned in annoyance at the invasion. It has to be said, however, that French children, being accustomed to eating out from an early age, are on the whole well behaved in restaurants, so it does help if one's own offspring are able to understand that they shouldn't run wild.

Many restaurants offer a **children's menu**; if not, they will often split a *prix-fixe* menu between two children. If travelling with very young children, you may find it practical to order nothing specific at all for them but just to request an extra plate and give them tasty morsels to try from your own dish. French meals are usually generous enough to allow you to do this, and you are unlikely to encounter any hostility from *le patron* (or indeed *la patronne*).

Most **hotels** have family rooms so that children do not have to be separated from parents; a cot *(lit bébé)* can often be provided for a small supplement, although it is a good idea to check availability if booking in advance.

Many of the seaside resorts have children's clubs on the beach, where for a fee children can be left for a few hours to take part in organised sports and fun events.

It is also possible to organise holidays for unaccompanied children, including stays in *gîtes d'enfants* or on farms, or activity holidays. It is very common for French children to spend large parts of their summer holidays away from their parents on holiday camps, so the country is well geared up for this type of activity. The tourist offices in each *département* also organise events and holiday camps for unaccompanied children. For contact numbers *see page 327*.

The following companies and organisations should be able

to give further information on activities for children:

CIDJ, Centre d'Information et de Documentation Jeunesse, 101, quai Branly, 75740 Paris Cédex 15, tel: 01 44 49 12 25, fax: 01 40 65 02 61.

Loisirs de France Jeunes, 30 rue Godot-de-Mauroy, 75009 Paris, tel: 01 47 42 51 81, fax: 01 42 66 19 74. For details on holiday centres for children and teenagers.

Disabled Travellers

Most travellers with disabilities will want to book **accommodation** in advance rather than arriving "on spec". Most of the official list of hotels (available from regional tourist offices – *see page 327*) include a symbol to denote wheelchair access, but it is always advisable to check directly with the chosen hotel as to exactly what facilities are available to guests.

Balladins is a chain of newly built, budget-priced hotels throughout France, which all have at least one room designed for guests with disabilities, and restaurants and all other public areas are easily accessible. For a complete list contact: Hotels Balladins (Hotels et Compagnie Nuit d'Hotel Balladins Climat de France Relais Bleus), 5 avenue du Cap Horn, 91943 Les Ulis, tel: 02 69 29 32 00, fax: 02 69 07 93 89.

An **information sheet** aimed at disabled travellers is published by the French Government Tourist Office; this lists accommodation suitable for the disabled (including wheelchair users) across France but if you have specific needs it is best to double check when booking.

The following organisations all offer advice and publish booklets specifically for people with disabilities wanting to take various kinds of holiday in France:

Association des Paralysés de France
Service Information
17 boulevard August Blanqui
75013 Paris
Tel: 01 40 78 69 00

CNFLRH (Comité Nationale Français de Liaison pour le Readaption de Handicapés)
236 bis rue de Tolbiac
75013 Paris
Tel: 01 53 80 66 66
Fax: 01 53 80 66 67
E-mail: cnrh@worldnet.net
This organisation offers a good information service.

Direction des Musées de France, Service Accueil des Publics Spécifiques, 6 rue des Pyramides, 75041 Paris Cédex
Tel: 01 40 15 35 88
For information on access to museums.

SNCF (French Rail) and the **Gîtes de France** organisation both publish practical guides for travellers with reduced mobility.

Michelin's *Red Guide France*, which covers hotel accommodation, and their camping guide, entitled *Camping-Caravanning – France*, include symbols showing which places are equipped with good facilities for disabled travellers.

RADAR (The Royal Association for Disability and Rehabilitation)
12 City Forum, 250 City Rd,
London EC1V 8AF
Tel: 0207 250 32222
Fax: 0207 250 0212
www.radar.org.uk
Useful information for tourists.
RADAR's sister organisation in France is CNFLRH (the Comité National Français de Liaison pour la Réadaptation des Handicapés – for address, see above).

SATH (Society for the Advancement of Travel for the Handicapped)
347 5th Avenue, Suite 610, New York
Tel: 212-447 7284
Fax: 212-725 8253
www.sath.org.

Students & Young People

Students and young people under the age of 26 can benefit from cut-price travel to France and rail cards for getting around the region – for details *see Getting There, page 325*.

If you wish to stay in the region for a prolonged amount of time, it

may be worthwhile finding out about an exchange visit or study holiday. Several organisations exist to provide information or arrange such visits. In the UK, the **Central Bureau for Educational Visits and Exchanges**, Seymour Mews House, Seymour Mews, London WIH 9PE, tel: 0207 486 5101, produces three useful books with information on working and studying in France: *Working Holidays* (note that opportunities in the region are fairly limited; it is the grape harvest further south that is still a big draw for young people). Employment opportunities are listed in the guide. *Home from Home* lists a wealth of useful information about staying with a French family and *Study Holidays*, gives details of language courses across the region.

Student Reductions

Once in France, students will find a valid student identity card is very useful in obtaining discounts on all sorts of activities, including admission to museums and galleries, cinemas, theatres, etc. Reductions are sometimes allowed if you can prove your status with a passport, but this is at the discretion of the individual organisation and cannot be counted on.

The following agencies specialise in helping young people to arrange their holidays in France and will help you with a youth card:

UFCV (Union Française des Centres de Vacances et de Loisirs)
10 Quai Charente
75019 Paris
Tel: 01 44 72 14 14
Fax: 01 40 34 53 49
Organises cultural, sporting and leisure holidays for young people from 4 to 18 years old.

USIT Campus Travel
Tel: 08702 401010
STA (London)
Tel: 0207 837 9666

STA (Australia)
Tel: 03 9347 6911
CIEE (Council on International
Educational Exchange)
205 E. 42nd Street
New York
NY 10017
Tel: 212-661 1414
American Council for International Studies Inc.
19 Bay State Road
Boston, Mass. 02215
Tel: 617-236 2051
Youth for Understanding International Exchange
3501 Newark Street NW
Washington DC 20016
Tel: 202-966 6800
Fax: 800 833 6243
Centre d'Information et Documentation de Jeunesse
(CIDJ), based at 101 Quai Branly, 75015 Paris, is a national organisation which disseminates information pertaining to youth and student activities. There are also **Centres d'Information Jeunesse** at 104 rue Neuve Saint-Jean, 14300 Caen, tel: 02 31 85 73 60, and at 84 rue Beauvoisine, 76000 Rouen, tel: 02 35 98 38 75. The centres hold information on all kinds of facilities in the region, including those for sports, accommodation and activity holidays, as well as riding and holiday centres for disabled youngsters.

Language Courses

General
Union Nationale des Organisations de Séjours Linguistiques
19 rue des Mathurins, 75009 Paris
Tel: 01 49 24 03 61
Fax: 01 42 65 39 38
A national association of organisations offering language courses. A list of schools can be obtained upon written request.

In Normandy
École des Roches
BP 710, 27137 Verneuil-sur-Avre
Tel: 02 32 23 40 00
Courses for 11 to 18 year olds that also offers many additional leisure facilities.

Envol Espace
Le Trifid, rue Claude-Bloch, 14050 Caen Cédex
Tel: 02 31 06 07 89
Fax: 02 31 43 81 31
Specialist tour operator for youth groups.

Doing Business

Business travel now accounts for roughly a third of all French tourism revenue. This important market has led to the creation of a special Conference and Incentive Department in the French Government Tourist Office in both London and New York (see page 327) to deal solely with business travel enquiries. They will help organise hotels, conference centres and incentive deals for any group, whether large or small.

For general information on business travel and facilities contact the regional or departmental tourist offices (see Useful Addresses, page 327). They will be able to provide details of hotels that have conference facilities and are suited to housing large parties.

Getting Around

Maps

A first essential in touring any part of France is a good map. The Institut Géographique National (IGN) is the French equivalent of the British Ordnance Survey and their maps are excellent; those covering the region are listed below:

Red Series (1:250,000, 1 cm to 2.5 km) sheet No. 102 covers the region at a good scale for touring.

Green Series (1:100,000, 1 inch to 4 miles or 1 cm to 1 km) maps are more detailed, local plans. Sheet Nos 6 and 7 cover the north and much of the centre of the region, Nos 16 and 17 the south, and Nos 18 and 8 the east.

The Green Series is also quite good for walking, although serious walkers will need IGN's highly detailed 1:50,000 and 1:25,000 scales in the **Blue Series**.

Another particularly good set of maps for touring are the **Telegraph** (Recta Foldex) ones which cover France on four maps; the northwest sheet is the best one for Normandy.

Michelin regional maps are published at a scale of 1;200,000 (1 cm to 2 km); sheet No. 231 covers the whole of Normandy. Local maps are published at the same scale; sheet No. 52 covers the northeast, Nos 55 and 60 the centre, No. 54 the Cherbourg peninsula and sheet No. 59 covers the southwest. Michelin also publish a special historical map, sheet No. 102, the Battle of Normandy map (1:200,000).

Town plans are often given away free at local tourist offices, but if you wish to purchase them in advance, they are available from Michelin or Blay.

Buying Maps

In France, most good bookshops should have a range of maps, but they may cost less in hypermarkets or service stations. Town plans can often be picked up free of charge in local tourist offices.

Stockists in London are **Stanfords International Map Centre**, 12–14 Long Acre, Covent Garden, WC2E 9LP, tel: 0207 836 1321; **The Travel Bookshop**, 13 Blenheim Crescent, London W11 2EE, tel: 0207 229 5260 (www.thetravelbookshop.co.uk).

World Leisure Marketing, 11 Newmarket Court, Derby, DE24 8NW, tel: freephone 0800 83 80 80, fax: 01332 573 399, which offers a mail-order service, is the agent for IGN.

T & V Holt Associates, Oak House, Woodnesborough, Sandwich, Kent CT13 0NJ, tel/fax: 01304 614 123, specialise in maps and guide books to the battlefields. Major and Mrs Holt also organise guided tours of the battlefields *(see page 353)*.

Bicycle Hire

Car hire can be expensive if rentals are organised locally *(see Driving, page 333)*, but bikes *(vélos)* are fairly readily available for hire, often from ordinary cycle shops. Note that you will almost certainly be required to leave a safety deposit. Local tourist offices keep information on hire facilities. French Railways have bikes for hire at several stations in the region and they do not necessarily have to be returned to the same station. Bikes can be carried free of charge on buses and some trains *(Autotrains)*; on other, faster services you will have to pay. Travelling by a combination of bike and bus or train can be an excellent way of touring, and relieves you of some of the legwork. For further details on cycling *(see page 356)*.

Taxis

Taxis are usually readily available in the main towns in the region. The best places to find taxis are at railway stations and at official taxi ranks in city centres.

By Bus

Details of routes and timetables are generally available free of charge either from bus stations *(gare routières)*, which are often situated close to railway stations, or from tourist offices. Details of coach tours and sightseeing excursions are also available from bus stations.

By Train

Information on services is available from stations *(Gares SCNF)*. If you intend to travel extensively by train it may be worth obtaining a rail pass before leaving home *(see page 326)*. Children under 4 travel free, while those aged between 4 and 12 travel for half fare.

Adults travelling in groups of six or more can also obtain discounts (between 20 and 40 percent, depending on the number of people travelling together). All tickets have to be put through the orange machines at the stations to validate them before boarding the train. These machines are marked *"compostez votre billet"*.

Rules of the Road

Visitors from the UK must remember to drive on the right: it doesn't take long to get used to, but extra care should be taken when crossing the carriageway, for instance, as it is very easy to come out and automatically drive on the left, especially if there is no other traffic around.

The minimum age for driving in France is 18 and foreigners are not permitted to drive on a provisional licence.

Full or dipped headlights must be used in poor visibility and at night; sidelights are not sufficient, unless the car is stationary. Beams must be adjusted for right-hand-drive vehicles, but yellow tints are not compulsory.

The use of seat belts (front and rear, if fitted), and crash helmets for motorcyclists is compulsory.

Children under 10 are not permitted to ride in the front seat unless it is fitted with a rear-facing safety seat or if the car has no rear seat.

Priorité à la Droite: An important rule to remember is that priority on French roads is always given to vehicles approaching from the right, **except where otherwise indicated**. In practice, on main roads the major road will normally have priority, with traffic being halted on minor approach roads with one of the following signs:
● *Stop*
● *Cédez le passage* – give way
● *Vous n'avez pas la priorité* – you do not have right of way
● *Passage protégé* – no right of way

Particular care should be taken in towns, where you may wrongly assume you are on the major road, and in rural areas where there may not be any road markings (watch out for farm vehicles). Note that if a driver flashes his headlights, it is to indicate that he has priority, *not* the other way round. Priority is always given to emergency services as well as public utility vehicles, e.g. gas, electricity and water companies.

A few years ago, the French changed the rules concerning roundabouts – in theory, drivers already on the roundabout now have priority over those entering it, but beware – some drivers still insist that priority belongs to the drivers entering a roundabout.

NB: A yellow diamond sign indicates that you have priority but the diamond sign with a diagonal black line indicates that you don't.

Fuel

As in the UK, leaded petrol is no longer available. Unleaded petrol *(essence sans plomb)* and lead replacement, as well as diesel, can be bought. Petrol is currently cheaper in France than in the UK. Main tourist offices can supply maps showing the location of filling stations.

Driving

British, US, Canadian and Australian licences are all valid in France and you should always carry your vehicle's registration document and valid insurance (third party is the absolute minimum and a green card – available from your insurance company – is highly recommended). Additional insurance cover, which can include a "get-you-home" service, is offered by a number of organisations including the British and American Automobile Associations and Europ-Assistance. In the UK, contact the latter at Sussex House, Perrymount Road, Haywards Heath, West Sussex RH16 1DN, tel: 01444 442 442

SPEED LIMITS

Speed limits are as follows, unless otherwise indicated: 130 kph (80 mph) on motorways; 110 kph (68 mph) on dual carriageways; 90 kph (56 mph) on other roads, except in towns where the limit is 50 kph (30 mph). There is also a minimum speed limit of 80 kph (50 mph) on the outside lane of motorways during daylight with good visibility and on level ground. Speed limits are reduced by (20 kph/12 mph on motorways) in wet weather.

On-the-spot fines can be levied for speeding; on toll roads, the time is printed on the ticket you take at your entry point and can thus be checked and a fine imposed on exit. Nearly all *autoroutes* (motorways) are toll roads.

Autoroutes are designated A roads and national highways are N

roads. D roads are usually well maintained, while C (local roads) may not always be so.

Carry a red warning triangle to place 50 metres (55 yards) behind the car in case of a breakdown or accident; this is compulsory if you are towing a caravan. In an accident or emergency, call the police (dial 17) or use the free emergency telephones (every 2 km/1 mile) on motorways. If another driver is involved, lock your car and go together to call the police. It is useful to carry a European Accident Statement Form (obtainable from your insurance company) which will simplify matters in the case of an accident.

MOTORCYCLES/MOPEDS

Rules of the road for those in charge of two-wheeled vehicles are largely the same as for car drivers. The minimum age for driving machines over 80cc is 18. National number plates must be shown and crash helmets are compulsory. Dipped headlights must be used at all times. Children under 14 years cannot be carried as passengers.

CAR HIRE

Hiring a car can be an expensive business in France, partly because of the high VAT (TVA) rate, which is 33 percent on luxury items. It can be considerably cheaper to arrange hire in the UK or US before leaving for France. The following are UK numbers of international companies with offices at the Channel ports and in major cities:
Avis: tel: 0870 590 0500
Europcar: tel: 0207 834 8484
Hertz: tel: 0870 599 6699

Some fly/drive deals work out reasonably well if you're only going for a short visit. French Railways offer a good deal on their combined train/car rental bookings. The minimum age to hire a car is 18, but most companies will not hire to anyone under 21. The hirer must also have held a full licence for at

least a year. You will usually be asked to leave your credit card details as a deposit, even if you are paying in cash. Apart from Avis, most companies have an upper age limit of 60 to 65.

TOURIST ROUTES

Following a tourist circuit, or route, is a sure way of getting to see the major sites of a region. Some are designed to help appreciate the countryside, such as the apple route *(Route de la Pomme)*, but many have an historical significance, such as those connected to World War II. Here are a few suggestions; local tourist offices will provide more complete itineraries and maps.

The **Historical Route of the Norman Master Builders** is contained in a leaflet published, in English by the Caisse Nationale des Monuments, 62 rue Sainte-Antoine, 75186 Paris Cédex 04, tel: 01 44 61 2000, fax: 01 44 61 21 81. This route largely follows the west coast from Cherbourg down to Mont-St-Michel, dipping inland to Valognes, a town of many noble houses, Coutances, with its splendid cathedral, and Hambye for its ruined abbey in classic Norman Gothic style.

The same organisation will also provide details of the **Route Historique des Ducs de Normandie**, covering much of Calvados and including many reminders of William the Conqueror, such as his birthplace at Falaise and the Abbaye-aux-Hommes and the Abbaye-aux-Dames, built for William and his wife in Caen.

Liberty Road follows the itinerary of the battles during the liberation of France in 1944, all the way to Bastogne in Belgium. Special kilometre markers show the route. Kilometre 302 stands in front of the town hall in Sainte-Mère-Eglise, which was liberated on the night of 5 June 1944; there is also a 3002 km marker at Utah Beach. Further information is available from the Manche Tourist office *(see page 327)*.

There are also eight separate routes of varying lengths, signposted **Normandie-Terre Liberté**, showing the different stages of the Battle of Normandy. A leaflet, *The D-Day Landings and the Battle of Normandy*, describing the routes, is available, along with a special pass giving discount entry to museums along the routes, from L'Association des Sites et Musées de l'Espace Historique de la Bataille de Normandie; the association is based at the tourist office in Caen *(see page 327)*.

La Route Normandie-Vexin offers a 200-km (124-mile) cultural tour from Rouen towards Paris ending at Monet's house and garden at Giverny, and taking in some spectacular sights en route; high points include the Cistercian abbey at Fontaine-Guérard, the majestic ruins at Les Andelys and the 18th-century Château de Bizy in Vernon.

Normandy is famed for its riding stables, and in the Orne you can follow the **Route Historique des Haras et des Châteaux de l'Orne**, which includes the important national stud farm *(haras)* at Le Pin-au-Haras. Other important sites on the route are Sées cathedral, Sassy Manor with its formal gardens, and the Château d'O at Mortrée.

Also in the Orne, the **Suisse Normande Route** is signposted through the lovely Orne valley, passing through Thury-Harcourt, Condé-sur-Noireau and Clécy with its narrow streets and museums.

The **Cider Route** is signposted, "*Route du Cidre*" in the Pays d'Auge, linking attractive country towns such as Cambremer, Beuvron-en-Auge and Beaufour-Druval. Along the way, many small farms offer tastings of their produce – not just cider, but also the apple brandy, Calvados, and pommeau, the aperitif made from cider apples.

The Seine-Maritime tourist board has come up with several routes around their *département*, including the **Route du Val de Seine et des Abbayes**, which takes visitors to some of the greatest abbeys in the Seine Valley. The Eure tourist board

has also produced its own guide to marked routes: **Circuits en Vallée de Risle et Alentours**. For further details, write to the tourist offices in the area concerned *(see page 327)*.

A further source of information on historic routes and monuments is Demeure Historique, 57 Quai de la Tournelle, 75005 Paris, tel: 01 55 42 60 00.

Ramblers

France has a network of waymarked footpaths, called *Grande Randonnées*, which are well signposted and offer good facilities for walkers en route.

The paths are classified with a GR number and there are countless opportunities for exploring Normandy by foot, either following a long route, or on one of the shorter circular tours. Suggested tours might be the GR2 Cliffs on the Seine; GR223 Cotentin tour from Avranches to Barfleur; GR261 Normandy Landing Beaches; GR36 Ouistreham to Ecouché via the Orne Valley or a 250-km (155-mile) tour of the Pays d'Auge. Other GR paths include the Pays de Caux (GR21, 211 and 212); Suisse Normande (GR221); Eure valley and forests (GR222); the Normandy-Maine Regional Park (GR22 and 36) and the GR26, which runs from Feucherolles via Evreux and Bernay to the coast at Deauville.

These GR routes come under the protection of the French Ramblers

Hitchhiking

With sensible precautions, hitchhiking can be an interesting and inexpensive way to get around France. As anywhere else, women should be wary of hitchhiking alone. Would-be hitchhikers may be discouraged by the difficulty of getting a lift out of the channel ports, so it may be worth taking a bus or train for the first leg of your journey. Hitching is forbidden on motorways, but you can wait on slip roads or at toll booths.

Association, Fédération Française de la Randonnée Pédestre (FFRP), which publishes Topoguides (guide books incorporating IGN 1:50,000 scale maps) to all France's footpaths (in French). The guides are available in good bookshops in France, or in the UK.

McCarta's *Footpaths of Europe* series are regional walking guides based on the Topoguides, in English, with IGN mapping. There are two titles for the region: *Normandy and the Seine,* covering the 700 km (435 miles) of footpaths along the Seine from Paris to the coast; and *Coastal Walks in Normandy and Brittany*, a guide to the 900 km (560 miles) of footpaths bordering the fascinating coastline across the two regions. The IGN Blue series maps at a scale of 1:25,000 are ideal for walkers *(see page 331)*.

Each *département* has its own ramblers' organisation (operating under the FFRP umbrella), which arranges a variety of activities throughout the year. There are guided walks taking a day, a weekend or more, as well as walks with a particular theme, flora, or wildlife for example.

For more information, contact: **Centre d'Information Sentiers et Randonnée**, 14 rue riquet, 75019 Paris, tel: 01 44 89 93 93, fax: 01 40 35 85 67; **Randonnées Normandes**, CRT, le Doyenné, 14 rue Charles Corbeau, 27000 Évreux; or local tourist offices.

Various walking holidays with accommodation either in hotels or under canvas are available. The following are useful addresses: **Office National des Forêts**, 36 rue St-Blaise, 61000 Alençon, tel: 02 33 82 55 00; **Inntravel**, Hovingham, York YO6 4JZ, tel: 01653 628 811, fax: 01653 628 741.

Visitors can take advantage of low-priced accommodation offered in *gîtes d'étapes*, hostels offering basic facilities which are to be found on many of the GR routes and in mountain regions. For more information contact the Gîtes de France organisation *(see Where to Stay, page 340)*.

Holiday villas beyond indulgence.

BALEARICS ~ CARIBBEAN ~ FRANCE ~ GREECE ~ ITALY ~ MAURITIUS
MOROCCO ~ PORTUGAL ~ SCOTLAND ~ SPAIN

If you enjoy the really good things in life, we offer the highest quality holiday villas with the utmost privacy, style and true luxury. You'll find each with maid service and most have swimming pools.

For 18 years, we've gone to great lengths to select the very best villas at all of our locations around the world.

Contact us for a brochure on the destination of your choice and experience what most only dream of.

INTERNATIONAL CHAPTERS

Toll Free: 1 866 493 8340
International Chapters, 47-51 St. John's Wood High Street, London NW8 7NJ. Telephone: +44(0)20 7722 0722
email: info@villa-rentals.com www.villa-rentals.com

Where to Stay

Hotels

Although hotels are plentiful in the main towns of the region and along the main highways, those tucked away in the smaller country villages are sometimes the best. All hotels in France conform to national standards and carry star-ratings, set down by the Ministry of Tourism, according to their degree of comfort and amenities. Prices are charged per room, rather than per person and range from as little as €32 for a double room in an unclassified hotel (i.e. its standards are not sufficient to warrant a single star, but it is likely to be clean, cheap and cheerful), to around €96 for the cheapest double room in a 4-star luxury hotel.

Hotels are required to display their menus outside, and details of room prices should be visible either outside or in reception, as well as on the back of bedroom doors. It is possible, and not uncommon, for a hotel to have a 1-star rating, with a 2-star restaurant. This is ideal if you are on a budget and more interested in food than wallpaper or plumbing.

When booking a room you should normally be shown it before agreeing to take it; this is common practice in France. Supplements may be charged for an additional bed or a cot (lit bébé). You may be asked when booking if you wish to dine, particularly if the hotel is busy. You are not obliged to take a meal along with the room but preference is often given to customers who are going to eat in the hotel dining room, as there is not a lot of profit in letting rooms alone.

Also, the simple request, "On peut dîner ici ce soir?" will confirm that the hotel's restaurant is open (many are closed out of season on Sunday or Monday evening).

Lists of hotels can be obtained from the French Government Tourist office in your own country or from regional or local tourist offices in France. It is also worth buying from the Tourist Office in London the Logis et Auberges de France guide (www.logis-de-france.fr). This is an invaluable guide to an excellent and reasonably priced network of family-run hotels, which aim to offer a friendly welcome and good local cuisine. The guide can also be bought in bookshops in France. It can be used to book hotels before travelling (for the central reservation office in Paris, tel: 01 45 84 83 84; UK, tel: 0207 287 3181); they also offer a "Logis en Liberté" or a "Go as you please" service, where you can book several hotels participating in the scheme for a flat rate.

Some tourist offices will make hotel bookings for you for a small fee. Several other hotel chains and associations offer central booking facilities. These range from the very cheap and simple groups such as the Balladins chain of modest but very modern 1-star hotels, to the Concorde group of 4-star and de-luxe hotels.

A brief list of central booking offices in the UK is given here.

Mercure, Reservations: 01 60 77 27 27. UK office, **Resinter**, 1 Shortlands, London W6 8DR, tel: 0208 283 4500; fax: 0208 283 4650.

Campanile, Reservations: 21 avenue Jean-Moulin, 77200 Torcy, tel: 01 64 62 46 46/0149 78 01 45, fax: 01 64 62 46 61; www.campanile.fr. Over 200 2-star to 4-star hotels. UK office, Red Lion Court, Alexandra Road, Hounslow TW3 1JS, tel: 0208 569 6969, fax: 0208 569 4888.

Climat de France, 5 rue Cap-Horn, 91943 Les Ulis, tel: 01 64 46 01 23. About 150 2-star hotels.

UK office, Voyages Vacances Int., 34 Saville Row, London W1X 1AG, tel: 0207 478 8213.

Concorde Hotels, 35–37 Grosvenor Gardens, London SW1W 0BS, tel: 0800 181 591 or 0207 630 1704, fax: 0207 630 0391.

Formule 1, Reservations: 35 rue Dr Babinski 93400 Saint-Ouen, tel: 01 49 21 90 75, fax: 01 49 21 90 79. One-star, budget-priced hotels, offering a booking service from one hotel to another in the chain.

Ibis Reservations, 91021 Evry tel: 08 03 88 22 22. More than 160 2-star hotels. UK office, **Resinter**, 1 Shortlands, London W6 8DR, tel: 0208 283 4500, fax: 0208 283 4650.

Price Guide

Prices are given for a double room. Breakfast is not usually included.

$	budget: under €50
$$	moderate: €50–€110
$$$	luxury: over €110

Hotel Listings by Area

The following is a selection of good hotels in Normandy to suit all budgets. The Normandy Tourist Board in Bristol (see page 327) offers a free booking service for a large selection of hotels in the region. Also look under restaurant listings (see page 343) because many places recommended mainly for their restaurants also have rooms and make useful overnight stops.

SEINE MARITIME

Criel-sur-Mer
Royal Albion Hotel
1 rue de la Mer, 76910 Mesnil-Val-Plage
Tel: 02 35 86 2142
Fax: 02 35 86 78 51
This attractive hotel in its own spacious grounds has a great location near the sea on the outskirts of Le Tréport. **$$**

Dieppe

Au Grand Duquesne
15 place St-Jacques, 76200
Tel: 02 32 14 61 10
Fax: 02 35 84 29 83
A dozen pleasant rooms, all en suite, with TV in a Logis de France hotel just a few steps from the port and St-Jacques church. **$**

Les Arcades de la Bourse
1–3 Arcades de la Bourse, Port de Plaisance, 76200
Tel: 02 35 84 14 12
Fax: 02 35 40 22 29
An attractive old building, right on the harbour side; 21 rooms, all with views of the port. Restaurant specialises in seafood. **$$**

La Présidence
boulevard de Verdun, 76200
Tel: 02 35 84 31 31
Fax: 02 35 84 86 70
Large hotel on the seafront with panoramic restaurant overlooking the sea. **$$**

Eu

Pavillon de Joinville
Route du Tréport, 76260
Tel: 02 35 50 52 52
Fax: 02 35 50 27 37
A former hunting lodge, set in delightful grounds. **$$**

Fécamp

Auberge de la Rouge
route du Havre, 76400
Saint-Léonard
Tel: 02 35 28 07 59
Fax: 02 35 28 70 55
A *Logis de France* inn, on the outskirts of town, with its own garden and terrace but only 8 rooms. **$$**

Relais et Châteaux

Relais et Châteaux is a group of independently owned hotels and restaurants in former castles and other historic buildings. The group publishes a guide, which is available by post from Grape Vine Publishing, Grosvenor Gardens House, 35 Grosvenor Gardens, London SW1W 0ES. For further information, tel: 0207 630 7667 or 0870 242 0052.

Hôtel Normandy
4 avenue Gambetta, 76400
Tel: 02 35 29 55 11
Fax: 02 35 27 48 74
In the heart of the old town, this pleasantly old-fashioned looking hotel has 30 en suite rooms with phone and TV; a large car park; belle époque-style Maupassant Brasserie and a very good restaurant. Narrow stairs and no lift are its only disadvantage **$$**

Le Havre

Clarine
quai Colbert, 76600
Tel: 02 35 26 49 49
Fax: 02 35 25 10 13
This 86-bed hotel has rooms overlooking the Bassin Vauban. The restaurant is good value and well worth trying. **$$**

Hotel Foch
4 rue de Caligny, 76600
Tel: 02 35 42 50 69
Fax: 02 35 43 40 17
Reasonably priced hotel in quiet surroundings near the marina, not far from the sea. **$**

Vent d'Ouest
4 rue de Caligny, 76600
Tel: 02 35 42 50 69
Fax: 02 35 42 58 00
A comfortable 3-star hotel furnished with marine-style antiques. Parking; conference rooms; sports club. **$$**

Martin Église

Auberge du Clos Normand
22 rue Henri IV, 76370
Tel: 02 35 04 40 34
Fax: 02 35 04 48 49
Leafy riverside inn with a rustic restaurant serving regional food. **$$**

Neufchâtel-en-Bray

Le Grand Cerf
9 grande rue Fausse Porte, 76270.
Tel: 02 35 93 00 02
Fax: 02 35 94 14 92
Hotel and restaurant set in its own pleasant grounds. **$$**

Pont-Audemer

Le Petit Coq aux Champs
la Pommeraie Sud, 27500
Campigny
Tel: 02 32 41 04 19
Fax: 02 32 56 06 25

This fairy-tale thatched cottage set in a wonderful garden is nicely situated for visiting the resorts of the Côte Fleurie. To find it, take the A13 from Pont-Audemer, then the D29 in direction of Campigny. **$$$**

Rouen

Hôtel Dandy
93 rue Cauchoise, 76000
Tel: 02 35 07 32 00
Fax: 02 35 15 48 82
In a central, pedestrianised street near the Place du Vieux Marché, the Dandy has 18 well-furnished rooms. **$$**

Hôtel des Carmes
33 Place des Carmes, 76000
Tel: 02 35 71 92 31
Fax: 02 35 71 76 96
Attractive small hotel (12 rooms) with colourful decor in quiet but central square. **$$**

Hôtel de Dieppe
place Bernard-Tissot, 76000
Tel: 02 35 71 96 00
Fax: 02 35 89 65 21
Convenient for the station, with quiet rooms. **$**

Hôtel de la Cathédrale
12 rue St-Romain, 76000
Tel: 02 35 71 57 95
Fax: 02 35 70 15 54
In a 17th-century building with a pleasant little courtyard, this friendly hotel stands on a cobbled street, close to historic sites and restaurants. **$$**

Hôtel de Lisieux
4 rue de la Savonnerie, 76000
Tel: 02 35 71 87 73
Fax: 02 35 89 31 52
Good-value accommodation in a modernised old building between the cathedral and river. **$**

Sassetout-Le-Mauconduit

Château de Sassetot
76540 Sassetout-Le-Mauconduit
Tel: 02 35 28 00 11
Fax: 02 35 28 50 00
Situated off the D925 between Fécamp and Dieppe, this splendid château was the home of Sissi, Empress of Austria, in the late 19th century. Impressive dining room, terrace, large garden and tennis courts. **$$–$$$**

Varengeville sur Mer
Des Sapins
Ste-Marguérite-sur-Mer, 76119
Tel: 02 35 85 11 45
Fax: 02 35 04 33 37
Sweet little seaside hotel with a garden. **$$**
La Terrasse
Vasterival, 76119
Tel: 02 35 85 12 54
Fax: 02 35 85 11 70
Approached down a narrow lane and perched on a cliff from which there are stupendous views, this hotel has 22 rooms and a large restaurant with a covered terrace. **$–$$**

Veules-les-Roses
Douce France
13 rue du Docteur Girard, 76980
Tel: 02 35 57 85 30
Fax: 02 35 57 85 31
A delightful 17th-century post house, lovingly restored, set by the river in this pretty village. Courtyard and garden. Small suites with kitchenettes. Restaurant. Disabled access. **$$**

CALVADOS

Arromanches
Hôtel de la Marine
2 Quai du Canada, 14117
Tel: 02 31 22 33 18
Fax: 02 31 22 98 80
Old-fashioned seafront hotel with sea-view restaurant; an ideal base for visiting the landing beaches. **$**

Audrieu
Château d'Audrieu
Audrieu, 14250
Tel: 02 31 80 21 52
Fax: 02 31 80 24 73
Eighteenth-century château with original decor, set in its own grounds. Convenient for Bayeux and Caen. Excellent restaurant. **$$$**

Bayeux
Grand Hôtel du Luxembourg
25 rue des Bouchers, BP 331, 14400
Tel: 02 31 92 00 04
Fax: 02 31 92 54 26
Classic grand hotel restored in over-

the-top Best Western glass-and-marble style. **$$**
Hôtel d'Argouges
21 rue St-Patrice
Tel: 02 31 92 88 86
Fax: 02 31 92 69 16
A stylish mansion with a quiet inner courtyard and a garden, yet within walking distance of the city centre. Parking; 25 rooms. **$$**
Le Lion d'Or
71 rue St-Jean, 14400
Tel: 02 31 92 06 90
Fax: 02 31 22 15 64
This splendid hotel was once a coaching inn – part of the building dates back to the 17th century. Comfortable rooms. The rather formal restaurant has a good reputation though it has lost its Michelin star. **$$**

Cabourg
Grand Hôtel
Promenade Marcel-Proust, 14390
Tel: 02 31 91 01 79
Fax: 02 31 24 03 20
It would be a shame not to include the hotel made famous by Marcel Proust, where his favourite Madeleine cakes are still served for breakfast. Right on the seafront, the Grand has all the comforts and facilities expected of a 4-star hotel, including a pool, tennis courts and business facilities. **$$$**
Hôtel du Golf
avenue de l'Hippodrome, 14390
Tel: 02 31 24 12 34
Fax: 02 31 24 18 51
Well-equipped resort hotel with garden and swimming-pool, near golf course. **$$**

Caen
Le Dauphin
29 rue Gemare, 14000
Tel: 02 31 86 22 26
Fax: 02 31 86 35 14

Set in an attractively renovated former priory close to the town centre. **$$**
Hôtel St-Etienne
2 rue de l'Academie, 1400
Tel 02 31 86 35 82
Fax: 02 31 85 57 69
Good-value hotel in 18th-century stone building in old quarter. **$$**

Cambremer
Château Les Bruyères
Route du Cadran, 14340
Tel: 02 31 32 22 45
Fax: 02 31 32 22 58
Period furnishings, large gardens, pool, 13 rooms. At the heart of the Cider Route. Closed January to first week in April. **$$–$$$**

Crepon
Ferme de la Rançonnière
Route de Creully, 14480
Tel: 02 31 22 21 73
Fax: 02 31 22 98 39
email: ranconniere@wanadoo.fr
www.ranconniere.com
A beautiful old country manor house (13th–15th century) just 13 km (8 miles) east of Bayeux, and in a good position for exploring the Normandy beaches. Attractive rooms, many with exposed beams and antiques. **$$**

Deauville
Etap Hotel
St Arnoult, Route de Deauville, 14800
Tel: 02 31 14 80 80
Fax: 02 31 14 80 90
A decent cheap hotel. **$**
Hôtel Royal
boulevard Cornuché, 14800
Tel: 02 31 98 66 33
Fax: 02 31 98 66 34
Star-studded grand hotel – one of the top places to stay in this

Bring Your Own

It is worth bearing in mind that tea- and coffee-making facilities and hairdryers, which are standard in most English hotels and B&Bs, are rarely found in budget and moderately priced French hotel rooms.

elegant resort. Sea views, chintz and chandeliers. **$$$**
L'Augeval
15 avenue Hocquart de Turtot, 14800
Tel: 02 31 81 13 18
Fax: 02 31 81 00 40
Typical Normandy seaside architecture. Central position, comfortable rooms, heated outdoor pool. **$$–$$$** (depending on season)

Falaise
Hôtel de la Poste
38 rue Georges Clémenceau, 14700
Tel: 02 31 90 13 14
Fax: 02 31 90 01 81
Logis de France post-house hotel opposite the chateau of Fresnaye. **$**
Le Château du Terte
St-Martin-de-Mieux, 14700
Tel: 02 31 90 01 04
Fax: 02 21 90 33 16
An imposing château set in formal gardens. Rooms named after famous writers of the region. Nine rooms and two family suites. Open April to end October only. **$$$**

Honfleur
L'Absinthe
10 quai de la Quarantaine, 14600
Tel: (hotel) 02 31 89 23 23,
(restaurant) 02 31 89 39 00
Fax: 02 31 89 53 60
This beautifully appointed hotel occupies a 16th-century former presbytery, only a short walk from the Vieux Bassin. The restaurant can also be recommended. Private parking 200 metres away. **$$/$$$**
La Ferme-St-Siméon
rue Adolphe Marais, 14600
Tel: 02 31 81 78 00
Fax: 02 31 89 48 48
Pleasing country hotel, once a favourite of artists such as Monet and Corot and now a luxury *Relais et Châteaux* hotel with indoor swimming-pool and health club with sauna, solarium, etc. **$$$**
Le Cheval Blanc
2 Quai des Passagers, 14600
Tel: 02 31 81 65 00
Fax: 02 31 89 52 80
Quaint old hotel overlooking the fishing harbour, with two restaurants. **$$**

Lisieux
La Bretagne
36 Place de la République, 14100
Tel: 02 31 61 07 51
Fax: 02 31 62 43 59
Has one ground floor room suitable for people with disabilities. **$**

Pont-L'Evêque
Climat de France
Centre du Loisir du Lac, 14130
Tel: 02 31 64 64 00
Fax: 02 31 64 12 28
Modern hotel in a lakeside leisure complex. **$$**

Port-en-Bessin
Chateau la Chenevière
Commes, 14520
Tel: 02 31 51 25 25
Fax: 02 31 51 25 20
Conveniently situated for Bayeux and the D-Day beaches, the hotel occupies a magnificent stone mansion in its own park. There are 21 rooms and the gourmet restaurant has an excellent reputation. **$$$**

Price Guide

Prices are given for a double room. Breakfast is not usually included.
$ budget: under €50
$$ moderate: €50–€110
$$$ luxury: over €110

Touques
Le Village
64 rue Louvel et Brière, 14800
Tel: 02 31 88 01 77
Another reliable *Logis de France* hotel and restaurant. Attractive half-timbered building with an attractive terrace, opposite the town hall. **$$**

Trouville
Hôtel Le Cavendish
28 rue de la Plage
Tel: 02 31 88 70 70
Small, pleasant and inexpensive hotel (14 rooms) near the beach. **$–$$**
Hôtel Le Flaubert
rue Gustave Flaubert
Tel: 02 31 88 37 23
Fax: 02 31 88 21 56

Comfortable hotel with 33 rooms that likes to make the most of its association with the writer. Closed from mid-November to mid-March. **$$**
Mercure
Place Foch, 14360
Tel: 02 31 87 38 38
Fax: 02 31 87 35 41
Large and friendly hotel, with 80 rooms, in this popular resort. **$$**

Vire
Des Voyageurs
47 avenue de la Gare, 14500
Tel: 02 31 68 01 16
Fax: 02 31 67 61 86
Inexpensive *Logis de France* hotel, conveniently close to the station; 12 rooms. **$**

EURE

Le Bec Hellouin
L'Auberge de l'Abbaye
Le Bec Hellouin, 27800
Tel: 02 32 44 8602
Fax: 02 32 46 32 23
Attractive 18th-century half-timbered inn on the village square with rooms overlooking the rolling Risle valley. **$$**

Evreux
Hôtel de France
29 rue Saint-Thomas, 27000
Tel: 02 32 39 09 25
Fax: 02 32 38 38 56
Old-fashioned town hotel. Its small restaurant, famous for its apple tart, looks out onto a garden. **$–$$**

Pont-Audemer
Auberge du Vieux Puits
6 rue Notre-Dame-du-Pré, 27500
Tel: 02 32 41 01 48
Fax: 02 32 42 37 28
Tudor-style mansion near the centre of this lovely old town. Pretty courtyard. **$$**

Pont-Saint-Pierre
La Bonne Marmite
10 rue René Raban, 27360
Tel: 02 32 49 70 24
Fax: 02 32 48 12 41
Pleasant hotel in the Andelle valley, convenient for visiting Les Andelys, Château Gaillard, etc. **$$**

Saint-Pierre-du-Vouvray
Hostellerie Saint-Pierre
1 Chemin des Amoureux
Tel: 02 32 59 93 29
Fax: 02 32 59 41 93
Traditional, half-timbered mansion
(a former coaching inn) on the
banks of the Seine. **$$**

Verneuil-sur-Avre
Hostellerie du Clos
98 rue de la Ferté-Vidame, 27130
Tel: 02 32 32 21 81
Fax: 02 32 32 21 36
Elegant, turreted chateau in the
Relais et Châteaux chain. Rooms
furnished with period furniture and
there is a garden and parkland.
Tennis court and sauna. Closed
mid-December to end January and
Monday in low season. **$$$**

Vernon
Hôtel Normandy
1 rue Pierre Mendès France, 27200
Tel: 02 32 51 97 97
Fax: 02 32 21 01 66
Reasonable hotel, with 45 rooms,
convenient for visitors to Monet's
house and garden at Giverny. **$$**

ORNE

Alençon
Le Grand Saint Michel
7 rue du Temple, 61000
Tel: 02 33 26 04 77
Fax: 02 33 26 71 82
Small Logis de France hotel. **$$**

Argentan
Le Pavillon de Gouffern
61310 Silly-en-Gouffern
Tel: 02 33 36 64 26
Fax: 02 33 36 53 81
There are few hotels in Argentan so
this one just outside (take the N26 in
the direction of Paris) is a good find.
Set in parkland, it has 19 rooms. Its
restaurant has a good reputation. **$$**

Bagnoles de L'Orne
Capricorne
allée Montjoie, 61140
Tel: 02 33 37 96 99
Fax: 02 33 38 19 56
Family-run modern hotel with garden
and restaurant. **$**

Bellême
Relais Saint Louis
1 boulevard Bansard-des-Bois,
61130
Tel: 02 33 73 12 21
Fax: 02 33 83 71 19
Small, good-value Logis de France
hotel and restaurant. **$**

Clecy
Moulin du Vey
Le Vey, 14570
Tel 02 31 69 71 08
Fax 02 31 69 14 14
In a gorgeous spot on the banks of
the Orne below the picturesque
town of Clecy, in the heart of the
Suisse Normande. Good-quality
rooms (12) and a respected
restaurant. **$$**

La Ferté-Macé
Auberge d'Andaine
La Barbère, Route de Bagnoles,
61600
Tel: 02 33 37 20 28
Fax: 02 33 37 25 05
Country resort hotel and restaurant
in own grounds. Closed Sunday in
low season. **$$**

L'Aigle
Le Dauphin
4–6 Place de la Halle, 61300
Tel: 02 33 84 18 00
Fax: 02 33 34 09 28
Magnificent 17th-century hotel with
wood-panelled salon and 4-star
restaurant. **$$**

Mortagne au Perche
Du Tribunal
4 Place du Palais, 61400
Tel: 02 33 25 04 77
Fax: 02 33 83 60 83
Country resort hotel in leafy
grounds. **$$**

Pont d'Ouilly
Hôtel du Commerce
rue de Falaise, 14690
Tel: 02 31 69 80 16
Fax: 02 31 69 78 08
A traditional, provincial town
hotel in the centre of Pont d'Ouilly.
Friendly staff, comfy rooms and
decent, inexpensive food, but
not much in the way of
atmosphere. **$**

Sées
Le Cheval Blanc
1 Place Saint-Pierre, 61500
Tel: 02 33 27 80 48
Fax: 02 33 28 58 05
Small, reliable hotel in this
interesting cathedral town. **$**
Le Dauphin
31 place des Anciennes Halles,
61500
Tel: 02 33 27 80 07
Fax: 02 33 28 80 33
This small hotel (with just seven
beautifully decorated rooms, some
with four-poster beds) is in the
former market place, handily
situated for the cathedral and other
historic sights. **$$**

MANCHE

Avranches
Du Jardin des Plantes
10 Place Carnot, 50300
Tel: 02 33 58 03 68
Fax: 02 33 60 01 72
In a good location just outside the
city's famous botanical gardens,
this family hotel has a children's
play area and menu. **$$**

Barneville-Carteret
Hôtel de la Marine
11 rue de Paris, 50270
Tel: 02 33 53 83 31
Fax: 02 33 53 39 60
In a prime spot overlooking the
harbour in Carteret, and well placed
for exploring the best beaches of
the Cotentin; 31 rooms, many with
sea views. An excellent fish
restaurant with picture windows
giving splendid sea views. **$$**

Briquebec
Hôtel du Vieux Château
4 cours du Chateau, 50260
Tel: 02 33 52 24 29
Fax: 02 33 52 62 71
Located inside the ramparts of the
medieval castle in the heart of
Bricquebec, close to Cherbourg and
the north Cotentin beaches.
Tasteful rooms, and a restaurant in
the original knights' hall. Queen
Victoria and Field Marshall
Montgomery are among past
visitors. **$$**

Cherbourg
Hôtel de la Croix de Malte
5 rue des Halles, 50100
Tel: 02 33 43 19 16
Fax: 02 33 43 65 66
A friendly hotel in a good, central location, with extremely comfortable, good-value rooms. **$**
Le Louvre
2 rue H. Dunant, 50100
Tel: 02 33 53 02 28
Fax: 02 33 53 43 88
Convenient for the port. No restaurant. **$**

Coutances
Cositel
Route de Coutainville, BP 231, 50200
Tel: 02 33 07 5164
Fax: 02 33 07 06 23
Modern hotel with restaurant and wine bar, just outside Coutances. Well-equipped for people with disabilities and with good facilities for children, including mini-golf. **$$**

Granville
Hôtel Le Grand Large
5 rue de la Falaise, BP 617, 50406
Tel: 02 33 91 19 19
Fax: 02 33 91 19 00
Close to the town centre and right by the beach; 36 rooms plus apartments and duplex rooms with kitchens, that can be rented by the week. Thalassotherapy centre. **$$**
Le Michelet
5 rue Jules-Michelet, 50400
Tel: 02 33 50 06 55
Fax: 02 33 50 12 25
A small and friendly hotel (20 rooms) near the sea, just north of the old town. Simple, cheerful rooms, not all en suite. There is no restaurant. **$**

Hambye
Auberge de l'Abbaye
route de l'Abbaye, 50450
Tel: 02 33 61 42 19
Fax: 02 33 61 00 85
Located between the village of Hambye and the ruins of its famous abbey, this small, rural hotel has attractive, comfy rooms and a personal touch. Come here for the food if nothing else. Meat

Price Guide

Prices are given for a double room. Breakfast is not usually included.
$ budget: under €50
$$ moderate: €50–€110
$$$ luxury: over €110

grilled over a wood fire is a favourite. **$$**

Mont-St-Michel
Auberge St-Pierre
Grande Rue, 50116
Tel: 02 33 60 14 03
Fax: 02 33 48 59 82
A comfortable 3-star hotel in a 15th-century timbered building; 21 guest rooms, many with breathtaking views. Some rooms are in separate buildings (as with many hotels on the island). Book ahead and be prepared to carry your luggage up from the causeway car park. Closed in January. **$$–$$$**
Les Terrasses Poulard
Intra Muros–Grande Rue, BP18, 50170
Tel: 02 33 60 14 09
Fax: 02 33 60 37 31
Modern, comfortable hotel. **$$**

Saint-Lô
Les Voyageurs
5–7 avenue de Briovère, 50000
Tel: 02 33 05 08 63
Fax: 02 33 05 14 34
Like most hotels with this name, this one is conveniently near the station. **$$**

Saint-Vaast-la-Hougue
De France et des Fuschias
20 rue Maréchal Foch, 50550
Tel: 02 33 54 42 26
Fax: 02 33 43 46 79
Delightful old hotel, offering a good fish menu. **$$**

Sainte-Cécile
Manoir de l'Acherie
Sainte-Cécile, 50800
Tel: 02 33 51 13 87
Fax: 02 33 61 89 07
A 17th-century manor house in a peaceful setting near Villedieu-les-Poêles. **$$**

Bed & Breakfast

Bed-and-breakfast accommodation is fairly widely available in private houses, often on working farms, whose owners are members of the **Fédération Nationale des Gîtes Ruraux de France**. All such accommodation is inspected by a local representative of the Fédération to ensure that standards are maintained in accordance with its "star" rating, which is shown by ears of corn (épis) on a scale of one to four. Bookings can be made for an overnight stop or a longer stay. Breakfast is included in the price and evening meals – usually made with local produce and extremely good value – are often, but not always, available.

B&B France is an Anglo-French affair with an office in Oxfordshire. Its guide, Le B&B, is available by post from PO Box 66, Bell Street, Henley-on-Thames, Oxon RG9 1XS, tel: 01491 578 803, fax: 01491 410806. B&B France offers its own booking service (details in Le B&B) or you can book accommodation directly with the hosts.

Several other guide books are also devoted to B&B listings, including: AA Bed and Breakfast in France, which features a sample booking letter, and two guides from Springfield Books: Chambres et tables d'hôtes (French Country

B&B

Bed and breakfast and chambre d'hôtes or tables d'hôtes are not exactly the same thing, because some B&B establishments provide just that, with no evening meal. However, they do overlap considerably. In terms of information available they also overlap with gîtes and you can get details of B&B and chambre d'hôtes accommodation from the addresses given for the Fédération des Gîtes de France in the box on the following page.

Welcome) and *Prestige B&B and Gîtes Accommodation*, which concentrates on the more luxurious end of the market. These guides are available from good bookshops or directly from the publisher: Springfield Books Limited, Norman Road, Huddersfield HD8 8TH, tel: 01484 864 955, fax: 01484 865 443.

If you do not wish to book anything in advance, just look out for signs along the road (usually in the country) offering *chambres d'hôtes*. You will be taking pot luck, but you may be delighted by the simple farm food and accommodation on offer.

Gîtes

France has what is probably the best network of self-catering holiday cottages anywhere in Europe. The **Fédération des Gîtes Ruraux de France** was set up in the 1950s with the aim of restoring rural properties (by means of offering grants to owners) on the condition that these properties would then be let as cheap holiday homes for the less well-heeled town and city dwellers. These *gîtes* (literally: a place to lay one's head) have now become extremely popular with the British in particular, as an inexpensive way of enjoying a rural holiday in France.

The properties range from very simple farm cottages to grand châteaux. They are all inspected by the *Relais Départemental des Gîtes Ruraux de France* (the county office of the national federation – for addresses *see box below* – and given an *épi* (ear of corn) classification. The *gîtes* are completely self-catering – in many cases, you should expect to supply your own bed-linen – but many of them have owners living nearby who will tell you where you can buy local produce.

Clévacances

This is a national organisation that arranges reasonably priced holiday lets. Members of the association

abide by a charter and the houses, flats or other accommodation are inspected regularly by the tourist authorities and awarded a key symbol on a rating of one to four. Bookings are made directly with the owners. For information contact the departmental tourist offices of Seine-Maritime, Calvados or Manche (*see page 327*). Details are also available from the **Fédération Nationale des Locations de Vacances Clévacances**, 54 boulevard de l'Embouchure, BP 2166, 31022 Toulouse. Tel: 05 61 13 55 66, fax: 05 61 13 55 94.

Many other tour operators and private individuals offer self-catering accommodation, ranging from a simple farm cottage to an apartment in a luxurious château, that is not subject to any form of inspection. Try the private advertisements in the national press for examples. A selection of UK-based companies, who will usually handle your travel arrangements as part of the package, are listed below:

AA Motoring Holidays
PO Box 128, Copenhagen Court, Basingstoke RG21 7DP
Tel: 01256 814433
Fax: 01256 493875

Allez France
27–31 West Street, Storrington RH20 4DZ
Tel: 01903 742345
Fax: 01903 745044
Individual Travellers' Company
Bignor, Pulborough, West Sussex RH20 1QD
Tel: 01798 869433
Fax: 01798 869343
Normandie Vacances
113 Sutton Road, Walsall WS5 3AG
Tel: 01922 725705
Fax: 01922 720278
VFB Holidays
Normandy House, High Street, Cheltenham GL50 3FB
Tel: 01242 240340
Fax: 01242 570340

Camping

There is a good choice of campsites in Normandy, many of them situated near the coast. The regional tourist offices produce a list of all recognised sites, with details of star ratings and information on facilities. The list is also available from the French Government Tourist Office in London (*see page 327*) – call first for details of postal arrangements. The sites can get booked up in high season, so try

Booking Gîtes

Gîtes can get heavily booked in high season, so start the process early. Some are bookable through Brittany Ferries at The Brittany Centre, Wharf Rd, Portsmouth, PO2 8RU, tel: 08705 360 360; brochure line: 0870 442 1859. Or *Maison de Gîtes de France*, 59 rue St Lazare, 75009 Paris Cédex 09, tel: 01 49 70 75 75, fax: 01 42 81 28 53, e-mail: info@gites-de-france.fr.

Addresses of the *Fédération des Gîtes de France* in individual *départements* are as follows:

Seine-Maritime: Immeuble Chambre d'Agriculture, Chemin de la Brétèque, BP 59, 76232 Bois Guillaume Cedex. Tel: 02 35 60 73 34, fax: 02 35 61 69 20, e-mail: gites.76@wanadoo.fr.

Calvados: 6 Promenade Madame-de-Sévigné, 14050 Caen Cedex. Tel: 02 31 83 57 64, fax: 02 31 83 57 64, e-mail: info@gites-de-france-calvacod.fr.

Eure: 9 rue de la Petite-Cité, BP882, 27008 Evreux Cedex. Tel: 02 32 39 53 38, fax: 02 32 33 78 13, e-mail: gites@eure.chambagri.fr.

Orne: 88 rue Saint-Blaise, BP 50, 61002 Alençon Cedex. Tel: 02 33 28 07 00, fax: 02 33 29 01 01, e-mail: orne-tourisme@wanadoo.fr.

Manche: Maison du Département, 50008 Saint-Lô Cedex. Tel: 02 33 56 28 80, fax: 02 33 56 07 03, e-mail: manchetourisme@cg50.fr.

and book well in advance if possible.

Members of the Camping Club or Camping and Caravanning Club of Great Britain may make use of the booking services offered by these organisations. The Michelin *Guide Guide – Camping/Caravanning (see box below)* lists sites that accept (or insist on) pre-booking.

A camping *carnet* is useful – indeed, some sites will not accept a booking without one. They are available in the UK to members of the AA, RAC or the Camping Clubs mentioned above, or for a small fee from the GB Car Club, PO Box 11, Romsey, Hants SO5 8XX.

Campsites, like hotels, have official classifications from 1-star (minimal comfort, water points, showers and sinks) to 4-star luxury sites, with extra space to each pitch, and offering above-average facilities, often including a restaurant or takeway food, games areas and swimming pools. The majority of sites nationwide are 2-star.

Some farms offer "official" sites too under the auspices of the **Fédération Nationale des Gîtes Ruraux** *(see page 341)* – these are designated *"Camping à la ferme"*. Facilities are usually limited, as farmers are only allowed to have six pitches. These sites are listed in the regional camping guide from tourist offices.

Another option, which is becoming increasingly popular, is to stay in a wooden hut on a site rather than in a caravan. There are several sites in Seine-Maritime where this is possible; write to the

Back to Basics

If you really like to get back to nature and are unimpressed by the modern trappings of hot water and electricity, you should look out for campsites designated *"Aire naturelle de camping"*, where facilities will be absolutely minimal, with prices to match.

tourist office in Rouen for details *(see page 327)*.

Packaged camping holidays are now very popular with British holidaymakers, as all the camping paraphernalia is provided on the site – you only have to take your personal luggage. Many companies now offer this type of holiday, mostly with ferry travel included in the all-in price. As with other package tours, the companies have couriers on the sites to help with any problems. It is interesting to note that where such companies have taken over sections of existing sites, the facilities have improved to meet the demands of their customers.

A lot of companies offer good opportunities for sports and leisure, such as wind-surfing or surfing; often the equipment, and sometimes instruction too is covered by the cost of the package. Be warned though that some of the sites are very large, so they might not suit people who wish to get away from it all. Here is a selection of the package operators, for others check the Sunday press:

Canvas Holidays
12 Abbey Park Place, Dunfermline KY12 7PD
Tel: 01383 644000
Fax: 01383 620075
Pioneers in the field; also offer a nanny service.
Eurosites
Wavell House, Holcombe Road, Helmshore BB4 4NB
Tel: 01706 830888
Fax: 01706 830248
French Life Holidays
26 Church Road, Horsforth, Leeds LS18 5LG
Tel: 0113 239 0077
Fax: 08704 441484
Does "multicentre" deals.
Keycamp Holidays
Ellerman House, 92 96 Lind Road, Sutton SM1 4PL
Tel: 020 8395 4000
Fax: 020 8395 8608
Bookings: 0870 7000
Sunsites, Canute Court
Toft Road, Knutsford, Cheshire WA16 0NL
Tel: 01565 625555
Fax: 01565 652874.

Youth Hostels

Holders of accredited Youth Hostel Association cards may stay in any of Normandy's hostels. Contact the following for more information:
Fédération Unie des Auberges de Jeunesse (FUAJ)
27 rue Pajol, 75018 Paris
Tel: 01 44 89 87 27
Fax: 01 44 89 87 49
Affiliated to the International Youth Hostel Federation.
Ligue Française pour les Auberges de Jeunesse (LFAJ)
38 boulevard Raspail, 75007 Paris
Tel: 01 45 48 69 84
Fax: 01 45 44 57 41.

The **British Youth Hostel Association** publishes the *International Youth Hostel Handbook*, which includes all the hostels in Normandy and is available from the Youth Hostel Association. You can obtain it by post from Youth Hostel Association, 8 St Stephen's Hill, St Albans, Herts, tel: 01727 845 047 or in person from 14 Southampton

Further Information for Campers

Other useful information for campers can be found in the highly informative *Michelin Green Guide – Camping/Caravanning France*. This book, which is published annually in March, also lists sites with facilities suitable for visitors with disabilities. It is available from Stanfords, 12–14 Long Acre, Covent Garden, WC2E

9LP or the travel section of any good bookshop.

The following organisations also offer practical information on camping in France: the Camping and Caravanning Club, 11 Lower Grosvenor Place, London SW1, tel: 01342 326944, and the Caravan Club, East Grinstead House, East Grinstead, Sussex RH19 1UA.

Street, London WC2E 7HA, tel:
0207 248 6547 and from 174 High
Street, Kensington, London W8
7RG. Call in advance – you may
need to send a stamped,
addressed envelope. The London
office also handles membership
queries, tel: 0207 938 2188.

In the US, apply to the **American
Youth Hostelling International**, 733
15th Street NW, Suite 840,
Washington DC 20005, tel: 202
783 6161, fax: 202 783 6171,
www.hiayh.org.

Gîtes d'Etape also offer hostel
accommodation and are popular
with ramblers and horse riders
(some offer stabling). All official
gîtes d'étape come under the
auspices of the **Relais
Départementaux des Gîtes
Ruraux** *(for addresses see page
341)*. These are a popular form of
cheap accommodation particularly
in the national parks. Prices are
similar to those at youth hostels,
and you do not have to be a
member of any organisation to use
them.

Where to Eat

French Cuisine

France enjoys a reputation
throughout the world for its fine
cuisine and good wine. The French
pay serious attention to their food,
even though fast foods have
started to creep into French
supermarkets, and onto the high
streets. It may be argued,
however, that the French have
always enjoyed convenience foods
provided by their splendid *traiteurs*
and *charcutiers*. Visit a
charcuterie (delicatessen) and
pick a selection of their prepared
dishes for a delicious picnic.

Normandy is noted in particular
for its dairy products, cheese and
cream, especially *crème fraîche*,
and anything to do with apples,
notably cider and Calvados, the
brandy distilled from cider. There is
abundant seafood available all
along the coast. As in neighbouring
Brittany, another notable speciality
of the region are *crêpes*
(pancakes), and there are many

Overnight Stops

When travelling around
Normandy, you will often find that
eating and sleeping go hand-in-
hand, as many hotels have good
kitchens and, as already
mentioned, may give preference
to customers who want to eat on
the premises. In small towns and
villages, the only place to eat
may be a hotel. Most (although
not the *chambres d'hôte*)
welcome people who are not
staying in the hotel, The list
below reflects this and there is,
therefore, some overlap with
hotels.

crêperies that offer an alternative to
a traditional restaurant meal – ideal
for a light lunch.

Restaurants

SEINE MARITIME

Aumale
Le Mouton Gras
2 rue de Verdun
Tel: 02 3593 4132
Fax: 02 35 94 52 91
Small half-timbered *Logis* on
Normandy's eastern border and an
agreeable stopover for motorists
using Boulogne or Calais. Rooms
are in a separate building from the
restaurant, which serves copious
Normandy fare marred by an
overpriced wine list. **$$**

Price Guide

The price ranges quoted are per
person for a three-course meal
with half a bottle of house wine.
They are intended only as a guide
$$$ Expensive: over €50
$$ Moderate: €25–€50
$ Inexpensive: under €25

Autigny
Heluin Chambre d'Hôte
Tel: 02 35 97 42 55
This barn, converted into five
accommodation units, is signposted
on the D142 5 km (3 miles) south
of Fontaine-le-Dun, 35 minutes from
Dieppe. The food is good and it
makes a useful overnight stop on
the way to or from the Dieppe
crossing. Breakfast is taken on the
ground floor, which is large enough
to accommodate children on a rainy
day. **$$**

Dieppe
Au Grand Duquesne
15 place St-Jacques, 76200
Tel: 02 32 14 61 10
Fax: 02 35 84 29 83
A small hotel of character situated
near St-Jacques. The restaurant
succeeds in bringing originality to
its fish-based menus. On their
cheapest menu are *saumon fumé
crêpes*. **$$**

Hôtel Windsor
18 boulevard de Verdun
Tel: 02 35 84 15 23
Fax: 02 35 84 74 52
Edwardian-style hotel on the sea front with a magnificent panoramic dining room overlooking lawns and the Plage. Food so good they even teach cooking. Prices more than justified for fish, *fruits de mer*, and apple-based *patisserie*. **$$$**

La Musadière
61 quai Henry IV
Tel: 02 3582 9414
Restaurant with covered pavement terrace. Friendly, welcoming service and a good choice of set menus featuring traditional Norman cuisine. The wine is expensive, but the lively entertainment from the passing crowds is free. **$$**

La Présidence
boulevard de Verdun
Tel: 02 35 84 31 31
Fax: 02 35 84 86 70
The Panorama Restaurant has splendid sea views and serves standard French cuisine, using fresh market produce. **$$$**

Les Ecamias
129 quai Henri IV
Tel: 02 35 84 67 67
This popular quayside restaurant is good value (especially if you opt for one of the set menus) and excels in down-to-earth Norman cooking – the *moules marinière* go down a treat,

Cheese

Wine drinkers are familiar with the term *appellation d'origine contrôlée*, but now other producers are adopting the same label, as a proof of quality, in particular for **cheeses**. Some of the best-known cheeses of the region are Camembert, Neufchâtel (the oldest-known cheese of Normandy), Livarot and Pont l'Evêque, but one of the delights of shopping in France, particularly in local markets, is to find all the individual cheeses that come from small producers. You are usually invited to try before you buy.

but there's also a good selection of fresh fish. **$**

Les Tourelles
43 rue du Commandant Fayolle
Tel: 02 35 84 15 88
Facing the medieval town gate of that name and behind the casino, a restaurant with an imaginitive menu, strong on seafood, including *marmite de pêcheur* and *fruits de mer*, couscous and paella. **$**

Étretat

Le Corsair
rue du Général Leclerc
Tel: 02 35 10 38 90
Fax: 02 35 28 89 74
A well-established hotel-restaurant with a good beach location and views of the sea and the cliffs. You can enjoy the seafood specialities either in the dining room or on the terrace. **$$**

Roches Blanches
rue de l'Abbé-Cochet
Tel: 02 35 27 07 34
Views of the rocky coastline are one of the advantages of this seaside restaurant. The main reason for coming here however is the wonderfully prepared fresh seafood – the prices are reasonable too. Reservations are essential at weekends. Closed Tuesday to Thursday. **$$**

Harfleur

L'Auberge du Prieuré
52 rue de la République
Tel: 02 35 42 40 62
An attractive restaurant in a 17th-century former pharmacy, with a courtyard, where meat is barbecued in the summer months. **$**

La Bouille

Le St-Pierre
4 Place du Bateau
Tel: 02 35 18 01 01
Fax: 02 35 18 12 76
This pretty spot on the Seine just outside Rouen has a number of restaurants and hotels but St-Pierre has the best views. The restaurant has a chic gastronomic menu, specialising in lobster and oysters. **$$$**

Menus

Menus must be displayed by law outside any establishment. Most places will offer a *prix-fixe* menu, a set meal at a particular price, sometimes including wine. Alternatively, you order separate items from *La Carte*. A set menu is usually the best value, unless you only want one dish.

There are usually cheaper menus available at lunchtime, when most French people eat their biggest meal of the day.

Le Havre

Aux Huit Viandes
20 quai Michel Féré
Tel: 02 35 42 12 39
In a town specialising in seaood, here's one for the carnivore. Booking recommended. Open every day. **$$**

Le Grignot
53 rue Racine
Tel: 02 35 43 62 07
Opposite Niemeyer's "Volcan" the Grignot has a heated outside terrace, a good fish and seafood menu, and serves meals till late. Closed Sunday. **$$**

Le Monaco
16 rue de Paris
Tel: 02 35 42 21 01
Fax: 02 35 42 01 01
The food served in this cheerful restaurant and brasserie is well above average, particularly the fish. Try the *cassoulet* of snails, oysters or home-made *foie gras*. **$$**

Odysée
41 rue du Général-Faidherbe
Tel: 02 35 21 32 42
Nothing special in the way of ambience, this seafood restaurant near the port is valued by those in the know for the quality of its fish dishes. Closed Monday, Sunday evening and Saturday lunch. **$$–$$$**

Jumièges

Auberge des Ruines
Place de la Mairie
Tel: 02 35 37 24 05
Fax: 02 35 37 87 34

This is a restaurant with rooms, just a stone's throw from the abbey ruins. The rooms are simple and inexpensive. The food is excellent and good value. **$–$$**

Lyons-la-Forêt
La Licorne
Place Bensérade
Tel: 02 32 49 62 02
Fax: 02 32 49 80 09
This is a picturesque 3-star hotel right in the centre of a very pretty town. Comfortable rooms are complemented by a busy restaurant serving traditional cuisine. **$$**

Martin Église
Auberge du Clos Normand
22 rue Henry IV
Tel: 02 35 04 40 34
Fax: 02 35 04 48 49
Once a farmhouse, this handsome red-brick building, now a first-class restaurant, still retains that character. Food is prepared at one end of the large dining room and eaten here or at tables under the trees in the orchard beside the trout stream at its borders. Closed Monday evening and Tuesday. A small number of beds available in the half-timbered annexe: a truly rural idyll. **$$–$$$**

Rouen
La Couronne
31 Place du Vieux Marché
Tel: 02 35 71 40 90
The building in which this restaurant is housed witnessed the immolation of Joan of Arc. The elegant interior matches the quality of the food, and is just right for a special occasion. Local duck and fish are especially recommended. **$$$**
La Pêcherie
29 Place de la Basse-Vieille-Tour
Tel: 02 35 88 71 00.
This is a great, highly unpretentious restaurant specialising in fish and seafood. **$$**
La Fine Auberge
76530 Moulineaux
Tel: 02 35 18 02 39
About 15 km (10 miles) outside Rouen, and handy for visiting the Chateau Robert le Diable, this country-style dining room with an

open fire serves standard French fare: oysters, *foie gras*, *magret de canard au poivre vert*, etc. Open for lunch only except Friday and Saturday. Booking advisable. **$$**
Le Queen Mary
1 rue du Cercle
Tel: 02 35 71 52 09
West of the Place du Vieux Marché, this is a friendly, no-nonsense restaurant. Majors in *moules* and *frites*, a good range of set menus and prompt service. **$**
Les Nymphéas
7–9 rue de la Pie
Tel: 02 35 89 26 69
This restaurant is the place to take yourself for a treat. In an old house off the market square, it is smartly furnished and has a small patio at the back. Try the Rouen duck or the apple and calvados souffle. **$$$**

St-Léonard
Auberge de la Rouge
on the D940 a few miles south of Fécamp
Tel: 02 35 28 07 59
Fax: 02 35 28 70 55
Six purpose-built ground-floor rooms surround a small garden. Booking is essential for both rooms and the superb restaurant, which serves duck, *foie gras* and menus according to season. Closed Sunday evening and Monday. **$$**

Valmont
Hôtel de l'Agriculture
Place du Docteur Dupont
Tel: 02 35 29 84 25
On the main square with views of the château from the front windows, which can be noisy at night. The restaurant is in a pleasant, half-timbered building and serves fine regional dishes. **$$**

Varangeville-sur-Mer
La Buissoniere
route du phare d'Ailly
Tel/fax: 02 35 83 17 13
On the road to the lighthouse near Ste-Marguerite-sur-Mer, this country restaurant lies in the heart of the Ailly forest. There's a choice of set menus and *à la carte* with a bias towards fish dishes. The speciality of the house is a smoked salmon and herb pie. **$$**

Veules les Roses
Les Galets
3 rue Victor Hugo
Tel: 02 35 97 61 33
Described as one of the best restaurants in Normandy, Les Galets has a contemporary twist on regional dishes. The price of menus reflects its reputation. Situated where France's shortest river reaches the *mini plage* in this most appealing of resorts on the Alabaster coast. Victor Hugo thought so, too. **$$$**

CALVADOS

Bayeux
La Table du Terroir Louis Bisson
42 rue St-Jean, Allée de l'Orangerie, 14400
Tel/fax: 02 31 92 05 53
A small and friendly but highly reputable restaurant owned by a professional butcher, whose shop is attached. Closed Sunday evening and Monday. **$$**

Le Luxembourg
25 rue des Bouchers, 14400
Tel: 02 31 92 00 04
Fax: 02 31 85 57 69
A quality 3-star hotel in the centre
of town, near the cathedral, with a
smartly furnished restaurant that
brings home the riches of
Normandy cuisine. Try the *foie gras*
with apples or *coquille St Jacques*.
$$$

Lion d'Or
71 rue St Jean, 14400
Tel: 02 31 92 06 90
Fax: 02 31 22 15 64
The rather formal restaurant of this
former coaching inn has a good
reputation though it has lost its
Michelin star. **$$**

Bénouville
La Pommeraie
18 avenue de la Côte-de-Nacre
Tel: 02 31 44 62 43
If you're staying near or visiting the
Pegasus Bridge or other D-Day
sites, this quality fish restaurant is
sure to appeal. An added attraction
is the setting, a former priory,
dating back to the 17th century.
Reservations and formal dress
essential. Closed Sunday evening
and Monday. **$$–$$$**

Fermes Auberges

These are farms with
restaurants, where customers
can expect a family atmosphere
and the most traditional Norman
food, often made with
ingredients bred or grown on the
farm. There will usually be just a
few tables and probably just one
menu. You should always phone
ahead – not so much to book a
table but to warn the owners how
many mouths they will need to
feed. There is a free brochure
*Bienvenue a la Ferme en
Normandie*, available from the
main tourist office in Évreux *(see
page 327)* that lists the two
dozen or so *fermes auberges* in
the region. As you tour
Normandy, look out for signs with
a yellow sunflower, symbol of the
fermes auberges.

Beuvron-en-Auge
Auberge de la Boule d'Or
Tel: 02 31 79 78 78
Fax: 02 31 39 61 50
In a gorgeous 18th-century, half-
timbered building in a prime spot
overlooking Beuvron's lovely *place*.
The unpretentious restaurant
serves good and reasonably priced
local food. With just three rooms
available, be sure to book well in
advance if you want to stay. **$**

Le Pavé d'Auge
Place du Village
Tel: 02 31 79 26 71
Awarded a Michelin star, Le Pavé
d'Auge is the smartest of several
restaurants in this picturesque
Auge village. It is at the top of the
range and serves absolutely
delicious food. **$$$**

Caen
Chez Michel
24 rue Jean-Romain
Tel: 02 31 86 16 89
Excellent value, which is why you
need to book or get here early to be
sure of a table. The staff are
welcoming and straightforward and
there's a large choice of French
dishes. Closed Saturday evening
and Sunday. **$**

Le Boeuf Ferré
10 rue Froide
Tel: 02 31 85 36 40
Tucked away in Caen's old quarter,
this has long been a favourite local
eating place; people are often
prepared to queue at weekends.
$–$$

La Bourride
15 rue du Vaugueux
Tel: 02 31 93 50 76
Small, top-class and reputable
restaurant in the city's old quarter
serving what they describe as
"cuisine de coeur et de passion".
$$$

La Ferlouche
Place Courtonne
Tel: 02 31 44 47 33
Eating here is great value if you opt
for one of the *plats du jour*, while
the warm old-fashioned ambience is
also appealing. If the weather is
good, try to find a table on the
terrace which overlooks the Bassin
Saint-Pierre. Closed Tuesday. **$**

Price Guide

The price ranges quoted are per
person for a three-course meal
with half a bottle of house wine.
They are intended only as a guide.
$$$ Expensive: over €50
$$ Moderate: €25–€50
$ Inexpensive: under €25

Naitre Corbeau
943 rue de Geole
Tel: 02 31 86 33 97
The "Crow's Nest" is a theme
restaurant devoted to cheese –
everything from fondues to flans, all
made with local produce. **$**

Camembert
La Camembertière
Tel: 02 33 39 31 87
A delightful rural restaurant in a
restored farm, and a perfect place
to stop off during a cheese tour of
the Pays d'Auge. Not surprisingly,
cheese dominates all areas of the
menu. The choice of camemberts
and other local cheeses is second
to none. Closed in winter. **$–$$**

Courseulles-sur-Mer
La Crémaillère
boulevard de la Plage
Tel: 02 31 37 46 73
Fax: 02 31 37 19 31
Large three-chimney *Logis* hotel on
the seafront with a seaview
restaurant serving locally caught
seafood. **$$**

Crepon
Ferme de la Rançonnière
Route de Creully, 14480
Tel: 02 31 22 21 73
Fax: 02 31 22 98 39
A beautiful old country manor house
(13th–15th century) just 13 km (8
miles) east of Bayeux, and in a good
position for exploring the Normandy
beaches. Attractive rooms, many with
exposed beams and antiques. **$$**

Deauville
L'Augeval
15 avenue Hocquart-de-Turot,
14800
Tel: 02 31 81 13 18
Fax: 02 31 81 00 40

A popular, well-recommended restaurant, where you can eat lunch and dinner on a terrace facing the swimming pool. Wheelchair access. **$$**

La Flambée
81 rue Généeral-Leclerc, 14800
Tel: 02 31 88 45 86
Fax: 02 31 88 07 94
Close to the casino. Well-cooked food that, in summer, can be enjoyed in a pleasant garden. **$$**

Le Normandie
38 rue Jean-Mermoz
Tel: 02 31 98 66 22
If money is no object, join the well-heeled (and discerning) clientele whose antecedents have been patronising this gourmet restaurant for the best part of a century. Regional cooking a speciality. **$$$**

Falaise

La Fine Fourchette
52 rue G. Clemenceau
Tel: 02 31 90 08 59
Beneath the rather garish décor and apparent formality, this is a relaxed and popular restaurant serving creative food based on tradition. Excellent value. **$–$$**

Honfleur

La Lieutenance
12 place Sainte Catherine
Tel/fax: 02 31 89 07 52
Located in a half-timbered 15th century building in the heart of the old port, this restaurant offers at least two set menus daily, featuring such dishes as monkfish medallions cooked in Muscadet, and smoked salmon in aspic with quail eggs. Calvados cheeses also available. **$$**

Les Bagues d'Argent
30–32 rue de l'Homme de Bois
Tel: 02 31 89 27 97
Friendly plant-filled restaurant with a limited but satisfactory menu. Pleasantly distant from the crowds circulating in the Vieux Bassin below. **$$**

Les Deux Ponts
20 quai de la Quarantine, 14600
Tel: 02 31 89 04 37
Fax: 02 31 89 08 64
In the centre of town, this restaurant is pleasant at any time of year, with a sunny terrace and a

dining room with an open fire. Closed Thursday. **$$**

Houlgate

Hôtel 1900
17 rue des Bains
Tel: 02 31 28 77 77
Fax: 02 31 28 08 07
This restaurant, as its names suggests, dates from the time of Proust's *A la Recherche du Temps Perdus* (he stayed in nearby Cabourg) and the décor harks back to the same period. As you would expect from a coastal resort, seafood and fish are the specialities. **$$**

Montreuil-en-Auge

Auberge la Route du Cidre
Cambremer, 14340
Tel/fax: 02 31 63 12 27
Tucked right in the middle of rolling cider country near Cambremer, the auberge consists of a *chambre d'hôte* in the grand old farmhouse, plus two *gîtes*. Inside the huge barn opposite the guest house is a friendly and unassuming restaurant serving simple Norman cooking and the best local ciders. It's worth coming just for the stupendous views of the valley through the picture windows. **$$**

Trouville

Les Vapeurs
160 quai F. Moreau
Tel: 02 31 88 15 24
Fax: 02 31 88 20 58
This restauant has been operating since 1927 and is *the* place to eat in Trouville. The place to be seen eating seafood or *moules frites*. Open late. **$$–$$$**

Carmen
24 rue Carnot, 14360
Tel: 02 31 88 35 43
Fax: 02 31 88 08 03
Located in a pleasant backstreet about 100 metres/yds from the beach, this *Logis de France* hotel restaurant serves traditional French cooking including seafood. **$$**

La Guinguette
52 quai Fernand Moureaux
Tel: 02 31 88 42 80
This fashionable terrace bistro with a prime site location is the place to come for racing tips as jockeys and

trainers make up a significant part of the clientele. When it's full to bursting, a marquee is erected to accommodate additional diners. **$$–$$$**

St-Pierre sur Dives

Auberge du Doux Marais
Le Doux Marais, Sainte-Marie-aux-Anglais
Tel: 02 31 63 82 81
Fax: 02 31 63 96 33
Housed in an old farmhouse with a large garden, just north of St Pierre. There is just one menu which, while comparatively expensive for a farmhouse restaurant, offers wholesome home-made food; the main course generally consists of meat cooked over a wood fire in the dining room. The atmosphere is relaxed and often lively, with Marinette and Bernard providing a warm welcome. Phone ahead. **$$**

EURE

Anet

Auberge de la Rose
6 rue Charles Lechevrel
Tel: 02 37 41 90 64
An eight-room hotel in this attractive château town. The classic cuisine of the restaurant is the main reason for staying here. **$$–$$$**

Beaumesnil

L'Etape Louis XIII
2 route de la Barre
Tel: 02 32 44 44 72

Vegetarians

In Normandy, as in the rest of France, vegetarians – at least those who do not eat fish – are not very well catered for. Despite the fresh vegetables available, salads and omelettes are often the only things on offer. While these are usually delicious, they can get a bit monotonous. If you are strictly vegetarian, beware of vegetable soups, as they often have a meat stock as a base.

The restaurant is housed in a former presbytery and dates from 1612. Traditional Norman cooking. **$$**

Le Bec Hellouin
L'Auberge de l'Abbaye
Tel: 02 32 44 86 02
Fax: 02 32 46 32 23
This wonderful old country inn, only a short walk from the monastery, dates from the 18th century and specialises in authentic regional cooking. This is a good place to sample the local cider. **$$$**

Les Andelys
La Chaîne d'Or
27 rue Grande
Tel: 02 32 54 00 31
Fax: 02 32 54 05 68
This attractively decorated, 12-room riverside hotel is a perfect place for a special weekend. Dining in the restaurant is definitely a high spot and one that can be enjoyed by non-residents as well. **$$**
Hostellerie St-Pierre
6 Chemin de la Digue, Saint-Pierre-du-Vauvray
Tel: 02 32 59 93 29
Fax: 02 32 59 41 93
Especially convenient if you happen to be visiting Les Andelys from Rouen. This excellent restaurant serves a delicious range of fish and meat dishes. Closed in winter months. **$$–$$$**

Pacy-sur-Eure
L'Etape
1 rue Isambard
Tel: 02 32 36 12 77
Fax: 02 32 36 22 74
This old 2-star hotel is in a fine situation right on the river and, if you want to stay, you may have to book one of its 17 rooms in advance. The food is good solid country fare, such as duck or pheasant with cabbage. **$$**

Pont-Audemer
Auberge du Vieux Puits
6 rue Notre-Dame-du-Pré
Tel: 02 32 41 01 48
Fax: 02 32 42 37 28
Famous 17th-century coaching

inn, featured in Flaubert's *Madame Bovary*. Excellent restaurant. **$$**

Vernon
Restaurant de la Poste
26 avenue de Gambetta
Tel: 02 32 51 10 63
Well suited for hungry customers after visiting Monet's house and garden at Giverny, which is nearby. Great value, with the local dishes appreciated by shoppers and stallholders on market day. **$**

Price Guide

The price ranges quoted are per person for a three-course meal with half a bottle of house wine. They are intended only as a guide
$$$ Expensive: over €50
$$ Moderate: €25–€50
$ Inexpensive: under €25

ORNE

Alençon
Au Peti Vatel
72 Place du Cdt Desmeulles
Tel: 02 33 26 23 78
This small restaurant on the outskirts of town is an institution, thanks to its genial proprieter. Good Normandy cooking. **$$–$$$**

Bagnoles de l'Orne
Lutétia
Boulevard Paul Chalvet
Tel: 02 33 37 94 77
Fax: 02 33 30 09 87
This 3-star hotel, open Easter to November, has rooms in an old house and a new annexe and retains an intimate atmosphere. The restaurant is good. **$$–$$$**

Carrouges
Du Nord
Place Gén de Gaulle
Tel: 02 33 27 20 14
Fax: 02 33 28 83 13
A small *Logis* on the main square with comfortable rooms. Local business people crowd the dining room at lunchtime. **$$**

Mortagne-au-Perche
Du Tribunal
4 Place du Palais, near St-Denis Gate and Notre-Dame cathedral
Tel: 02 33 25 04 77
Fax: 02 33 83 60 83
The rooms in this 18th-century half-timbered building are pretty if somewhat small. The kitchen is excellent. **$$**

Pont d'Ouilly
Auberge St Christophe
St Christophe
Tel: 02 31 69 81 23
Fax: 02 31 69 26 58
About 2 km (1 mile) north of Pont d'Ouilly. Good-value, traditional Norman food (chicken in cider sauce, *salade normande*, etc.) with a few modern twists. Service can be slow. Popular at weekends so book ahead. Also has a handful of rooms overlooking the garden. **$**

Putanges-Pont-Écrepin
Du Lion Verd
Place de l'Hôtel de Ville
Tel: 02 33 35 01 86
Fax: 02 33 39 53 32
At the southern end of the Suisse Normande, a large, confident *Logis* with a spacious restaurant and terrace overlooking the river, and with its own pedaloes. For the restaurant, book ahead on summer weekends. **$$**

Vimoutiers
La Maison du Vert
Ticheville, 61120 Vimoutiers
Tel: 02 33 36 95 84
This vegetarian restaurant prides itself on using organic produce as far as possible, mostly from the hotel gardens. Eggs are from free-range chickens and there's always a vegan dish on the menu. This is worth knowing about if you are in the area as vegetarians may have a lean time in Normandy. Try the baked feta cheese with red onion chutney or the gruyere soufflé. Good selection of organic wines. The location is Ticheville, a village a few kilometres to the south-east of Vimoutiers. **$$**

MANCHE

Avranches
Jardin des Plantes
10 Place Carnot
Tel: 02 33 58 03 68
Fax: 02 33 60 01 72
Located just outside the city's famous botanical gardens, with ample parking. The restaurant is popular with locals, which is always a good sign, but it means that service can be slow. **$–$$**

Barneville-Carteret
Hôtel de la Marine
11 rue de Paris, 50270
Tel: 02 33 53 83 31
Fax: 02 33 53 39 60
Overlooking the harbour in Carteret, this hotel has an excellent fish restaurant with picture windows. **$$**

Cherbourg
Hôtel de la Croix de Malte
5 rue des Halles, 50100
Tel: 02 33 43 19 16
Fax: 02 33 43 65 66
Good-value meals are to be had in this friendly hotel. **$**
Le Grand Gousier
21 rue de l'Abbaye
Tel: 02 33 53 19 43
Fax: 02 33 53 04 74
This busy port is not immediately associated with top-notch French cooking, but Le Grand Gousier is widely regarded as one of the best restaurants on the Contentin Peninsula. Excellent wine list. **$$–$$$**

Coutances
La Verte Campagne
Trelly, 50660
Tel: 02 33 47 65 33
An 18th-century farmhouse in a deliciously rural spot a few miles east of Villedieu. The main reason to come here is to eat in the excellent and unassuming Michelin-starred restaurant. There are also 7 rooms, which are largely unmodernised and mostly on the small side, but atmospheric and excellent value. **$$**

Domfront
Hôtel De France
7 rue du Mont-St Michel
Tel: 02 33 38 51 44
Fax: 02 33 30 49 54
Comfortable *Logis* in the centre of town near the station and within walking distance of the old town. Good for those travelling without a car. Restaurant serving traditional Normandy cuisine. **$$**

Granville
Creperie Grill l'Echauguette
22/24 rue St Jean
Tel: 02 33 50 51 87
Tucked away down one of the old streets of the Haute Ville, this popular restaurant serves excellent buckwheat crêpes and a range of meats grilled in the open fireplace *(au feu de bois)*. **$$**

Le Nez de Jobourg
Auberge des Grottes
Tel: 02 33 52 71 44
Small restaurant close to the cliffs, deservedly popular as a lunch stop for motorists touring the Hague peninsula. **$$**

Mont-St-Michel
Auberge St-Pierre
Grand Rue
Tel: 02 33 60 14 03
Comfortable, welcoming hotel. Restaurant specialities include omelettes and gigot of lamb. **$$$**
Hôtel du Guesclin
Grand-rue
Tel: 02 33 60 14 10
Fax: 02 33 60 45 81
One of the better value restaurants on the Mount, the du Guesclin has the added advantage of a first-floor dining room with outstanding views of the Baie du St-Michel. **$–$$**
La Granitière
74 rue Maréchal Foch
Tel: 02 33 54 58 99
Fax: 02 33 20 34 91
Smart but friendly hotel with a small restaurant. Good for a special treat. **$$$**
La Mère Poulard
Grand Rue
Tel: 02 33 60 14 03
This hotel restaurant is conveniently located near the main gate. As for the menu, the omelettes are the stuff of legend, though you pay handsomely for the privilege of enjoying them. Reservations essential in season. **$$**

St-Lô
L'Auberge Normande
20 rue de Villedieu
Tel: 02 33 05 10 89
This restaurant, right in the heart of town, is excellent value. The typically French dishes (mainly fish and seafood) are given a surprisingly imaginative twist. Closed Monday. **$–$$**

Valognes
Le Louvre
28 rue des Religieuses
Tel: 02 33 40 00 07
Fax: 02 33 40 1373
Thoroughly old-fashioned market-town hotel that gets packed out with locals for Sunday lunch. Comfortable rooms. **$–$$**

Villedieu-Les-Poêles
St-Pierre et St-Michel
12 Place de la République
Tel: 02 33 61 00 11
Fax: 02 33 61 06 52
Comfortable *Logis* in the centre of town with parking facilities. Weekend evenings and Sunday lunch finds the dining rooms full of both visitors and local people. **$$**

Gastronomic Holidays

Several UK companies offer holidays in the region which include gastronomic tours or cookery courses. A selection is given below:
Allez France, 27–31 West Street, Storrington RH20 4DZ. Tel: 01903 742345, fax: 01903 745044.
Powder Byrne Travel, 4 Alice Court, 116 Putney Bridge Road, London SW15 2NQ. Tel: 0208 871 3300, fax: 0208 871 3322.
InnTravel, Hovingham, York YO6 4JZ. Tel: 01653 628 811, fax: 01653 628 741. Organises three-night, self-drive holidays.

Price Guide

The price ranges quoted are per person for a three-course meal with half a bottle of house wine. They are intended only as a guide

$$$ Expensive: over €50
$$ Moderate: €25–€50
$ Inexpensive: under €25

Manoir de l'Acherie
Sainte-Cécile, 50800
Tel: 02 33 51 13 87
Fax: 02 33 51 89 07
A restored 17th-century granite manor in the peaceful countryside just east of Villedieu, and a popular stop-off for visitors en route to or from the Channel ports. Unfussy, comfortable rooms (15), some on the small side. The excellent restaurant serves traditional Norman food, with meat often grilled over a wood fire. **$–$$**

Drinking

CIDER

This traditional alcoholic drink, made from the juice of apples, is often drunk as an accompaniment to meals in preference to wine. It is produced all over Normandy, but predominantly in the Auge region. To discover more about the drink, follow the "cider route" *(see Tourist Routes, page 333)* and visit the producers and museums devoted to this golden, sparkling liquid.

Particular varieties of apples are used, harvested in October. The juice is squeezed out and left to mature so the sugar can turn to alcohol (around 5 percent by volume). It is left to ferment for just a short while before being bottled.

The best-quality cider, *cidre bouché* (literally "corked cider") continues to ferment after corking. It is drunk fairly young, preferably the following summer, the length of fermentation determining whether the cider will be sweet *(doux)*, medium dry *(demi-sec)* or dry *(brut or sec)*.

CALVADOS

Calvados is produced by evaporating the alcohol from cider and condensing it in a still. When removed from the still, the alcoholic content of Calvados is around 70 percent, but this is reduced to around 40 to 45 percent after being aged in oak casks. The Calvados is then blended with brandies of various ages to create a full flavour.

There are two recognised *appellation contrôlée* labels for Calvados: *Appellation contrôlée Calvados* and *Appellation contrôlée Calvados du Pays d'Auge* – the latter undergoing a double distillation in a traditional pot still.

There is a custom in Normandy of taking a small glass of Calvados halfway through a copious meal, as an aid to digestion. This is known

Wine Labels

Wines are graded according to their quality and this must be shown on the label. The grades are as follows:

Vin de Table, usually inexpensive everyday table wine. Quality can be variable.

Vin de Pays, local wine.

Vin délimité de qualité supérieure or **VDQS**, wine from a specific area and generally of higher quality than a *vin de table*.

Appellation d'origine contrôlée or **AOC**, used to describe good-quality wine from a specific area or château where very strict controls are imposed on the amount of wine produced each year.

If the label bears the words "*mis en bouteille au château*" it has been bottled at the vineyard. This is also indicated by the words *récoltant* or *producteur* around the cap; the term *négociant* means that it has been bought by a dealer and usually bottled away from the estate. However, this is not necessarily to the detriment of the wine, as there are many fine *négociants* in business today.

as a *trou Normand* (literally, a "Norman hole"). For those who find this custom a bit overpowering, it is sometimes served as Calvados-flavoured sorbet, rather than as a drink.

POMMEAU

This sherry-strength apéritif is made by blending the "must" of cider and Calvados in the ratio of two to one. Matured in oak casks, it is an ideal companion to oysters and *foie gras*.

WINE

Vines have been cultivated in France since the ancient Romans first planted them. To exclude cider or wine from the dinner table is almost like forgetting the salt and pepper. It is not regarded as a luxury; everyday wine *(vin de table)* is produced for everyday consumption. On the other hand, France produces some of the finest vintages in the world, and the pomp, ceremony and snobbery that accompany their production show just how important it is to the culture and economy of France. Normandy is one of the few regions of France that doesn't produce its own wine. It is common to see people drink cider instead of wine with a meal, particularly in *ferme auberges*.

Nightlife

Nightlife

The most lively nightlife in the region is to be found in the more sophisticated seaside resorts, such as Deauville and Trouville, and the major cities, notably Rouen and Caen. Here you will find a variety of nightclubs, discos and, especially around the coast, casinos – some of which also offer other entertainment away from the gaming tables.

Many towns around the region organise cultural festivals during the summer for the local people and tourists; also popular are *son-et-lumière* displays often staged in the grounds of châteaux.

If you are staying on a farm or in a country area, you may be invited to join in local festivities. Almost every town and village has its own fête during the summer; these range from simple *boules* competitions finished off with a dance, hosted by a band playing traditional music, to a full-blown carnival with street theatre, fireworks and sophisticated entertainment. Up-to-date information about all kinds of entertainment is available from tourist offices and hotels.

Casinos

The following casinos are open all year; there are plenty of others which are only open in the high season. You may be required to show your passport to gain admittance and most require you to be over 21. Many of them offer other forms of entertainment under the same roof, such as nightclubs and discos.

SEINE MARITIME

Dieppe
Tel: 02 35 82 33 60. Roulette, baccarat, *chemin de fer*, blackjack, gaming machines.

Forges-les-Eaux
Tel: 02 35 89 50 51. Gaming machines, baccarat, roulette, blackjack; regular entertainment in summer including magicians and dinner dances; restaurant.

CALVADOS

Deauville
Tel: 02 31 14 31 15. Roulette, blackjack, *chemin de fer*, over 200 gaming machines. Le Régine's nightclub is downstairs. Also a cinema.

Luc-sur-Mer
Tel: 02 31 97 32 19. Roulette, blackjack, gaming machines; disco and restaurant.

Ouistreham
Tel: 02 31 36 30 00. Place Alfred Thomas: gaming machines, billiards; disco, bars and a brasserie.

Trouville-sur-Mer
Tel: 02 31 87 75 00. Blackjack, 200 gaming machines, roulette, craps; disco, restaurant and cinema.

ORNE

Bagnoles-de-l'Orne
Tel: 02 33 37 84 00. Blackjack, roulette, *chemin de fer*, gaming machines; also offers old-time dancing and tea dances.

MANCHE

Cherbourg
Tel: 02 33 20 53 35. Gaming machines; pub, disco and restaurant.

Granville
Tel: 02 33 50 00 79. Blackjack, lots of gaming machines and American Roulette.

Festivals

Diary of Events

Listed below are brief details of the main annual events. For more specific information on events across the region, contact the local tourist offices listed on page 327.

January
Ste-Opportune-la-mare: Eure, Apple Fair.

February
Granville: Manche, Carnival.

March
Caen: Calvados, *Aspects de la Musique Contemporaine* (contemporary music festival).
Lisieux: Calvados, *Foire aux Arbres* (tree fair).
Mortagne: Orne, *Foire au Boudin* (black pudding fair); Livestock fair.

April
Caen: Calvados, Easter fair.
Deauville: Calvados, Classical music festival.
Domfront: Orne, *Foire des Rameaux* (Palm Sunday fair).
Fécamp: Seine-Maritime, cultural festival.
Lisieux: Calvados, Easter celebrations at the Basilica.

May
Beuvron: Calvados, Geranium festival.
Coutances: Manche, *Jazz sous les Pommiers* (jazz festival).
Evreux: Eure, May festival and carnival at the end of the month.
Honfleur: Calvados, *Bénédiction de la Mer* (sailors' festival).
Mont-St-Michel: Manche, Spring festival (religious and folk festival).

Pont-l'Evêque: Calvados, Cheese fair.
Saint-Sever: Calvados, Music festival.
Rouen: Seine-Maritime, International fair; Jeanne d'Arc festival.

June
Annual D-Day landings celebrations feted across France on 6 June.
Balleroy: Calvados, International hot-air balloon festival (every two years: the next one will be in 2003).
Cabourg: Calvados, International romantic film festival.
Caen: Calvados: Caen festival.
Le Havre: Seine-Maritime, Festival of the Sea.
Luneray: Seine-Maritime, Jazz festival.
Le Perche: Orne music festival.

July
Bastille Day: celebrated throughout France on the 14th.
Bayeux: Calvados, *Marché Médiéval* (market in medieval style); *Eté Musical de Bayeux* (Summer Music Festival), continues into August.
Deauville: Calvados, world Bridge championships; Jazz festival.
Dives-sur-Mer: Calvados, Puppet festival.
Fécamp: Seine-Maritime, *Fête de la Mer* (marine festival).
Le Havre: Seine-Maritime, Festival of wind instruments.
La Haye de Routot: Eure, Saint Clair festival and bonfire.
Honfleur: Calvados, Music festival, continues in August.
Gavray: Manche, Marché Normand (colourful market).
Mont-St-Michel: Manche, *Festival des Heures Musicales* (music festival), continues in August, pilgrimage across the sands.
Trouville: Calvados, Jazz festival.

August
Bagnoles-de-l'Orne: Orne, Lancelot of the Lake festival.
Berville-sur-Mer: Eure, Sailor's festival.
La Colombe: Manche, Harvest festival.
Dieppe: Seine-Maritime, Early music festival.

Le Havre: Seine Maritime, *Corso fleuri* (flower festival parade).
Lion-sur-Mer: Calvados, Music festival.
Saint-Vaast-la-Hougue/Ile de Tatihou: Manche, Festival of the sea.
Savigny: Manche, Harvest festival (also at La Colombe, Manche).

September
Alençon: Orne, Normandie-Maine Agricultural Show.
Musical de l'Orne: concerts all around the *département*.
Bellême: Orne, *Mycologiades de Bellême* (mushroom festival).
Deauville: Calvados, American film festival.
Lessay: Manche, Holy Cross fair.
Lisieux: Calvados, *Grandes fêtes de Ste-Thérèse*.
Neufchâtel: Seine-Maritime, Cheese festival.

October
Calvados: Horse festival throughout the *département*.
La Chapelle d'Andaines: Orne, *Journées Mycologiques* (mushroom fair).
Rouen: Seine-Maritime, Music and dance festival, also in Dieppe and Le Havre.
Vimoutiers: Orne, Apple fair.

November
Liery: Eure, Herring fair.
Le Havre: Seine-Maritime, Apple fair.

December
La Chapelle-d'Andaines and **Sées:** Orne, Turkey fair.
Evreux: Eure, St Nicholas fair.

Sites

Museums

The most important museums are mentioned, with details of opening hours, etc., in the relevant chapters. Of course, there are other, local museums and the tourist offices in the relevant towns will give you a complete list. Remember, most museums close for a long lunch from noon or 12.30pm to around 2.30pm. Most museums charge an entrance fee; reductions are usually given for children, senior citizens and students – on production of a valid card. Some major towns and cities offer a multi-site ticket; again, you should enquire at tourist offices for further details.

Military Cemeteries and Monuments

The following is a selection of military cemeteries and monuments across Normandy, listed alphabetically by nationality. For a comprehensive list of all the military sites in the region, contact the Normandy tourist office (*see page 327*) and ask for the brochure *Espace Historique de la Bataille de Normandie.*

American
Colleville-Saint-Laurent, on the coast between Arromanches and Grandcamp: 9,386 graves.
St-James (Montjoie St Martin), between Avranches and Fougères: 4,410 graves.

British
Banneville-Sannerville, between Caen and Troarn: 2,175 graves.
Bayeux, 4,868 graves.

Brouay, between Caen and Bayeux: 377 graves.

Cambes-en-Plaine, between Caen and Courseulles: 224 graves.

Chouain (Jerusalem), between Bayeux and Tilly-sur-Seulles: 40 graves.

Douvres-la-Délivrande, located between Caen and Luc-sur-Mer: 927 graves.

Fontenay-le-Pesnel, situated between Caen and Caumont-l'Eventé: 520 graves.

Hermanville-sur-Mer, on the coast: 986 graves.

Hottot-Longraye, between Caen and Caumont-l'Eventé: 965 graves.

Ranville, near Pegasus Bridge: 2,151 graves.

Ryes, between Bayeux and Arromanches: 987 graves.

St-Charles-de-Percy, near Bény-Bocage: 792 graves.

St-Désir-de-Lisieux, near Lisieux: 589 graves.

St-Manvieu, situated between Caen and Caumont-l'Eventé: 2,186 graves.

Secqueville-en-Bessin, between Caen and Bayeux: 117 graves.

Tilly-sur-Seulles, between Caen and Balleroy: 1,224 graves.

Canadian

Bény-sur-Mer, Reviers, near Courseulles: 2,048 graves.

Bretteville-sur-Laize-Cintheaux, located between Caen and Falaise: 2,959 graves.

French

Alençon, Memorial to the 2nd Armoured Division.

Battlefield Tours

A long-established company that runs sensitive and well-organised guided tours of the battlefields is Major and Mrs Holt's Battlefield Tours, 15 Market Street, Sandwich, Kent CT13 9DA, tel: 0304 612248. The same company organises battlefield tours for schoolchildren. Contact Galloway Coach Travel Ltd, Denters Hill, Mendlesham, Stowmarket IP14 5RR, tel: 0449 767778.

German

La Cambe, between Bayeux and Isigny: 21,160 graves.

La Chapelle-en-Juger, Marigny, located between Saint-Lô and Coutances: 11,169 graves.

Huisnes-sur-Mer, near Mont-St-Michel: 11,956 graves.

Orglandes, south of Valognes: 10,152 graves.

St-Désir-de-Lisieux, near Lisieux: 3,735 graves.

Polish

Grainville-Langannerie, between Caen and Falaise: 650 graves.

Craft Workshops

Craft lovers may wish to visit the following workshops, which organise demonstrations and exhibitions on subjects as diverse as glass blowing and bread-making. Workshops are listed by *département*.

Seine Maritime

Blagny-sur-bresle, Manoir de Fontaine. Tel: 02 35 94 44 79. Glassworks museum where glass-blowing demonstrations are given. Open: March to November. Closed Tuesday and Sunday morning.

Calvados

Noron-la-Poterie. Near Cerisy-la-Forêt, this is an important centre for the local salt-glaze pottery industry. Several workshops are open to the public, free of charge, Monday to Friday 9am–noon, 2–6pm.

Eure

La Maison des Métiers, Bourneville. Tel: 02 32 57 40 41. A showcase for local crafts and trades, which also includes the regional **Musée des Métiers** with demonstrations and a gift shop. Open: every afternoon from February–October; closed: Tuesday except in July and August; weekends open in November and December only.

Moulin de Hauville, Hauville, Eure. Tel: 02 35 37 23 16. One of the few stone windmills left in Normandy. Constructed in the 13th century, it has since been restored and is open afternoons in July and August plus Saturday and Sunday from September to June for demonstrations.

La Haye de Routot. Tel: 02 32 57 35 74. In the Seine Valaley, 50km (32 miles) from Le Havre, two buildings have been restored as living history exhibitions: one is a bakery where bread is baked in the traditional manner every Sunday from March to November; the other is a clog-maker's workshop; there is also a flax and linen centre nearby.

Mont-St-Michel

One of the most important sites of Normandy, indeed of the whole of France. The spectacular **abbey** rises on a rock in the St-Michel Bay, well fortified against the sea and invaders. It had a functioning religious community until the Revolution, when the monastery became a prison. However, it has been well preserved since 1874, when it was declared a national monument and it remains remarkably intact. The foot of the mount is crowded with souvenir shops, but those with the fortitude to climb to the top and enter the abbey itself will be rewarded, as the tourist hordes thin out somewhat and the views are splendid. Open daily; tel: 02 33 89 80 00 for times of tours.

Shopping

What to Buy

Most major towns in France have made the wise decision to keep town centres for small boutiques and individual shops; many of these areas are pedestrianised and very attractive, although beware – some cars ignore the *voie piétonnée* signs. The large supermarkets, hypermarkets, furniture stores and do-it-yourself outlets are grouped on the outskirts of the town, which are mostly designated as a *Centre Commercial*. The biggest centres are vast and are to be found on the edge of the major conglomerations such as Rouen and Caen.

These centres, although aesthetically quite unappealing, are fine for bulk shopping, for self-catering or for finding a selection of wine to take home at reasonable prices. However, for gifts and general window-shopping, town centres are usually far more interesting. It is here that you will find the individual souvenirs with a particularly local flavour, alongside the beautifully dressed windows of delicatessens and *patisseries*.

Opening Times

Food shops, especially bakers, tend to open early; boutiques and department stores open about 9am, but sometimes not until 10am. In most town centres, almost everything closes from noon until 2.30 or 3pm but in seaside resorts and other tourist areas, it is becoming more common for shops to remain open over lunch. Most shops close in the evening at 7pm. Out of town, the hypermarkets are usually open all day until 8 or even 9pm. Most shops are closed Monday morning and many all day. If you want to make a picnic lunch, remember to buy everything you need before midday. Good delicatessens (*charcuteries*) have a selection of delicious ready-prepared dishes, which make picnicking a delight.

Caen is said to have one of the best shopping centres outside Paris, and is very well served both by large department stores and individual boutiques.

Clothing

You'll find all the chain stores and labels you are used to in the UK and more, specifically French, ones besides. Children's sizes tend to be small compared with UK and US age ranges. Hypermarkets usually have good-value children's clothes. When buying adults' clothing, you will find that most garments have Continental, UK and US sizes on their labels. For useful phrases when shopping, *see Language section, page 360.*

General Markets

The heart of every French town is its market; most start early and close at midday, although some of the bigger ones are also open in the afternoon, or at least until 2pm. The French themselves usually visit early to get the best of the produce.

Markets are full of colour and bustle; the finest have all kinds of stalls from flowers to rabbits, chicken and ducks. Do not be deceived, however, into thinking these creatures are being sold as pets – they are for the pot. There are usually stalls selling household linen and cheap clothes, as well. Local cheeses, honey, cider, sausage, pâté and other

Buying Direct

As you travel around Normandy you may be tempted by the signs you see along the road for *dégustations* (tastings). Many cider producers and farmers will invite you to try their cider, Calvados, and other produce before you buy. You may also be invited to look around the farm, or distillery, which is usually interesting.

Don't think that because you are buying directly from the suppliers that you will pay less. Farm produce may be more expensive than supermarket goods, but remember that it is home produced and not factory processed – and this guarantee is worth a lot.

specialities are often offered for tasting, to tempt browsers to buy. It often works, too. Fish markets are often held daily by the harbour early in the morning in many coastal towns, e.g. Ouistreham, Trouville and Courseulles. Rouen has markets either for second-hand goods or fresh produce and flowers, or both, every day except Monday, at different sites in the town. The food markets are always in the Place du Vieux-Marché.

Some of the best weekly markets in the region are:

Monday
Seine-Maritime: Buchy.
Calvados: Pont-l'Evêque, Saint-Pierre-sur-Dives.
Eure: Bourg-Achard, Gisors, Pont-Audemer.
Orne: Briouze (livestock), Vimoutiers (afternoon).
Manche: Bricquebec, Carentan.

Tuesday
Seine-Maritime: Goderville.
Calvados: Deauville, Dives-sur-Mer (summer only), Grandcamp-Maisy.
Orne: L'Aigle, Argentan, Soligny-la-Trappe.
Manche: Cherbourg, Hambye, Lessay, Villedieu-les-Poêles.

Wednesday
Seine-Maritime: Yvetot.
Calvados: Villers-Bocage, Luc-sur-Mer (summer only), Trouville.
Eure: Evreux (centre), Le Neuborg, Vernon.
Orne: Carrouges, Flers, Le Mêle-sur-Sarthe.
Manche: Cérisy-la-Forêt, Granville.

Thursday
Seine-Maritime: Etretat, Forges-les-Eaux, Saint-Saëns.
Calvados: Condé-sur-Noireau, Houlgate, Le Molay-Littry.
Eure: Lyons-la-Forêt.
Orne: Alençon, Bellême, La Ferté-Macé.
Manche: Coutances, Sainte-Mère Eglise.

Friday
Seine-Maritime: Auffay, Eu.
Calvados: Caen (Place St-Sauveur), Cambremer, Deauville, Vire.
Eure: Broglie, Tillières-sur-Avre.
Orne: Argentan, Courtomer, Domfront, Ecouché.
Manche: Agon, Valognes.

Saturday
Seine-Maritime: Caudebec-en-Caux, Dieppe, Fécamp.
Calvados: Bayeux, Beuvron (afternoon), Deauville, Falaise, Honfleur, Lisieux.
Eure: Les Andelys, Bernay, Evreux, Louviers, Verneuil-sur-Avre.
Orne: Alençon, Bagnoles de L'Orne, Carrouges (afternoon), Flers, Gacé and Mortagne-au-Perche (afternoon), Sées.
Manche: Avranches, Granville, Mortain, Saint-Lô.

Sunday
Seine-Maritime: Harfleur.
Calvados: Caen (Place St Pierre), Cabourg, Trouville.
Eure: Brionne, Cormeilles.
Orne: Alençon, Mortrée.
Manche: Barenton, Hauteville-sur-Mer.

Antiques Markets

There is an increasing number of antique or second-hand *(brocante)* markets in the provinces, as well as flea markets *(marché aux puces)*, which are great fun to look around – you may even find a genuine bargain antique among all the old junk. Try the market at Saint-Pierre-sur-Dives, in Calvados, held on the first Sunday in every month. Annual antique and bric-à-brac fairs are usually held as below:
February: Lisieux and Honfleur (Calvados).
April: L'Aigle (Orne), Neufchâtel-en-Bray and Rouen (Seine-Maritime), Bernay (Eure).
May: Argentan (Orne).
June: Beaumont-le-Roger (Eure), Le Tréport (Seine-Maritime).
August: Mortagne-au-Perche (Orne).

Special Fairs

Look out for special fairs held all over the country throughout the year, such as at harvest times. In Seine-Maritime, for example, you'll find cherry markets in July, plum markets in August and apple markets in October.

Sport

Participant Sports

Normandy offers opportunities for all kinds of sporting activities. Most medium-sized towns have swimming-pools and even small villages often have a tennis court, but you may have to become a temporary member to use it – enquire at the local tourist office or *mairie* (town hall), which will also provide details of other local sports.

It seems to be a quirk of the French tourist industry that they do not always take full advantage of their facilities. Even though there may be good weather in early summer and autumn, open-air swimming-pools and other venues often limit their seasons to the period of the summer school holidays (July and August). Some also close in the middle of the day.

Wind-surfing is popular along the coast and inland; many of the sailing schools also offer courses. Sand yachting is mostly practised on the sandy stretches of beach in Calvados and Manche.

Activity holidays can also be taken at the **Center Parcs** site, at Les-Bois-France in Verneuil-sur-Avre, which is open all year round. For information contact: Center Parcs, 17–19 Place de Catalogne, 75014 Paris. Tel: 01 42 18 12 12, fax: 01 42 18 12 01.

Many companies offer sporting and activity holidays; a selection, with sports organised by type, is given as follows:

WATERSPORTS

With miles of coastline, Normandy offers many opportunities for sailing, wind-surfing and other kinds of water sports. It is impossible to list all the facilities here, but a selection is given to start you off.

Sailing

The regional tourist office *(see page 327)* publishes a leaflet detailing all the yachting harbours in the region and their facilities. Another useful address is the Yacht Club de France, 4 rue Chalgrin, 75116 Paris. Tel: 01 45 01 28 46, fax: 01 45 00 12 86. It is possible to hire a self-skippered yacht or one with a crew for a week or a weekend; try the companies listed below:

Aries Location, Port-Chantereyne, 50100 Cherbourg. Tel: 02 33 01 63 63, fax: 02 33 01 63 60.

Centre Nautique, Krischarter, Port-Deauville, 14800 Deauville. Tel: 02 31 88 67 32, fax: 02 31 88 89 37.

Granville Plaisance, Port de Hérel, 50400 Granville. Tel: 02 33 50 23 82.

There are almost 100 sailing clubs and sailing schools in the region, offering courses at all levels; information is available from departmental tourist offices or try the following:

Club Nautique de Trouville-Hennequeville, École de Voile, Digue des Roches Noires, 14360 Trouville. Tel: 02 31 88 13 59.

Deauville Yacht Club, Quai de la Marine, 14800 Deauville. Tel: 02 31 88 38 19.

Canoeing

The national organisation for the sport is **Canoë-Kayak de France**, 47 Quai Ferber, 94360 Bry-sur-Marne. Tel: 01 48 81 54 26. Tourist offices in the individual *départements* will also give details of courses, possibilities of hire and advice about which stretches of water are well suited to canoeing.

In **Seine-Maritime**, good facilities and opportunities to hire equipment exist on the Varenne, Béthune, Eaulne and Yères. In **Calvados**, there's a respected kayaking club at Thury Harcourt. In **Eure**, there are recreation centres for canoeing in Poses, Dangu, Brionne and La Bonneville; navigable rivers are the Risle, Epte, Eure, Andelle and Charentonne. There are also good facilities in Damigny, Orne and the Normandie-Maine Regional park, while in Granville (**Manche**) a sea kayak club offers courses in July and August.

Swimming & Diving

The national organisation for the sport is the **Fédération Française de Natation**, 148 Avenue Gambetta, 75020 Paris. Tel: 01 40 31 17 70. There are hundreds of swimming-pools throughout the region. Sea bathing is usually controlled by means of flags on supervised beaches.

Several clubs offer facilities and courses for deep-sea diving; these are usually based at swimming-pools.

Water Skiing

The national organisation for the sport is the **Fédération Française de Ski Nautique**, 16 rue Clément-Marot, 75008 Paris. Tel: 01 47 20 05 00. The Léry-Poses leisure in Eure offers the best inland facilities in the region *(see the Leisure Centres box)*.

Sand Yachting & Windsurfing

The Cotentin Peninsula is the place to practise these sports. Contact the **L'école du Vent en Côte des Isles**, Portbail, tel: 0233 04 86 15 or **Eolia Wind Sports Centre**, 14710 Colleville-sur-Mer, tel: 02 31 22 26 21, fax: 02 31 22 00 25 for sand yachting on Omaha Beach (catamaran courses also available).

Angling

Sea-fishing trips are widely available on the coast – look out for signs advertising trips on the quayside. Fécamp, Dieppe, Le Tréport and

Crossing the Bay

You can cross the bay of Mont-St-Michel on foot, as pilgrims used to do. From mid-April to October, experienced guides lead groups across the sands at low tide. The round trip is 14km (8 miles) long and takes about 4½ hours, including an hour at Mont-St-Michel. For reservations, contact Chemin de la Baie du Mont-St-Michel, 14 Places des Halles, 50530 Genets. Tel: 02 33 89 80 88, fax: 02 33 89 80 87.

Saint-Valéry-en-Caux offer good sport. A permit *(permis)* is usually required for coarse fishing: enquire at local tourist offices. The Orne *département* is particularly popular for trout fishing, with its well-stocked rivers.

Fishing is such a popular sport in Normandy that the regional tourist board has produced a handbook giving information about trips, accommodation and the best sites to fish. For details, contact the tourist office in Évreux *(see page 327)*.

CYCLING

Taking your bicycle *(vélo)* to France is easy, as they are carried free on most ferries and trains. You can also rent cycles for a reasonable cost; some railway stations have them for hire – you can often arrange to pick a bike up at one station and leave it at another.

Alternatively, try bicycle retailers/repairers or the local tourist office for bike hire. Some hirers have signed a charter to enable them to become a *"Point-Vélo Accueil"*, offering a high standard of service and information for cyclists. Some youth hostels rent cycles and also arrange tours with accommodation in hostels or under canvas. For more details, contact the YHA *(see page 342)*.

There are almost 20 marked cycle routes in Seine-Maritime – the tourist office in Fécamp (tel: 02 35 28 51 01) can supply details, plus

Children

Most of the resorts have beach clubs for children where youngsters can be entrusted to the care of supervisors for all kinds of fun and games. Although a fee is normally payable, prior booking is not usually necessary.

information about cycle hire and accommodation. Cycling holidays are offered by various organisations; with campsite or hotel accommodation with the advantage that your luggage is often transported for you to your next destination. Some operators are listed below:

Fédération Française de Cyclotourisme (FFCT), 8 rue Jean-Marie-Jégo, 75013 Paris. Tel: 01 44 16 88 88. Tours of 40–60 miles (60–100 km) per day. Bring your own bike.

Fédération Française de Cyclisme, Bâtiment Jean-Monnet, 5 rue de Rome, 95561 Rosny-Sous-Bois. Tel: 01 49 35 69 00, fax: 01 48 94 09 97, www.ffc.fr.

Cyclists Touring Club, Cotterell House, 69 Meadrow, Godalming, Surrey GU7 3HS. Tel: 01483 417217, fax: 01483 426994.

Sherpa Expeditions, 131a Heston Road, Hounslow TW5 0RD. Tel: 0208 577 2717, fax: 0208 572 9788. "Inn to Inn" holidays.

It is advisable to take out insurance before you go. Normal rules of the road apply to cyclists *(see page 332)*; cycle paths must be used where available. Advice and information can be obtained from **The Touring Department of the Cyclists Touring Club**. Their service to members includes competitive cycle and travel insurance, free detailed touring itineraries and general information sheets about France. The club's French counterpart, **Fédération Française de Cyclotourisme** offers a similar service. Rob Hunter's book *Cycle Touring in France* is also a very useful handbook.

Such is the French passion for cycling that local clubs organise many trips lasting a day or more, and visitors are often more than welcome to join in. Lists of clubs and events are also organised by local members of the *Fédération Française de Cyclotourisme*, who also produce leaflets giving suggested cycle tours for independent travellers, ranging from easy terrain to very hard going for the more experienced

Leisure Centres

Inland, there are many *Base de Loisirs* (leisure centres), where water and other types of sports can be practised. On lakes and quiet river stretches, they also offer various activities, including tennis, riding and mini-golf. They usually have a café or bar, and sometimes also a restaurant, picnic areas, and often a campsite.

Many centres offer tuition in the various sports available and fees are usually charged at an hourly or half-hourly rate. Where boating and windsurfing is permitted, equipment is often available for hire, or you may take your own.

The following is just a selection; tourist offices will give you details of others in their area:

Seine Maritime

Cany-Barville – Lac de Caniel: offers sports including sailing, rowing, water skiing and pedaloes. Tel: 02 35 97 40 55.

Jumièges-le-Mesnil – Base de Loisirs: sailing, windsurfing, catamarans, canoes, plus tennis, archery, golf and climbing. Tel: 02 35 37 93 84.

Saint-Aubin-le-Cauf – Étang de la Varenne: sports on offer include sailing, windsurfing, canoeing/kayaking. Tel: 02 35 85 69 05.

Calvados

Clécy: the Lionel Terray Outdoor Centre offers numerous outdoor activities: canoeing/kayaking, cross-country cycling, rock climbing, orienteering, archery; accommodation also available. Tel: 02 32 69 72 82, fax: 02 31 69 86 30

Condé sur Vire: Écluse Leisure Centre offers canoeing/kayaking – unaccompanied or with qualified staff – rock climbing, walking, cycling, plus mini-golf, giant chess and draughts. Accommodation open all year round. Tel/fax: 02 33 57 33 66.

Pont l'Evêque: leisure centre around a lake of almost 56

hectares (140 acres); sailing, punting, wind-surfing. Tel: 02 31 65 29 21.

Eure

Brionne: leisure centre with sailing, fishing, pedaloes and supervised bathing.

Conches – Domaine de la Noé: leisure centre offers canoeing and windsurfing and other amenities such as pony rides, golf and tennis. Open: May to end September.

Dangu: water sports centre on Gisors lake: canoeing, wind-surfing, fishing, mini-golf and a play area; good campsite. Tel: 02 32 55 43 42.

Poses – Les Étangs des Deux Amants: the Léry-Poses leisure centre offers the best inland water-skiing facilities in the region on its two lakes. Also many other sports facilities and a campsite. Tel: 02 32 59 13 13.

Toutainville – Centre Nautique de Toutainville: sports include sailing, windsurfing and water skiing.

Venables: Aubevoye water sports centre on 86 hectares (300 acres) of water running into the Seine: power boats, sailing, windsurfing, water skiing and fishing. Open 15 April to 21 November.

Orne

La Ferté-Macé: a lake of almost 28 hectares (70 acres) in a large park, with a sandy beach, bathing, pedaloes, windsurfing and other attractions. Tel: 02 33 37 10 97.

Le Mele-sur-Sarthe: leisure centre based around a lake: sailing, windsurfing, bathing, tennis. Tel: 02 33 27 61 02.

Soligny-la-Trappe: a small lake with supervised bathing, punts, pedaloes and mini-golf. Tel: 02 33 34 50 29.

Vimoutiers: Éscale du Vitou leisure centre in a pleasant setting with a small lake, swimming pool, riding centre, tennis and children's games; accommodation available. Tel: 02 33 39 12 04.

cyclist, with details of accommodation en route, cycle repairers and other facilities.

Mountain Biking

This sport has really taken off in recent years, particularly among the French, many of whom are already dedicated cyclists. Many of the organisations listed under Cycling above offer mountain bike holidays or, in the UK, contact: **Rough Tracks**, Bremhill, Calne, Wiltshire SN11 9LA. Tel/fax: 07000 560749. This firm offers holidays in the Normandy Regional Park.

Mountain bikes (in French called VTT – *Vélo Tout Terrain*) and protective gear can be hired locally, try the local tourist office, or cycle shops/repairers.

There are several special terrains suitable for mountain biking. In particular, the **Centre de Loisirs VTT** at Domfront offers 950 km (590 miles) of marked routes at four levels of difficulty. Other marked trails are to be found in the Valcongrain forest in Calvados; at the Ferrière-Harang 200-km (125-mile) circuit; and at Amayé-sur-Orne.

Bungee Jumping

Europe's first bungee-jumping centre, still going strong, is on the Souleuvre Viaduct near Le Bény-Bocage, in Calvados. The centre also runs "bosun's chair" rides across the valley at 100 kph (60mph). If this is your idea of fun, contact A.J. Hackett, tel: 02 31 66 31 66, or visit www.ajhackett.fr

HORSE-RIDING

Normandy, and in particular the *département* of Orne, is real horse country and there are countless opportunities for those who wish to ride or watch equestrian events. Treks lasting a day or more – as well as longer holidays on horseback – can be organised locally. Further information can be obtained from tourist offices (see

page 327). Alternatively, you could try the following riding centres:
Ferme Equestre de la Corbière, 76720 Auffay. Tel: 02 35 32 82 82, fax: 02 35 34 98 25.
Le Village du Cheval, 61100 St Michel-des-Andaines. Tel: 02 33 37 12 79, fax: 02 33 37 15 50. Offers all kinds of equestrain activities, including courses for children and senior citizens, trips to nearby Bagnoles-de-l'Orne in a horse-drawn carriage, etc. Open all year.
Poney Club de Bois Gilberts des Vallés, Thierry de Pas, 76750 Buchy. Tel: 02 35 34 42 51, fax: 02 35 32 65 72; Thierry.depas@wanadoo.fr specialises in riding holidays in forest terrain for children aged between 5 and 12.
Poney Club de Port-Bail, Ferme de Mielles, 50580 Port-Bail. Tel: 02 33 04 85 96, fax: 02 33 04 26 71; equitation.portbail@wanadoo.fr offers accompanied half-day, whole-day and three-day treks during summer months, including exhilarating rides on the sands.

Local tourist offices will provide details of stables if you simply wish to hire a horse by the hour or day.

GOLF

Golf has caught on in a big way in France and the regional tourist boards have joined forces with the French Golf Federation in an effort to promote the sport and set higher standards. The resulting organisation, **France Golf International**, embraces over 100 golf courses around the country, which must provide a certain standard of facilities. The courses must have weekend reservation systems and multilingual staff must be on hand to help foreigners.

Many tour operators offer golfing holidays in the region, and the following is just a selection:
Brittany Ferries, The Brittany Centre, Wharf Board, Portsmouth, Hants PO2 8RU. Tel: 0990 360 360, fax: 01705 873237.

Driveline Europe, Greenleaf House, Darkes Lane, Potters Bar EN6 1AE. Tel: 01707 660011, fax: 01707 649126.

Below are the principal courses in each *département*:

Seine Maritime

Golf de Dieppe, 51 Route de Pourville, 76200 Dieppe. Tel: 02 35 84 25 05, fax: 02 35 84 97 11. 18 holes. Driving range, equipment rental.
Golf d'Étretat, Route du Havre, BP7, 76790 Etrétat. Tel: 02 35 27 04 89, fax: 02 35 29 49 02. 18 holes.
Golf de la Forêt Verte, 76710 Bosc-Guérard. Tel: 02 35 33 62 94, fax: 02 35 33 16 52. 18 holes. Driving range, equipment rental.
Golf du Havre, Hameaux St-Supplix, BP 10, 76930 Octeville-sur-Mer. Tel: 02 35 46 36 50, fax: 02 35 46 32 66. 18 holes. Driving range.
Golf de Rouen Mont-St-Aignan, Rue Francis Poulenc, 76130 Mont-St-Aignan. Tel: 02 35 76 38 65, fax: 02 35 75 13 86. 18 holes. Driving range.
Golf Public du Parc Régional des Boucles de la Seine Normande, 76480 Jumièges. Tel: 02 35 05 32 97, fax: 02 35 37 99 97. 18 holes. Driving range.
Golf de Saint-Saëns, Domaine du Vaudichon, BP 20, 76680 Saint-Saëns. Tel: 02 35 34 25 24, fax: 02 35 34 43 33. 18 holes. Driving range, equipment rental.

Calvados

Golf d'Omaha Beach (PG), La Ferme St-Sauveur, 14520 Port-en-Bessin. Tel: 02 31 22 12 12, fax: 02 31 22 12 13. Three 9-hole courses. Equipment rental.
Golf de Cabourg Le Home (PG), 38 avenue du Président René Coty, Le Home Varaville, 14390 Cabourg. Tel: 02 31 91 25 56, fax: 02 31 91 18 30. 18 holes. Driving range, equipment rental.
Golf de Caen (PG), Le Vallon, 14112 Biéville-Beuville. Tel: 02 31 94 72 09, fax: 02 31 47 45 30. 27 holes. Driving range, lessons in school holidays.

Golf de Clécy-Cantalou (PG), Manoir de Cantelou, 14570 Clécy. Tel: 02 31 69 72 72, fax: 02 31 69 70 22. 18 holes. Described as one of the most beautiful in France. Driving range, lessons available, equipment rental, accommodation.

New Golf Barrière de Deauville (PG), 14800 Saint-Arnoult. Tel: 02 31 14 24 24, fax: 02 31 14 24 25. 27 holes. Driving range, equipment rental, accommodation.

Golf de Deauville-l'Amirauté, Tourgeville, 14800 Deauville. Tel: 02 31 14 42 00, fax: 02 31 88 32 00. 18 holes. Driving range, equipment rental, lessons available.

Golf de Garcelles, Route de Lorgui-chon, 14540 Garcelles-Secqueville. Tel: 02 31 39 09 09, fax: 02 31 39 09 10. 18 holes. Driving range, putting, lessons, 4 covered tennis courts.

Golf de Deauville-St-Gatien (PG), La Ferme du Mont St-Jean, 14130 Saint-Gatien-des-Bois. Tel: 02 31 65 19 99, fax: 02 31 65 11 24. 27 holes. Driving range, lessons in school holidays.

Golf de St-Julien (PG), St-Julien-sur-Calonne, 14130 Pont-l'Evêque, BP 76. Tel: 02 31 64 30 30, fax: 02 31 64 12 43. 27 holes. Driving range, equipment rental.

Eure

Golf du Champ de Bataille, 27110 Le Neubourg. Tel: 02 32 35 03 72, fax: 02 32 35 83 10. Private club, 18 holes.

Golf de Center Parcs, Domaine des Bois-Francs, 27130 Verneuil-sur-Avre. Tel: 02 32 60 50 02, fax: 02 32 60 14 28. 9 holes; 3-hole beginners' training course; equipment rental.

Golf de Léry-Poses, Base de Loisirs de Léry-Poses, BP 7, 27740 Poses. Tel: 02 32 59 47 42, fax: 02 32 61 20 34. 18 holes. Driving range, equipment rental.

Golf du Vaudreuil, 27100 Le Vaudreuil. Tel: 02 32 59 02 60, fax: 02 32 59 43 88. 18 holes. Course designed by the English golf architect Hawtree in 1961.

Orne

Golf de Bagnoles-de-l'Orne, Route de Domfront, 61140 Tesse La Madeleine. Tel: 02 33 37 81 42. 9 holes. Driving range and equipment rental.

Golf de Bellême, Les Sablons, 61130 Bellême. Tel: 02 33 73 12 79, fax: 02 33 85 13 20. 18 holes. Driving range, equipment rental.

Manche

Golf de Coutainville, Chalet du Golf 50230 Agon-Coutainville. Tel: 02 33 47 03 31, fax: 02 33 47 38 42. 18 holes. Driving range.

Golf de Granville, Chalet du Golf, 50290 Bréville-sur-Mer. Tel: 02 33 50 23 06, fax: 0233 61 91 87. 27 holes. Lessons and training.

Other Sports

There are opportunities for all kinds of less-common sports in the region. For example, the Suisse Normande area and the Seine Valley are particularly good for rock climbing. If your particular kind of exercise is not featured here, try contacting **Insolite**, 7 rue des Basnages, 76000 Rouen. Tel: 02 35 71 20 20, or the ever-helpful tourist office in Évreux. Tel: 02 32 33 79 00, fax: 02 32 31 19 04.

Spectator Sports

EQUESTRIAN EVENTS

There are numerous equestrian events in the region, particularly in Orne. There are races almost all year round at Argentan race course and there is an important horse show in September in the grounds of the Château de Carrouges in the Normandie-Maine Regional Park, which also stages other events. A three-day event is held in Caen in October and the Harcourt four-in-hand competition is held annually in June. There are international jumping events at Flers in August, and at Val-de-Reuil and Beaumont-le-Roger. Many competitions are also held at the **Haras du Pin** national stud.

The best known races, of course, are at **Deauville**, where the Prix Jacques le Marois and the Prix Morny are among the most important events of their kind in Europe. There's a great atmosphere, enjoyed even by those who don't usually go to the races, and the entrance charge is surprisingly low.

BOATING EVENTS

There is a 24-hour speed boat race at Rouen at the end of April, and the prestigious Cowes–Deauville yacht race takes place at the end of May.

CYCLES AND CARS

The Paris–Camembert cycle race takes place in June; and the Paris–Deauville vintage car race is staged in October.

Details of sporting events can be obtained from the nearest tourist office (*see page 327*), or from national organisers of specific events.

Language

French is the native language of more than 90 million people and the acquired language of 180 million. It is a Romance language descended from the Vulgar Latin spoken by the Roman conquerors of Gaul. It still carries the reputation of being the most cultured language in the world, and the most beautiful. People often tell stories about the impatience of the French towards foreigners not blessed with fluency in their language. In general, however, if you attempt to speak in French, you will be helpful.

Since much of our vocabulary is related to French, thanks to the Norman Conquest, travellers will often recognise many helpful cognates, such as *hôtel*, *café* and *bagages*. You should be aware, however, of some misleading "false friends" *(see page 362.*

Words & Phrases

How much is it? *C'est combien?*
What is your name? *Comment vous appelez-vous?*
My name is... *Je m'appelle...*
Do you speak English? *Parlez-vous anglais?*
I am English/American *Je suis anglais/américain*
I don't understand *Je ne comprends pas*
Please speak more slowly *Parlez plus lentement, s'il vous plaît*
Can you help me? *Pouvez-vous m'aider?*
I'm looking for... *Je cherche*
Where is...? *Où est...?*
I'm sorry *Excusez-moi/Pardon*
I don't know *Je ne sais pas*
No problem *Pas de problème*
Have a good day! *Bonne journée!*
That's it *C'est ça*

Here it is *Voici*
There it is *Voilà*
Let's go *On y va. Allons-y*
See you tomorrow *A demain*
See you soon *A bientôt*
yes *oui*
no *non*
please *s'il vous plaît*
thank you *merci*
(very much) *(beaucoup)*
you're welcome *de rien*
excuse me *excusez-moi*
hello *bonjour*
OK *d'accord*
goodbye *au revoir*
good evening *bonsoir*
here *ici*
there *là*
today *aujourd'hui*
yesterday *hier*
tomorrow *demain*
now *maintenant*
later *plus tard*
this morning *ce matin*
this afternoon *cet après-midi*
this evening *ce soir*

The Alphabet

Learning the pronunciation of the French alphabet is a good idea. In particular, learn how to spell out your name.
a=ah, **b**=bay, **c**=say, **d**=day **e**=er, **f**=ef, **g**=zhay, **h**=ash. **i**=ee, **j**=zhee, **k**=ka, **l**=el, **m**=em, **n** =en, **o**=oh, **p**=pay, **q**=kew, **r**=ehr, **s**=ess, **t**=tay, **u**=ew, **v**=vay, **w**=dooblah vay, **x**-=eex, **y** ee grek, **z**=zed

On Arrival

I want to get off at... *Je voudrais descendre à...*
Is there a bus to the Louvre? *Est-ce qui'il ya un bus pour le Louvre?*
What street is this? *A quelle rue sommes-nous?*
Which line do I take for...? *Quelle ligne dois-je prendre pour...?*
How far is...? *A quelle distance se trouve...?*
Validate your ticket *Compostez votre billet*
airport *l'aéroport*
train station *la gare*
bus station *la gare routière*

Métro stop *la station de Métro*
bus *l'autobus, le car*
bus stop *l'arrêt*
platform *le quai*
ticket *le billet*
return ticket *aller-retour*
hitchhiking *l'autostop*
toilets *les toilettes*
This is the hotel address *C'est l'adresse de l'hôtel*
I'd like a (single/double) room... *Je voudrais une chambre (pour une/deux personnes) ...*
....with shower *avec douche*
....with a bath *avec salle de bain*
....with a view *avec vue*
Does that include breakfast? *Le prix comprend-il le petit déjeuner?*
May I see the room? *Je peux voir la chambre?*
washbasin *le lavabo*
bed *le lit*
key *la cléf*
lift/elevator *l'ascenseur*
air conditioned *climatisé*

On the Road

Where is the spare wheel? *Où est la roue de secours?*
Where is the nearest garage? *Où est le garage le plus proche?*
Our car has broken down *Notre voiture est en panne*
I want to have my car repaired *Je veux faire réparer ma voiture*
It's not your right of way *Vous n'avez pas la priorité*
I think I must have put diesel in the car by mistake *Je crois que j'ai mis du gasoil dans la voiture par erreur*
the road to... *la route pour...*
left *gauche*
right *droite*
straight on *tout droit*
far *loin*
near *près d'ici*
opposite *en face*
beside *à côté de*
car park *parking*
over there *là-bas*
at the end *au bout*
on foot *à pied*
by car *en voiture*
town map *le plan*
road map *la carte*
street *la rue*
square *la place*

Emergencies

Help! *Au secours!*
Stop! *Arrêtez!*
Call a doctor *Appelez un médecin*
Call an ambulance *Appelez une ambulance*
Call the police *Appelez la police*
Call the fire brigade *Appelez les pompiers*
Where is the nearest telephone? *Où est le téléphone le plus proche?*
Where is the nearest hospital? *Où est l'hôpital le plus proche?*
I am sick *Je suis malade*
I have lost my passport/purse *J'ai perdu mon passeport/porte-monnaie*

give way *céder le passage*
dead end *impasse*
no parking *stationnement interdit*
motorway *l'autoroute*
toll *le péage*
speed limit *la limitation de vitesse*
petrol *l'essence*
unleaded *sans plomb*
diesel *le gasoil*
water/oil *l'eau/l'huile*
puncture *un pneu de crevé*
bulb *l'ampoule*
wipers *les essuies-glace*

Shopping

Where is the nearest bank (post office)? *Où est la banque/Poste la plus proche?*
I'd like to buy *Je voudrais acheter*
How much is it? *C'est combien?*
Do you take credit cards? *Est-ce que vous acceptez les cartes de crédit?*
I'm just looking *Je regarde seulement*
Have you got...? *Avez-vous...?*
I'll take it *Je le prends*
I'll take this one/that one *Je prends celui-ci/celui-là*
What size is it? *C'est de quelle taille?*
Anything else? *Avec ça?*
size (clothes) *la taille*
size (shoes) *la pointure*
cheap *bon marché*
expensive *cher*

enough *assez*
too much *trop*
each *la pièce (eg 15F la pièce)*
bill *la note*
chemist *la pharmacie*
bakery *la boulangerie*
bookshop *la librairie*
library *la bibliothèque*
department store *le grand magasin*
delicatessen *la charcuterie/le traiteur*
fishmonger's *la poissonerie*
grocery *l'alimentation/l'épicerie*
tobacconist *tabac*
market *le marché*
supermarket *le supermarché*
junk shop *la brocante*

Sightseeing

town *la ville*
old town *la vieille ville*
abbey *l'abbaye*
cathedral *la cathédrale*
church *l'église*
keep *le donjon*
mansion *l'hôtel*
hospital *l'hôpital*
town hall *l'hôtel de ville/la mairie*
nave *la nef*
stained glass *le vitrail*
staircase *l'escalier*
tower *la tour (La Tour Eiffel)*
walk *le tour*
country house/castle *le château*
Gothic *gothique*
Roman *romain*
museum *la musée*
art gallery *la galerie*
exhibition *l'exposition*

Basic Rules

It is worth trying to master a few simple phrases before holidaying in France. The fact that you have made an effort is likely to get you a better response. More and more French people like practising their English on visitors, especially waiters and the young. Pronunciation is the key; they really will not understand if you get it very wrong. Remember to **emphasise each syllable**, but not to pronounce the last consonant of a word as a rule (this includes the plural "s") and always drop your "h"s. Whether to use **"vous"** or **"tu"** is a vexed question; increasingly the familiar form of "tu" is used by many people. However it is better to be too formal, and use "vous" if in doubt. It is very important to be polite; always address people as **Madame** or **Monsieur**, and address them by their surnames until you are confident first names are acceptable. When entering a shop always say, "Bonjour Monsieur/ Madame," and "Merci, au revoir," when leaving.

tourist information *l'office de tourisme/le*
office *syndicat d'initiative*
free *gratuit*
open *ouvert*
closed *fermé*
every day *tous les jours*
all year *toute l'année*
all day *toute la journée*

Dining Out

Table d'hôte (the "host's table") is one set menu served at a set price. **Prix fixe** is a fixed-price menu. **A la carte** means dishes from the menu are chosen and charged separately.

breakfast *le petit déjeuner*
lunch *le déjeuner*
dinner *le dîner*
meal *le repas*
first course *l'entrée/les hors d'oeuvre*
main course *le plat principal*
made to order *sur commande*
drink included *boisson compris*
wine list *la carte des vins*
the bill *l'addition*
fork *la fourchette*
knife *le couteau*
spoon *la cuillère*
plate *l'assiette*
glass *le verre*
napkin *la serviette*
ashtray *le cendrier*

Breakfast and Snacks
baguette **long thin loaf**
pain **bread**

petits pains **rolls**
beurre **butter**
poivre **pepper**
sel **salt**
sucre **sugar**
confiture **jam**
oeufs **eggs**
...à la coque **boiled eggs**
...au bacon **bacon and eggs**
...au jambon **ham and eggs**
...sur le plat **fried eggs**
...brouillés **scrambled eggs**
tartine **bread with butter**
yaourt **yoghurt**
crêpe **pancake**
croque-monsieur **ham and cheese toasted sandwich**
croque-madame **...with a fried egg on top**
galette **type of pancake**
pan bagna **bread roll stuffed with salad Niçoise**
quiche **tart of eggs and cream with various fillings**
quiche lorraine **quiche with bacon**

First course

An *amuse-bouche*, *amuse-gueule* or appetiser is something literally to "amuse the mouth", which is served before the first course. Typical delicacies include:
anchoiade **sauce of olive oil, anchovies and garlic, served with raw vegetables**
assiette anglaise **cold meats**
potage **soup**
rillettes **rich fatty paste of shredded duck, rabbit or pork**
tapenade **spread of olives and anchovies**
pissaladière **Provençal pizza with onions, olives and anchovies**

Viandes (Meat)

bleu **rare**
à point **medium**
bien cuit **well done**
grillé **grilled**
agneau **lamb**
andouille/andouillette **tripe sausage**
bifteck **steak**
boudin **sausage**
boudin noir **black pudding**
boudin blanc **white pudding (chicken or veal)**
blanquette **stew of veal, lamb or chicken with a creamy egg sauce**

boeuf à la mode **beef in red wine with carrots, mushroom and onions**
à la bordelaise **beef with red wine and shallots**
à la bourguignon **cooked in red wine, onions and mushrooms**
brochette **kebab**
caille **quail**
canard **duck**
carbonnade **casserole of beef, beer and onions**
carré d'agneau cassoulet **rack of lamb stew with beans, sausages, pork and duck, from the southwest**
cervelle **brains (food)**
chateaubriand choucroute **thick steak with sauerkraut, bacon and sausages from the Alsace region**
confit **duck or goose preserved in its own fat**
contre-filet **cut of sirloin steak**
coq au vin **chicken in red wine**
côte d'agneau **lamb chop**
daube **beef stew with red wine, onions and tomatoes**
dinde **turkey**
entrecôte **beef rib steak**
escargot **snail**
faisan **pheasant**
farci **stuffed**
faux-filet **sirloin**
feuilleté **puff pastry**
foie **liver**
foie de veau **calf's liver**
foie gras **goose or duck liver pâté**

False Friends

False friends are words that look like English words but mean something different.
le car **coach, also railway carriage**
le conducteur **bus driver**
la monnaie **change (coins)**
l'argent **money/silver**
ça marche **can sometimes mean walk, but is usually used to mean working (the TV, the car etc.) or going well**
actuel **"present time"**
(la situation actuelle **the present situation)**
rester **to stay**
location **hiring/renting**
personne **person or nobody, according to context**
le médecin **doctor**

Non, non, Garçon

Garçon is the word for waiter but it is never used directly; say *Monsieur* or *Madame* to attract his or her attention.

gardiane **rich beef stew with olives and garlic, from the Camargue**
cuisses de grenouille **frog's legs**
grillade **grilled meat**
hachis **minced meat**
jambon **ham**
lapin **rabbit**
lardon **small pieces of bacon, often added to salads**
magret de canard **breast of duck**
médaillon **round pieces of meat**
moelle **beef bone marrow**
mouton navarin **stew of lamb with onions, carrots and turnips**
oie **goose**
perdrix **partridge**
petit-gris **small snail**
pieds de cochon **pig's trotters**
pintade **guinea fowl**
pipérade **Basque dish of eggs, ham, peppers, onion**
porc **pork**
pot-au-feu **casserole of beef and vegetables**
poulet **chicken**
poussin **young chicken**
rognons **kidneys**
rôti **roast**
sanglier **wild boar**
saucisse **fresh sausage**
saucisson **salami**
veau **veal**

Poissons (Fish)

armoricaine **made with white wine, tomatoes, butter and cognac**
anchois **anchovies**
anguille **eel**
bar (or loup) **sea bass**
belon **Brittany oyster**
Bercy **sauce of fish stock, butter, white wine and shallots**
bouillabaisse **fish soup served with grated cheese, garlic croutons and rouille, a spicy sauce**
cabillaud **cod**
calmars **squid**
colin **hake**
coquillage **shellfish**
coquilles Saint-Jacques **scallops**
crevette **shrimp**

daurade **sea bream**
flétan **halibut**
fruits de mer **seafood**
hareng **herring**
homard **lobster**
huître **oyster**
langoustine **large prawn**
limande **lemon sole**
lotte **monkfish**
morue **salt cod**
moule **mussel**
moules marinières **mussels in white wine and onions**
raie **skate**
saumon **salmon**
thon **tuna**
truite **trout**

Légumes (Vegetables)

ail **garlic**
artichaut **artichoke**
asperge **asparagus**
aubergine **aubergine/eggplant**
avocat **avocado**
bolets **boletus mushrooms**
céleri rémoulade **grated celery with mayonnaise**
champignon **mushroom**
cèpes **ceps**
chanterelle **wild mushroom**
cornichon **gherkin**
courgette **courgette/zucchini**
chips **potato crisps**
chou **cabbage**
chou-fleur **cauliflower**
concombre **cucumber**
cru **raw**
crudités **raw vegetables**
épinard **spinach**
frites **chips, French fries**
gratin dauphinois **sliced potatoes baked with cream**
haricot **dried bean**
haricots verts **green beans**
lentilles **lentils**
maïs **corn**
mange-tout **snow pea**
mesclun **mixed leaf salad**
navet **turnip**
noix **nut, walnut**
noisette **hazelnut**
oignon **onion**
panais **parsnip**
persil **parsley**
pignon **pine nut**
poireau **leek**
pois **pea**
poivron **bell pepper**
pomme de terre **potato**

Slang

métro, boulot, dodo nine-to-five syndrome
McDo McDonald's
branché trendy (literally "connected")
C'est du cinéma It's very unlikely
une copine/un copain friend/pal
un ami friend but **mon ami**, boyfriend; also **mon copain**
un truc thing, "whatsit"
pas mal, not bad, good-looking
fantastic! fantastic! terrible!

radis **radish**
roquette **arugula, rocket**
ratatouille **stew of aubergines, courgettes and tomatoes**
riz **rice**
salade Niçoise **egg, tuna, olives, onions and tomato salad**
salade verte **green salad**
truffe **truffle**

Fruits (Fruit)

ananas **pineapple**
cavaillon **fragrant sweet melon from Cavaillon in Provence**
cerise **cherry**
citron **lemon**
citron vert **lime**
figue **fig**
fraise **strawberry**
framboise **raspberry**
groseille **redcurrant**
mangue **mango**
pamplemousse **grapefruit**
pêche **peach**
poire **pear**
pomme **apple**
raisin **grape**
prune **plum**
pruneau **prune**
Reine claude **greengage**

Sauces Sauces

aioli **garlic mayonnaise**
béarnaise **sauce of egg, butter, wine and herbs**
forestière **with mushrooms and bacon**
hollandaise **egg, butter and lemon sauce**
lyonnaise **with onions**
meunière **fried fish with butter, lemon and parsley sauce**
meurette **red wine sauce**

Mornay **sauce of cream, egg and cheese**
Parmentier **served with potatoes**
paysan **rustic style**
pistou **Provençal sauce of basil, garlic and olive oil; vegetable soup with the sauce.**
provençale **sauce of tomatoes, garlic and olive oil.**
papillotte **cooked in paper**

Puddings (Dessert)

Belle Hélène **fruit with ice cream and chocolate sauce**
clafoutis **baked pudding of batter and cherries**
coulis **purée of fruit or vegetables**
gâteau **cake**
île flottante **whisked egg whites in custard sauce**
crème anglaise **custard**
pêche melba **peaches with ice cream and raspberry sauce**
tarte tatin **upside down tart of caramelised apples**
crème caramel **caramelised egg custard**
crème Chantilly **whipped cream**
fromage **cheese**
chèvre **goat's cheese**

In the Café

If you sit at the bar (le zinc), drinks will be cheaper than at a table. Settle the bill when you leave; the waiter may leave a slip of paper on

Table Talk

I am a vegetarian Je suis végétarien
I am on a diet Je suis au régime
What do you recommend? Que'est-ce que vous recommandez?
Do you have local specialities? Avez-vous des spécialités locales?
I'd like to order Je voudrais commander
That is not what I ordered Ce n'est pas ce que j'ai commandé
Is service included? Est-ce que le service est compris?
May I have more wine? Encore du vin, s'il vous plaît?
Enjoy your meal Bon appétit!

the table to keep track of the bill.
The French enjoy bitter-sweet
aperitifs, often diluted with ice and
fizzy water.

drinks *les boissons*
coffee *café*
...with milk or cream *au lait or
crème*
...decaffeinated *déca/décaféiné*
...black/espresso *express/noir*
...American filtered coffee *filtre*
tea *thé*
...herb infusion *tisane*
...camomile *verveine*
hot chocolate *chocolat chaud*
milk *lait*
mineral water *eau minérale*
fizzy *gazeux*
non-fizzy *non-gazeux*
fizzy lemonade *limonade*
**fresh lemon juice served with
sugar** *citron pressé*
fresh squeezed orange juice
orange pressé
full (eg full cream milk) *entier*
fresh or cold *frais, fraîche*
beer *bière*
...bottled *en bouteille*
...on tap *à la pression*
pre-dinner drink *apéritif*
**white wine with cassis,
blackcurrant liqueur** *kir*
***kir* with champagne** *kir royale*
with ice *avec des glaçons*
neat *sec*
red *rouge*
white *blanc*
rose *rosé*
dry *brut*
sweet *doux*
sparkling wine *crémant*
house wine *vin de maison*
local wine *vin de pays*
Where is this wine from? *De
quelle région vient ce vin?*
pitcher *carafe/pichet*
...of water/wine *d'eau/de vin*
half litre *demi-carafe*

Time

At what time? *A quelle heure?*
When? *Quand?*
What time is it? *Quelle heure
est-il?*
● *Note that the French generally
use the 24-hour clock.*

quarter litre *quart*
mixed *panaché*
after dinner drink *digestif*
brandy from Armagnac *Armagnac*
Normandy apple brandy *calvados*
cheers! *santé!*
hangover *gueule de bois*

Days of the Week

Monday *lundi*
Tuesday *mardi*
Wednesday *mercredi*
Thursday *jeudi*
Friday *vendredi*
Saturday *samedi*
Sunday *dimanche*

Capitalisation

Note that days of the week,
seasons and months are not
capitalised in written French.

Seasons

spring *le printemps*
summer *l'été*
autumn *l'automne*
winter *l'hiver*

Months

January *janvier*
February *février*
March *mars*
April *avril*
May *mai*
June *juin*
July *juillet*
August *août*
September *septembre*
October *octobre*
November *novembre*
December *décembre*

Numbers

0	*zéro*
1	*un, une*
2	*deux*
3	*trois*
4	*quatre*
5	*cinq*
6	*six*
7	*sept*
8	*huit*
9	*neuf*

10	*dix*
11	*onze*
12	*douze*
13	*treize*
14	*quatorze*
15	*quinze*
16	*seize*
17	*dix-sept*
18	*dix-huit*
19	*dix-neuf*
20	*vingt*
21	*vingt-et-un*
30	*trente*
40	*quarante*
50	*cinquante*
60	*soixante*
70	*soixante-dix*
80	*quatre-vingts*
90	*quatre-vingt-dix*
100	*cent*
1000	*mille*
1,000,000	*un million*

*Note that the number 1 is often
written as an upside down V and the
number 7 is usually crossed*

On the Telephone

How do I make an outside call?
*Comment est-ce que je peux
téléphoner à l'exterieur?*
**I want to make an international
(local) call** *Je voudrais une
communication pour l'étranger
(une communication locale)*
What is the dialling code? *Quel
est l'indicatif?*
**I'd like an alarm call for 8
tomorrow morning**. *Je voudrais
être réveillé à huit heures
demain martin*
Who's calling? *C'est qui à
l'appareil?*
Hold on, please *Ne quittez pas
s'il vous plaît*
The line is busy *La ligne est
occupée*
**I must have dialled the wrong
number** *J'ai dû faire un faux
numéro*

Further Reading

History and Travel

France Today, by John Ardagh.
London: Secker and Warburg. Up-to-date, hefty tome on modern France.
Writers' France, by John Ardagh.
London: Hamish Hamilton. A region-by-region guide to the literature and great writers of France.
The Identity of France, by Fernand Braudel. London: Fontana Press.
A Traveller's History of France, by Robert Cole. London: The Windrush Press. Slim volume for background reading.
Pierre Deux's Normandy, by Dannenberg, Moulin and LeVec. London: Phaidon. Photographic record of Normandy today.
A Holiday History of France, by Ronald Hamilton. London: The Hogarth Press. Illustrated guide to history and architecture.
*Holt's Battlefield Guides:
Normandy-Overlord* and *Holt's Visitor's Guide to the Normandy Landing Beaches*, by Tonie & Valmai Holt. Both available from T & V Holt Associates, Oak House, Woodnesborough, Sandwich, Kent CT13 0NJ.
Six Armies in Normandy, by John Keegan. Jonathan Cape (hardback), Pimlico (paperback). The story of the Battle for Normandy.
The Bayeux Tapestry, by David M. Wilson. London: Thames and Hudson. A full colour representation of the complete tapestry, its history and commentary by the Director of the British Museum.
The French, by Theodore Zeldin. New York: Random House. How the French live today.
Walking in France, by Rob Hunter is a good basic guide book for serious walkers. Oxford: Oxford University Press.

Fiction

For details of the authors from the area, see the **Writers** chapter on page 104. Other novels include:

Odo's Hanging, by Peter Benson. London: Hodder & Stoughton. Historical novel about the making of the Bayeux Tapestry.
Madame Bovary, by Gustave Flaubert. Translated by Gerard Hopkins. Oxford University Press. This novel is the best place to start with this essential Norman writer.
The Looking Glass, by Michèle Roberts. London: Virago. A novel set in Rouen and Étretat at the beginning of the 20th century, full of the atmosphere of the times.
The Longest Day, by Cornelius Ryan. Simon & Schuster, New York.

Food

Edible France: A Traveller's Guide, by Glynn Christian. London: Grub Street. An entertaining region by region guide to local food and wine, including recommended shops, plus market days.
The Food Lover's Guide to France, by Marc and Kim Millon. London: Little, Brown & Company. Excellent background on regional food, with selection of the best producers, shops and restaurants.
Normandy Gastronomique, by Jane Sigal. Conran Octopus.

Other Insight Guides

Apa Publications has more travel guide titles in print than any other guide book publisher, with over 200 *Insight Guides*, more than 100 *Pocket Guides* and over 200 *Compact Guides*.

Insight Guide: France is the major book in the French series covering the whole country, with features on food and drink, culture and the arts as well as a broad picture of the nation. Other Insight Guide titles cover **Alsace**, **Brittany**, **Burgundy**, **Corsica**, the **Côte d'Azur**, the **Loire Valley**, **Paris** and **Provence**.

Insight Pocket Guides are written by host authors who show you the best of the places they know well. The books are designed in a series of day trips and excursions, and are particularly useful for people with only a short time to make the most of their visit. Titles include **Alsace**, **Brittany**, **Corsica**, the **Côte d'Azur**, the **Loire Valley**, **Paris** and **Provence**. Complete with pull-out map.

Compact Guides are the handiest guide books around. These inexpensive, full-colour mini-encyclopaedias give you the best routes of the region with a star-rated system of all the sites worth seeing, plus all the practical information you will need for your stay. Titles include **Brittany**, **Burgundy**, **Normandy**, **Provence** and **Paris**.

ART & PHOTO CREDITS

INSIGHT GUIDE
NORMANDY

Cartographic Editor **Zoë Goodwin**
Production **Linton Donaldson**
Design Consultant **Klaus Geisler**
Picture Research **Hilary Genin, Britta Jaschinski**

Index

Numbers in italics refer to photographs

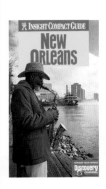